Law on the battlefield

Melland Schill Studies in International Law
Series editor Professor Dominic McGoldrick

The Melland Schill name has a long-established reputation for high standards of scholarship. Each volume in the series addresses major public international law issues and current developments. Many of the Melland Schill volumes have become standard works of reference. Interdisciplinary and accessible, the contributions are vital reading for students, scholars and practitioners of public international law, international organizations, international relations, international politics, international economics and international development.

Law on the battlefield

second edition

A. P. V. ROGERS

The first edition was jointly awarded the
Paul Reuter Prize 1997
by the International Committee of the Red Cross

Juris Publishing

Manchester University Press

Copyright © A. P. V. Rogers 1996, 2004

The right of A. P. V. Rogers to be identified as the author of this work has been asserted by him in accordance with the Copyright, Designs and Patents Act 1988.

First edition published 1996 by Manchester University Press

This edition published by Manchester University Press
Oxford Road, Manchester M13 9NR, UK
www.manchesteruniversitypress.co.uk

British Library Cataloguing-in-Publication Data
A catalogue record for this book is available from the British Library

ISBN 0 7190 6135 0 *hardback*
     0 7190 6136 9 *paperback*

First published in the USA and Canada by Juris Publishing, Inc.
71 New Street, Huntington, New York 11743
www.jurispub.com

Library of Congress Cataloging-in-Publication Data applied for

ISBN 1-929446-57-8 *hardback*
     1-929446-58-6 *paperback*

This edition first published 2004

13 12 11 10 09 08 07 06   10 9 8 7 6 5 4 3 2

Typeset in 10/12pt Times
by Graphicraft Limited, Hong Kong
Printed in Great Britain
by Biddles Ltd, King's Lynn

To Annekatrin

Contents

Contents

Series editor's preface

The very title of this book is a challenging one. Many observers of world events will take much convincing that the 'law on the battlefield' is not a contradiction in terms. Yet General Rogers presents a powerful and informed case. On the basis of his extensive practical experience he offers expert guidance on how international humanitarian law can, and should, be integrated into military planning and doctrine. The civilizing influence of that law needs to be firmly embedded in legal analysis and military planning. Political and military leaders need to be ever conscious of the restraints it imposes on them.

It is one of the tragic ironies of our time that continuing conflicts have heightened interest in the interpretation, application and function of international humanitarian law. The clarity and wisdom of this work will ensure that it attracts wide interest across a range of disciplines concerned with international conflicts.

Dominic McGoldrick
International and European Law Unit
University of Liverpool

Foreword to the first edition

by

General Sir Michael Rose, KCB, CBE, DSO, QGM, MA

Although the idea that there can be any law governing something as conjectural and murderous as war may be regarded as surprising, the concept that behaviour under conditions of war should be subject to some sort of *jus in bello* can be traced back at least to the Age of Chivalry, when clear rules were developed for the treatment of prisoners and civilian populations following sieges. These rules were based not so much on natural law as on a perception among the combatants that there was some mutual benefit to be gained by recognizing some element of restraint. Over the centuries these restraints have become encapsulated in a law of war. The advent of weapons of mass destruction clearly challenged many of the legal assumptions contained in the various treaties, but the idea that there should be a law of war nonetheless survived, and continues to this day to be enshrined in a number of treaties and protocols.

However, it is clear that nowadays the majority of conflicts are increasingly taking the form of civil war, and this has made the laws of war more difficult to uphold. This is because these new forms of warfare not only have the savage character of the Hundred Years War in Europe but are marked by a total absence of any respect for human values or, indeed, the law of war. Such conflicts have combined to create chaotic situations of anarchy in which hatred and a spirit of revenge run unbridled. The extreme horrors caused by these changed circumstances need no further description, for they are daily illustrated on our TV screens. Within days, modern cities are reduced to rubble by bombardment and entire populations are compelled to exist in conditions of total misery.

Inevitably there is an increasing tendency for the United Nations to become involved in these conflicts – often for humanitarian reasons. The Security Council resolutions on which all United Nations humanitarian and peacekeeping operations are founded *de facto* have the force of international law and provide the legal framework for all mission activities. In Bosnia the United Nations Protection Force is able to establish safe areas and exclusion zones and oblige the combatants to allow free passage for aid convoys through the practical application of the law of war. Any military force used by the United Nations in support of its mandate is required to comply with the guidelines which underpin all peacekeeping operations. Only a minimum level of force can be used to achieve a specific objective. Warning must be given where possible, all collateral damage must be avoided, and all use of force must be proportional, relevant and timely. Only by strict adherence to these rules can a mission avoid becoming party to the conflict itself as happened with such disastrous results in Somalia in 1993. On a more general note, the civilian and military personnel who were taken hostage by the Iraqis in Kuwait in 1990 probably owe their release to the diplomatic pressure brought to bear through the Geneva Convention of 1949, under whose protective status they found themselves. In sum, the aim of the law of war is to save life and limb by encouraging humane treatment and by preventing unnecessary suffering and destruction.

As war has become more complicated, so, sadly, has the language of the treaties and protocols. If the law of war is to be successfully applied, it must clearly be understood by those to whom it is addressed. It is important that the language used should not be obscure. This book makes a most useful contribution to the understanding of the law of war. It takes key provisions of the 1977 Geneva Protocol I and explains their context, their negotiating history as well as their meaning and relevance today. I commend it not only to military lawyers but also to those who plan and conduct operations of peacekeeping and war. The book will also appeal to those who would like to resolve in their own minds the apparent incompatibility between law and war.

M. R.
April 1995

Preface to the first edition

As a military lawyer I first became interested in the law of war when I attended the congress of the International Society for Military Law and the Law of War in The Hague in 1973. Preparation the following year of a paper entitled Penal and Disciplinary Sanctions against Prisoners of War was my first academic foray in this field. A posting to the international legal staff of Supreme Headquarters Allied Powers Europe prompted me to read the *Manual of Military Law* Part III (*The Law of War on Land*) from cover to cover, which stood me in good stead. There followed a specialist appointment in the United Kingdom where I was responsible for law-of-war training and advice within the army. This included being a delegate at the UN Weapons Conference in 1979 and 1980. My interest in the law of war in the following years was kept alive by my involvement in the International Society, as an occasional lecturer at the International Institute of Humanitarian Law or at seminars arranged by the International Committee of the Red Cross and the British Red Cross Society and as a regular attender at the Law of Armed Conflict discussion group of the British Institute of International and Comparative Law. From 1987, further appointments at the Ministry of Defence, where I was responsible for law-of-war advice, especially during the Gulf War of 1990–91, gave me an opportunity to practise the theory that I had absorbed over the years. I also attended meetings of experts arranged by the International Committee of the Red Cross to discuss laser weapons and anti-personnel mines.

However, my education in law of war had been entirely 'on the job'. I had developed a special interest in the decisions that have to be made by commanders, staff officers and military lawyers in the context of land warfare, often under severe time pressure, which require a careful balancing of military and humanitarian requirements and was looking for an opportunity to study these problems in greater depth, so was glad to embark, on a part-time basis, upon a thesis of the same title as this book which eventually led to the award of the degree of Master of Laws by Liverpool University in July 1994.

I am grateful to Major General M. T. Fugard, then Director of Army Legal Services, for launching me on this project and to him and his successors for providing financial support for my studies; to my supervisor, Professor Peter Rowe of Liverpool University, for his many suggestions, guidance and wise counsel; to Dr Dominic McGoldrick of Liverpool University for his energy in persuading the publishers to accept this work; to Richard Purslow, the editorial director, for his patience; to Miss Kim Spreadbury for her dedicated work on the word processor; especially to the many authorities I have quoted for enlightening me; and, not least, to my wife, Annekatrin, for her patient support and encouragement for work done almost entirely in my spare time, often in the early hours of the morning!

I take full responsibility for the final result, which is not a statement of British Government policy nor to be seen as official endorsement of any facts stated or conclusions reached but is solely a reflection of my personal views.

The scope of this book is limited. It does not deal with the law relating to the protection of the victims of war, civil wars, naval warfare or the use of weapons. It is a critical study of the key provisions of the law relating to the conduct of combat in international armed conflicts on land, illustrated by reference to problems that have arisen in recent armed conflicts. The study that led to this book has helped to clear my mind on a number of issues and enabled me to see things more clearly. My only hope is that the book will assist readers in the same way to a better understanding and so facilitate, in a very modest way, the ultimate aims of the laws of armed conflict, which is to reduce the sufferings of war.

A. P. V. R.
Tidworth, January 1995

Foreword to the second edition

by

Professor Frits Kalshoven

It gives me great pleasure to write this foreword to the second edition of *Law on the Battlefield*. I must have met the author at the congress of the International Society for Military Law and the Law of War held in The Hague in 1973, where, as noted in the preface to the first edition, he became interested in the law of war. However, I really got to know him at the UN Conventional Weapons Conference, 1979–80, where he and I were delegates for our respective governments. Indeed, far from being just a delegate, Tony Rogers stood out as the patient yet determined leader who steered the conference through the difficult negotiations that resulted in the adoption of the Mines Protocol.[1]

At the time, the Mines Protocol represented an excellent compromise between military necessity and the requirements of humanity. True, it applied solely in international armed conflict, and it had nothing to say about violations of its terms. Most important, however, it was applicable by a professional armed force playing the game by the rules.

This, of course, is where it went wrong. Not all warfare is conducted by well-trained, law-abiding armed forces. Rather, widespread violation of the rules of the game, whether on purpose or by negligence, has become a common feature of much of contemporary warfare. Especially with weapons like anti-personnel mines and booby-traps, the effects have been disastrous, as evidenced in countries like Afghanistan and Angola.

One usual reaction to such patterns of law infringement is to ask for better compliance; another is to ask for improved rules, and a third, for a total prohibition of the incriminated means or method of warfare. In the case of the mines, rather than focusing first and foremost on compliance with the 1980 Protocol (which few people knew), two lines of action were vigorously pursued. One led

[1]Protocol on Prohibitions or Restrictions on the Use of Mines, Booby-Traps and Other Devices (Protocol II), annexed to the Convention on Prohibitions or Restrictions on the Use of Certain Conventional Weapons which May be Deemed to be Excessively Injurious or to Have Indiscriminate Effects, adopted 10 October 1980, reprinted in A. Roberts and R. Guelff (eds.), *Documents on the Laws of War*, 3rd edn, 2000, pp. 514–34.

to improved law: the Amended Mines Protocol of 1996 refines the substantive rules on use of landmines and booby-traps, expands the scope of the rules to cover internal armed conflict as well, and invites parties to provide for 'appropriate measures to ensure the imposition of penal sanctions'.[2]

The other, more radical campaign resulted in the adoption, in 1997, of the Ottawa Convention, which completely bans anti-personnel mines from use and, indeed, if all goes well, from the face of the earth.[3] As of today, as noted by Kofi Annan, Secretary-General of the United Nations, more than two-thirds of all countries are party to the Convention.[4]

The point is that although neither result could have been achieved without the support of governments, the initiative and driving force lay elsewhere: with the ICRC, as well as with groups of private persons and NGOs in many countries, who in 1992 bundled their efforts in the International Campaign to Ban Landmines: civil society at work.

The Ottawa Convention in particular stands out as one of these totally unpredictable events that mark our times. Other examples are the establishment, in rapid succession, of the ad hoc International Tribunals for the former Yugoslavia and Rwanda, followed by the adoption of the Rome Statute establishing the International Criminal Court. While it remains to be seen what will be the impact of these events on the battlefield, another event had instant and dramatic effect. On 11 September 2001, civilian airplanes used as weapons of war crashed into the World Trade Center in New York and the Pentagon in Washington, causing several thousand casualties and untold human misery. In reaction, the President of the United States declared a 'war on terror', with an elusive al-Qa'ida as the enemy and the whole world as the battlefield. Questions arose immediately: would international humanitarian law apply in every single action relating to this 'war', or was there room for human rights law? Where would the responsibility for compliance with applicable law lie, and who would enforce it? And, of an entirely different order: should the existing body of international humanitarian law not be declared defunct and replaced with a modern set of rules empowering governments involved in the war on terror to do whatever seemed required to pursue the goal of overcoming the enemy wherever he might be believed to be hiding?

Subsequent events confirm that today, as in the past, terrorists select their targets with utter disregard of any law. However, events also demonstrate that armed forces best carry out their military operations with due regard for the well-established principles of avoidance of unnecessary suffering and respect for civilians. Armed forces therefore need to be trained, and military operations

---

[2]*Ibid.*, at p. 535.

[3]Convention on the Prohibition of the Use, Stockpiling, Production and Transfer of Anti-Personnel Mines and on Their Destruction, adopted at Ottawa on 18 September 1997, *ibid.*, at p. 645.

[4]UN News Service Message, Monday, 15 September 2003, 21.01: Message to the Fifth Meeting of States Parties to the Convention being held in Bangkok.; UNNews@un.org.

planned, with an eye to implementing these principles and the detailed rules of battlefield law that elaborate them. This is not merely to keep the soldiers out of the clutches of the Prosecutor of the International Criminal Court, but first and most importantly to prevent the needless, senseless suffering that nonchalant warfare may entail.

Critical observers, whether among the media or in academe, are also in need of expert exposition of the intricacies of battlefield law as it has evolved over time. For all these reasons, the second, enlarged and enriched, edition of this book is to be warmly welcomed.

In his Introduction, Tony Rogers wonders whether, within the whole of law, international battlefield law is perhaps no more discernible than the third power of a vanishing point. Sir Hersch Lauterpacht might have thought so, had he paid special attention to this part of the law of war. Given the current keen interest on all sides for the actuality of warfare, I do not share this concern. Indeed, battlefield law may well have turned into the most glaringly visible part of international law!

Professor Frits Kalshoven

Preface to the second edition

The purpose of the first edition was to provide a critical study of the key provisions of the law relating to the conduct of combat in international armed conflicts on land, illustrated by reference to problems that had arisen in recent armed conflicts. It was intended to bridge the gap between the legal theory propounded in academic works and the conduct of military operations as evidenced in military manuals or in actual practice.

The purpose of the second edition remains the same. When the first edition went out of print, it seemed inappropriate just to reprint it, as so much had happened in the field of the law of war in the intervening years. This is not, however, a comprehensive rewrite; it is more of an updating of the first edition. I have tried to leave the text of the first edition undisturbed as far as possible but bring it up to date in the light of recent events, especially the judgments of the International Criminal Tribunals for the former Yugoslavia, the Rome Statute of the International Criminal Court, including its new rules on superior orders, and the conflicts concerning Kosovo in 1999, Afghanistan in 2001 and Iraq in 2003. I have taken the opportunity to add two new chapters: on the rules relating to the conduct of combat against members of enemy armed forces and on the rules relating to the conduct of combat in internal armed conflicts.

The approach I have adopted is to take a proposition of the law of war, examine its historical origins and current exposition, deal with problems of interpretation and application, especially in the light of recent conflicts, and reach conclusions about how it should be applied in practice. As Professor Sir Adam Roberts commented on the first edition of the book, it 'is stronger on law than it is on history'. That is intentional. Historians need to look elsewhere, perhaps at the works of Professor Geoffrey Best, but I have found it necessary to refer briefly to the historical context in which the treaty law has developed and to incidents in some of the conflicts in which the law has been applied in order to illustrate its application.

Most armed conflicts are internal. The customary and treaty rules relating specifically to conduct of combat in internal conflicts are very limited. In recent

years there has been a growing realization on my part that applying the fundamental principles of customary law can often lead to the same result as applying
the detailed rules applicable in international armed conflict. The *Tadić* judgment,
where the Yugoslav tribunal held that criminal responsibility also applied to
internal armed conflicts, was a milestone in the development of the law of armed
conflict and there has been a readiness on the part of the tribunal to apply
customary law principles to internal armed conflicts. This is a phenomenon that
needs detailed examination and the International Committee of the Red Cross
(ICRC) customary law study, unfortunately not published as this edition goes to
press, should provide this. In the meantime, I hope that Chapter 9 of this book
will provide some basic guidelines.

I hesitated about retaining Chapter 7 on environmental protection as much
more comprehensive studies have been published since the first edition of this
book, especially the important book *The Environmental Consequences of War*,
edited by J. E. Austin and C. E. Bruch, which was published by Cambridge
University Press in 2000. However, I decided that Chapter 7 might still serve as
a brief introduction to the subject.

Professor Leslie Green, in his review of the first edition, commented that at
times it is necessary to measure my comments against my English legal background and, to some extent, the impact of Western ideology. I make no apology
for that deficiency, if it be one, for everybody is a product of his or her upbring-
ing, environment, education and experience. But I hope that I am able to
approach the issues addressed in this book objectively and with an open mind.
Readers will also find that my illustrations have been drawn from a narrow
selection of conflicts, generally those in which British sailors, soldiers and avia-
tors have been involved, men and women incidentally for whom I have the
greatest admiration. Of course, there have been many other recent conflicts
around the world, in Asia, Africa and South America, which I regret I have not
had time to study.

In preparing the second edition, I have tried to make good some of the defi-
ciencies of the first edition pointed out by reviewers. I am particularly grateful
to Professors Leslie Green, Sir Adam Roberts and Michael Schmitt for their
thoughtful comments.

Professor Michael Schmitt, in his review, expressed disappointment that, while
relying heavily on Protocol I, I devoted little, if any, attention to the status of
that instrument in international law and that there should have been some
mention of whether or not the cited articles of the protocol were controversial.
At that stage the United States, the United Kingdom and France were not parties.
Indeed, the only state party involved in the Gulf War of 1991 was Syria. As this
edition goes to press, the United States has still not ratified the Protocol, though
161 states, including the United Kingdom and France, have done so. Nevertheless, the Protocol does reflect, though perhaps in slightly different language,
some principles of customary law that non-parties, such as the United States,

consider binding. A useful indication of the United States view of customary law is to be found in the Department of Defence's Military Commission Instruction No. 2 of 30 April 2003.

I have tried to respond to other criticisms of the first edition by including in Chapters 8 and 9 material on the *ad hoc* tribunal for the former Yugoslavia and the International Criminal Court, which were at an early stage in their development when the first edition went to press; and the new Chapter 2 enables me to say something about psychological operations. Chapter 10, 'The military lawyer's perspective' has been extended a little to cover some legal aspects of peace support operations. However, I have resisted the temptation to discuss UN peace-keeping operations in any detail, weaponry except where it touches upon environmental protection, or the implementation of the law and the punishment of violations, as I feel that these topics fall outside the scope of this book, which is intended to be a guide to the law relating to the conduct of combat.

I would like to express publicly my appreciation to the Lauterpacht Research Centre for International Law at the University of Cambridge for taking me into their tranquil academic harbour when, having retired from the Army I felt, like the Flying Dutchman, adrift on the storm-tossed seas of international law. I am very pleased that another Dutchman, Professor Frits Kalshoven, who has always been a great inspiration to me, agreed to write the foreword to this edition. Thanks also go to Susan Lamb, for guiding me through the thickets of the jurisprudence of the Yugoslav tribunal, to Roger Marsh for his help with air operations, to Charles Garraway for his comments on Chapter 9 and to Tony Mason for his flexibility over deadlines.

A. P. V. R.
Cambridge, 30 June 2003

Abbreviations

AbiH   The Muslim Army of Bosnia-Herzegovina

AFP 110-31   International Law – The Conduct of Armed Conflict and Air Operations, US Department of the Air Force, 1976

AFP 110-34   Commander's Handbook on the Law of Armed Conflict, US Department of the Air Force, 1980

Air Warfare Rules   Hague Rules of Aerial Warfare, 1923 (UK Misc. 14 of 1924 (Cm. 2201)

Annual Digest   H. Lauterpacht (ed.), *Annual Digest and Reports of Public International Law Cases*, Butterworth

Brussels Code   Project of an International Declaration Concerning the Laws and Customs of War attached to the Final Protocol of the Brussels Conference of 1874 (65 *British and Foreign State Papers* 1005)

CBW   Chemical and bacteriological warfare

CDDH   Diplomatic Conference on the Reaffirmation and Development of International Humanitarian Law applicable in Armed Conflicts, Geneva, 1974–77

CIA   Central Intelligence Agency

Civilian Convention   Geneva Convention relative to the Protection of Civilian Persons in time of War, 1949 (75 UNTS (1950) 287 (No. 973))

CO   commanding officer

CPC   Cultural Property Convention

Cultural Property Convention   Convention for the Protection of Cultural Property in the Event of Armed Conflict, The Hague, 1954 (249 UNTS 214 at p. 240 (No. 3511))

Cultural Property Regulations   Regulations for the Execution of the Cultural Property Convention (249 UNTS 270)

DA PAM 27-161-2   International Law vol. II, US Department of the Army, October, 1962

Despatch   P. Hine, Despatch by Joint Commander of Operation Granby, 2nd Supplement to the *London Gazette*, 28 June 1991

DOD   Department of Defence

DOD Interim Report   Conduct of the Persian Gulf Campaign, US Department of Defence Interim Report to Congress, July 1991

DOD Report   Conduct of the Persian Gulf War, US Department of Defence Final Report to Congress, April 1992

ENMOD Convention   Convention on the Prohibition of Military or Any Other Hostile Use of Environmental Modification Techniques, 1977 (1108 UNTS 151–78 (No. 17119))

First Cultural Property Protocol   Protocol to the Cultural Property Convention (249 UNTS 358–64)

FM 27-10   The Law of Land Warfare, US Department of the Army, 1956

GYIL   *German Yearbook of International Law*

Hague Regulations   Regulations annexed to Hague Convention IV of 1907 (100 *British and Foreign State Papers* 338)

HMSO   Her Majesty's Stationery Office

HVO   Croatian Defence Council

ICC Statute   Rome Statute of the International Criminal Court 1998, 37 ILM (1998) 999

ICRC   International Committee of the Red Cross

ICRC *Commentary*   ICRC *Commentary on the Additional Protocols of 1977 to the Geneva Conventions of 1949*, Nijhoff, 1987

ICRC Draft Rules   ICRC Draft Rules, ICRC, 1956

ICTY   International Criminal Tribunal for the former Yugoslavia

ILC   International Law Commission

ILM   International Legal Materials

ILR   International Law Reports

IMT   International Military Tribunal

JSM   Joint Service Manual on the Law of Armed Conflict (JSP 383) [to be published]

KLA   Kosovo Liberation Army

Lieber Code   Instructions for the Government of Armies of the United States in the Field, prepared by Francis Lieber and promulgated by President Lincoln as General Orders No. 100 on 24 April 1863

MUP   Yugoslav Interior Forces (i.e., Special Police)

NATO   North Atlantic Treaty Organization

Naval Bombardment Convention   Hague Convention IX of 1907 Concerning Bombardment by Naval Forces in Time of War (100 *British and Foreign State Papers* 401)

POW   Prisoner of War

Prisoner of War Convention   Geneva Convention III relative to the Treatment of Prisoners of War, 1949 (75 UNTS (1950) 135–285)

Protocol I   First Additional Protocol of 1977 to the Geneva Conventions of 1949 (UK Misc. No. 19 (1977), Cmnd. 6927; 1125 UNTS (1979) 3–608

Protocol II Second Additional Protocol of 1977 to the Geneva Conventions of 1949 (UK Misc. No. 19 (1977), Cmnd 6927; 1125 UNTS (1979) 609–99

RAF Royal Air Force

ROE rules of engagement

Roerich Pact Treaty on the Protection of Artistic and Scientific Institutions and Historic Monuments, Washington, 1935 (reproduced in C. I. Bevans, Treaties & Other International Agreements of the United States of America, 1776–1949, Department of State, vol. 3, p. 254)

Rome Statute See ICC Statute

RPG rocket-propelled grenade

Second Cultural Property Protocol Second Protocol to the Hague Convention of 1954 for the Protection of Cultural Property in the Event of Armed Conflict, 38 ILM (1999) 769

St Petersburg Declaration St Petersburg Declaration of 1868 renouncing the Use, in Time of War, of Explosive Projectiles Under 400 Grammes Weight (58 *British and Foreign State Papers* 16)

UNESCO UN Educational, Scientific and Cultural Organization

VRS Army of Republika Srpska

WCR Law Reports of Trials of War Criminals, selected and prepared by the UN War Crimes Commission, 15 vols., HMSO, 1946–49

Weapons Convention Convention on Prohibitions or Restrictions on the Use of certain Conventional Weapons which may be deemed to be excessively injurious or to have indiscriminate effects, 1980 (UK Misc. No. 23 (1981), Cmnd. 8370)

Wounded Convention Geneva Convention I for the Amelioration of the Condition of Wounded and Sick in Armed Forces in the Field, 1949 (75 UNTS (1950) 31–83)

ZDv 15/2 *Humanitäres Völkerrecht in bewaffneten Konflikten* (also available in English as Humanitarian Law in Armed Conflicts), German Ministry of Defence, August 1992

ZDv 15/9 The Protection of Cultural Property in Armed Conflicts, German Ministry of Defence, July 1964

1

General principles

Writers delve back through the history of centuries to the ancient civilizations of India and Egypt to find in their writings evidence of practices intended to alleviate the sufferings of war. This evidence is to be found in agreements and treaties, in the works of religious leaders and philosophers, in regulations and articles of war issued by military leaders and in the rules of chivalry.[1] It is said that the first systematic code of war was that of the Saracens and was based on the Koran.[2] The writers of the Age of Enlightenment, notably Grotius[3] and Vattel,[4] were especially influential. It has been suggested that more humane rules were able to flourish in the period of limited wars from 1648 to 1792 but that they then came under pressure in the drift towards continental warfare, the concept of the nation in arms and the increasing destructiveness of weapons from 1792 to 1914.[5] Efforts had to be made in the middle of the last century to reimpose on war limits, which up to that time had been based on custom and usage.[6]

The most celebrated attempt at codifying the customs and usages of war was the Lieber Code of 1863 issued by President Lincoln to the Union Forces in the American Civil War. In the second half of the nineteenth century more reliance was placed on codifying the rules of the law of war in treaty form, starting with the Geneva Convention of 1864, the St Petersburg Declaration of 1868 and continuing with the Brussels Conference of 1874 and the Hague Conferences of

[1] I. Detter, *The Law of War*, 2nd edn, Cambridge University Press, 2000, pp. 151–4.

[2] See R. C. Algase, Protection of civilian lives in warfare: a comparison between Islamic law and modern international law concerning the conduct of hostilities, *Military Law and Law of War Review*, 1977 at p. 246.

[3] H. Grotius, *De Jure Belli ac Pacis*, 1642. A translation into English by F. W. Kelsey was published by Wildy & Sons in 1964.

[4] E. de Vattel, *Le Droit des gens*, 1758.

[5] United States, *International Law*, vol. II, Department of the Army, 1962, DA Pam 27-161-2.

[6] See further, G. I. A. D. Draper, Humanitarianism in the modern law of armed conflict, in M. A. Meyer (ed.), *Armed Conflict and the New Law*, British Institute of International and Comparative Law, 1989, at p. 3. A useful summary of the historical development of the law of armed conflict is to be found in H. McCoubrey and N. D. White, *International Law and Armed Conflict*, Dartmouth, 1992, pp. 209–23.

1899 and 1907. It was during this period that some European states were developing powerful armies and navies and expanding their influence throughout the
world. Some theorists, mainly German and notably Lueder, advanced the view
that such military power should not be restrained by the usages and customs
of war. These theorists influenced German thinking as late as 1914 when the
chancellor is reported to have said of the invasion of Belgium: 'we are now in
a state of necessity and necessity knows no law . . .'.[7] Conversely, today, the less
technologically advanced states sometimes see the law of war as an instrument
for emasculating the mighty. One delegation at the CDDH – the Diplomatic
Conference on the Reaffirmation and Development of International Humanitarian
Law applicable in Armed Conflicts, Geneva, 1974–77 – even suggested that
where one nation in an armed conflict had an air force and the other did not, the
nation with the air force should be prohibited from using it.[8]

The modern international law of war on land is to be found for the most part
in treaties, notably the Hague Regulations of 1907, the Geneva Conventions of
1949, Protocol I of 1977 to those conventions and the various treaties dealing
with weapons, culminating in the Conventional Weapons Convention of 1981.

That is not to say that customary law is replaced by treaty law. Treaties, of
course, only bind the parties. Customary law continues to develop and binds all
states. Treaty law may in two senses be helpful in interpreting customary law:
in being in some cases a codification of customary law; in others, new treaty
rules may by sufficient ratification become regarded as universally accepted and,
therefore, indicative of customary law. They will not, however, if they have
been the subject of reservations.[9] Customary law cannot be excluded by treaty.[10]
Treaty provisions that have never been applied in practice may, by custom, be
rendered obsolete. The problem with customary law is ascertaining with any
certainty what it is[11] and here the opinions of writers may differ.

The tenuous nature of the law of war was admirably summarized by Professor
Lauterpacht in the following words: 'If international law is, in some ways, at the
vanishing point of law, the law of war is, perhaps even more conspicuously, at
the vanishing point of international law'.[12] At the time he wrote this, a considerable effort had just been expended in bringing up to date the rules relating to the

---

[7]M. Walzer, *Just and Unjust Wars*, 2nd edn, Basic Books, 1992, p. 240.

[8]W. H. Parks, Air war and the law of war, 32 *Air Force Law Review* 1 (1990), p. 218.

[9]See, e.g. S. Kadelbach, Zwingende Normen des humanitären Völkerrechts, *Humanitäres
Völkerrecht Informationsschriften*, 1992, No. 3, p. 118.

[10]Art. 53 of the Vienna Convention on the Law of Treaties.

[11]For an interesting article on this subject, see C. Bruderlein, Custom in international humanitarian
law, *International Review of the Red Cross*, November/December 1991, p. 579. See also C. J.
Greenwood, Customary international law and the First Geneva Protocol of 1977 in the Gulf conflict,
in P. J. Rowe (ed.), *The Gulf War 1990–91 in International and English Law*, Routledge, 1993,
pp. 66–9, who explains when the provisions of a multilateral treaty are to be treated as authoritative
statements of customary law.

[12]H. Lauterpacht, The problem of the revision of the law of war, *British Yearbook of International
Law*, 1952, p. 382.

protection of the victims of war contained in the Geneva Conventions. Apart from the Wounded Convention, those conventions did not deal with law on the battlefield, or the law relating to the conduct of combat, which was to be found in principles derived from customary international law and in the Hague Regulations. Extending the Lauterpacht *dictum*, one could perhaps add that if the law of war were at the vanishing point of international law, the law on the battlefield would be at the vanishing point of the law of war.

Early treatises[13] contained very little on the conduct of hostilities, but a lot of the rules relating to the conduct of combat are now codified in Protocol I. Some of the more important of those rules will be examined but first it is necessary to deal with general principles and with some expressions that will be used in the following chapters.

The great principles of customary law, from which all else stems, are those of military necessity, humanity, distinction and proportionality. According to the UK *Manual of Military Law*, the principles of military necessity and humanity as well as those of chivalry have shaped the development of the law of war.[14] Chivalry may, however, be classified as an element of the principle of humanity. These principles will dominate much of the discussion in later chapters, so need to be explained here.

Military necessity[15]

Views about military necessity vary. Some argue that too much emphasis has been placed on military necessity to the detriment of the development of the law of war and the protection of war's victims. They say that 'the elasticity of the term "military necessity" under the laws of war has enabled belligerents to legally justify virtually any conduct otherwise available to the proponents of kreigsraison [*sic*]'.[16] Others, such as the author, take a more pragmatic view. States are reluctant to give up anything that gives them a military advantage, so the search is always for common ground where states can agree on some measures that can afford a little protection for the victims of war. Although the results are often disappointing, every little gain helps. Even the critics seem to accept this

---

[13]See, e.g. J. Westlake, *International Law* Part II (War), Cambridge University Press, 1913, Chapter IV of which devotes some sixty-four pages to law of war on land but only very few pages to the conduct of combat.

[14]United Kingdom, *Manual of Military Law*, Part III, HMSO, 1958 (*Manual of Military Law*), para. 3. See Draper, Humanitarianism, p. 6, on the gradual elimination of the ideals of chivalry. See also R. W. Gehring, Loss of civilian protection, *Military Law and Law of War Review*, 1980, p. 14.

[15]For a more detailed treatment of the subject, see E. Rauch, Le concept de nécessité militaire dans le droit de la guerre, *Military Law and Law of War Review*, 1980, p. 209; H. McCoubrey, The nature of the modern doctrine of military necessity, *Military Law and Law of War Review*, 1991, p. 215.

[16]See C. Jochnick and R. Normand, The legitimation of violence: a critical history of the laws of war, *Harvard International Law Journal*, vol. 35, 1994, p. 64.

in the end: 'even minor limitations on belligerent conduct and marginal humanitarian gain are worth pursuing'.[17]

Dr Francis Lieber defined military necessity as long ago as 1863 as 'those measures which are indispensable for securing the ends of the war, and which are lawful according to the modern laws and usages of war'.[18]

The principle of military necessity is encapsulated in the preamble to the St Petersburg Declaration: that the only legitimate object which states should endeavour to accomplish in war is to weaken the military forces of the enemy and that for this purpose it is sufficient to disable the greatest possible number of men.

While it was formerly argued by some that necessity might permit a commander to ignore the laws of war when it was essential to do so to avoid defeat,[19] to escape from extreme danger or for the realization of the purpose of war,[20] such arguments are now obsolete since the modern law of war takes full account of military necessity. For example, the preamble to the Hague Regulations speaks of 'the desire to diminish the evils of war, as far as military requirements permit' and Protocol I, Art. 41, para. 3, prohibits the execution of prisoners of war whose presence would hamper or endanger the operations of special forces.

When writers refer to the suspension of the rules of the law of war because of military necessity,[21] they must be referring only to the last vestiges of usages of war that have not been codified in treaty form: 'what may be ignored in case of military necessity are not the laws of war, but only the usages of war'.[22]

Now that practically all such usages have been codified in the Hague Regulations, Geneva Conventions and Protocols I and II, it is hard to see that this exception has any practical significance nowadays. Although some treaties, such as Protocol I and the Weapons Convention allow for denunciation by a party, the denunciations do not take effect until the end of an armed conflict in which the denouncing party is engaged.

---

[17]*Ibid.*, p. 416.

[18]Lieber Code, Art. 14.

[19]See Westlake, *International Law*, pp. 126–8; cf. J. S. Risley, *The Law of War*, Innes & Co, 1897, p. 125; L. Oppenheim, *International Law*, vol. 2, 7th edn by H. Lauterpacht, Longman, 1952, pp. 231–3.

[20]Such arguments were mainly advanced by German theorists between 1871 and 1914 and are summed up in the maxim *Kriegsraison geht vor Kriegsmanier* (see United States, *International Law*, p. 9). For an interesting review of this doctrine, see G. Best, *Humanity in Warfare*, Methuen, 1983, pp. 172–9.

[21]E.g., Detter, *Law of War*, p. 398, who states: 'It is not only treaties and conventions that may be suspended in their application by dubious claims of military necessity but also general uncodified rules on methods, including rules on targets, and humanitarian rules. The legal position today, after a considerable body of case law has developed, appears to be that rules of the Law of War must only be suspended in case of 'clear' military necessity; that the burden of proof is increased for the suspension of any rules exempting targets from attack; and an especially enhanced burden of proof applies in the case of suspension from humanitarian rules. The degree of military necessity is also increased in proportion to the violation of these three groups; the presumption exists that no military necessity can justify violations of rules of the Law of War.'

[22]See Oppenheim, *International Law*, p. 233.

Holland pithily summarizes the modern view in these words: 'military necessity justifies a resort to all measures which are indispensable for securing [the submission of the enemy]; provided that they are not inconsistent with the modern laws and usages of war'.[23]

De Visscher, writing in 1917, took the view that the old arguments could at best be applied to usages of war, but not to the law of war whether in treaty or customary form.[24]

References to military necessity are to be found in the Hague Regulations, which prohibit the destruction or seizure of the enemy's property, unless it be imperatively demanded by the necessities of war[25] and which prohibit the use of weapons calculated to cause *unnecessary* suffering.[26]

Allowances for military necessity may be found in the Geneva Conventions, the Cultural Property Convention of 1954 and in Protocol I.[27]

Military necessity has been described as the principle that a belligerent is justified in applying compulsion and force of any kind, to the extent necessary for the realization of the purpose of war, that is, the complete submission of the enemy at the earliest possible moment with the least possible expenditure of men, resources and money.[28] Best comments that this approach is old-fashioned, which it is in light of recent developments in the law of war, and provides 'no soothing syrup for civilians'.[29] The reference to the complete submission of the enemy, written in light of the experience of total war in the Second World War, is probably now obsolete since war can have a limited purpose as in the termination of the occupation of the Falkland Islands in 1982 or of Kuwait in 1991. In the US Air Force manual,[30] it is stated that the concept of military necessity has four basic elements:

1 That force is regulated.
2 That force is necessary to achieve as quickly as possible the partial or complete submission of the adversary.
3 That the force is no greater than needed to achieve this.
4 That it is not otherwise prohibited.

In other words, it is not possible for military commanders to do anything they like in war. What they do must be justified in every case by military necessity,

---

[23]T. E. Holland, *The Laws of War on Land*, Clarendon, 1908, p. 12. See also G. Schwarzenberger, *International Law*, vol. II, Stevens, 1968, pp. 135–6; M. Greenspan, *The Modern Law of Land Warfare*, University of California Press, 1959, p. 314.
[24]C. de Visscher, Les lois de la guerre et la théorie de la nécessité, *Revue Général de Droit International Public*, vol. 24 (1917), at p. 99.
[25]Art. 23(g).
[26]Art. 23(e).
[27]Detter, *Law of War*, pp. 393–6, lists various exceptions for military necessity. So does McCoubrey, Military necessity, pp. 229–37.
[28]*Manual of Military Law*, para. 3.
[29]Best, *Law and War since 1945*, Clarendon Press, 1994, p. 271.
[30]*International Law – the Conduct of Armed Conflict and Air Operations*, AFP 110-31, 1976, pp. 1–6.

that is the military requirement to undertake the action in question.[31] The rule has been stated thus: 'in every case destruction must be *imperatively* demanded by the necessities of war, and must not merely be the outcome of a spirit of plunder or revenge.'[32] Attacking civilians is not normally a military requirement because it does not weaken the military forces of the enemy. Destroying a cathedral or museum does not usually contribute to the defeat of the enemy's armed forces. McCoubrey[33] leaves open the possibility that military necessity might be a defence in cases of imperative military defensive need in response to an overwhelming threat.[34] Schwarzenberger emphasizes, however, that the defence, which is of very limited scope, is personal necessity rather than the broader concept of military necessity.[35]

Military necessity has threefold significance in the law of war. First, and foremost, no action may be taken which is not militarily necessary. Second, the law of war sometimes allows exceptions to its rules for good military reasons. Third, it is an element of the rule of proportionality (dealt with below) in trying to achieve a balance between the, sometimes conflicting, aims of military success and humanitarian protection.

In reviewing the first edition of this book, Schmitt commented that the author had allowed himself 'to fall into an archetypal morass when discussing the principle of military necessity'. He wrote that military necessity had been characterized variously: as a *limitation* on military operations, as an *enabler* to allow exceptions to the rules in specified circumstances and as *an element of the rule of proportionality*. 'Rather than distinguishing between the three, and proffering an opinion on the appropriate way to portray this seminal principle of law, Rogers asserts that military necessity is significant to all three interpretations.' Schmitt considers that only the *fact* of military necessity operates in these three ways but that as a *legal principle* it operates only as a limitation,[36] that is 'the principle that forbids destructive acts unnecessary to secure a military advantage.'[37]

---

[31]In fact, attacks must be directed at military objectives, see Chapter 3.

[32]Oppenheim, *International Law*, p. 414.

[33]McCoubrey ends his study on military necessity with the following definition: 'Military necessity is a doctrine within the laws of armed conflict which recognizes the potential impracticability of full compliance with legal norms in certain circumstances and, accordingly, may mitigate or expunge culpability for *prima facie* unlawful actions in appropriate cases in armed conflict. Its precise effects in any given case will rest upon the combination of issues of circumstances, fact and degree and the strength of the claims of the norms concerned. The effect of the doctrine is limited to particular events and circumstances and does not have a general suspensory effect upon the law of armed conflict' (McCoubrey, Military necessity, p. 240).

[34]McCoubrey, *International Humanitarian Law*, pp. 198–203.

[35]Schwarzenberger, *International Law*, pp. 129–30.

[36]M. N. Schmitt, Book review: law on the battlefield, US Air Force, 8 (1998) *Journal of Legal Studies*, at pp. 256–8.

[37]M. N. Schmitt, War and the environment: fault lines in the prescriptive landscape, in J. E. Austin and C. E. Bruch (eds.), *The Environmental Consequences of War*, Cambridge University Press, 2000, at p. 101.

That seems a valuable and succinct explanation of the significance of the term 'military necessity' in the law of war.

Humanity

The preamble to Hague Convention IV of 1907 respecting the laws and customs of war on land contains a clause, known, after its drafter,[38] as the Martens clause, which provides that in cases not covered by the attached regulations the belligerents 'remain under the protection and the rule of the principles of the law of nations' which, according to Martens, was derived from the usages established among civilized people, the laws of humanity and the dictates of the public conscience.[39]

The purpose of the clause was not only to confirm the continuance of customary law,[40] but also to prevent arguments that because a particular activity had not been prohibited in a treaty it was lawful. Humanity is, therefore, a guiding principle that puts a brake on undertakings which might otherwise be justified by the principle of military necessity. For example, a military commander might say that military necessity required him to put to death wounded enemy combatants in enemy-controlled hospitals on the grounds that when they recovered they would be able to continue fighting. The principle of humanity, however, intercedes on behalf of the wounded, recognizing that those *hors de combat* do not pose an immediate threat and requiring their lives to be saved.[41] They are, of course, protected under the Wounded Convention, which specifically applies the principle of humanity to the treatment of the wounded.

Rule of distinction

The idea of humanity comes most sharply into focus in the rule of distinction. It follows from the preamble to the St Petersburg Declaration that war is to be waged against the enemy's armed forces, not against its civilian population. Attacks are to be directed at military targets, not at civilian objects.

---

[38]Professor de Martens of the University of St Petersburg, legal adviser to the Russian imperial foreign ministry during the Hague conferences.

[39]The clause is also found in the Geneva Gas Protocol, the Geneva Conventions of 1949, Protocol I and the Weapons Convention of 1981, see H. Spieker, Martens'sche Klausel, *Humanitäres Völkerrecht Informationsschriften*, October 1988, p. 46.

[40]Spieker, Martens'sche Klausel.

[41]See the *Peleus* trial, 1 WCR 1, where the court rejected the defence of the captain of a submarine that he was justified in firing on the survivors of a ship he had torpedoed to remove all traces of the sinking so that his submarine would not be sought and attacked. See also Best, *War and Law*, p. 253.

Civilians and combatants

Since military operations are to be conducted against the enemy's armed forces, there must be a clear distinction between the armed forces and civilians, or between combatants and non-combatants, and between things that might legitimately be attacked and things protected from attack.

Customary law has always made a distinction between combatants and the civilian population, or at least certain parts of it such as children and women and unarmed priests.[42] By at least the eighteenth century, the rule had emerged that non-combatants should not be directly attacked.[43]

These principles hold good today having been confirmed by the Lieber Code[44] and in the preamble to the St Petersburg Declaration.[45]

Non-combatants are not permitted to take part in hostilities and are at the same time protected from attacks and shielded from the indirect effects of war.

The current definition of a combatant is any member of the armed forces of a party to the conflict except medical personnel and chaplains.[46] All other persons are considered to be civilians.[47]

Only combatants are permitted to take a direct part in hostilities.[48] It follows that they may be attacked. Civilians may not take a direct part in hostilities and for so long as they refrain from doing so are protected from attack.[49] Taking a direct part in hostilities must be more narrowly construed than making a contribution

---

[42]See the authorities quoted by T. Meron in Henry the Fifth and the law of war, *American Journal of International Law*, 1992, at pp. 21–34. As late as 1897, Risley, *Law of War*, p. 108, wrote that 'old men, women, and children, and perhaps ministers of religion, are always regarded as non-combatants'.

[43]Oppenheim, *International Law*, p. 346. See also the review of the writers of the Age of Enlightenment in Best, *Humanity*, pp. 53–67. Emerich de Vattel, *Le Droit des gens*, 1758, wrote about the rule of distinction in the eighteenth century saying: 'At the present day, war is carried on by the regular army; the people, the peasantry, the towns folk, have no part in it, and as a rule have nothing to fear from the sword of the enemy. Provided the inhabitants submit to him who is master of the county, and pay the contributions demanded, and refrain from acts of hostility, they live as safely as if they were on friendly terms with the enemy; . . . the peasants go freely into the enemy camp to sell their provisions and they are protected as far as possible from the calamities of war. Such treatment is highly commendable and well worthy of nations which boast of their civilization; it is even of advantage to the enemy. A general who protects unarmed inhabitants, who keeps his soldiers under strict discipline, and who protects the country is enabled to support his army without trouble and is spared many evils and dangers.'

[44]Art. 22.

[45]'the only legitimate object which States should endeavour to accomplish during war is to weaken the military forces of the enemy'.

[46]Additional Protocol I of 1977 (Protocol I), Art. 43.

[47]*Ibid.*, Art. 50, para. 1.

[48]*Ibid.*, Art. 43, para. 2.

[49]*Ibid.*, Art. 51, paras. 2 and 3. Para. 3 reads: 'Civilians shall enjoy the protection afforded by this Section, unless and for such time as they take a direct part in hostilities.' The author would not go so far as Zegveld in suggesting that this means that civilians have a *right* to participate in hostilities, see L. Zegveld, *The Accountability of Armed Opposition Groups in International Law*, Cambridge University Press, 2002, p. 76.

to the war effort[50] and it would not include taking part in arms production or military engineering works or military transportation. However, as discussed below, these production plants, engineering works or transports would be legitimate military objectives despite the fact that civilians were working in them.

Nevertheless, civilians share the general dangers of war in the sense that attacks on military personnel and military objectives may cause incidental damage. It may not be possible to limit the radius of effect of an attack entirely to the objective to be attacked, a weapon may not function properly or may be deflected by defensive measures, or a civilian object may be attacked by mistake because of faulty intelligence. Similarly, civilians working in military objectives, though not themselves legitimate targets, are at risk if those objectives are attacked. Such incidental damage is controlled by the rule of proportionality, which is dealt with below.

Since combatants may be attacked, and to protect civilians, who may not, combatants are obliged to distinguish themselves from the civilian population while engaged in an attack or in a military operation preparatory to an attack.[51] They do so by wearing military clothing and equipment or at the very least by carrying their weapons openly at such times.[52]

Parks[53] complains that this reflects an extreme and unrealistic view of the rule of distinction as applied to personnel. He cites, as an example, the case of a civilian driving a military truck filled with ammunition. If the truck is attacked and the driver is killed, all is well; but if the truck driver is attacked directly and killed, the soldier who fired at him has committed a grave breach of Protocol I. He says that 'some legal scholars', and the writer is probably one of them, 'have endeavoured to avoid the issue' by suggesting that the scenario in the example is perfectly logical. He takes the view that the current rules do not reflect history and suggests that an attack on a civilian ought to be lawful 'if his immunity from military service is based upon the conclusion that continued service in his civilian position is of greater value to a nation's war effort than that person's service in the military'.[54]

This is an extreme view. The idea that civilians should have a quasi-combatant status depending on the job they do seems to take little account of the confusion that it would cause. If there is to be any hope that the law will be complied with, the rules must be as simple and straightforward as possible.[55] At least the present law is clear: combatants may be attacked directly; civilians who are in or near military objectives run the risk of being killed as a side effect of attacks on those objectives.

[50]F. Kalshoven and L. Zegveld, *Constraints on the Waging of War*, 3rd edn, ICRC, 2001, p. 99.
[51]Protocol I, Art. 44, para. 3.
[52]For further discussion of this problem, see M. H. F. Clarke, T. Glynn and A. P. V. Rogers, Combatant and prisoner of war status, in Meyer, *Armed Conflict*, p. 120.
[53]Parks, Air war, at p. 134.
[54]*Ibid.*, p. 135.
[55]In this the writer agrees with Best, *Law and War*, p. 262.

Taking a direct part in hostilities

In the example of the civilian driving the ammunition truck, it is the truck that is the target. Depending on the weapons available to him, the range and other factors, the soldier attacking the truck is likely to follow his training and fire at the centre of the target, perhaps with an anti-tank missile. If the truck driver is killed, it will be incidental to the attack on that target, proportionate and lawful. If, on the other hand, the attacking soldier is armed only with a sniper's rifle, his only way of stopping the truck might be to fire at the driver.[56] At the range at which the target is likely to be engaged, the soldier would not be able to identify the driver as a civilian – and if the truck was a military vehicle the presumption of civilian status cannot realistically apply – so a war crime would not be committed because of lack of knowledge and intent. Taking the legal analysis one stage further and posing the unlikely scenario that the sniper knew that the driver was a civilian, technically that would be a war crime. However, it would be difficult to secure a conviction. Given differences of opinion about what is meant by 'taking a direct part in hostilities', the defence might argue that the civilian had forfeited his protected civilian status by taking a direct part in hostilities in driving military supplies. The argument would be quite strong if the driving had been in the combat zone. A grave breach would only be committed if the accused 'wilfully, in violation of the relevant provisions of' the Protocol made an individual civilian the object of attack.[57]

Because the scenario of the civilian ammunition truck driver highlights the problem so well, it became a focal point of discussion at a conference of experts convened at The Hague in 2003 to consider the question of what is meant by 'taking a direct part in hostilities'.[58] While everybody agreed that the truck was a legitimate target, there was no consensus about the lawfulness of attacking the driver: some thought that he had forfeited his protected status while others did

---

[56]Some readers interpreted this passage in the first edition of this book as saying that the driver had forfeited his protected status. That was not the author's intention, which was to point out that, even if a violation of the law of war had been committed by the soldier, it would be difficult to secure a conviction in court. For the record, the passage read as follows: 'In the example of the civilian driving the ammunition truck, it is the truck that is the target. Depending on the weapons available to him, the soldier attacking the truck may follow his training and fire at the centre of the target. If the truck driver is killed, it will be incidental to the attack on that target, proportionate and lawful. If, on the other hand, the attacking soldier is armed only with a sniper's rifle, his only way of stopping the truck might be to fire at the driver. In the unlikely event that the sniper knew that the driver was a civilian – and if the truck was a military vehicle the presumption of civilian status cannot realistically apply – it could be argued in the sniper's defence that the civilian is an unlawful combatant who has forfeited his protected civilian status by taking a direct part in hostilities by driving military supplies. The argument would be quite strong if the driving had been in the combat zone even if the vehicle had been a civilian vehicle. A grave breach would only be committed if the accused "wilfully, in violation of the relevant provisions of" the Protocol made an individual civilian the object of attack.'

[57]Protocol I, Arts. 43 para. 2, 51, paras. 2 and 3.

[58]Meeting of experts at the TMC Asser Institute on 2 June 2003 on direct participation in hostilities under international humanitarian law. The unfortunate truck driver became affectionately known as 'Bob'.

not. Though there was general agreement that working in a munitions factory should not be regarded as taking a direct part in hostilities but that opening fire at members of the enemy armed forces should be so regarded, the experts at the Asser Institute meeting were not able to reach any conclusion as to what activity between those two extremes would result in loss of protected status. The problem really only arises in connection with attacks on individuals. In other words, has the individual forfeited his civilian protection so that he can be directly attacked? This problem can best be illustrated by a list:

1 Attacking or trying to capture members of the enemy armed forces.
2 Attacking or trying to capture the weapons, equipment or locations of members of the enemy armed forces.
3 Laying mines, planting or detonating bombs.
4 Sabotaging military lines of communication.
5 Deploying to or recovering from places where the activities listed in 1 to 4 are carried out.
6 Becoming member of a guerrilla groups or armed faction involved in attacks against enemy armed forces.
7 Children throwing petrol bombs or stones at enemy military patrols.
8 Acting as armed guards at military installations.
9 Collecting weapons on behalf of a party to the conflict.
10 Carrying and using small arms for the purpose of defending themselves or their families against banditry, rape and pillage.
11 Driving ammunition trucks to supply enemy armed forces.
12 Hiding weapons on behalf of a party to the conflict.
13 Providing the armed forces with technical assistance in the maintenance of weapons systems or military transportation.
14 Providing assistance in the gathering and processing of intelligence data, for example, assessing aerial photography for likely targets.
15 Working in scientific laboratories developing new weapons.
16 Working in depots and canteens providing food and clothing for the armed forces.
17 Working as civilian officials in the Ministry of Defence.
18 Working in factories producing weapons platforms, weapons and ammunition.
19 Working in factories producing components that directly assist the enemy's war effort.
20 Working in commercial institutions that indirectly support the war effect by financing the government through taxation.

The author is inclined to the view that taking 'a direct part in hostilities' should be narrowly construed both in terms of the activity and its duration as, otherwise, civilian protection is placed severely at risk, and would draw the line after point 6. In cases 1 to 5, civilian protection would be lost for the duration of the activity concerned. In case 6, it would be lost so long as participation in the activities of the group continued. Items 7 to 9 are borderline cases and the correct response will depend on the circumstances. In case 7, at the very least, the soldiers under attack have the right to use necessary force in self-defence. In case 8, protection would only be lost if the civilian guards tried by force to prevent attacks on, or attempts to capture, the military installation by members of the opposing armed forces. Case 9 would not result in loss of protection though members of the opposing armed forces would be entitled to prevent them doing so, by force if necessary. The civilians concerned also run the risk of being mistaken for combatants. Cases 10 onwards do not result in the forfeiture of protection, though the trucks, caches, workshops and installations in question may be legitimate targets so the civilians concerned run the risk of death of injury resulting from attacks on those targets. For the reasons given in Chapter 3, the institutions in case 20 are not legitimate targets.

Civilian property and military targets

As with personnel, the attacker also has to distinguish between civilian property and military targets. The frequent use by commentators during the 1991 Gulf war of the expression 'civilian target' indicates a lack of understanding of this basic principle. The fact that civilians are killed as a result of mistaken attacks on civilian property, or as an incidental effect of attacking military targets, also leads to muddled thinking.

The preamble to the St Petersburg Declaration[59] placed great emphasis on attacks against military personnel. In the intervening years, attacking military personnel has, in some conflicts, become less important.

Military objectives such as tanks, missile sites, munitions factories and dumps and communications installations have become correspondingly more significant, so that one could say that in the twentieth century objects became militarily more crucial targets than personnel. During the course of this development, the old-fashioned clear distinction between combatants and non-combatants seems, to some observers, to have become blurred. Perhaps more important now is the distinction between military objectives and civilian objects. That is not to say that the rule of distinction as applied to personnel has become obsolete. It remains in force, but it does not have the dominating position it had in 1868.

Civilians and civilian objects protected

The Hague Regulations prohibit the unnecessary destruction of enemy property, attacking undefended towns, dwellings or buildings, and pillage. The parties to

---

[59] 'for this purpose it is sufficient to disable the greatest possible number of men; ... this object would be exceeded by the employment of arms which uselessly aggravate the sufferings of disabled men ...'

the conflict are also required to spare buildings dedicated to religion, art, science or charity and hospitals and also places where the wounded and sick are cared for.[60] Westlake commented as early as 1913 that, even in fortified towns, firing at homes, when it can be avoided, is cruel and useless and ought to be forbidden unless there is reason to suspect that the houses are occupied by troops or are used as magazines.[61]

By 1938 the British Prime Minister, Neville Chamberlain, was able to say in the House of Commons that:

1 The bombing of civilians as such and deliberate attacks upon civilian populations is against international law.
2 Targets which are aimed at from the air must be legitimate military objectives and must be capable of identification.
3 Reasonable care must be taken in attacking these military objectives so that by carelessness a civilian population in the neighbourhood is not bombed.[62]

These principles were confirmed in a resolution of the Assembly of the League of Nations later that year.[63] As late as 4 June 1940, the British Chief of Air Staff reminded his commanders that the intentional bombing of the civilian population was illegal, targets being limited to enemy forces, fortifications, supply depots, shipyards, power stations, oil refineries, munitions factories and railway lines.[64]

State practice in the Second World War seemed to undermine this clear view of customary law.[65] It involved large numbers of civilian casualties and a tendency to bomb centres of population.[66] In brief,[67] this practice was due to the following factors:

1 Confusion over the concept of undefended towns. The Hague Regulations prohibited the bombardment of undefended towns but left open the question of what was defended and whether, if it were defended, the town itself could be bombarded or only military objectives in the town. Some thought that a town could be regarded as defended if it were protected by anti-aircraft guns, or if it were behind the enemy front line so that ground troops could not

[60]Hague Regulations, Arts. 22–8.
[61]Westlake, *International Law*, p. 89.
[62]House of Commons Debates, vol. 337, col. 937.
[63]League of Nations paper A.69, 1938, IX, 28 September 1938, entitled Protection of civilian populations against air bombardment.
[64]This message is cited in P. S. Meilinger, Winged defence, answering the critics of air power, *Air Power Review*, winter 2000, 41, at p. 43.
[65]H. M. Hanke, The 1923 Hague Rules of Air Warfare, *International Review of the Red Cross*, No. 292, January–February 1993, pp. 33–5, describes the gradual relaxation of the instructions on naval and air bombardment issued to the RAF in August 1935. See also Best, *Law and War*, pp. 199–205.
[66]For a brief summary of state practice during the Second World War, see E. Rosenblad, Area bombing and international law, *Military Law and Law of War Review*, 1976, p. 66.
[67]For a more detailed analysis, see Parks, Air war, p. 44.

occupy it without resistance. Some thought that undefended meant without military value or without military objectives.[68]

2 The concept of total war where civilians worked in the armaments industry or in administrative or logistic capacities to release more soldiers for actual combatant duties.

3 The need to attack objectives supporting the war effort such as factories, ports, means of supply and communications, as well as purely military targets. This inevitably affected civilians who worked in those installations or who lived nearby. Spaight argued that this need extended to private property, the aim of warfare being by 'direct action to paralyse the enemy's higher administration, to interrupt his munitionment, to interfere with his life and business, to disturb and disorganize his productivity, to destroy his morale, to weaken his will and capacity as a national organism to continue the struggle'. However, he qualifies this later by saying that international law 'should refuse to countenance any departure from the principle that Air Force necessity permits the destruction of non-military property only when non-combatants in the vicinity have at least the opportunity to provide for their safety, and that attack upon such property is absolutely banned when it must involve necessarily the sacrifice of innocent life'.[69]

4 It was argued that target area bombing was justified, first, because at night it was impracticable to aim at a precise objective and, second, for tactical reasons. Anyway, the areas concerned were 'industrial urban centres manufacturing the requirements of the German war machine'.[70] Greenspan suggested in 1959 that target area bombing could be justified on two grounds. First, that the area is 'so preponderantly used for war industry as to impress that character on the whole neighbourhood, making it essentially an indivisible whole'. The second factor must be that the area is so heavily defended from air attack that the selection of specific targets within the area is impracticable.[71]

5 The doctrine of belligerent reprisals,[72] which leads to confusion about legitimate targets. The doctrine allows a belligerent, after a warning has remained unheeded, to take proportionate measures that would ordinarily be unlawful, in order to redress violations of the law of war by the enemy.[73] Such measures could include attacks on the enemy's civilian population. The German air attack on Coventry was said to be a reprisal for British attacks on German

---

[68] See Jochnick and Normand, Legitimation of violence, pp. 72, 76, 80.

[69] J. M. Spaight, The doctrine of air force necessity, undated paper from the Air Ministry Archive.

[70] Some notes on the policy regarding the bombing of towns in enemy countries with special reference to the effect of such bombing on civilians as well an objects of non-military significance on the areas attacked, dated 4 December 1943 on Air Ministry File No. ACAS(G)/DW/.

[71] Greenspan, *Modern Law*, p. 336.

[72] For a more extensive treatment of the subject, see, e.g., C. J. Greenwood, Reprisals and reciprocity in the new law of armed conflict, in Meyer, *Armed Conflict*, p. 227.

[73] Draper, Humanitarianism, p. 16, has expressed it much better as: 'a reprisal is an act, otherwise illegal, taken as a last resort to compel the enemy to desist from previous illegalities'.

cities. British bomber command retaliated by attacking the centre of Mannheim.[74] There are accusations and counter-accusations about who started the practice of target area bombing,[75] but the fact is that the German air force was primarily designed as a tactical arm in close support of the ground forces while the Royal Air Force concept had always been strategic.[76]

6 The allies found that the bombing of targets in Germany involved heavy losses in aircraft.[77] The RAF switched to night attacks, which increased the difficulty of identifying targets. Targets were attacked at increasing distances to reduce the risks to the attacking forces but to the detriment of accuracy. This resulted in high civilian casualties. It is estimated that about 42,000 civilians were killed in Hamburg in August 1943 because of the firestorms, which were impossible to bring under control.[78]

7 The reluctance of the attackers to accept risks means that they tend to rely on the information they have been given and presume that the object to be attacked is military rather than civilian.[79] One author mentions a symposium in which officers were asked to discuss a hypothetical helicopter attack on a village they had reason to believe was undefended. Their response was that they would never allow themselves to get close enough to the target at a speed slow enough to tell whether the target was legitimate or not. They knew that if the village were defended they would be imperilled if they were to approach it too slowly or too close.[80] This unwillingness is offset by the greater sophistication in target intelligence, often by satellite, and in guidance and tracking systems. Reports of the accuracy of cruise missiles and guided bombs used by the United States in conflicts since 1991 are quite astonishing.[81] The responsibilities of the attackers in cases such as this will be examined in Chapter 4.

[74]Rosenblad, Area bombing, p. 66.

[75]The British directive on bombardment policy of 29 October 1942, on file C.S. 15803/A.S.P.1, seems to be based on a principle of reciprocity. It sets out rules for attacks against targets in enemy occupied France, Belgium and Holland that carefully reflect the Chamberlain principles but concludes, with regard to German, Italian and Japanese territory, 'consequent upon the enemy's adoption of a campaign of unrestricted air warfare, the Cabinet have authorised a bombing policy which includes the attack of enemy morale'.

[76]See Best, *Humanity*, pp. 271–2. However, Parks notes that the German air force also planned for strategic bombing (Parks, Air war, p. 54).

[77]Precision-bombing raids caused severe losses, for example the British dam raids and the United States raid against the ball-bearing industry in Schweinfurt in 1943; see Rosenblad, Area bombing, p. 67.

[78]Rosenblad, Area bombing, p. 67. See also Best, *Law and War*, p. 280.

[79]There was such a case during the NATO air campaign during the Kosovo conflict of 1999, when a column of civilian tractors was attacked from 15,000 feet; see A. P. V. Rogers, Zero-casualty warfare, *International Review of the Red Cross*, March 2000, p. 165.

[80]P. Karsten, *Law, Soldiers and Combat*, Greenwood, 1978, at p. 93.

[81]See, for example, the report of a cruise missile attack on the Jumhouriyah bridge in Baghdad in the *Daily Telegraph* of 7 February 1991. Protocol I, of course, now re-establishes the presumption of civilian status, see Arts. 48 and 52, para. 3.

8   There is also the theory, discussed by Walzer, that the decision to bomb
     German cities was taken at a time of supreme emergency when German forces
     were victorious everywhere and Bomber Command was the only possibility
     for offensive action to defeat those forces.[82] As noted above, there was an
     argument at the time that customs and usages of war could be suspended by
     military necessity. Parks, makes the point with characteristic forcefulness
     that during the Second World War air planners were simply unable to ascer-
     tain what the law was. They would not have found a list of legitimate targets
     or a definition of the distinction between combatants and non-combatants; at
     best they 'would have found considerable disagreement and confusion among
     scholars'. Similarly there would have been uncertainty about whether attacking
     civilians to lower morale and bring pressure to bear on their military leaders
     to surrender was a legitimate object of warfare, or whether undermining morale
     was simply a legitimate by-product of attacks on military objectives as they
     were then understood.[83] Best refers to the philosophical idea of double-effect
     and concludes that hitting civilian morale was often as important as hitting
     military objectives and sometimes the principal purpose.[84] Parks adds that
     the law had failed to keep pace with technological developments.[85]

All these factors led to a generation of soldiers and civilians who were under
the misapprehension that civilians and civilian objects might legitimately be
attacked. While a delegate at the United Nations Conference on Conventional
Weapons in 1979, the writer was told by a senior diplomat that it was only when
the diplomat became involved in arms control matters two years previously that
he had realized for the first time that it was not permissible to attack civilians.

Guerrilla warfare has tended to cause confusion. During the Rhodesian civil
war, for example, observation patrols watched a guerrilla armed and in uniform
disappear behind a bush and at the next sighting, five minutes later, appear in
red shirt and dark trousers, having peeled off his uniform and hidden it with his
weapon, leaving the patrol uncertain whether it was the same man.[86]

Media reports can also convey a misleading impression. If, quite rightly, they
focus on civilian casualties caused, for example, by indiscriminate artillery fire
or by a deliberate policy of terrorizing the civilian population, the uninformed
may come to believe that attacks on civilians are a part of normal warfare.

Commentators who tried to rationalize these activities were, perhaps, led astray
into thinking that the rule of distinction had changed. As has been pointed out
elsewhere,[87] they might more profitably have concentrated on what was a

---

[82]Walzer, *Just and Unjust Wars*, pp. 255–63.
[83]See Jochnick and Normand, Legitimation of violence, pp. 78, 82, 86–9, 92.
[84]Best, *Law and War*, p. 280.
[85]Parks, Air war, p. 50.
[86]T. Arbuckle, Rhodesian bush war strategies and tactics, *Journal of the Royal United Services Institute*, 1979.
[87]A. P. V. Rogers, Conduct of combat and risks run by the civilian population, *Military Law and Law of War Review*, 1982, p. 295.

legitimate target.[88] A military aircraft factory is clearly a legitimate target.[89] The factory may, of course, be manned entirely by civilians. However, it is only direct attacks on civilians that are prohibited.[90] Loss of civilian life caused by the destruction of the factory is incidental because civilians were not the object of the attack. It is here that the rule of proportionality, dealt with below, comes into play. If the incidental casualties expected are out of proportion to the military gain anticipated, the attack becomes unlawful.[91]

The credibility of the concept of civilian immunity was stretched by the bombing techniques of the Second World War and steps had to be taken subsequently to reinforce that principle by making indiscriminate attacks unlawful. Whatever the legal position may have been in 1945, attempts have been made by the drafters of Geneva Protocol I of 1977 to restate and reinforce the customary rules protecting civilians. It is clear now that attacks on individual civilians or on the civilian population are prohibited.[92] Even reprisals against civilians and civilian objects are now prohibited by Protocol I.[93]

Rule of proportionality[94]

This rule is an attempt to balance the conflicting military and humanitarian interests (or military necessity and humanity) and is most evident in connection with the reduction of incidental damage caused by military operations.[95] It has been described as the nub of the law of armed conflict, which may itself be regarded as a development of the rule.[96] It may be inferred from Arts. 15 and 22 of the Lieber Code and is to be found elsewhere, such as the customary rules on reprisals and in the concept of self-defence in the *jus ad bellum*.[97] It is considered to be part of the customary law of armed conflict[98] and is reflected in the Hague Air Warfare Rules of 1923.[99]

---

[88]This subject is dealt with in Chapter 3.

[89]Within the definition of military objective in Protocol I, Art. 52.

[90]*Ibid.*, Art. 51.

[91]See Protocol I, Art. 51, para. 5(b).

[92]Oppenheim, *International Law*, p. 346; Protocol I, Art. 51.

[93]Arts. 51 para. 6, 52 para. 1, 53 para. c, 54 para. 4, 55 para. 2, 56 para. 4, unless a reservation be entered to any or all of these paragraphs.

[94]For a more detailed essay on the subject, see F. Krüger-Sprengel, Le concept de proportionalité dans le droit de la guerre, *Military Law and Law of War Review*, 1980, p. 179.

[95]See D. Fleck, Die rechtlichen Garantien des Verbots von unmittelbaren Kampflandlung gegen Zivilpersonen, *Military Law and Law of War Review*, 1966, vol. I, pp. 98–9.

[96]D. H. N. Johnson, The legality of modern forms of aerial warfare, *Royal Aeronautical Society Journal*, August 1968, p. 685.

[97]The *Caroline* case, 29 British and Foreign State Papers 1129.

[98]F. Kalshoven, The reaffirmation and development of international humanitarian law, *Netherlands Yearbook of International Law*, 1978, at p. 116; W. J. Fenrick, The rule of proportionality and Protocol I in conventional warfare, 98 *Military Law Review* (1982), at p. 96.

[99]Art. 24.

An example of the practical application of the rule of proportionality is given by Masters.[100] In Iraq, in 1941, the author's battalion had just completed a successful assault on a feature known as the Big House. They saw wicker boats being launched onto the inland floods and were about to call up artillery fire when the commanding officer (CO) told them to wait because there might be women and children in the boats. As the boats were setting out from a concealed village, this was quite possible. Masters protested that, whether or not the boats contained women and children, they certainly contained enemy soldiers. Nevertheless, the CO gave the order not to fire. Disgusted at the time by his CO's attitude, Masters later thought he had acted honourably. Strangely, the CO was not pleased with himself because his character had prevented him from doing what a real ball-of-fire soldier would have done.

From the legal point of view, the CO acted correctly. He instinctively adopted the presumption that there were civilians in the boats as well as soldiers and concluded that to kill those civilians would have been out of proportion to the military gain achieved by killing the enemy soldiers, who posed no immediate threat to his unit.

A munitions factory is such an important military objective that the death of a large proportion of the civilians working there cannot be said to be disproportionate to the military gain achieved by destroying the factory. A more significant factor is the number of incidental casualties and the amount of property damage caused to civilians living nearby if the factory is in a populated area. The explosion of a munitions factory may cause serious collateral damage, but that is a risk of war that would not infringe the proportionality rule.

Parks describes a United States air attack, during the Vietnam war in 1972, on a hydroelectric plant at Lang Chi. It was estimated to supply up to 75 per cent of Hanoi's industrial and defence needs. On the other hand, it was thought that if the dam at the site were breached, as many as 23,000 civilians could die, presumably in the resultant floods. President Nixon's military advisers said that if laser-guided bombs were used there was a 90 per cent chance of the mission's being accomplished without breaching the dam. On that basis, the President authorized the attack, which successfully destroyed the electricity generating plant without breaching the dam.[101] This seems a good example of the proportionality rule at work.

Collateral damage may be even more severe if a factory produces nuclear, chemical or biological weapons. It is to be hoped that such factories would not be sited in populated areas,[102] but if they are, the enemy must be entitled to attack them even though the consequences for the civilian population may be severe. What, therefore, does the rule of proportionality require of the attacker

---

[100]J. Masters, *The Road past Mandalay*, Michael Joseph, 1961, p. 35.

[101]Parks, Air war, pp. 168–9.

[102]For the responsibilities of the defenders in such cases, see Chapter 5.

in the case of targets such as these? The answer is that the attacker must use precision weapons, for example, camera-guided missiles, aimed at the factory itself. If the attacking state does not possess such weapons, its obligations are to consider the feasibility of other methods or means of attack that would achieve the same result but reduce incidental damage as far as possible. In the Gulf war of 1991, for example, the Royal Air Force used Buccaneer aircraft fitted with laser target designators to pinpoint targets.[103] In certain situations it may be possible to put targets such as these out of action by sabotage raids by commandos. Further, the attacker must, so far as possible, carry out the attack in such a way as to prevent the escape of dangerous substances, radiation, or chemical or biological contamination. An example of such a precision attack was the United States air attack on vital equipment near the oil terminal at al-Ahmadi during the Gulf war to prevent oil escaping into the Gulf.[104]

Attacking isolated targets in populated areas is one thing, but what of fighting between ground forces in populated areas? It is an unfortunate feature of war in populated areas that large numbers of civilians are killed. The death and destruction caused by artillery and mortar fire during the Yugoslav civil war of 1991–95 is all too obvious from media reports. Fenrick describes the capture of Manila in 1945 in the face of tenacious opposition by Japanese troops. United States forces had frequently to resort to the use of artillery to protect the lives of their own soldiers. An estimated 100,000 civilians were killed, mainly in the crossfire, compared with 17,000 soldiers on both sides. In Fenrick's words 'No one wanted these people to die or derived any military benefit from their death. It just happened'.[105]

The rule of proportionality was first set out in treaty form in Arts. 51, para. 5(b) and 57, para. 2(b) of Protocol I.[106] The precise scope of the rule before that is not entirely clear, but it probably prohibited military acts that were grossly disproportionate to the object to be obtained.[107] The Pentagon put it thus: 'It prohibits military action in which the negative effects (such as collateral civilian casualties) clearly outweigh the military gain'.[108] This formulation has been criticized as more relaxed than the statements of the rule appearing in the United States military manuals and in Protocol I.[109] But it seems to the author that the Department of Defence report represents a reasonable attempt to articulate the

[103]P. Hine, Despatch by the Joint Commander of Operation Granby, second supplement to the *London Gazette*, 28 June 1991 (Despatch), p. G42.

[104]United States Department of Defence, *Conduct of the Persian Gulf War*, Final Report to Congress, April 1992 (Department of Defence report), p. 625.

[105]Fenrick, Proportionality, p. 92.

[106]But it had its roots in the ICRC draft rules of 1956, Art. 8.

[107]W. E. Hall, *A Treatise on International Law*, Clarendon Press, 8th edn by A. Pearce Higgins, 1924, at p. 635.

[108]Department of Defence report, p. 611.

[109]See R. K. Goldman, The legal regime governing the conduct of Operation Desert Storm, *University of Toledo Law Review*, vol. 23, 1992, no. 2, p. 337.

rule of proportionality as it stood before its codification in Protocol I. Green-wood[110] comments that not too much significance should be attached to language in a report to Congress, which was not a piece of precise legal drafting.

Despite its importance, no separate article of Protocol I is devoted to the rule of proportionality. It is to be found in two different places. First, it is merely given as an example of an attack prohibited because it is indiscriminate. The example is 'an attack which may be expected to cause incidental loss of civilian life, injury to civilians, damage to civilian objects, or a combination thereof, which would be excessive in relation to the concrete and direct military advantage anticipated'.[111] Second, the proportionality rule is also to be found, in almost identical language, in the article dealing with precautions in attack. That article requires commanders to cancel attacks if they may be expected to offend the proportionality rule.[112]

As Kalshoven has pointed out, the word 'proportionality' does not even appear in these articles because of opposition by some delegations at the diplomatic conference at which Protocol I was negotiated (CDDH) to the very concept of proportionality.[113] They were reluctant to include any reference to the proportion-ality rule because of the difficulty of comparing things that were not comparable (i.e. military advantage and civilian losses) and because it precluded objective judgement, leaving it to military commanders to overemphasize the military advantage. Doswald-Beck sums it up well by saying that it is 'impossible to state that a factory is worth X civilians . . . If, for example, the destruction of a bridge has a crucial importance for the success of a particular campaign, higher casualties will be tolerable to achieve this than, for example, the destruction of a munitions factory of secondary importance.'[114] The concept of excessive civilian loss was eventually accepted as a compromise.[115]

The rule is more easily stated than applied in practice, especially in a case where in adopting a method of attack that would reduce incidental damage the risk to the attacking troops is increased. The rule is unclear as to the degree of care required of the soldier and the degree of risk he must take. It is suggested, however, that the risk to the attacking forces is a factor to be taken into con-sideration when applying the proportionality rule. Nor is it clear what level of civilian casualties would be regarded as disproportionate. In the case of Manila mentioned above the ratio of civilian to military deaths was nearly 6:1. The problem is more acute nowadays given the firepower available to relatively small units. Parks raises two interesting further points: first, that civilians work-ing within a legitimate military target who are killed when it is attacked should

---

[110]Greenwood, Gulf conflict, p. 78.
[111]Art. 51, para. 5(b).
[112]Art. 57, para. 2(a)(iii) and (b); see further Chapter 4.
[113]Kalshoven, Reaffirmation, p. 117.
[114]The value of the 1977 Protocols, in Meyer, *Armed Conflict*, p. 156.
[115]Fenrick, Proportionality, pp. 103–6.

not be regarded as collateral casualties and, therefore, should not be taken into account when applying the proportionality rule; and, second, that the attacking commander should be given credit for any civilian casualties caused through the failure of the defenders to take adequate precautions against the effect of attacks.[116] Both these points are valid though there would still be an obligation on the attacker to take feasible precautions to minimize the risk to civilians working within the military target.[117] Schmitt[118] is doubtful of the legitimacy of the failure of the defenders being taken into consideration as part of the proportionality equation. He may be right on the basis of the formulation of the proportionality rule in Protocol I,[119] but, in the author's opinion, a tribunal considering a person's criminal responsibility would be interested in all the circumstances of the case, including the actions of the defenders. An interesting recent phenomenon is that of civilian volunteers deploying to protect potential military objectives. In the Kosovo conflict of 1999, civilians went and stood on bridges that they thought might be attacked by NATO aircraft. In the event, the bridges were not attacked while these civilians were standing there but, if they had been, it could be argued that the civilians had forfeited their protected status under the law of armed conflict.

The International Committee of the Red Cross (ICRC) *Commentary* contains the following passage:[120]

The idea has been put forward that even if they are very high, civilian losses and damages may be justified if the military advantage at stake is of great importance. This idea is contrary to the fundamental rules of the Protocol; in particular it conflicts with Article 48 (Basic Rule)[121] and with paragraphs 1[122] and 2[123] of the present Article 51. The Protocol does not provide any justification for attacks which cause *extensive* civilian losses and damage. Incidental losses and damages should never be *extensive*.

This passage introduces a new idea, of extensive damage, which cannot be supported by reference to Protocol I. Had the word 'excessive' been used for 'extensive' the last two sentences of the passage quoted above would be legally accurate. Otherwise this passage makes nonsense of the rule of proportionality, the whole idea of which is to achieve a balance between the military advantage and the incidental loss. Clearly, the more important the military objective, the

---

[116]Parks, Air war, p. 174.

[117]Protocol I, Art. 57 para. 2(a)(ii). See further Chapter 4.

[118]Schmitt, Book review, pp. 261–2.

[119]Incidental loss of civilian life, injury to civilians, damage to civilian objects, or a combination thereof, which would be excessive in relation to the concrete and direct military advantage anticipated.

[120]Y. Sandoz, C. Swinarski, B. Zimmerman, with J. Pictet, *Commentary* on the Additional Protocols of 8 June 1977, ICRC, 1987 (ICRC *Commentary*), para. 1980.

[121]'The rule of distinction.

[122]General protection of the civilian population.

[123]Civilian population and civilians not to be attacked.

greater the incidental losses before it could be said that the rule of proportionality had been violated. Greenwood[124] says that the above statements of the ICRC represent only the views of certain ICRC lawyers and that the comments of Air Vice-Marshal Wrattan are probably closer to the interpretation which most states would place on the proportionality principle. Air Vice-Marshal Wrattan said in evidence to the House of Commons Defence Committee that certain targets: 'were not ... in my judgement and that of the Americans of a critical nature. That is to say, they were not fundamental to the timely achievement of victory. Had that been the case then, regrettably, irrespective of what collateral damage might have resulted, one would have been responsible and had a responsibility for accepting those targets and for going against them.'[125] Another problem is whether the humanitarian and military limbs of the proportionality rule must be looked at in the longer or shorter term. The answer probably is that it does not matter so long as the same timescale is applied to both limbs.[126]

The author has made the following attempt elsewhere to summarize the practical application of the proportionality rule:

It is relatively easy to think of extreme situations such as the counter-attack on an enemy stronghold in a village. If the commander directs his attack at the stronghold, the risk of excessive incidental loss is minimal. If he destroys the whole village, there is a much greater risk of infringing the proportionality rule.

It is the commander who has to make the decision. He must weigh up the military advantages and the incidental loss. He must decide what steps are feasible to verify that the objects to be attacked are military objectives and what feasible precautions can be taken to minimize incidental loss. He may be able to make a comparison between different methods of attack, so as to be able to choose the least excessive method compatible with military success.

But his decision may be questioned later by a tribunal dealing with grave breaches under Art. 85 of the Protocol. It would seem that such a tribunal would have to look at the situation as it appeared to the military commander at the time, and then decide whether, in its opinion, the proportionality and feasibility tests were satisfied. If the tribunal found that the civilian object damaged was clearly separate, or that the military advantage was either nil or negligible, it might take the view that the commander had failed to do everything feasible or take all feasible precautions. The commander should, of course, be given the benefit of any doubt.[127]

---

[124]Greenwood, Gulf conflict, p. 78.

[125]House of Commons Defence Committee, Tenth Report, *Preliminary Lessons of Operation Granby*, HMSO, 1991 (Defence Committee Report), p. 38.

[126]Rogers, Conduct of combat, p. 311.

[127]Rogers, Conduct of combat, p. 311. See Protocol I Art. 75.4(d) on the presumption of innocence. Green is critical of this sentence in his review of *Law on the Battlefield* in the summer 1997 edition of the *Naval War College Review*, at p. 132, where he says that it is contrary to the view of the ICRC, and possibly the wording of Protocol I. In referring to a commander's being given the benefit of the doubt, I am trying to say that, while the commander is required to apply the rule of proportionality in the conduct of combat, a tribunal subsequently considering his criminal responsibility would also have to apply the presumption of innocence in a borderline case.

Factors to be taken into account are numerous: for example, the military importance of the target or objective, the density of the civilian population in the target
area, the likely incidental effects of the attack, including the possible release of
hazardous substances, the types of weapon available to attack the target and their
accuracy, whether the defenders are deliberately exposing civilians or civilian
objects to risk, the mode of attack and the timing of the attack, especially in the
case of a mixed target. If civilian workers are absent at night, that might be the
best time to launch the attack so as to reduce civilian casualties.[128] In the Gulf
war of 1991, allied attacks on dual-use facilities (i.e. military and civilian) were
normally scheduled at night because fewer people would be inside or on the
streets outside.[129] The rule of proportionality will be considered again in the
context of precautions in attack in Chapter 4.

Indiscriminate attacks

Having decided what the military objectives are, the military commander then
has to consider whether they can be attacked jointly or whether they must be
attacked separately. The rule of distinction, and possibly the rule of proportionality, is violated if the attack is indiscriminate.

Customary law

Whether there existed a customary rule prohibiting indiscriminate attacks is a
debatable question. Probably only blind attacks were prohibited under customary
law since they would have violated the principle of distinction.[130] Other, direct,
attacks would have had to conform to the rule of proportionality.[131] It could be
argued, however, that the rule of distinction implies that reasonable care must
be taken to ensure that the military target is, in fact, attacked.[132] In 1919, the
Committee of Imperial Defence expressed the view that it should be illegal
to bomb the civilian population indiscriminately without attempting to attack
military objectives. The drafters of the Air Warfare Rules obviously thought so
too, because they provided that where military objectives were situated so that
they could not be bombarded 'without the indiscriminate bombardment[133] of the

---

[128] ICRC *Commentary*, para. 2023.

[129] Department of Defence report, p. 100.

[130] In the *Blaškič* case, 122 ILR 1, 168 (para. 512), the Yugoslavia tribunal inferred from the
shelling of Stari Vitez with 'baby-bombs' (homemade mortars), which could not be aimed accurately, that there was a deliberate attack on civilians.

[131] Rogers, Conduct of combat, p. 298.

[132] Hanke, Air Warfare, p. 24.

[133] In an earlier draft 'indiscriminate bombing' was rendered as 'bombing without distinction', see
Hanke, Air Warfare, p. 25.

civilian population, the aircraft must abstain from the bombardment'.[134] The Rules were never adopted in treaty form so the argument cannot be advanced with complete conviction, especially in light of state practice in the Second World War, but it could be argued that the rule of distinction implies a third requirement, namely that the method or means selected for the attack must be such as to enable the target to be struck. Blix has described these three elements as follows:

1   Targets must be *identified* with some certainty as military objectives.
2   Attacks must be *directed* to such identified targets, and
3   The weapons and methods must be such that the target may be hit with some
    degree of *likelihood*.[135]

Treaty law

The three elements identified by Blix are to be found in Protocol I, which prohibits indiscriminate attacks.[136] These are attacks which:

1   are 'not directed at a specific military objective';
2   'employ a method or means of combat which cannot be directed at a specific
    military objective'; or
3   'employ a method or means of combat the effects of which cannot be limited
    as required' by the protocol;
    'and consequently, in each such case, are of a nature to strike military
    objectives and civilians or civilian objects without distinction.'

The first of these elements would prohibit a missile attack directed at an area the size of a town such as the notoriously inaccurate Scud missiles used by Iraq in the Gulf war of 1991. The second might prohibit the area-bombing technique used to attack several military targets in a populated area. Green makes the point[137] that just because a built-up area exists that does not mean that the larger area is no longer a military objective. He says that the civilian area within it should always be clearly defined and the rule of proportionality must be observed. It is difficult to know what to make of this statement. If civilian areas are defined, steps would have to be taken to avoid incidental damage in those areas, which might negate an area-bombing technique unless they were so small as to be insignificant in relation to the surrounding military objectives. The third element deals with two situations: where the attacker is unable to control the effects of the attack, such as dangerous forces released by it, or where the

---

[134]Art. 24(3).
[135]H. Blix, Area bombardment: rules and reasons, *British Yearbook of International and Comparative Law*, 1978, at p. 48.
[136]Art. 51, para. 4.
[137]L. C. Green, *The Contemporary Law of Armed Conflict*, 2nd edn, Manchester University Press, 2000, p. 150.

incidental effects are too great. In either case, the problem would seem to be covered by the rule of proportionality[138] and, of course, there is a specific article dealing with dangerous forces.[139]

The protocol goes on to give two examples of indiscriminate attacks. The first of these is 'an attack by bombardment which treats as a single military objective a number of clearly separated and distinct military objectives located in a city, town, village or other area[140] containing a similar concentration of civilians or civilian objects'. It has been pointed out that while 'bombardment' was understood at the CDDH to mean bombardment by artillery as well as from the air, the meaning of 'clearly separated and distinct' was far less certain.[141] The second example is where the attack would violate the rule of proportionality.

In considering whether there has been a breach of the rule prohibiting indiscriminate attacks, it suffices if 1, 2 or 3 is violated provided the attack is 'of a nature' to strike military objectives and civilians or civilian objects without distinction. This is a curious provision because it takes no account of the *actual* consequences of an attack. On a strict construction, if the attack is indiscriminate by its nature, it would seem to matter not whether any civilians are actually killed as a result. It is suggested that this would be an absurd and unintended result of the drafting. Certainly, to amount to a grave breach the indiscriminate attack must *affect* the civilian population.[142]

No hard-and-fast rules can be laid down since so much depends on the facts of each case. If, for example, the military objective consists of widely scattered enemy tank formations in the desert, it would be clearly permissible to use weapons having a wider range of effect than would be possible were the attack to be directed at a single communications site in the centre of a heavily populated area. Military objectives dispersed about densely populated areas would normally have to be treated as separate military objectives requiring separate attacks.[143] One commentator has adverted to the difficulty of getting information about the exact location of enemy military objectives and the consequent use of an area-covering method.[144] Of course, there is nothing in the protocol to prevent the use of artillery-covering fire or mine laying[145] to deny an area of land to the enemy. That area of land is a military objective. Other rules of the protocol, such as the rule of proportionality, might, however, impinge on that practice.

---

[138] Set out in Art. 51, para. 5(b).

[139] Art. 56.

[140] 'Other area' covers refugee camps and columns (Kalshoven and Zegveld, *Constraints*, p. 103).

[141] G. Aldrich, New life for the laws of war, *American Journal of International Law*, 1981, at p. 780.

[142] Protocol I, Art. 85, para. 3(b).

[143] C.-I. Skarstedt, Armed forces and the development of the law of war; R. Barras, S. Erman, Forces armées et développement du droit de la guerre: *Military Law and Law of War Review*, 1982, pp. 231, 261 and 270.

[144] Skarstedt, Armed forces, p. 231.

[145] For restrictions on the use of mines, see Chapter 7.

Another writer has referred to the difficulty in the choice of means when attacking several targets by artillery fire. He concludes that it is not feasible to separate artillery units below battery level.[146]

Aldrich expresses the view that 'if the objectives are sufficiently separated so that they can feasibly be attacked separately with the weapons available and if this degree of separation is evident to the attacker, then they must be attacked separately in order to reduce the risks to the civilian population'.[147]

The first two points in the definition of indiscriminate attacks referred to above and the first example of indiscriminate attacks may be regarded as a development of the traditional rule, which prohibited aimless attacks. In the second example of indiscriminate attacks, elements of proportionality have been introduced by the deeming as indiscriminate those attacks that would cause excessive incidental damage. Although this is likely to cause confusion, it may be regarded as simply a revised version of the customary proportionality rule in another guise.

But Protocol I goes further in point 3 of the definition by prohibiting as indiscriminate those attacks 'which employ a method or means of combat the effects of which cannot be limited as required by the Protocol'.[148] This provision, which is new to international law, is unfortunately vague. There is no provision of Protocol I that specifically limits the effects of methods and means. It may be a reference to the rule of proportionality in Art. 57 (precautions in attack). If so, it is superfluous because Art. 57 applies anyway. If it is a reference to Protocol I as a whole, it lacks the precision necessary for a provision the breach of which may result in a person's being charged with a war crime.[149]

The language of Protocol I is unsatisfactory because it confuses the distinction and proportionality principles. Parts 1 and 2 of the definition articulate the rule of distinction, but part 3 strays into considerations of proportionality.

The precise relationship between the rules in Protocol I of proportionality and prohibiting indiscriminate attacks has been closely scrutinized.[150] Some believe that indiscriminate attacks will be illegal even if the proportionality rule has not been offended.[151] Others believe that the proportionality rule prevails, so that even if an attack is actually indiscriminate, there is no violation of the law if the proportionality rule has not been broken.

While it is difficult, applying the language of Protocol I, to come to the same conclusion as those in the second group, one has considerable sympathy for their

---

[146]E. L. Gonsalves, Armed forces and the development of the law of war, *Military Law and Law of War Review*, 1982, p. 192.

[147]Aldrich, New life.

[148]Art. 51, para. 4(c).

[149]Compare Art. 85, para. 3(b).

[150]Krüger-Sprengel, Proportionality, p. 179; Rauch, Necessité, p. 205.

[151]E. Rauch, Conduct of combat and risks run by the civilian population, *Military Law and Law of War Review*, 1982, p. 68. The precise view of Kalshoven and Zegveld on this point in *Constraints*, pp. 103–4, is not entirely clear.

argument. After all, who is concerned about the attack's technically being indiscriminate if no civilian is killed as a result?

Perhaps it is better to regard the various provisions of Protocol I as cumulatively requiring commanders to take care in their planning of an attack to ensure that separate military objectives are separately attacked, with incidental damage reduced as much as possible, and that if the incidental damage is likely to outweigh the military advantage, the attack must be replanned. Basically, the commander will have to ask himself three questions before he proceeds with the attack:

1 Is the target a military objective?
2 Is the attack indiscriminate?
3 Is the rule of proportionality likely to be offended?[152]

The United Kingdom made a declaratory statement on ratification of Protocol I to the effect that, in considering whether an attack is indiscriminate, the attack as a whole should be looked at, not merely isolated or particular parts of the attack, and that commanders must necessarily make their decisions on the basis of their assessment of the information from all sources which is available to them at the relevant time.[153]

The responsibility of commanders is dealt with in Chapter 8.

Definition of attack

The word 'attack' has already been used. It will be used many times in the course of this work. It would be useful, therefore, to define it now.

'Attacks' are currently defined, for the purposes of the law of war, as 'acts of violence against the adversary, whether in offence or in defence'.[154] Kalshoven explains that 'act of violence' involves the use of means of warfare (i.e., weapons) and does not include taking prisoners of war even though that might involve the application of force.[155] The words 'in offence or in defence' ensure that forces who open fire to repel an attack or invasion are themselves engaged in an attack

---

[152]Rogers, Conduct of combat, p. 303.

[153]A. Roberts and R. Guelff, *Documents on the Laws of War*, 3rd edn, Oxford University Press, 2000, p. 511. Doswald-Beck, The value of the 1977 protocols, pp. 156–7, explains the need to look at the whole attack thus: 'This approach should be acceptable if seen within the context of a given tactical operation: such an operation may necessitate, for example, the destruction of six military objectives, one of which, being particularly difficult to get at, might involve far greater casualties than the other five. The attack of that one objective on its own might be of no great use, but within the context of the operation as a whole, absolutely essential. The yardstick, in this example, would be the number of casualties overall in relation to the value of the operation as a whole.' The reference here to casualties must, in the context, include collateral casualties.

[154]Protocol I, Art. 49, para. 1.

[155]Kalshoven and Zegveld, *Constraints*, p. 97.

and equally responsible for compliance with all the rules of Protocol I that deal with attacks.[156]

Those rules apply to all attacks, even attacks in a party's national territory that is under adverse occupation,[157] and apply equally to sea and air warfare directed at targets on land.[158] The *a contrario* argument that since the Protocol applies to attacks on national territory under the control of an adverse party, it does not apply to attacks on national territory not under the control of an adverse party is inadmissible since it is clear from the wording that it applies 'to all attacks in whatever territory conducted'.

The definition of attack is wide enough to include a whole range of attacks, from that of a single soldier opening fire with his rifle to that of an army group's major offensive. However, Fenrick[159] points out that the context of certain provisions of Protocol I[160] is such that the attacks referred to cannot relate to the acts of a single soldier. He hazards the opinion that they can only apply to a formation the size of a division. On the other hand, Switzerland made a declaration on ratification that the provisions of Art. 57, para. 2, of Protocol I create obligations only for commanding officers at battalion or group level and above.[161] The Swiss authorities consider that commanders at lower levels do not have the necessary means, in terms of reconnaissance, to comply with all the requirements of this paragraph.[162] The Swiss military manual places the responsibility on battalion and group commanders or higher commanders to ensure that civilians are warned if possible and that they are not injured and do not suffer harm and that the rule of proportionality is complied with.[163] However, it does not seem possible in practice to apply such a blanket rule since so much will depend on the situation on the ground. The Swiss reservation might make sense in the context of a large-scale attack. The individual company or platoon commander will not have an overview of the tactical situation. That is why the United Kingdom approached the problem from a different angle and made a statement on ratification of Protocol I that the commander must be judged in the light of the information available to him. A commander at a lower level, perhaps a corporal in command of a section, may be involved in an isolated attack when advancing through a town on, say, a small enemy position in a school.[164] In those circumstances the

---

[156]The writer, perhaps obtusely, fails to follow Parks's contention that by so defining attacks maximum constraints were placed on a force engaged in offensive military operations (Parks, Air war, p. 115).

[157]Protocol I, Art. 49, para. 2.

[158]*Ibid.*, para. 3.

[159]Fenrick, Proportionality, p. 102.

[160]E.g. Arts. 51(5)(b) and 57(2).

[161]Roberts and Guelff, *Documents*, p. 509.

[162]Switzerland, *Botschaft über die Zusatzprotokolle zu den Genfer Abkommen*, Swiss Federal Council, 1981 (81.004), p. 52.

[163]Switzerland, *Gesetze und Gebräuche des Krieges*, Swiss Army regulation 51.7/lld, 1987.

[164]As postulated by G. J. Cartledge, *The Soldier's Dilemma*, Australian Department of Defence, 1992, pp. 171–3.

corporal would have to consider whether there were civilians (including children) in the school or whether it had been abandoned. In the former case, he would have to think very carefully about how and with what weapons he should attack the enemy or, indeed, whether he should attack at all if not fired upon. In the latter case, he would still need to consider the possibility of incidental damage being caused by his attack. The better view must be that the level of responsibility will depend on the precise circumstances of the incident under examination in its broader context.

An attack can consist of combined infantry, tanks, artillery, helicopters and other close support aircraft involving many combatants in many different but coordinated actions, each of which would fall within the definition of 'attack'. An offensive would amount to an attack, but so would all its constituent elements. A battle group[165] attack might contravene the provisions of Art. 57 and the question would arise as to whether the corps commander responsible for the whole offensive was also responsible for that small part of it.

Italy made a declaratory statement on ratification, as did other states, 'that the military advantage anticipated from an attack is intended to refer to the advantage anticipated from the attack considered as a whole and not only from isolated or particular parts of the attack'.[166] The United Kingdom made a similar statement.[167] What does this statement mean? The ICRC *Commentary* suggests that it is redundant and that 'it goes without saying that an attack carried out in a concerted manner in numerous places can only be judged in its entirety' but goes on to say that 'this does not mean that during such an attack actions may be undertaken which would lead to severe losses among the civilian population or to extensive destruction of civilian objects'.[168]

At first sight the Italian statement would seem to exculpate the corps commander where the battle group commander has acted outside his authority but it would also seem to exculpate the battle group commander, which would seem to go too far. The statement probably means that, when judging the responsibility of a commander or soldier at a particular level, one has to look at that part of the attack for which he was responsible, but in the context of the attack as a whole. The responsibility of the commander is dealt with in more detail in Chapter 8.

---

[165]Combined armour and infantry.
[166]See Roberts and Guelff, *Documents*, p. 507.
[167]*Ibid.*, p. 511.
[168]ICRC *Commentary*, para. 2218.

2

Enemy armed forces

Law on the battlefield conveniently falls into two parts: how you fight the enemy armed forces and how you protect the enemy's civilian population. The first edition of this book concentrated on the second part. It was written after the Gulf war of 1991, which gave rise to many interesting legal questions about targeting from the air but few relating to the conduct of ground operations. The same was true of the Kosovo conflict of 1999, at least from the point of view of the coalition forces. But then operations in Afghanistan in 2001 and, more so, in Iraq in 2003 resulted in allegations of violations of the law relating to surrender, the flag of truce, perfidy and the treatment of captured persons, making this chapter, dealing with the first part of law on the battlefield, a necessary addition to the book.

Although, as mentioned in Chapter 1, the only legitimate object which states should endeavour to accomplish in war is to weaken the military forces of the enemy,[1] that does not mean that, in fighting the enemy armed forces, international law is silent. The law does impose some limitations. These may conveniently be grouped under the general headings of 'good faith' between the belligerents and 'humanity' towards those who are out of action because of wounds, illness, surrender or capture.

I   Good faith

The reason for the good faith provision of the law of armed conflict is to prevent the abuse, and the consequent undermining, of the protection afforded by the law.

The attack on retreating Iraqi forces on the Basra road during the night of 26 to 27 February 1991 has been the subject of some criticism on the basis that it was not really necessary to attack a retreating column.[2] There are three principal

---

[1]The preamble to the Declaration of St Petersburg of 1868.
[2]F. Smyth, The Gulf War, in R. Gutman and D. Rieff (eds.), *Crimes of War*, W. W. Norton & Company, 1999, at p. 162.

legal issues in relation to this attack: whether the Iraqi column was a legitimate military target, whether the customary rule of proportionality was violated and whether the allies were guilty of bad faith. There can be no question that the column was a legitimate target. It comprised enemy soldiers who had not surrendered. They represented a military threat to coalition operations. As for proportionality, it is true that the column contained civilian vehicles that had been looted from Kuwait but it was reasonable for the allies to assume that they contained members of the Iraqi armed forces. It turned out later that some cars did contain Palestinians and Indians and even some Kuwaiti prisoners, but their unfortunate deaths were not disproportionate to the scale of the military target. As for the question of bad faith, this is not established by examination of the facts. On 22 February 1991, President Bush presented Saddam Hussein with an ultimatum, which expired the following day. It required the Iraqis to commence their withdrawal from Kuwait before expiry of the ultimatum and complete it within one week. In return, the allies undertook not to attack withdrawing troops so long as the withdrawal continued according to the ultimatum. Iraq did not accept these terms, so the conditions of the ultimatum lapsed and the ground attack started on 24 February. Even after that the allies announced that the retreating Iraqis would be safe so long as they abandoned their weapons and vehicles. Needless to say, those on the Basra road did not do so.

Who is a member of the enemy armed forces?

Generally speaking, wars are fought between the armed forces of the parties to the conflict. Members of the armed forces, other than medical personnel and chaplains, are combatants and have the right to take a direct part in hostilities; they may also be made the object of attack at any time, even when off-duty. If captured, they become prisoners of war. It is thus important to be able to identify members of the armed forces. In a conventional conflict between states, such as the Falklands war of 1982, this is not difficult. It is difficult when guerrilla tactics are adopted or irregular militias, paramilitary groups or resistance movements are involved in the fighting.

Two cases on combatant status were decided by the Privy Council (in this context the supreme appellate court for Commonwealth cases) in 1968. In the first case, the accused was a Malaysian national in the Indonesian armed forces operating in Malaysia. It was held that he was not entitled to prisoner-of-war status as he owed allegiance to the detaining power and that he could be tried for an offence against the security laws of Malaysia.[3] In the second case, the accused was a member of the Indonesian armed forces. While wearing civilian clothes he committed sabotage in an office building in Singapore, killing three

[3]*Public Prosecutor* v. *Koi*, 1968 All ER 419.

civilians. It was held that, as he was not operating as a member of the Indonesian armed forces at the time and he did not comply with the requirements of Article 4A paragraph 2 of the Geneva Prisoner of War Convention of 1949, he had neither combatant nor prisoner-of-war status and could be tried for murder under Malaysian domestic law.[4] While the second case turned on its facts, the first case seems objectionable under international law since the prisoner-of-war convention does not make a distinction according to the nationality of the captured person. Nevertheless, even though entitled to prisoner-of-war status, he was, as a Malaysian national, susceptible to trial before the Malaysian courts.

These decisions probably have not survived Protocol I, which states that the 'armed forces of a Party to the conflict consist of all organized armed forces, groups and units which are under a command responsible to that Party for the conduct of its subordinates . . .'.[5] The Protocol makes no reference to nationality, nor is the question mentioned in the ICRC *Commentary* on the Protocol. It would seem, therefore, that so long as a person is a member of the armed forces of a party to the conflict, or of armed forces for which a party to the conflict is responsible, irrespective of his nationality, he is entitled to combatant, and prisoner-of-war, status. There is no real problem in the case of members of the armed forces of a state or of armed groups that are controlled by a party to the conflict. More problematic is the case of volunteers who, without joining the armed forces, fight for a party to the conflict, either as individuals or as formed groups. If those individuals or groups come under command of a party to the conflict, in the sense of accepting and carrying out the orders of that party, it can be argued that they are lawful combatants, unless they are mercenaries.[6] If they are mercenaries or they are not under command, they are not lawful combatants and the party on whose behalf they participate should take all steps in its power to expel them. Of course, if an independent armed group participating in hostilities is large, powerful and organized enough, it may itself become a party to the conflict.

Identifying members of the opposing armed forces is problematic if they conduct guerrilla operations and are farmers by day and fighters by night. It is not clear if they are to be regarded as part-time soldiers or as civilians who have forfeited their protection. While they are involved in guerrilla operations they

[4]*Mohammed Ali* v. *Public Prosecutor*, 1968 All ER 488.

[5]Additional Protocol I of 1977 (Protocol I), Art. 43, para. 1.

[6]According to Protocol I, Art. 47, para. 2, a mercenary is any person who: (a) is specially recruited locally or abroad in order to fight in an armed conflict; (b) does, in fact, take a direct part in the hostilities; (c) is motivated to take part in the hostilities essentially by the desire for private gain and, in fact, is promised, by or on behalf of a Party to the conflict, material compensation substantially in excess of that promised or paid to combatants of similar ranks and functions in the armed forces of that Party; (d) is neither a national of a Party to the conflict nor a resident of territory controlled by a Party to the conflict; (e) is not a member of the armed forces of a Party to the conflict; and (f) has not been sent by a State which is not a Party to the conflict on official duty as a member of its armed forces.

may, of course, lawfully be attacked but how about when they are tilling their fields? This issue was discussed at a meeting of experts in The Hague in 2003,[7] but no consensus could be reached as to whether it was legitimate to attack such fighters in their homes. In the author's opinion, there is a strong argument that if a person belongs to a group of guerrilla fighters that carries out attacks on opposing armed forces, he may be considered a combatant if the group conducts its operations in accordance with the law of war. If it does not so conduct its operations, he may be considered to have forfeited his civilian status for the duration of his membership of, or participation in the actions of, that group. Membership could be established by, for example, his participation in the planning for, or otherwise assisting, in the military operations of the group.

In the Iraq war of 2003, some of the stiffest resistance was put up, not by the Iraqi army, but by the Fedayeen Saddam militia forces. Protocol I did not apply to that conflict because neither Iraq nor the United States is a party to the protocol. Had it applied, these forces might have fallen within the definition of 'armed forces' in the sense of being under command, but they probably did not fulfil the further requirement that they be subject to an internal disciplinary system which enforces compliance with the law of armed conflict. Such forces probably also failed to comply with the requirements of the Hague Regulations: responsible command, fixed distinctive sign recognizable at a distance, carrying arms openly and conducting their operations in accordance with the laws and customs of war.[8]

A member of the armed forces of a state that is not a party to the conflict but who happens to be captured or detained during the conflict is actually regarded as a civilian. When Iraqi forces invaded Kuwait in 1990 they captured some British military personnel who had been seconded by the British authorities for service with the Kuwaiti armed forces as part of the training and liaison team. Because they had been sent on official duty, they would not have been mercenaries if Geneva Protocol I had applied.[9] In fact, because the United Kingdom was not at that stage involved in an armed conflict with Iraq, the Geneva Civilian Convention of 1949 applied to those personnel and they were protected persons. After some diplomatic negotiations, they were released by the Iraqis and repatriated to the United Kingdom.

There is the continuing issue of the Taliban and al-Qa'ida captives held at the United States base at Guantanamo Bay, Cuba. It seems that the former are being held as prisoners of war but not the latter because, according to Ari Fleischer, they belong to a terrorist group, not a state. In fact, the more likely justification for denying them prisoner-of-war status is that they did not fulfil the requirements

---

[7] Expert meeting at the TMC Asser Institute, The Hague, on direct participation in hostilities under international humanitarian law, 2 June 2003.

[8] Hague Regulations 1907, Art. 1.

[9] The United Kingdom was not a party to Protocol I and, at that stage, was not involved in the armed conflict.

of Article 4 of the Geneva Prisoner of War Convention of 1949.[10] So are they protected by the Geneva Civilian Convention of 1949? That applies, in general, to persons who find themselves in the hands of a party to the conflict of which they are not nationals. However, the status of 'protected person' does not apply to nationals of neutral and co-belligerent states that maintain normal diplomatic relations with the detaining power.[11] So that would exclude, for example, al-Qa'ida suspects from the United Kingdom, Pakistan or Algeria. They would be entitled only to the more limited protection of Part II of the Civilian Convention, as well as human rights law. Some United States citizens who were captured fighting for the former Afghan regime were not detained at Guantanamo Bay but at Norfolk, Virginia, on the basis that, as citizens of the United States, they were not entitled to prisoner-of-war status. This appears to follow the Privy Council decision in the *Koi* case. So far, the United States courts have not intervened on behalf of the detainees, either because they do not wish to interfere with the acts of the executive *durante bello* or because Guantanamo Bay is outside their jurisdiction. The English Court of Appeal also decided it had no jurisdiction to interfere, although it was prepared to review judicially the acts of the Foreign and Commonwealth Office in looking after the interests of British nationals detained there.[12] It seems that the conflict in Afghanistan between the coalition and Taliban forces is now over and that persons detained should either be released or put on trial in respect of offences relating to the conflict.[13]

Child fighters

According to a report from Reuters,[14] during the Iraq war of 2003 a United States soldier killed, by machine-gun fire, an Iraqi boy aged about 10 who stooped to pick up a rocket-propelled grenade (RPG) launcher from the body of a dead paramilitary. This was against a background of children being used as fighters and, more often, as scouts and weapons collectors.

The use of children to fight has plagued recent conflicts,[15] but there must be a presumption of civilian status in respect of a 10-year-old. Obviously, if he

---

[10]The US expert on the law of armed conflict, W. H. Parks, called them unprivileged belligerents; see the Department of Defence news briefing of 7 April 2003 on www.defenselink.mil. As to the possible use of military courts to try these captives, see A. P. V. Rogers, The use of military courts to try suspects, *International and Comparative Law Quarterly*, October 2002.

[11]Geneva Civilian Convention 1949 (Civilian Convention), Art. 4. See also Art. 5 on restrictions that can be placed for security reasons on those entitled to protected person status.

[12]*R. (Abassi and another)* v. *Secretary of State for Foreign and Commonwealth Affairs and another* [2002] EWCA Civ159.

[13]The publication of the US Military Commission Instructions of 30 April 2003, see www.nimj.org, is an indication that trials may be contemplated.

[14]K. Murray, US troops face children, and hard calls, in battle, 7 April 2003 at 11:29 p.m. ET, posted on www.reuters.com.

[15]See A. Cataldi, Child soldiers, and C. Dufka, Children as killers, in Gutman and Rieff, *Crimes of War*, at pp. 76 and 78.

picked up an RPG launcher with the intention of using it against the United States troops, he would forfeit his civilian immunity and become a legitimate target. However, he might have picked it up as a weapons collector for the militia[16] or even out of idle curiosity. A lot depends on what had just been happening on the battlefield, for example, whether United States troops had been attacked in the recent past by child fighters in civilian clothes. Also, much would depend on the actual situation and the time for response. So it is difficult to put oneself in the situation. If, for example, the soldier had his machine gun trained on the child as he went to pick up the RPG launcher, that might have been a case for a warning shot; if, on the other hand, his attention was elsewhere and he only became aware through the corner of his eye of the child turning the RPG launcher in his direction, he would have had to act immediately.

Perfidy and ruses of war

Perfidy

The Hague Regulations provide that it is 'especially forbidden . . . to kill or wound treacherously individuals belonging to the hostile nation or army'[17] but go on to say that 'ruses of war are considered permissible'.[18] They do not define treachery or ruses of war.

Protocol I repeats the rule in slightly different language, saying that it is 'prohibited to kill, injure or capture an adversary by resort to perfidy'.[19] It defines perfidy as 'acts inviting the confidence of an adversary to lead him to believe that he is entitled to, or is obliged to accord, protection under the rules of international law applicable in armed conflict, with intent to betray that confidence'.[20] It then gives the following examples of perfidy, if done with intent to betray the enemy's confidence:

(a)   the feigning of an intent to negotiate under a flag of truce or of surrender;
(b)   the feigning of an incapacitation by wounds or sickness;[21]
(c)   the feigning of civilian, non-combatant status; and
(d)   the feigning of protected status by the use of signs, emblems or uniforms of the United Nations or of neutral or other States not Parties to the conflict.[22]

---

[16]This may not be sufficiently proximate to military action to classify it as taking a direct part in hostilities, see Chapter 1.

[17]Hague Regulations, Art. 23(b).

[18]Hague Regulations, Art. 24.

[19]Protocol I, Art. 37, para. 1.

[20]According to the ICRC *Commentary*, para. 1500, there are three elements here: inviting the confidence of the adversary, the intent to betray that confidence (the subjective element) and the actual betrayal of that confidence (the objective element).

[21]The feigning of incapacity with the motive not of attacking the enemy but of surviving to fight another day is permitted.

[22]Protocol I, Art. 37, para. 1.

United States officials have alleged that, during the Iraq war of 2003, the Iraqi regime sent forces carrying white flags as if to indicate an intention to surrender to draw coalition forces into ambushes.[23] In another case, it is alleged that Fedayeen militia dressed in civilian clothes appeared to surrender before opening fire on US marines, nine of whom died.[24] If true, these would be classic examples of perfidy.

Ruses of war

Protocol I confirms that ruses of war are permitted. It defines them as 'acts which are intended to mislead an adversary or to induce him to act recklessly but which infringe no rule of international law applicable in armed conflict and which are not perfidious because they do not invite the confidence of the adversary with respect to protection under the law'. It then gives the following examples: 'the use of camouflage, decoys, mock operations and misinformation'.[25]

Ruses of war are ploys to obtain a tactical advantage by misleading the enemy but without involving the abuse of any legally protected status.

According to the *Manual of Military Law*, legitimate ruses include:

surprises; ambushes; feigning attacks, retreats or flights; simulating quiet and inactivity; assigning large strong-points to a small force; constructing works, bridges etc., which it is not intended to use; transmitting bogus signal messages, and sending bogus despatches and newspapers with a view to their being intercepted by the enemy; making use of the enemy's signals, watchwords, wireless code signs and tuning calls, and words of command; conducting a false military exercise on the wireless on a frequency easily interrupted[26] while substantial troop movements are taking place on the ground; pretending to communicate with troops or reinforcements which do not exist; moving landmarks; constructing dummy airfields and aircraft; putting up dummy guns or tanks; laying dummy minefields; removing badges from uniforms; clothing the men of a single unit in the uniforms of several units so that prisoners and dead may give the idea of a much larger force; giving false ground signals to enable airborne personnel or supplies to be dropped in a hostile area, or to induce aircraft to land in a hostile area.[27]

---

[23]Parks, Department of Defence briefing. According to the *International Herald Tribune* of 24 March 2003, in one incident, a flag of surrender was displayed and was followed by artillery fire and in another, Iraqi troops dressed in civilian clothes appeared to welcome US troops but then ambushed them. Similar claims were made during the Gulf war of 1991: see P. de la Billière, *Storm Command*, HarperCollins, 1992, p. 250. He also refers on this page to duplicity by Iraqi tank commanders advancing with the gun barrels pointing to the rear, indicating that they did not mean to fight, and resulting in coalition second-line forces delaying coming to grips with them. It seems that leaflets dropped by coalition forces in the Iraq war of 2003 required surrendering troops to ensure that tanks turrets were reversed: see A. Buncombe, US army chief says Iraqi troops took bribes to surrender, *The Independent*, 24 May 2003.

[24]Ben Rooney, *The Daily Telegraph, War on Saddam*, Robinson, 2003, p. 64.

[25]Protocol I, Art. 37, para. 2.

[26]Perhaps 'intercepted' is meant.

[27]United Kingdom, *Manual of Military Law*, Part III, HMSO, 1958 (*Manual of Military Law*), para. 312.

A feint attack to mislead the enemy as to the point of the main attack would also be a legitimate ruse. During the Gulf war 1991, the allies carried out a deception plan of naval and artillery bombardments in the east as if in preparation for an amphibious assault while, in fact, the main attack was to be a wide sweep across the desert to the West, coupled with an airborne landing well inside Iraq.[28]

Difference between perfidy and ruses of war

The essence of perfidy is the abuse of protected status to effect the killing, wounding or capture of the enemy; ruses of war, while involving deception, do not involve the abuse of protected status.

The author has tried to explain the difference elsewhere[29] by contrasting the following cases: (a) the camouflaging of a tank so that the enemy pass by unaware of its existence and are then fired on at short and lethal range (a ruse) and (b) the soldier who feigns wounds so that he can fire at short and lethal range on an enemy soldier who comes to his assistance (perfidy). In the first case the tank crew do not feign protected status at all; in the second, the soldier lures the adversary into danger by pretending to have the protected status of someone *hors de combat*.

Tactics: ambush, sniping, sabotage

Ambush is a legitimate tactic, even if done by way of a suicide-bombing mission, provided it is carried out by members of the armed forces in uniform. It is not legitimate if carried out by soldiers masquerading as civilians[30] or by civilians.[31]

The use of snipers is also legitimate as long as they fire at military personnel or at military objectives.[32] The reason why General Galić was indicted in respect of the sniping of targets in Sarajevo during the period September 1992 to August 1994 was because, according to the indictment, the attacks were aimed at civilians in a campaign to terrorize the population of the city.[33]

---

[28]De la Billière, *Storm Command*, p. 283.

[29]A. P. V. Rogers, P. Malherbe and B. Doppler, *Fight it Right* (Model Manual on the Law of Armed Conflict for Armed Forces), ICRC, 1999, para. 1011.2.

[30]Four US soldiers were reported killed in a suicide bomb explosion on 29 March 2003 involving a taxi driven by Ali Jaffar al-Nomani, said to be a non-commissioned officer of the Iraqi army (D. MacIntyre, Suicide bomb threats by women are linked to deaths of American soldiers, *The Independent*, 5 April 2003).

[31]Another three US soldiers were reported killed in a suicide bombing involving a pregnant woman on 3 April 2003 (*Ibid.*).

[32]For further discussion of the subject, see A. P. V. Rogers, What is a legitimate military target? in R. Burchill, N. White and J. Morris (eds.), *Peace, Security and Law: Essays in Honour of Hilaire McCoubrey*, Cambridge University Press, 2004.

[33]*Prosecutor* v. *Stanislav Galić*, Case No. IT-98-29, see the decision of the trial chamber on 3 October 2002.

Sabotage attacks behind enemy lines are also legitimate but the normal rules of the law of armed conflict apply, that is, they must be carried out by uniformed combatants against military objectives[34] and precautions must be taken to minimize death and injury among the civilian population and damage to civilian property.[35]

Uniform

The Hague Regulations are silent about the requirement for members of the armed forces to wear uniform. Perhaps this was regarded as so obvious as not to require stating.[36] The only requirement was for members of militias or volunteer corps to have a fixed distinctive emblem recognizable at a distance.[37] This was repeated, albeit with the use of the word 'sign', rather than 'emblem', in the Geneva Prisoner of War Convention.[38]

At the trial of Werner Rohde and others, it was held that the fact that persons in civilian clothes had been parachuted into occupied territory to assist a military liaison officer to a resistance movement did not excuse the accused for their execution because the captured personnel had not been put on trial.[39]

Protocol I provides that 'combatants are obliged to distinguish themselves from the civilian population while they are engaged in an attack or in a military operation preparatory to an attack'.[40] How they distinguish themselves is left to the good sense of the military authorities. Obviously the resplendent uniforms of the Crimean war have no place on the modern battlefield, but soldiers in combat fatigues with a combat helmet, webbing and, perhaps in temperate regions, lots of foliage to break up their silhouette, would look quite different from any self-respecting civilian. Even militia fighters, at least those appearing before cameras, such as the Kosovo Liberation Army or the Peshmergas in Northern Iraq, seem to wear some type of combat dress with distinctive patches. That is all the law requires.

In the Afghanistan conflict of 2001, however, it was often difficult for Western eyes to distinguish, by their dress, militia fighters belonging to the Northern Alliance from local inhabitants. The local dress sense seems to have infected members of coalition forces fighting alongside the Northern Alliance. For example, television pictures were shown on 26 November 2001 of persons identified by

---

[34]See Chapter 3.

[35]See Chapter 4.

[36]Protocol I, Art. 44, para. 7, refers to the generally accepted practice of states with respect to the wearing of uniform by combatants assigned to the regular, uniformed, armed units of a party to the conflict.

[37]Hague Regulations, Art. 1.

[38]Art. 4(A)(2)(b).

[39]5 *Law Reports of Trials of War Criminals* (WCR) 54.

[40]Protocol I, Art. 43, para. 3.

the reporter as members of coalition special forces who assisted in putting down the uprising at the Qalai Janghi prison and who were wearing a motley collection of civilian, military and mixed clothing. When questioned about this later the Pentagon spokesman said: 'Most of the Special Forces in Afghanistan operated in uniform, full uniform. There were some who worked in what we referred to as non-standard uniform that was at least a partial uniform so that they could be identified. They also carried their arms openly.'[41] He contrasted this with the activities of Iraqi militias in 2003 as follows:

The basic distinction between those types of operations where there was no attempt to conceal their combatant status, and what we're saying with the Fedayeen Saddam in Iraq is that they are purposely concealing their combatant status, concealing their weapons, wearing no part of a uniform, wearing no distinctive device, in order to engage in acts of treachery or perfidy ... They are purposely using the soldiers' – the US soldiers' – respect for civilians as a way to conceal their intent and engage in treacherous killing of coalition forces. So there is a big difference between the two.[42]

In answer to a further question he referred to the following requirements for soldiers fighting alongside indigenous troops to comply with the rule of distinction: 'Wear some sort of distinctive device, which can be a hat, a scarf, an armband, something like that, with an American flag on their body armour; and carry their arms openly; and ... carry out their operations in accordance with the law of war ... and [not intend] to pose as a civilian.'[43] Protocol I does deal with situations where it is not possible for combatants to wear uniform, in the following terms:

there are situations[44] in armed conflicts where, owing to the nature of hostilities an armed combatant cannot so distinguish himself, shall retain his status as a combatant, provided that, in such situations, he carries his arms openly:
   (a) during each military engagement, and
   (b) during such time as he is visible[45] to the adversary while he is engaged in a military deployment[46] preceding the launching of an attack in which he is to participate.

---

[41]Parks, Department of Defence briefing.
[42]*Ibid.*
[43]*Ibid.*
[44]The UK, Germany, Canada, Ireland, Republic of Korea and New Zealand take a narrow view of these situations, declaring on ratification of Protocol I that these situations can arise only in occupied territory or in national liberation conflicts. For the latter, see Chapter 9. Italy and Spain take an even narrower view, saying that the situations can arise only in occupied territory.
[45]Some states, notably Australia and New Zealand, put on record at ratification their understanding that 'visible' includes visible with the aid of binoculars, by infra-red or image intensification devices or means of electronic or other surveillance.
[46]Some states, including the UK, Germany, Canada, Ireland, Italy, Republic of Korea, Netherlands, New Zealand and Spain made statements on ratification of Protocol I that 'deployment' includes any movement towards a place from which an attack is to be launched.

Writing in 1982,[47] the author commented on this exceptional rule as follows:

If a combatant fails to comply with these two conditions and he is an irregular combatant[48] he will not only have committed a punishable act but he will also forfeit prisoner of war status. Having taken away prisoner of war status, however, the Article effectively gives it back to him in paragraph 4 where it says that people captured in these circumstances are entitled to protection equivalent in all respects to that accorded to prisoners of war. This seems nonsensical. The Article, unfortunately, is open to abuse by irregulars and could, as a result, be detrimental to the interests of the civilian population since regular troops might take no risks in verifying whether persons in civilian clothes are guerrillas or peaceful civilians. If a guerrilla being pursued merges into the civilian population and later emerges from his sanctuary to attack regular forces he is using the protection given to the civilian population by law to gain a military advantage over his opponent. It is difficult to see why such action is any less perfidious than any of the actions castigated by Article 37 of Protocol I. It would have been much better if the wearing of uniform had been a mandatory requirement for combatant status. It is inconsistent for parties to the conflict to be required to avoid locating military objectives near populated areas and yet be allowed to hazard the civilian population by not distinguishing combatants and non-combatants.

The United Kingdom, probably because of its concerns about terrorism, considered that this exceptional rule should only apply in very limited circumstances, stating, on ratification that the situation 'can only exist in occupied territory or in armed conflicts covered by paragraph 4 of Article 1'.[49] It did not enter any reservation for special-forces operations. Perhaps it was thought that Art. 44, para. 6 would provide protection.[50] It seems to the author that special forces are likely, in certain types of operations, to decide to operate under cover and take their chances, if captured, on whether they would be accorded prisoner-of-war status. At first sight, Parks seems to make a hair-splitting distinction between the operations of United States special forces in Afghanistan and those of Iraqi forces in Iraq. His reference to hats or scarves sufficing to distinguish combatants from civilians is unconvincing. Nevertheless, as Parks hints, establishing the facts of what happened is one thing; establishing that a war crime has been committed is quite another. If it is customary, as it seems in Afghanistan, for the militia forces of the various factions to fight in clothing that does not resemble Western perceptions of combat clothing and if US or UK special forces fighting alongside them are dressed the same, this is hardly going to deceive the opposition into thinking that they are dealing with civilians. Deception lies at the heart of

[47]A. P. V. Rogers, Armed forces and the development of the law of war, 1982 *Military Law and Law of War Review*, 201 at p. 218.

[48]It seems that, because of Protocol I, Art. 44, para. 6, members of the regular forces never forfeit prisoner-of-war status, *ibid.*, p. 219.

[49]Protocol I, Art. 1, para. 4, deals with liberation struggles. It seems unlikely that the interpretation of the UK statement could be stretched to 'enemy occupied territory'.

[50]'This Article is without prejudice to the right of any person to be a prisoner of war pursuant to Article 4 of the Third Convention.'

perfidy or treachery. It relates to the *mens rea* of the alleged war criminals; it relates also to whether the enemy was deceived. So in the case of the Iraqi soldiers, both aspects would have to be examined. Relevant questions would include: were the soldiers concerned members of the regular armed forces or members of a *levée en masse* or foreign irregular fighters who had gone to help (who might be mercenaries)? Why did they did they adopt civilian clothing? Was it any different from what civilians customarily wear? What effect did it have on the opposition? What was the intent behind it?

Use of enemy uniform

The Hague Regulations prohibit the 'improper use of the military insignia and uniform of the enemy'.[51] The meaning of the word 'improper' is thus important.

In 1944, Major Skorzeny's troops were ordered to penetrate United States lines during the Ardennes offensive and capture bridges over the river Meuse. The men were dressed in US uniforms, drove US jeeps and carried US equipment. They were instructed to avoid contact and combat until they reached their objective. The plan was later abandoned and the brigade was employed as infantry in an attack towards Malmédy. In a later trial before a US war crimes tribunal, the ten accused were charged with taking part in combat disguised as Americans and treacherously killing US personnel as a result. The accused were acquitted, mainly because of lack of evidence that they had actually opened fire on US troops.[52]

The *Skorzeny* case was seen as authority for the proposition that enemy uniform could be used during deployments but not in actual combat. However, that interpretation is no longer valid for parties to Protocol I, which prohibits the use:

a. 'in an armed conflict of the flags or military emblems, insignia or uniforms of neutral or other States not Parties to the conflict'; and
b. 'of the flags or military emblems, insignia or uniforms of adverse Parties while engaging in attacks or in order to shield, favour, protect or impede military operations'.[53]

This rule is expressed as not affecting the existing generally recognized rules of international law applicable to espionage or to the use of flags in the conduct of armed conflict at sea. Under the Hague Regulations,[54] a spy who succeeds in rejoining his own forces cannot, if subsequently captured, be tried for his earlier spying offences. That means that he could not be punished for wearing enemy uniform while committing those offences.

[51]Hague Regulations, Art. 23(f).
[52]*US* v. *Skorzeny*, 9 WCR 90.
[53]Protocol I, Art. 39.
[54]Art. 31.

The rule would not prevent enemy uniforms being worn in rear areas for training purposes or by a prisoner of war to facilitate his escape. Members of the armed forces using enemy uniforms on long-range reconnaissance patrols in enemy-held territory would contravene this provision but would not forfeit prisoner-of-war status.[55]

Misuse of emblems

The misuse of United Nations emblems is a war crime,[56] as in the case of Bosnian Serb soldiers who, disguised as UN troops, captured French UN soldiers on 26 May 1995. It is likewise prohibited to make improper use of the red-cross, or red-crescent, emblem, the flag of truce[57] or the protective emblem of cultural property.[58]

According to the manuals and textbooks, use of the white flag, or flag of truce, means nothing more than an indication of a wish to enter into communication with the enemy.[59] In practice, it is often displayed by soldiers wishing to surrender or by civilians wishing to indicate their civilian status.

Care has to be exercised by both sides. In the engagement at Goose Green during the Falklands war of 1982 some Argentinean soldiers showed the white flag without the permission of their commander. British soldiers who went to investigate were shot and killed by other Argentinean forces in the area who were unaware that the white flag had been raised. There is no need to expose oneself to unnecessary risk. It is for those showing the white flag to come forward under its protection.

It would be improper to make use of an armoured ambulance marked with the red-cross emblem to transport ammunition to troop positions, to use the cultural property emblem on a building used as a military headquarters, to use the flag of truce to redeploy forces, or to use United Nations emblems to infiltrate enemy positions.

Intelligence-gathering

Gathering information about the enemy in order to secure a tactical advantage is an important aspect of warfare. It was recognized as a legitimate activity in

[55] See Protocol I, Art. 44, para. 6.

[56] Protocol I, Art. 38 paras. 1 and 2.

[57] Hague Regulations, Art. 23(f).

[58] Protocol I, Art. 38, para. 1. The prohibition extends to other emblems, signs or signals provided for by the Geneva Conventions or the protocol. That would include the special signals for the protection of medical aircraft.

[59] See *Manual of Military Law*, para. 394.

the Hague Regulations.[60] It is also necessary to enable commanders to fulfil their legal requirement to verify potential targets as military objectives and take precautions to protect civilians. Information is obtained in many different ways, through published information, aerial photography, captured documents or personnel, intercepted messages, reconnaissance patrols or through informers or agents in enemy territory. If acting clandestinely, these agents are usually referred to as spies.[61] A person operating in the uniform of his armed forces is not a spy.[62] Some protection for spies is provided by the Hague Regulations and Protocol I. Although liable to be tried and punished if captured, spies may not be summarily executed.[63] A member of the armed forces who, after spying, rejoins his forces cannot, if subsequently captured, be dealt with for his previous spying activities.[64]

During operations behind enemy lines in Burma during the Second World War, a commando unit was about to cross a road heavily used by the enemy when a monk appeared from a hidden path, saw members of the unit and walked away down the road. In a previous campaign, monks had often acted as spies and there was a danger that this monk would inform the enemy of the unit's position. He was too far away to be captured, so the options were to let him go or shoot him. The unit commander decided to let him go. This decision was correct because the monk could not have been executed without a trial, he was not overtly taking a direct part in hostilities and there was no evidence that he was passing information to the enemy.

In 1999, three American soldiers were captured close to the border between Kosovo and Macedonia. At first, it was claimed by the Yugoslav authorities that they were spies and would be put on trial. They appeared, battered and bruised, on television.[65] It was said that they had sustained these injuries trying to evade capture.

They could not have been spies since they were not acting clandestinely. They were wearing military uniform and travelling in a military vehicle at the time of capture. That meant that they were entitled to be treated as prisoners of war. There was no suggestion that they had committed any war crimes so it was not clear for what they might be tried. In the event, no proceedings were taken against them.

---

[60]Hague Regulations, Art. 24.

[61]A spy is defined as a person who, acting clandestinely or on false pretences, obtains or endeavours to obtain information in the zone of operations of a belligerent, with the intention of communicating it to the hostile party (Hague Regulations, Art. 29).

[62]Protocol I, Art. 46, para. 2.

[63]Hague Regulations, Art. 30. However, if members of the armed forces, they forfeit prisoner-of-war status (Protocol I, Art. 46, para. 1).

[64]Hague Regulations, Art. 31; Protocol I, Art. 46, paras. 3 and 4 – though this excludes from this protection residents of territory occupied by the adverse party if caught while engaging in espionage.

[65]Prisoners of war should not be paraded on television. They must be protected against public curiosity (Geneva Prisoner of War Convention 1949 (Prisoner of War Convention), Art. 13).

ICRC delegates visited the soldiers on 26 April and it was reported that they had been allowed to send family messages. They were eventually released on 2 May, following the intervention of the Reverend Jesse Jackson.

Assassination

When the word assassination is used, readers from the United States probably think of Abraham Lincoln or John F. Kennedy. For European readers perhaps the classic case of assassination was that of the Austrian Archduke, Franz Ferdinand, in Sarajevo on 28 June 1914 by the Serbian nationalist, Gavrilo Princip. That happened in peacetime so, presumably, was a case of murder. More relevant to the law of armed conflict, perhaps, was the assassination of Reinhard Heydrich, the German governor of Bohemia and Moravia, by Czech partisans, Jan Kubis and Josef Gabcik, in Prague on 29 May 1942, during a period of belligerent occupation. The partisans were trained in Britain and parachuted into Czechoslovakia by the RAF. According to Hamilton,[66] they held the rank of warrant officer.

Some writers, like Green, say that assassination is contrary to the customary law of armed conflict.[67] He cites Art. 148 of the Lieber Code, which, although it has the heading 'assassination' really deals with outlawry. He also cites Art. 23(b) of the Hague Regulations, which deals with treachery. [68]

The United Kingdom *Manual of Military Law* states, also under the heading 'assassination':[69] 'Assassination, the killing or wounding of a selected individual behind the line of battle by enemy agents or partisans,[70] and the killing or wounding by treachery of individuals belonging to the opposing nation or army, are not lawful acts of war'. It is not clear whether this deals with three separate activities: assassination, partisan killings and treacherous killings or whether the reference to partisan killings and treacherous killings is an attempt to define assassination.

The dictionary definition of 'assassinate' is 'to kill by treacherous violence', the emphasis being on treachery.

The manual goes on to distinguish the case of the attack by British commando forces on the headquarters of General Rommel at Beda Littoria in 1943 since it was carried out by military personnel in uniform, had as part of its objective the seizure of Rommel's operational headquarters, including his own residence, and the capture or killing of enemy personnel therein.

---

[66] J. D. Hamilton, How Britain helped kill Heydrich, on www.theherald.co.uk/perspective/archive.

[67] L. C. Green, *The Contemporary Law of Armed Conflict*, Manchester University Press, 2nd edn, 2000, p. 144.

[68] It provides: 'it is forbidden to kill or wound by treachery individuals belonging to a hostile nation or army'.

[69] Para. 115.

[70] According to the Manual, the reference to agents or partisans is a reference to illegal combatants.

So an attack by members of the armed forces in uniform against an individual member of the enemy armed forces, whether by dropping a bomb on his command post, using a sniper to fire at him or sending in a commando party, does not amount to assassination,[71] provided it is not done perfidiously.[72]

There probably is no independent war crime of assassination. If an officer is killed by partisans posing as civilians, that would amount to treachery or perfidy; if a civilian is singled out for attack, that would be a violation of the principle of civilian immunity. Perhaps, to avoid confusion, it would be better, as Gross does,[73] to speak of 'selected' or 'targeted' killings. These, according to Gross, 'must meet the same conditions demanded of any form of legitimate warfare. Only insofar as Israel targets aggression or a clear threat of aggression, responds proportionately and respects humanitarian law will targeted killings excite little moral outrage'.

The reported attack, in October 2001, on the house in Afghanistan of Mullah Omar, in which his stepfather and nephew were reported killed,[74] raises the question of whether Mullah Omar, or his house, was a legitimate target. Perhaps one should consider this as an attack on the house, which may have been a legitimate target if it were a place, or command post, from which the operations of the Taliban and al-Qa'ida forces were directed.

A curious case was the reported attack, via an unmanned drone, of the suspected al-Qa'ida leader, Qaed Salim Sinan al-Harethi, in Yemen in November 2002, apparently by Central Intelligence Agency (CIA) officials.[75] It may be that this was a peacetime anti-terrorism operation conducted in support of the Yemeni authorities under Yemeni law. To legitimize the attack under the law of war, one would have to construct an argument, first, that the United States was at war with al-Qa'ida, or that this was a continuation of the war in Afghanistan, second, that Qaed Salim Sinan al-Harethi was a legitimate target because he was a member of the enemy armed forces and, third, that the attack was carried out by the

[71]Y. Shany, Israeli counter-terrorism measures: are they 'kosher' under international law?, in M. Schmitt and G. L. Beruto (eds.), *Terrorism and International Law: Challenges and Responses*, International Institute of Humanitarian Law, 2003 argues that the Israeli policy of targeted killings is based on the notion that those 'who take up arms and participate in armed activities against Israel are legitimate military targets'. That must mean that he takes the view that (a) there is an armed conflict or occupation to which the law of war applies and (b) that persons taking part in the planning and execution of the current recent wave of suicide attacks are regarded as taking a direct part in hostilities and as having forfeited any protected status that they might otherwise have, not just for the duration of any suicide mission in which they have been involved. Shany, however, considers that targeted killings should only be carried out as a last resort if the Israeli defence force does not have the practical ability to arrest the person concerned.

[72]That is, killing an enemy by inviting his confidence that he is entitled to give or receive protection under the law of war and then abusing that confidence (see Protocol I, Art. 37).

[73]M. L. Gross, Fighting by other means in the Mideast: a critical analysis of Israel's assassination policy, *Political Studies*, 2003, vol. 51, no. 1, at p. 8.

[74]*The Independent*, 17 October 2001.

[75]This was reported in *The New York Times*, *The Washington Post* and *The Independent* of 6 November 2002. See also the article by A. Dworkin, The Yemen strike: the war on terrorism goes global, on www.crimesofwar.org/onnews/news-yemen.html.

United States armed forces. Even if one could establish that this was a situation to which the law of war applied, and some leading academics are scornful of the very idea that a 'war on terrorism' is a war in the legal sense, it would be difficult to put forward a convincing argument on the other points. In particular, only members of the armed forces of a party to an armed conflict may take a direct part in hostilities. So the question arises: were the CIA officials concerned members of the US armed forces? If not, the whole argument starts to crumble and one searches in vain for any other authority for this attack in international law.

During the Iraq war of 2003 there were two reported attempts by United States Air Force aircraft to kill the Iraqi president, Saddam Hussein, by bombing places where he was thought to be.[76] Would these have been legitimate attacks? Although the attacks were behind enemy lines, they were not carried out treacherously or by illegal combatants and it is quite likely that Saddam Hussein controlled the Iraqi armed forces. But is it legitimate to single out for attack an enemy head of state? Both the United Kingdom Manual and Green refer to the offer to the British government by a foreigner in 1806 to assassinate Napoleon. The man was detained and the French Ministry of Foreign Affairs informed.

Although the point is controversial, it seems to the author that if an enemy head of state were, for example, the actual, rather than the ceremonial, commander-in-chief of the armed forces, then it would be lawful to direct an attack against him. Even if he were not, *de jure*, the commander-in-chief but, *de facto*, commanded and controlled the operations of the armed forces, that would suffice, in the author's opinion, to make him a legitimate target.

Outlawry

On 8 April 2003 the BBC reported that people had been offered £3000 for killing British soldiers operating in Iraq. While, if it were done, this might be a case of assassination if carried out by illegal combatants, it is more likely to be a case of 'outlawry'.

Dr Francis Lieber, in his Instructions for the Government of the Armies of the United States in the Field of 24 April 1863 (Lieber Code), wrote:

The law of war does not allow proclaiming either an individual belonging to the hostile army, or a citizen, or a subject of the hostile government, an outlaw, who may be slain without trial by any captor . . . Civilized nations look with horror upon offers of rewards for the assassination of enemies as relapses into barbarism.

This formulation treats outlawry and assassination as connected but really dwells on the offers of rewards, rather than the method of killing or the status of the

---

[76]P. Cockburn, Bomber crew kills nine in the 'big one' but was Saddam Hussein among them? *The Independent*, 9 April 2003.

persons carrying it out. The authors of the *Manual of Military Law*,[77] however, see the prohibition of outlawry as a consequence of the prohibition of assassination: 'In view of the prohibition of assassination, the proscription or outlawing or the putting of a price on the head of an enemy individual or an offer for an enemy "dead or alive" is forbidden'. The authors of the Manual go on to express the view that this prohibition would extend to rewards for the killing of classes of individuals, such as officers. That would apply, in the context of the Iraq war, to offers of rewards for killing British soldiers. They also say that there would be no objection to rewards for capturing individuals unharmed. At the root of the objection to outlawry probably is the fact that it would encourage non-combatants to attack members of the opposing armed forces and thus undermine the rule of distinction.

Psychological warfare

Psychological operations[78] are perfectly legitimate provided they do not involve abuse of any protection afforded under the law of war, see, for example, what is written about interrogation of prisoners of war (pp. 55–6). There can no objection, therefore, to broadcasts, or the dropping of leaflets, encouraging the enemy to surrender, or even the payment of bribes to induce enemy commanders to surrender.[79] There was some criticism of United States failure in Afghanistan to have sufficient linguists and experts on the sensitivities and attitudes of the factions in Afghanistan and the surrounding nations. However, deployment of psychological operations teams on the ground to create local support and reduce support for al-Qa'ida and the Taliban were useful.[80] The coalition efforts to win 'hearts and minds' in Iraq in 2003 did not convince all Iraqis, some of whom were critical of the coalition's failure to restore law and order and support the effective distribution of aid and the medical effort. Leaflets were dropped to the Iraqi population telling them to put down their weapons so they would not be mistaken for Iraqi Fedayeen Saddam.[81] Whether due to psychological operations of not, many Iraqi soldiers sent to defend Basra preferred peace to war. One

---

[77] At para. 116.

[78] In his review of the first edition, Roberts comments that there 'is surprisingly little about aspects of the 1991 Gulf operations that powerfully affected war on land, particularly the successful air-dropping of leaflets telling Iraqi soldiers that they would not be targets if they walked away from their military vehicles'. So this paragraph is an attempt to remedy the defect.

[79] See D. Usborne, US 'psy-ops' division rolls out its weapons of mass persuasion, *The Independent*, 21 March 2003; A. Buncombe, US army chiefs. During the war in Afghanistan in 2001, US psychological operations staff were reported to be broadcasting directly on Afghan television and dropping leaflets telling fighters that if they wanted to surrender they should approach US forces with their hands in the air, their weapons slung, muzzle down, across their backs with magazine removed and rounds expelled (see *The Independent*, 20 October 2001).

[80] A. H. Cordesman, *The Lessons of Afghanistan*, CSIS Press, 2002, pp. 136–40.

[81] Parks, Department of Defence briefing.

British officer is reported as saying that 'they don't want to shoot us and we
don't want to shoot at them'.[82]

II   Humanity

Attacking food and water used by members of enemy armed forces

There is a prohibition on attacking food and water facilities in order to deny
them to the civilian population, but this does not apply to such objects as are
used by the enemy as sustenance solely for the members of its armed forces, or,
if not as sustenance, then in direct support of military action. In the latter case,
no action may be taken against these objects if it may be expected to cause the
starvation of the civilian population or force its movement.[83]

It would be permissible to destroy a supply depot containing rations for the
enemy armed forces or, for example, to use a corn field or orchard as cover for
advancing infantry or for troops to take cover behind a barn containing grain.[84]

Surrender

Sir James Turner, a student of warfare, wrote as long ago as 1671 that 'the fear
of bad quarter, of hard and cruel usage, and of the breach of treaties and articles,
hath made many resolve to take no quarter and to choose to die fighting'.[85]
However, it has long been recognized that if an enemy soldier wanted to surrender,
he should be allowed to do so and, so long as he laid down his weapons and
remained peaceful, he should not be attacked. The rule was rendered in the
Hague Regulations as: 'it is especially forbidden ... to kill or wound an enemy
who, having laid down his arms, or having no longer means of defence, has
surrendered at discretion'.[86]

Safeguard of persons *hors de combat*

Protocol I goes on to state that a person who is recognized or who, in the
circumstances, should be recognized to be *hors de combat* shall not be made the
object of attack. A person is *hors de combat* if he is in the power of an adverse

---

[82]P. Bishop, Diehards keep allies at bay, in *The Daily Telegraph, War on Saddam*, Robinson,
2003, p. 52.
[83]Protocol I, Art. 54, para. 3. See also, ICRC *Commentary*, para. 2112.
[84]See ICRC *Commentary*, para. 2110.
[85]P. Karsten, *Law, Soldiers and Combat*, Greenwood, 1978.
[86]Hague Regulations, Art. 23(c).

party, he clearly expresses an intention to surrender, or has been rendered unconscious or is otherwise incapacitated by wounds or sickness, and therefore is incapable of defending himself. However, he must abstain from any hostile act and must not attempt to escape.[87]

No procedure is laid down, but normally a soldier surrendering would be expected to put down his weapons and come out into the open with his hands raised above his head. Television footage of United States armoured vehicles moving towards Baghdad during the Iraq war of 2003 included clear instructions from a commander to his soldiers not to open fire on Iraqi soldiers emerging from the undergrowth with their hands up. In the case of the wounded, it is only those who either stop fighting, or are prevented by their wounds from fighting, who are protected. Those who carry on fighting despite their wounds, like Lieutenant Maurice Dease, who 'five times wounded before he was killed, worked his machine-gun to the end'[88] are not protected from attack. He was posthumously awarded the Victoria Cross for defending the canal north of Mons on 23 August 1914. A plaque in his memory is still to be seen on the Nimy railway bridge.

Occupants of aircraft and vehicles

There has been confusion in the past about whether it was permissible to fire at a person parachuting from an aircraft. The principle of humanity would make a distinction between those parachuting to safety because their aircraft had been shot down and those, like airborne troops, parachuting into action. Protocol I deals with problem as follows:

No person parachuting from an aircraft in distress shall be made the object of attack during his descent. Upon reaching the ground in territory controlled by an adverse Party, a person who has parachuted from an aircraft in distress shall be given an opportunity to surrender before being made the object of attack, unless it is apparent that he is engaging in a hostile act. Airborne troops are not protected by this Article.[89]

Members of the civilian population may well be on the scene first, but they must also respect this rule. Protection would be lost if a pilot ejecting from his aircraft opened fire during his descent. The normal rules on surrender apply once a person parachuting from an aircraft in distress reaches the ground. Once he has disentangled himself from his parachute harness, he would clearly have to indicate an intention to surrender to be protected from attack. He would not be protected if he opens fire or tries to escape. Hostile acts would include trying to destroy

---

[87]Protocol I, Art. 41, paras. 1 and 2.
[88]A. C. Doyle, *The British Campaign in France and Flanders 1914*, Hodder and Stoughton, 1916, p. 20.
[89]Protocol I, Art. 42.

an aircraft that has been forced down[90] or trying to burn important military documents. Parachuting airborne troops are legitimate targets, unless descending from an aircraft in distress and clearly showing an intention to surrender.[91]

Quarter

Two incidents in the Afghanistan conflict of 2001 stand out as particularly bloody: the so-called 'massacre' at Mazar-i-Sherif, when tanks were sent in because the defenders refused to surrender,[92] and the uprising at the Qalai Janghi prison.[93] The latter resulted in an estimated 450 Taliban and al-Qa'ida deaths and 40 deaths and 100 wounded among the Northern Alliance fighters. In these cases one would need to know if the fighters who were killed had surrendered or whether they fought to the end. If the high death toll was due to the tenacious fighting and unwillingness to surrender of those involved, their deaths were not caused unlawfully. It would be a different matter if the deaths were caused by the execution of those who had surrendered.

It is considered that military necessity is satisfied once enemy soldiers have stopped fighting and surrendered. Further violence against them then becomes unnecessary.[94] From this point they are to be respected and protected. The Hague Regulations provided that: 'It is especially forbidden ... to declare that no quarter will be given.'[95] This rule was confirmed in Protocol I as follows: 'It is prohibited to order that there shall be no survivors, to threaten an adversary therewith or to conduct hostilities on this basis.'[96]

Unusual conditions of combat

It was sometimes argued in the past that military necessity required a departure from the rule on quarter in cases like long-range reconnaissance patrols or commando raids in enemy-held territory because it was not possible to treat captured persons in accordance with the legal requirements in those circumstances. They could not be evacuated to prisoner-of-war camps, their presence would endanger, or at least encumber, the mission and to release them would be to reveal to the enemy the existence and location of the patrol or commando force.

[90]ICRC *Commentary*, para. 1650.

[91]See S. Oeter, Methods and means of combat, in D. Fleck (ed.), *The Handbook of Humanitarian Law in Armed Conflicts*, Oxford University Press, 1995, p. 156.

[92]*The Independent*, 16 November 2001.

[93]*The Independent*, 26 November 2001.

[94]Making a person the object of attack in the knowledge that he is *hors de combat* is a grave breach of Protocol I: see Art. 85, para. 3(e). Under the Rome Statute of the International Criminal Court (ICC Statute), Art. 8, para. 2(b)(vi) it is a war crime to kill or wound a combatant who, having laid down his arms or having no longer means of defence, has surrendered at discretion.

[95]Hague Regulations, Art. 23(d).

[96]Protocol I, Art. 40.

Protocol I deals with this situation as follows: 'When persons entitled to protection as prisoners of war have fallen into the power of an adverse Party under unusual conditions of combat which prevent their evacuation as provided for in Part III, Section I, of the Third Convention, they shall be released and all feasible precautions[97] shall be taken to ensure their safety.'[98] In these cases captured persons may not be killed. They must be released. There is, however, no requirement to release them immediately, so it can be done when it is safe to do so. Also, the use of the word 'feasible' indicates that there may be flexibility, depending on the circumstances, as to the precautions to be taken for their safety. Consideration may have to be given to providing them with water and rations, map, compass, shelter and information about unexploded ordnance in the area.

Wounded, sick and dead

One of the main purposes of the law of armed conflict, ever since the first Geneva Convention of 1864, has been to ensure the treatment of the wounded and sick.[99] It places an obligation to do so on all parties to the armed conflict in respect of all the wounded and sick, whether own or enemy, whether soldiers or civilians, only medical reasons dictating priority of treatment. That is why medical personnel, medical units and medical transports have a protected status and are permitted to display the red-cross or red-crescent protective emblem:[100] to enable them to carry out this essential function efficiently.

The most important rule is the following: 'At all times, and particularly after an engagement, Parties to the conflict shall, without delay, take all possible measures to search for and collect the wounded and sick, to protect them against pillage and ill-treatment, to ensure their adequate care, and to search for the dead and prevent their being despoiled.'[101] Equally important is respect for the dead. There have, unfortunately, been cases of mutilation of the dead, of dead bodies being dragged behind vehicles, of public jubilation over dead bodies and of theft of personal possessions and clothing of the dead.[102] The legal requirement is for

---

[97] The UK has on ratification placed on record its understanding that 'feasible' means that which is practicable or practically possible, taking into account all circumstances ruling at the time, including humanitarian and military considerations.

[98] Protocol I, Art. 41, para. 3.

[99] The obligations are now laid down in the Geneva Wounded and Sick Convention 1949 (Wounded Convention); in the Geneva Shipwrecked Convention 1949; and in Protocol I, Arts. 8–34.

[100] The red shield of David, which is used by Israel, though not formally a protective emblem, is recognized in practice as such.

[101] Wounded Convention, Art. 15.

[102] See H. W. Elliott, Dead and wounded, in Gutman and Rieff, *Crimes of War*, pp. 118–20. In the author's opinion, maltreatment of bodies, though not a grave breach, is a war crime, being a serious violation of the law of war. It is of interest in this connection that United States Military Commission Instruction No. 2 of 30 April 2003, makes degrading treatment of a dead body a war crime.

death to be verified, bodies to be respected, identified and honourably interred, or cremated if imperative reasons of hygiene or religious reasons so dictate. Bodies are not to be looted. One half of a double identity disc, or the disc itself if there is only one, is to remain on the body. Wills and other documents of importance to the next of kin, money and articles of intrinsic or sentimental value are to be collected and passed, with all other information about the deceased, through military channels, to the National Information Bureau.[103]

Prisoners of war

Most of the Geneva Prisoner of War Convention 1949 is taken up with the running of prisoner-of-war camps. These must be far enough from the battlefield to be out of danger,[104] so fall outside the scope of this book. Perhaps the most important articles of the convention are those that deal with the initial stages of captivity (Arts. 13–20). They are summarized, with commentary, below. It is in the early stages of captivity that captured persons are most vulnerable to abuse of their legal rights, especially if they fall into the hands of civilian mobs or poorly trained militia forces. Once they are in the proper prisoner-of-war evacuation and handling process, their identity is known and their capture registered, they are much safer. In the Iraq war of 2003, it was interesting to compare media pictures: the calm and efficient manner in which British Royal Marines dealt with Iraqis who were clearly surrendering in the early days of the war; the frightened expressions of members of a United States maintenance unit who were captured and shown on al-Jazeera television; the equally frightened Iraqis, hooded and bound, who were captured by British forces after the fighting in Basra; or the armed groups, many in civilian clothes, who were searching the river bank for the crew after reports that a US aircraft had been shot down. In Afghanistan in 2001 there were allegations of the ill-treatment of captives and even summary executions by both Taliban and Northern Alliance fighters.[105]

The general rule is that members of the enemy armed forces, other than medical personnel and chaplains,[106] are entitled to prisoner-of-war status on capture.[107] It

---

[103]Wounded Convention, Arts. 15–18.

[104]Prisoner of War Convention, Art. 19.

[105]The UN Assistance Mission in Afghanistan was reported to be investigating an allegation that mass graves near Sheberghan contained the bodies of Taliban fighters who surrendered at Kunduz and died of suffocation when being transported in unventilated metal containers: see Claims of torture and intimidation against witnesses to Afghan war crimes on the Crimes of War website, www.crimesofwar.org; K. Morris, 'Threats' to kill Afghan killing witnesses, BBC news online, 14 November 2002. According to R. Gutman, in an e-mail dated 24 June 2003 to the author, the investigation had not got underway owing to security concerns.

[106]Who, if interned, are entitled to the special status of 'retained personnel': see Prisoner of War Convention, Art. 33.

[107]Protocol I, Arts. 43, 44.

is sometimes difficult to decide whether members of paramilitary groups or persons not wearing uniform or civilians who have taken up arms are entitled to prisoner-of-war status. However, the capturing troops do not need to concern themselves with these questions. The captured persons should be treated as prisoners of war until their status has been determined by a competent tribunal.[108]

Humane treatment

Prisoners of war must at all times be humanely treated and protected, particularly against acts of violence or intimidation and against insults and public curiosity. They are entitled to respect for their persons and their honour. Women are to be treated with all the regard due to their sex and must have treatment as favourable as that granted to men. All prisoners of war are entitled to equal treatment, without any adverse distinction based on race, nationality, religious belief or political opinions, or any other distinction founded on similar criteria. Reprisals against prisoners of war are prohibited.

Is it permissible to show prisoners of war on television? This issue arose during the Gulf war of 1991. There was adverse reaction in the West to the showing of captured pilots on Iraqi television as humiliating and degrading treatment.[109] The interests of prisoners of war have to be balanced against the legitimate interest of the media in reporting on developments in a war, so the policy was adopted in the coalition forces of allowing photographs of prisoners of war to be shown so long as they were not close-up enough for individuals to be identified. That lesson was obviously forgotten in the early days of the Iraq war 2003 as British marines were shown on television searching surrendering Iraqis who could be identified and the press published clear pictures of members of the Iraqi 51st and 32nd mechanised infantry divisions surrendering near Az Bayer.[110] Eventually, after captured American soldiers were shown on al-Jazeera television, and United States defence secretary, Donald Rumsfeld, protested that it was illegal for prisoners of war to be shown in humiliating circumstances,[111] the Ministry of Defence in London requested journalists to ensure that the faces of Iraqi prisoners of war were pixillated or obscured to prevent their being identified.[112] Apart from the interests of the prisoners of war themselves, there was concern that reprisals might be visited by the Iraqi authorities on the families of prisoners of war who were known to have surrendered.

---

[108] Prisoner of War Convention, Art. 5.
[109] According to the ICC Statute, Art. 8, para. 2(b)(xxi), humiliating and degrading treatment is a war crime.
[110] E.g., the Associated Press photograph in *The Independent* of 22 March 2003.
[111] D. MacIntyre, Chilling images 'breach Geneva Convention', *The Independent*, 24 March 2003.
[112] G. Keleny, Enshrined in the Geneva Convention is a protection which all PoWs are owed, *The Independent*, 25 March 2003.

Maintenance and medical treatment

Captured persons who are wounded or sick must be given the medical care required by their condition, without discrimination, only medical reasons dictating the priority of treatment.[113] Beyond that they are entitled to free maintenance and any medical attention required by their state of health. They must not be subjected to physical mutilation or to medical or scientific experiments of any kind, which are not justified by their medical, dental or hospital treatment and carried out in their interest.

Searching

It is normal procedure to search and disarm captured persons. Weapons[114] and ammunition, military equipment, other than protective equipment and clothing, and military documents, other than identity documents, may be removed. The latter may be useful for intelligence purposes.

Prisoners of war must be allowed to keep all their personal effects, such as private letters or family photographs, their protective equipment, such as combat helmets and protective clothing, masks and equipment, their clothing, their feeding equipment, their badges of rank and nationality and decorations, and their identity documents. Identity documents are to be issued to prisoners of war who possess none.

Sums of money and articles of value carried by prisoners of war may not be taken away from them except by order of an officer, and after the amount and particulars of the owner have been recorded in a special register and an itemized receipt has been given, legibly inscribed with the name, rank and unit of the person issuing the receipt. Sums in the currency of the detaining power, or which are changed into such currency at the prisoner's request, are be placed to the credit of the prisoner's account.[115] Other sums of money, as well as valuables, are to be returned to prisoners of war at the end of their captivity. It is likely that at the point of capture there will be little time to do more than remove weapons and ammunition. British military doctrine envisages a more detailed process, including the completion of a capture tag, with details of the prisoner of war, the place and circumstances of capture and of items removed, at unit headquarters.[116]

---

[113] Wounded Convention, Art. 12; Protocol I, Art. 10.

[114] That would include not only military issue guns and bayonets but also privately owned knives, since these could be used to attack guards or facilitate escape. The uprising at the Qalai Janghi prison in Afghanistan in November 2001 was said to have been due to the fact that captives were able to smuggle weapons into the fort: see *The Independent* of 26 November 2001.

[115] See Prisoner of War Convention, Art. 64.

[116] United Kingdom, Joint Warfare Publication 1–10, *Prisoners of War Handling*, March 2001, para. 3B8. A unit is a battalion or equivalent body of troops.

Security

The Prisoner of War Convention permits prisoners of war to be interned or confined to certain areas[117] and permits weapons to be used, after warning, against those escaping from internment or confinement.[118] However, it is silent on the question of what measures can be taken during the early stages of captivity to prevent prisoners of war from escaping, gathering military information or conspiring together to overwhelm their captors. Nevertheless, it has been customary to escort prisoners of war under armed guard, to blindfold them if necessary and to segregate officers from other ranks.

Is it permissible to hood and manacle prisoners of war? The United Kingdom armed forces' instructions on prisoner-of-war handling do not refer to hooding but there is a reference, in the section on guidelines for the movement of prisoners of war: 'If the use of restraints is specifically authorised, PW hands may be secured in front of them using "Plasticuffs"'.[119] It seems to the author permissible to fetter, hood or blindfold prisoners of war as a temporary measure during the capture and evacuation process if it is necessary for security reasons, for example to prevent escape, attacks on those guarding them or access to classified information.[120]

Interrogation

Prisoners of war are bound to give only their surname, first names and rank, date of birth, and army, regimental, personal or serial number, or equivalent information. That is to enable their identity to be established. Those who, owing to their physical or mental condition, are unable to state their identity are to be handed over to the medical service so that their identity can be established by other means. Prisoners of war must show their identity card on demand, but this must be returned to them. No physical or mental torture, nor any other form of coercion, may be inflicted on prisoners of war to secure from them information of any kind. Prisoners of war who refuse to answer may not be threatened, insulted, or exposed to unpleasant or disadvantageous treatment of any kind. The questioning of prisoners of war must be done in a language that they understand.

[117]Prisoner of War Convention, Art. 21.
[118]Prisoner of War Convention, Art. 42.
[119]United Kingdom, *Prisoner of War Handling*, para. 3B3-1.
[120]Commenting on the policy of placing hoods on prisoners of war, W. H. Parks, at the Department of Defence briefing, said: 'It is standard procedure in most militaries to either blindfold or hood prisoners at the time of capture because every soldier is trained that the best time to escape is at the time of capture. So the idea is, first, not to give them the opportunity to escape, and second, not to . . . give them the opportunity to collect military intelligence in the event that they should escape. Obviously, the hooding is one method for doing that; the other I mentioned is blindfolding. They obviously can still breathe. It's not a matter of trying to abuse them in any way, it's a standard security procedure for most militaries it not all, upon capture'.

None of the above rule prevents the interrogation of prisoners of war.[121] As the author has written elsewhere:[122]

There seems to be a popular misconception ... that you cannot interrogate prisoners of war. This is not so. Prisoners of war are often a valuable source of military intelligence and there is nothing in the Geneva Prisoners of War Convention that prohibits questioning them. However, under Article 17, they are not obliged to answer questions (only to give their number, rank, name and date of birth) and no torture, coercion, threats, insults or unpleasant or disadvantageous treatment may be used to secure information from them. The situation is no different in the case of people classified as illegal combatants. They can be questioned but if they refuse to answer questions, basic human rights standards prevent torture or cruel, inhuman or degrading treatment.

While torture and other forms of coercion may be easy to spot, the precise meaning of terms like 'unpleasant treatment' or 'inhuman treatment' is more open to debate.[123] An indication is provided by the judgment of the European Court of Human Rights when it considered interrogation techniques such as wall-standing, sleep deprivation and hooding used by the British security forces in Northern Ireland.[124] The court decided that they amounted to inhuman and degrading treatment. While the precise language of the two treaties differs, a court considering war crimes might find the European Court's views of persuasive value.

After the Iraq war of 2003, there were media allegations that the United States forces, as an interrogation technique, subjected uncooperative prisoners of war to prolonged periods of heavy metal music and popular American children's songs. Sergeant Mark Hadsell is reported as saying: 'They can't take it. If you play it for 24 hours, your brain and body functions start to slide, your train of thoughts slows down and your will is broken. That's when we come in and talk to them'.[125] Although there might be argument about whether such pre-interrogation techniques as keeping prisoners of war standing, kneeling or in uncomfortable positions for hours or depriving them of sleep is torture,[126] there seems little doubt that such treatment, or 'softening them up' by subjecting them to loud noises for long periods, amounts to coercion.

---

[121]I. Detter, *The Law of War*, 2nd edn, Cambridge University Press, 2000, p. 331 states baldly 'Prisoners of war must not be subjected to interrogation.' But this may be qualified in the next sentence, which reads 'All "illegal" methods of obtaining information are prohibited.' Perhaps she regards the use of illegal methods as interrogation. However, the dictionary definition of 'interrogate' is to ask questions of a person, especially closely or formally.

[122]Letter to *The Independent* published on 31 January 2002.

[123]Committing outrages upon personal dignity, in particular humiliating and degrading treatment, is a war crime according to the ICC Statute, Art. 8, para. 2(b)(xxi).

[124]*Republic of Ireland* v. *United Kingdom* (1979–80) 2 EHRR 25.

[125]Sesame Street breaks Iraqi POWs, BBC news online, of 20 May 2003, quoting *Newsweek*.

[126]V. Ladisch, 'Stress and duress': drawing the line between interrogation and torture, 24 April 2003, on www.crimesofwar.org.

Evacuation

Prisoners of war are to be evacuated, as soon as possible after their capture, to prisoner-of-war camps far enough from the combat zone to be out of danger. Periods spent in transit camps should be as brief as possible. Only prisoners of war who, owing to wounds or sickness, would run greater risks by being evacuated than by remaining where they are, may be temporarily kept back in a danger zone. Prisoners of war must not be unnecessarily exposed to danger while awaiting evacuation from a fighting zone.

The evacuation of prisoners of war is to be effected humanely and in conditions similar to those for the forces of the detaining power in their changes of station.

The detaining power must supply prisoners of war who are being evacuated with sufficient food and potable water, and with the necessary clothing and medical attention, take all suitable precautions to ensure their safety during evacuation, and establish as soon as possible a list of the prisoners of war who are evacuated.

3

Military objectives

It follows from the rule on the protection of civilians and civilian objects that attacks must be limited to military objectives.[1] The word 'limited' does not mean that there must be no collateral damage. Limitation of collateral damage is dealt with under the rule of proportionality.[2]

The term 'military objective' is a relatively recent addition to the law of war. The St Petersburg Declaration merely referred to weakening 'the military forces of the enemy'. Even in military manuals published after the Second World War,[3] the term is only obliquely referred to in connection with bombardments and is not defined; the emphasis of those manuals seems to be on defended and undefended localities.[4] However, even in the case of bombardment of defended localities, it is clear that the manuals envisaged such bombardments being directed against military objectives therein.[5] A definition of military objectives appeared for the first time in the Air Warfare Rules.[6] That definition was probably an attempt to rationalize the practice of states but, since the rules never became legally binding, they were probably ignored by manual writers. It is necessary, therefore, to trace developments in state practice and treaty law before examining the current definition of the term.

Early texts such as the Lieber Code did not contain the concept of the military objective. Presumably, as indicated by the preamble to the St Petersburg Declaration, it was assumed that war would be waged between the enemy armed

[1]Protocol I, Art. 52, para. 2.

[2]See, further, Chapter 1. See also M. Bothe, K. J. Partsch and W. Solf, *New Rules for the Victims of Armed Conflicts*, Martinus Nijhoff, 1982, p. 322.

[3]See, e.g., the UK *Manual of Military Law* Part III, HMSO, 1958 (*Manual of Military Law*), Chapter VII; *The Law of Land Warfare*, United States Department of the Army (FM 27-10), 1956, Chapter 2 s. IV.

[4]See, further, Chapter 5.

[5]See *Manual of Military Law*, para. 288. Para. 289 might mislead the reader into supposing that a defended town as such may be bombarded. This would be an erroneous deduction since para. 289 must be read in the light of para. 288.

[6]Art. 24.

forces.[7] The only exception to this was the rule that permitted the bombardment of fortified and defended places.[8] This, of course, involved the civilian population of those places. In the nineteenth century it was considered by some permissible to bombard civilian houses during a siege since this might hasten the reduction of the enemy,[9] the inhabitants being considered temporarily to have lost their non-combatant status because of their close association with the garrison.

In modern wars, however, the enemy soldier has become a less important target than the weapons, such as tanks and aircraft, which he operates, the depots and lines of communication which keep the troops supplied and the civilian manufacturing industries which provide the raw materials, fuel and goods without which the armies cannot survive. In 1870 courts recognized the justification for destroying Confederate cotton during the American civil war since cotton sales provided funds for importing almost all Confederate arms and ammunition.[10] The importance of military objectives was recognized, first, in the Hague Naval Bombardment Convention of 1907, which for the first time acknowledged that the military significance of the target was a more relevant factor than whether a town or place was defended. The convention did not limit bombardment to purely military objects. It encompassed industrial objects of military value.[11] The convention permitted bombardment of military works, military or naval establishments, depots of arms or war *matériel* and certain workshops and plant.

The right of a belligerent to destroy the enemy's war *matériel*, railways and telegraphs has long been acknowledged as well as barracks and accommodation for troops, military stores and factories and foundries manufacturing military supplies.[12]

Fauchille in 1917 considered that aerial bombardment was permitted against military works, military or naval establishments, depots of arms or war materials, workshops (*les ateliers*) and installations suitable for use by the enemy army or fleet, ships of war, the head of the government or his representative, soldiers and other persons officially attached to the army or fleet.[13]

According to Parks[14] the practice of the First World War showed that the following were regarded as legitimate targets: 'military and naval bases; warehouses, airfields and docks; lines of communication; and industrial targets that

---

[7]See L. Oppenheim, *International Law*, vol. 2, 7th edn by H. Lauterpacht, Longman, 1952, paras. 105, 107. In fact, one looks in vain through Oppenheim for a definition of military objective.

[8]See, e.g., Arts. 15–16 of the Brussels Conference Draft Code of 1874 (Brussels Code).

[9]See, e.g., J. S. Risley, *The Law of War*, Innes & Co., 1897, p. 116; and J. R. Baker and H. G. Crocker, *The Laws of Land Warfare*, Department of State, Washington, 1919, p. 199, who castigated this practice.

[10]US Department of the Air Force, *Commander's Handbook on the Law of Armed Conflict*, (AFP 110-34), 1980, p. 2–1.

[11]See W. H. Parks, Air war and the law of war, 32 *Air Force Law Review* 1 (1990), p. 18.

[12]See J. M. Spaight, *War Rights on Land*, Macmillan, 1911, pp. 113 ff.

[13]P. Fauchille, Le bombardement aérien, *Revue Générale de Droit International Public*, vol. 24 (1917), p. 73.

[14]Parks, Air war, p. 21.

offered a contribution to the enemy's war effort'. In preparing the Hague Air Warfare Rules, according to Parks, the British delegation's draft included the term 'military objective' without defining it, while the United States draft contained a list of objects that might be attacked without using the term 'military objective'.[15] The final text is obviously a compromise between the two approaches because the Hague rules contained a definition which prepared the way for later, more comprehensive definitions: 'an object of which the destruction or injury would constitute a distinct military advantage to the belligerent'.[16]

The rules go on to give a list of military objectives. It is worth setting out the list in full: 'military forces; military works; military establishments or depots; factories constituting important and well-known centres engaged in the manufacture of arms, ammunition or distinctively military supplies; lines of communication[17] or transportation used for military purposes'.[18] The preamble to the list states that aerial bombardment is legitimate only when 'directed exclusively at' the listed objects. The context in which the word 'exclusively' appears makes it ambiguous. Does it mean that only objects on the list may be attacked or that an attack on a listed object must be limited to that object and nothing else? Schwarzenberger seemed to think that the list was intended to be exhaustive,[19] while Rousseau refers to it as examples.[20] An examination of the remainder of the article does not help to resolve this ambiguity, but it does seem that it was the intention of the drafters that the list should be exhaustive.[21]

Art. 24(3) prohibits the bombardment of cities, towns, villages and dwellings not in the immediate neighbourhood of the operations of land forces, but does permit the attacking of the listed military objectives in such rear areas, provided the attackers are discriminate. The writer does not share the view of Parks[22] that the Art. 24(3) 'specifically prohibited the attack of targets "not situated in the immediate vicinity of the operations of land forces"' or the similar view of Doswald-Beck.[23]

Art. 24(4) relaxes the requirement for discrimination in the contact zone. It envisages the bombardment of cities, towns, villages and dwellings in the

---

[15]Parks, Air war, p. 28.

[16]Art. 24(1).

[17]Detter refers to various discrepancies between the English, French and German texts. For instance the German text *Nachrichten* and *Vekehrsmittel* clearly refers to radio stations and other news media while the English 'lines of communication' is more vague (I. Detter, *The Law of War*, 2nd edn, Cambridge University Press, 2000, p. 281).

[18]Art. 24(2). This is similar to the list appearing in United States, *Law of Land Warfare*, at p. 19, of objects that may be attacked even if they are not defended.

[19]G. Schwarzenberger, *International Law*, vol. 2, Stevens, 1968, p. 153.

[20]C. Rousseau, *Le Droit des conflits armés*, Pedone, 1983, p. 130.

[21]H. M. Hanke, The Hague Rules of Air Warfare, *International Review of the Red Cross*, 1993, pp. 21–2.

[22]Parks, Air war, p. 138.

[23]The value of the 1977 protocols, in M. A. Meyer (ed.), *Armed Conflict and the New Law*, British Institute of International and Comparative Law, 1989, p. 143.

immediate neighbourhood of the operations of land forces but then goes on to add the proviso that 'the *military concentration*' must be sufficiently important to justify such bombardment, having regard to the danger thus caused to the civilian population. This was probably an attempt to adapt the defended town concept to air warfare.

This use of the words 'the military concentration' drives one to the conclusion that Art. 24(4) makes concessions for military necessity but does not enlarge the list of military objectives in Art. 24(2).

It does seem that the drafters of the rules, like the International Law Association in their draft convention of 1938 for the protection of civilian populations against new engines of war, did not envisage attacks on the broader manufacturing base of the enemy's industry.

Of course, the rules were never adopted in treaty form so they would have to be tested against customary law and state practice. In that light, the definition of military objectives cannot be regarded as anything more than an incomplete indication of what amounts to such objects. Spaight, as early as 1924, provided a long list of objects attacked during the First World War which fell outside the list in the Air Warfare Rules, including iron and steel works and oil production facilities.[24] The problem, as the British Prime Minister, Neville Chamberlain, acknowledged, was that there was no agreed definition of military objectives.[25]

Stone[26] refers to the Anglo-French view during the World Wars that legitimate military objectives included: 'docks and dockside warehouses; blast furnaces; iron works and foundries, steel works, coke ovens; power stations, gasworks, waterworks; motor and engineering works; oil wells, refining and oil storage depots; benzol works and depots; granaries'. But practice in the Second World War seems to have indicated a broader understanding of what amounted to a military objective. After the war a French court decided that a lighthouse attacked by German forces was a military objective because it could have provided navigational assistance to allied forces.[27] The strategic bombing concept decided upon at Casablanca in January 1943 envisaged the progressive disruption of the military, industrial and economic system of Germany, thereby enfeebling the German people to such an extent that the effectiveness of the German armed forces would be irreversibly undermined.[28] The resultant advent of target area bombing, of course, does not affect the contemporary understanding of what amounted to a military objective. In terms of accuracy it was merely an inefficient method of attacking military objectives. Parks, after an exhaustive review of the authorities, concludes that by the end of the Second World War the contemporary understanding of what was meant by 'military objectives' was as follows:

[24]J. M. Spaight, *Air Power and War Rights*, Longman, 1924, pp. 233–5.
[25]Spaight, *Air Power and War Rights*, Longman, 1947, at p. 258.
[26]J. Stone, *Legal Controls of International Conflict*, Stevens, 1954, p. 624.
[27]See the case of Gross-Brauckmann, *Annual Digest*, 1948, Case No. 223.
[28]Rousseau, *Le Droit des conflits armés*, p. 366.

military equipment, units, and bases; economic targets;[29] power sources (coal, oil, electric, hydroelectric);[30] industry (war supporting manufacturing, export and/or import); transportation (equipment, lines of communication, and petroleum, oil, and other lubricants necessary for transportation); command and control; geographic;[31] personnel;[32] military;[33] and civilians taking part in the hostilities, including civilians working in industries directly related to the war effort.[34]

However, in the words of Blix,[35] 'if the view is taken . . . that practically the whole productive force of the belligerent is sufficiently relevant to justify attacks, the basic immunity of the civilian population is immediately placed in jeopardy'. An effort has to be made to draw a line somewhere.[36]

A US war crimes tribunal considered military objectives in the following passage: 'A city is bombed for tactical purposes; communications are to be destroyed, railroads wrecked, ammunition plants demolished, factories razed, all for the purpose of impeding the military.'[37] The Geneva Conventions use the term 'military objective', but do not define it. Art. 18 of the Civilian Convention contains a recommendation that hospitals should be situated as far as possible from military objectives. The ICRC state[38] that although the concept of a military object was accepted, opinions differed widely as to what amounted to a military objective. Pictet[39] comments that military objectives must be understood in the strictest sense as clearly defined points of actual or potential military importance. It might, perhaps, be inferred from the Prisoner of War Convention that metallurgical, machinery and chemical industries are legitimate objects of attack because prisoners of war may not be employed in those industries.[40] Kalshoven, however, counsels caution in jumping to any conclusion that these objectives may always be attacked since the circumstances must be such that their elimination contributes to 'weakening the military forces of the enemy'[41] and thus represent a clear military advantage for the attacker.[42]

---

[29]Presumably this should be a colon.

[30]Presumably this should be a comma.

[31]Presumably this refers to areas of land.

[32]Presumably this should be a colon.

[33]Presumably this should be a comma.

[34]Parks, Air war, p. 55.

[35]H. Blix, Area bombardment: rules and reasons, *British Yearbook of International Law*, 1978, at p. 33.

[36]Spaight, *Air Power*, 1947, at p. 277, commented that it was 'the special, not the general, war potential of the enemy that is still the objective'.

[37]*US* v. *Ohlendorf (Einsatzgruppen Case)*, IV *Trials of War Criminals Before the Nürnberg Military Tribunals*, Washington, 1949, p. 467.

[38]Y. Sandoz, W. Swinarski, B. Zimmerman and J. Pictet, *Commentary on the Additional Protocols of 8 June 1977 to the Geneva Conventions of 12 August 1949*, Martinus Nijhoff, 1987, (ICRC *Commentary*), para. 2000.

[39]In his *Commentary* on the Convention (ICRC, 1958).

[40]Art. 50.

[41]Wording from the St Petersburg Declaration.

[42]F. Kalshoven and L. Zegveld, *Constraints on the Waging of War*, 3rd edn, ICRC, 2001, p. 45.

Another indication of what amounts to a military objective is to be found in treaty form in Art. 8 of the Cultural Property Convention.[43] This provides that refuges for cultural property are to be situated an adequate distance from: 'any large industrial centre or from any important military objective constituting a vulnerable point, such as, for example, an aerodrome, broadcasting station, establishment engaged upon work of national defence, a port or railway station of relative importance or a main line of communication'. The ICRC draft rules of 1956[44] included a list of categories of military objectives which contained some objects of a civilian nature: war and supply ministries, lines of communication of military importance, broadcasting and television stations and telephone and telegraph exchanges of military importance, industries producing transport and communications material or metallurgical, engineering or chemical industries or installations producing energy (including gas and electricity) for mainly military purposes or use.[45]

The authors of the United States Department of Defence report on the Gulf war of 1991 summarize the above treaties by saying 'cultural and civilian objects are protected from direct, intentional attack unless they are used for military purposes, such as shielding military objects from attack'.[46] That summary might give a misleading impression. If, for example, the enemy were to hide its mobile missile launchers in a museum, one might have no alternative but to attack the museum since the object of attack would be hidden from view; but if they placed a military helicopter close to a church, the helicopter would be the object of the attack, not the church, though the church might well suffer in the process.

The above examples are static objectives. But means of transportation may be a military objective. The taxis commandeered by the military governor of Paris to transport reservists to the front in 1914[47] became military objectives when used for that purpose. Civilian oil tankers, lorries and railway wagons are not normally military objectives, but it is submitted that if intelligence reports suggest that the enemy plan to use such vehicles for military purposes, they can be attacked to prevent them being used for those purposes.

The term 'military objective' is not limited to inanimate objects. It also includes persons belonging to the enemy armed forces. It does not include members of the enemy civilian population. Even if the latter share the dangers of war, they are never in themselves military objectives.[48] In this respect, McCoubrey's reference

---

[43]Dealt with in Chapter 6.

[44]Sometimes known as the New Delhi draft rules.

[45]See ICRC *Commentary*, p. 632.

[46]United States, *Conduct of the Persian Gulf War*, Department of Defence Final Report to Congress, April 1992 (DOD Report), p. 611.

[47]See Schwarzenberger, *International Law*, p. 112.

[48]However, civilians may forfeit their protection if they take a direct part in hostilities, see Chapter 1.

to the civilian workforce actually working in military targets as military objectives is, in the writer's opinion, misconceived.[49] This is rather like Stone's attempt at rationalization with 'the work force of military objectives'.[50]

Another attempt at a definition which, because of its language, is obviously a precursor to the definition in Protocol I, is that adopted by the Institute of International Law in 1969: 'There can be considered as military objectives only those which, by their very nature or purpose or use, make an effective contribution to military action, or exhibit a generally recognized military significance, such that their total or partial destruction in the actual circumstances gives a substantial, specific and immediate military advantage to those who are in a position to destroy them.'[51] Kalshoven has pointed out[52] that this definition falls into two disjunctive parts so that objectives qualify as military objectives if either they make an effective contribution to military action – and that presumably covers objects of a civilian nature – or they exhibit a generally recognized military significance. It is not clear from the drafting whether the last part of the definition qualifies both of the earlier alternatives (which it probably does) or only the second.

Current law

Military objectives[53] are now defined, so far as objects are concerned, as those which by their location, nature, purpose or use make an effective contribution to military action and whose total or partial destruction, capture or neutralization, in the circumstances ruling at the time, offers a definite military advantage.[54]

This abstract definition has been criticized as being not very constructive and that an abstract definition coupled with a non-exhaustive list of examples would be better.[55] However, it is clear from this definition that military objectives are not limited to those in the vicinity of the opposing armed forces; they include objects in the hinterland, and any remaining doubts on this issue have been dissolved.[56]

---

[49]See H. McCoubrey, *International Humanitarian Law*, Dartmouth, 1990, p. 115.

[50]As to which see Stone, *Legal Controls*, p. 627.

[51]See D. Schindler and J. Toman, *The Laws of Armed Conflicts*, Sijthoff & Noordhoff, 3rd edn, 1988, p. 265.

[52]F. Kalshoven, Reaffirmation and development of international humanitarian law, *Netherlands Yearbook of International Law*, 1978, p. 110.

[53]Military objective is used in the sense of the target rather than the overall military task – see ICRC *Commentary* paras. 2009, 2010.

[54]Protocol I, Art. 52, para. 2.

[55]E. Rosenblad, Area bombing and international law, *Military Law and Law of War Review*, 1976, p. 90.

[56]E. Rauch, Attack restraints, target limitations, etc., *Military Law and Law of War Review*, 1979, vol. 1-2, p. 55.

The United Kingdom made a statement on ratification of Protocol I to the effect that an area of land could be a military objective.[57] The author analysed the definition of military objectives in 1982.[58] That analysis is brought up to date below. At first sight this seems a very wide definition. It does, however, have certain limitations:

1   The second part of the definition limits the first part which otherwise would be limitless. The term 'definite' was eventually chosen from among various other suggestions such as 'distinct', 'clear', 'direct', 'substantial', 'obvious' and 'specific'. There seemed to be no special significance about the final choice,[59] but it has been suggested that 'definite' rather than 'relative' had the effect of excluding the rule of proportionality as a criterion for the interpretation of the term 'military objective', for an attack may offer a definite military advantage whether or not excessive collateral damage is caused by it.[60] Once it has been established that the object to be attacked is a military objective, one then has to consider the rule of proportionality in respect of the incidental damage that the attack might cause. Having established that attacking the object concerned would confer a definite military advantage, the military commander, when considering the rule of proportionality, is then confronted with similar wording in that the collateral damage expected must not be excessive in relation to the concrete and direct military advantage expected.[61] 'Definite' also excludes a fanciful estimate of the military advantage or one that is not based on proper information;[62] or it means a concrete and perceptible military advantage rather than a hypothetical and speculative one.[63]

2   It must be read in conjunction with the prohibition on attacks against civilians and the civilian population in Art. 51, para. 2, of Protocol I. This rules out attacks directed against such civilians. But, subject to the rule of proportionality, it does not prevent attacks directed at military objectives that cause incidental damage to civilians.

3   There is no apparent reason for the inclusion of the words 'so far as objects are concerned' since the definition is sufficiently wide to include areas

---

[57]A similar statement was made on ratification by Canada, Germany, Italy, the Netherlands, New Zealand and Spain: see A. Roberts and R. Guelff, *Documents on the Laws of War*, 3rd edn, Oxford University Press, 2000, at pp. 499–512.

[58]A. P. V. Rogers, Conduct of combat and risks run by the civilian population, *Military Law and Law of War Review*, 1982, p. 304.

[59]Kalshoven, Reaffirmation, pp. 110–12; ICRC *Commentary*, para. 2019. The German translation *eindeutig* (see, e.g., Switzerland *Botschaft über die Zusatzprotokolle zu den Genfer Abkommen*, Swiss Federal Council, 1981, p. 123), meaning 'unequivocal', adds yet another dimension to the understanding of this term.

[60]E. Rauch, Conduct of combat and risks run by the civilian population, *Military Law and Law of War Review*, 1982, p. 67.

[61]See Chapter 4.

[62]See ICRC *Commentary*, para. 2024.

[63]Bothe *et al.*, *New Rules*, p. 326.

of land, enemy combatants and their equipment, which are quite clearly military objectives.[64] It could, of course, be argued that the word 'object' does not include combatant personnel.[65] The German manual lists the enemy armed forces separately from objects as military objectives.[66] The ICRC *Commentary*[67] states that 'object' means something tangible and visible, rather than something abstract like the object of a military operation. Rauch[68] hints at a difference between combatants and military objectives. If so, attacks on enemy military personnel would not be limited in any way by the definition, for example, the need to show a definite military advantage by killing a single enemy combatant.

4   The words 'in the circumstances ruling at the time' are also a limiting factor.[69] A cathedral, for example, would not normally be an object of military importance and could not be attacked. If, however, the enemy moved its divisional headquarters into the cathedral, it would become a military objective in view of the circumstances ruling at the time, that is, the presence of the enemy headquarters.

5   The presumption of civilian status in Arts. 50 and 52 of Protocol I, which applies even in the contact zone. This presumption was accepted despite some reservations in the negotiating committee to the effect that soldiers are unlikely to place their lives at risk because of the presumption, especially as in the front-line civilian buildings may be incorporated in the defensive works.[70]

There are various key words in Art. 52. The first of these is *limited*. This word means that care must be used in directing attacks only against military objectives. Art. 52 does not deal with the question of collateral damage, which is regulated by Art. 57.[71]

The words *nature, location, purpose or use* need explanation. According to the ICRC, 'nature' refers to all objects directly used by the armed forces, e.g. weapons, military equipment, transports, headquarters, communication centres, etc.;[72] 'location' includes sites which are militarily important because they must be seized or denied to the enemy or because the enemy must be forced to retreat from them;[73] and 'purpose' means future intended use of an object, while 'use' means its present function.[74] It is hard to think of an example of a case where 'purpose' will be the deciding factor, especially given the limitation of 'in the

---

[64]CDDH, Report of Committee III, second session, para. 64, under reference CDDH/215/Rev. 1. See also ICRC *Commentary*, para. 2017.
[65]Rauch, Conduct of combat; Kalshoven, Reaffirmation.
[66]*Humanitäres Völkerrecht in bewaffneten Konflikten*, ZDv 15/2, 1992, para. 442.
[67]Para. 2007.
[68]Attack restraints.
[69]Kalshoven, Reaffirmation, pp. 110–12.
[70]*Ibid.*
[71]See Chapter 4.
[72]See ICRC *Commentary*, para. 2020.
[73]*Ibid.*, para. 2021.
[74]*Ibid.*, para. 2022.

circumstances ruling at the time'. If, for example, a military commander received intelligence that the enemy were about to use a school as a munitions depot, it is unlikely that he would want to attack it until the munitions had been moved in.

The words 'nature', 'location' and 'purpose or use' are sufficiently wide to give the military commander considerable room for manoeuvre, but are subject to the qualifications later in the definition of *effective contribution to military action* and the offering of a 'definite military advantage'.

It has been suggested that there is no connection between effective contribution and military advantage. This means that it is permissible to attack bridges, fuel dumps and airfields in the rear areas since these targets make an effective contribution to the enemy's military power in the area of operations. Similarly, diversionary attacks are permitted because by diverting enemy attention away from the point of attack they confer a definite military advantage on the attacker.[75] Industry producing goods used by the armed forces and facilities supporting those factories are military objectives, but the precise extent to which industry can be made the object of attack is far from clear.[76]

The term *military action* appears to have a wide meaning equating to the general prosecution of the war. Meyrowitz, however, points out that while the definition of military objective in Protocol I allows more latitude than would be the case if the definition were based on a list of targets, the requirement that there be a definite military advantage also imposes some limitations on the war aims of a party to the conflict.[77]

It has always been difficult to define military objectives with sufficient precision for military commanders and for some commentators[78] who feel that a non-exhaustive list would be useful. An annex listing such objectives was provided for in the ICRC draft rules of 1956 but never drafted.[79] There are so many variable factors. The only certainties are as follows:

1   A purely civilian object contains neither military personnel nor things of military significance.
2   A civilian object which contains military personnel or things of military significance is considered a military objective.[80]

A tentative list of military objectives and of objects protected from attack is set out in the conclusions to this chapter.

---

[75]B. M. Carnahan, Protecting civilians under the draft Geneva protocol, 18 *Air Force Law Review*, 1976, p. 61.

[76]E.g. the Confederate cotton referred to above (see p. 59).

[77]See Buts de guerre et objectifs militaires, *Military Law and Law of War Review*, 1983, vol. 1-2, p. 108.

[78]See E. Rosenblad, Area bombing and international law, *Military Law and Law of War Review*, 1976.

[79]See Schindler and Toman, *Laws of Armed Conflicts*, p. 253.

[80]R. Barras and S. Erman, Forces armées et developpement du droit de la guerre, *Military Law and Law of War Review*, 1982, pp. 262, 271.

In case of doubt about objects that are normally civilian, such as churches, houses or schools, they should be presumed to have civilian status.[81] Bothe *et al.*[82] point out that in the ICRC draft 'installations and means of transport' were also included in the presumption, but the phrase was later deleted because means of transport fell into a category where their use for military purposes could not be excluded by a presumption. Greenwood[83] comments that it is very doubtful whether the rule of doubt represents customary law. Green's statement that 'the location and surrounding situation may make the object a military objective, as would be the case of a dwelling-house in the centre of a combat area or in the event of street and house-to-house fighting'[84] needs to be treated with caution. Everything depends on the circumstances. It is not possible to lay down general exemptions.

One reporter has mentioned that making a distinction between military objectives and civilian objects often involves a lot of effort. If it calls for a disproportionate consumption of men, ammunition, or loss of time as a tactical factor, commanders, especially at lower levels, may be inclined to be less careful in their selection of targets.[85]

There continues in some quarters to be some inexplicable doubt about whether an area of land can be a military objective. Würkner-Theis[86] discusses these doubts by saying that to recognize an area of land as a military objective would be to legalize area bombardment and negate the principle of distinction; that the recognition of an area of land in the Mines Protocol might be regarded as being limited to the purposes of that protocol; on the other hand use of words like 'location' and 'neutralization' in the definition of military objectives seem to imply areas of land, the denying of which to the enemy could be of considerable military importance; but since the precise effect of a mine cannot be forecast at the time of laying, it is difficult to say that there is a definite military advantage to be gained by laying a mine, unless the tactical situation is such that the enemy's manoeuvrability can be hindered by the laying of mines. After considering the authorities, he comes to the conclusion that an area of land *can* be a military objective.[87]

A study of armed conflict reveals that areas of land have always featured very prominently in combat. The German official manual of the First World War laid

---

[81]Protocol I, Art. 52, para 3.

[82]*New Rules*, p. 326.

[83]C. J. Greenwood, Customary international law and the first Geneva protocol of 1977 in the Gulf conflict, in P. J. Rowe (ed.), *The Gulf War 1990–91 in International and English Law*, Routledge, 1993, p. 75.

[84]L. C. Green, *The Contemporary Law of Armed Conflict*, 2nd edn, Manchester University Press, 2000, p. 156.

[85]E. L. Gonsalves, Armed Forces and the development of the law of war, *Military Law and Law of War Review*, 1982, p. 192.

[86]G. Würkner-Theis, *Fernverlegte Minen und humanitäres Völkerrecht*, Lang, 1990, at p. 121.

[87]*Da die Neutralisation eines für die Bewegung des Gegners bedeutsamen Gebietes einen militärischen Vorteil bedeutet, ist ein Landgebiet daher ein militärisches Objekt.*

down that it was permissible to bombard an area when it was intended to guard a passage, to defend approaches, to protect a retreat or to prepare or cover a tactical movement.[88] The United States *Handbook*[89] confirms that it is permissible to deny an area to enemy troops by planting land mines on it, or destroy a mountain pass that is crucial to the enemy's lines of communication. The definition of 'attack' given earlier emphasizes this prominence. Denying land to enemy forces is often a principal consideration in military operations. Bothe *et al.* refer to the word 'neutralization' in the definition of military objective and point out that an area of land may be neutralized by laying mines on it.[90] In this respect Protocol I has changed nothing. If an area of land has military significance, for whatever reason, it becomes a military objective. This has been described as a reasonable interpretation: 'as no objection has been voiced against it either in the formal procedure by a State party to Protocol I or in literature, it is deemed to be generally acceptable'.[91] Such an area of land may be attacked or occupied. It would, therefore, be wrong to say[92] that 'civilian intervening areas' can never be a military objective. The ICRC *Commentary* seems to accept that an area of land may be a military objective provided it is of limited size and in the combat zone.[93] The reference to the combat zone is, in the opinion of the author, an inadmissible restriction because it is not a limitation that appears in the definition of military objective itself. Art. 4 of the Mines Protocol to the Weapons Convention, for example, envisages the laying of mines outside the combat zone if certain precautions are taken. In these cases, it is not the definition of military objective but the other rules of Protocol I that provide the necessary protection. If, for example, an area of land contains civilian objects, the military commander will be obliged to ensure that those civilian objects are not directly attacked and that precautions are to be taken to minimize incidental loss. If the rule of proportionality would be infringed the action would have to be replanned.

Although the 'subjective' approach adopted in Protocol I has been criticized,[94] it is difficult, however, to see how objective criteria could be drafted without adopting the enumerative approach, which, first, can never be exhaustive and, second, cannot adapt to changing circumstances and technological and other

[88]See *Kriegsbrauch im Landkriege*, in the translation entitled *The German War Book*, by J. H. Morgan, John Murray, 1915, at p. 81.

[89]United States, *Commander's Handbook on the Law of Armed Conflict*, Department of the Air Force, Pamphlet 110-34, 1980, p. 2-1.

[90]*New Rules*, p. 325.

[91]H. P. Gasser, Some legal issues concerning ratification of the 1977 Geneva protocols in M. A. Meyer (ed.), *Armed Conflict and the New Law*, British Institute of International and Comparative Law, 1989, p. 87.

[92]Rauch, Conduct of combat, p. 68.

[93]ICRC *Commentary*, p. 2026.

[94]Detter, *Law of War*, p. 283, asks: 'How is [a party] expected to know the planned use of any particular installation? Surely objective criteria must be preferred rather than those which presuppose a detailed knowledge of enemy strategies. It is almost better to resort to large presumption of use and thus classify all industrial centres as military objectives'.

developments. At best, lists can only be illustrative. Objective criteria based on a non-enumerative approach would probably render almost nugatory the provisions for the protection of the civilian population, which is assured, to some extent, by the 'subjective' definition of military objectives coupled with the rule of doubt and the principle of proportionality. As will be seen in the next section (pp. 71–6), the subjective approach seems to have caused no difficulty in the Gulf war of 1991.

Parks also criticizes the definition of military objectives in Protocol I, saying that it is intended to limit targets to objectives connected to a nation's military effort rather than its war effort and that this does not reflect state practice.[95] He says that if certain lines of communication used by enemy armed forces are destroyed, they will simply transfer to other lines of communication; that electric grids are so complex that it is not possible to ascertain whether a given power plant is providing energy for national defence; that motorways may be used as airstrips for military aircraft; that nations export materials in order to pay for the purchase of weapons; that nations import raw materials to manufacture tanks, ships and aircraft; that dispersal of petroleum products or of the manufacture of parts for weapons systems add to the problems of the attacker; that attacks of relatively slight military importance can have untold psychological value. He refers to the Doolittle raids on Japan in 1942, which caused Japan to switch aircraft to home defence and unleashed a chain of events that enabled the United States to stem the tide of Japanese conquests. Of course, that result may not have been foreseen by the Doolittle planners, who may have been concerned mainly with giving US forces a morale boost.[96]

The author does not share all those concerns,[97] taking the view that the definition of military objectives is sufficiently wide to allow most of the above targets to be attacked. Obviously an attacker will wish to concentrate his efforts in such a way as to derive the maximum benefit. He will not attack a country's entire lines of communication, motorway system or electric grid only because it might be used by the armed forces or to move supplies. He will attack those points that will give him the best advantage.[98] Dispersal of possible objectives makes things more difficult for the attacker, but this is not a problem that arises from the definition of military objectives. There is no difficulty about attacking raw materials used in the armaments industry, nor does the motive (i.e. the psychological advantage) for attacking a *military* objective matter.

The only potential area of difficulty is with regard to economic targets.[99] If a country relies almost entirely on, say, the export of coffee beans or bananas for

[95]Parks, Air war, p. 138.
[96]Parks, Air war, p. 142.
[97]Nor does G. Best, *Law and War since 1945*, Clarendon Press, 1994, pp. 274–5.
[98]This question will be discussed later in this chapter in the light of events in the Gulf war 1991 (see pp. 71–6).
[99]Such as the Confederate cotton previously referred to.

its income and even if this income is used to great extent to support its war effort, the opinion of the author is that it would not be legitimate to attack banana or coffee bean plantations or warehouses. The reason for this is that such plants would not make an *effective* contribution to *military* action nor would their destruction offer a *definite* military advantage. The definition of military objectives thus excludes the general industrial and agricultural potential of the enemy. Targets must offer a more specific military advantage. Green puts it as economic targets that indirectly but effectively support enemy operations.[100] None of this, however, would prevent attacks on military objectives, such as means of transportation or ports, which would indirectly affect the export of agricultural products.

The Gulf war 1991

It is relatively easy to single out military objectives of a purely military nature. Before the Gulf war, a leader writer urged allied forces to attack Iraqi military potential – 'airfields, missile sites, military bases and factories producing chemicals or nuclear materials' but also advised that they should not bomb 'dams, factories or centres of civilian population . . . or attempt the defoliation of the country'.[101]

In practice things are not so simple in a modern society. According to Roberts,[102] many of the objects attacked by the allies during the air campaign served the needs of both the armed forces and the civilian population, such as oil storage sites, power stations and factories, and that it is difficult to neutralize the military effectiveness of those targets without simultaneously harming the civilian population. Schachter,[103] comments that 'the hostilities revealed how difficult it can be to make a sharp separation between the military target and civilian objects, especially in an industrial society where their commingling is widespread'. Attacks on the electric power system meant that electric power was severely curtailed resulting in shortages and contamination of the water supply.[104] Roads, railways, bridges, airports and ports are used for the deployment of military forces and the movement of military supplies as well as for civilian purposes. It has been pointed out that bombing to cut the enemy off from its supplies is more effective than attacking the enemy forces themselves, which, through digging in and camouflage can remain largely protected from air attack.[105] The attacks on bridges

[100]Green, *Contemporary Law*, p. 191.

[101]*The Independent*, 11 January 1991.

[102]A. Roberts, Failures in protecting the environment, in Rowe (ed.), *Gulf War*, p. 139.

[103]O. Schachter, United Nations law in the Gulf conflict, *American Journal of International Law*, 1991, at p. 466.

[104]See report of the UN Secretary-General to the President of the Security Council of 20 March 1991, UN Document S/22366.

[105]E. Luttwak, Supplies, not troops should be the main target of jets in Kuwait, *The Times*, 16 February 1991.

and supply lines were to prevent reinforcements and supplies reaching the Kuwaiti theatre of operations.[106] Microwave towers used for civilian communications can also be used as part of the military command and control system; and electric power grids can be used for civilian and military purposes simultaneously.[107] Some have been critical of the bombing of Iraq's electrical system[108] on the grounds that the civilian population suffered unduly as a result. But such a system is a military objective if by destroying it the enemy's military effectiveness is reduced.[109] Protection of the civilian population is provided by the rule of proportionality, see Chapter 1.

In the Gulf war it was considered that because of the highly centralized Iraqi command arrangements the communications system was a very important target, since if it were rendered inoperative the Iraqi leaders would be unable to direct their forces. Bridges over the river Euphrates in Baghdad carried the fibre optic cables, which provided communications with the forces. Destruction of the bridges served two ends: to sever those cables and to impede the deployment of Iraqi forces and their supplies.[110]

Targets actually attacked during the allied air campaign included the following:

1 Military targets – Iraqi military aircraft both in the air and on the ground,[111] some in hardened shelters,[112] air bases and runways, Scud missiles, naval vessels, tanks, military vehicles and artillery pieces, army and Republican Guard positions in the Kuwait theatre of operations,[113] barracks,[114] surface-to-air and anti-ship missile bases and their radars, military production facilities and ammunition storage areas, chemical weapons facilities, military headquarters and command posts[115] and minefields.[116]

2 Dual-use targets –[117] leadership command facilities such as the Iraqi intelligence service headquarters,[118] refined oil production installations, nuclear, chemical

[106]See DOD Report, p. 98.

[107]*Ibid.*, p. 612.

[108]E.g. Middle East Watch, *Needless Deaths in the Gulf War*, Human Rights Watch, 1991.

[109]Protocol I, Art. 52, para. 2, speaks of the object making an effective contribution to military action and whose neutralization, etc. offers a definite military advantage.

[110]DOD Report, p. 612.

[111]*Ibid.*, pp. 95–9.

[112]C. Allen, *Thunder and Lightning*, HMSO, 1991, p. 137.

[113]DOD Report, pp. 95–9.

[114]P. Hine, Despatch by the joint commander of Operation Granby, second supplement to the *London Gazette*, 28 June 1991, p. G42; Allen, *Thunder and Lightning*, p. 137.

[115]DOD Report, pp. 95–9.

[116]Apparently, some were attacked with fuel-air explosive, see Hansard (Commons), 2 May 1991 at col. 484 and Hansard (Commons), 17 Jun 1991 at col. 16; and DOD Report, p. 196.

[117]These must, of course, be military objectives. Greenwood rightly emphasizes that, legally, there is no intermediate category of dual-use objects: either something is a military objective or it is not (Greenwood, Gulf conflict, p. 73).

[118]Greenwood, Gulf conflict, states that ministries are not necessarily military objectives. It depends on the circumstances: what ministries they are and what contribution they make to the enemy's military action.

and biological sites,[119] bridges,[120] communications towers, exchanges and lines, supply lines, including railway and road bridges between Baghdad and Basra, radio and television installations and electricity production facilities.[121]

According to media reports, dual-use targets that might have been attacked but which were not for fear of the consequences for the civilian population included dams.[122] A dam is not necessarily a military objective.[123] It depends on its purpose. If it is purely to create a reservoir of drinking water, it will not be a military objective. If it were only to provide hydro-electric power, the situation would be different. It is more likely to provide both: water and electric power. There is, however, the danger from flooding to the civilian population to be considered if the dam is attacked. In the circumstances, it is better to attack the hydro-electric power installations with precision weapons rather than the dam itself.[124] According to Middle East Watch, other objects that were removed from the target list included statues of Saddam Hussein and triumphal arches.[125] According to one account, it seems that the statue was removed from the list mainly because of the fear of incidental damage.[126] Middle East Watch seems to assume that the definition of military objectives in Protocol I applied to the Gulf conflict[127] but, of course, Protocol I did not apply in that conflict. The less clear customary law understanding of the term, which did apply, may have permitted potential or indeterminate factors such as enemy morale to be taken into account.

In the Gulf war the United States air warfare plan was to strike first at Iraqi command and control and communications facilities, second to gain air supremacy, third to destroy the nuclear, bacteriological and chemical warfare capability, fourth to eliminate Iraq's offensive warfare capability by attacking military production plants and fifth to attack lines of communications to Iraqi forces in Kuwait. Only after that were enemy armed forces attacked.[128]

British aircraft attacked airfields, barracks, radar control centres, ammunition dumps, petroleum storage sites, power stations, Scud missile sites, bridges,

---

[119]DOD Report, pp. 95–9.

[120]Allen, *Thunder and Lightning*, pp. 113–16.

[121]DOD Report, pp. 95–9.

[122]*The Times*, 15 February 1991. The Secretary of State for Defence confirmed that the allies did not attack water supplies, see *Preliminary Lessons of Operation Granby*, House of Commons Defence Committee 10th Report, HMSO, 1991, p. 10.

[123]Special provisions protecting dams are to be found in Protocol I, Art. 56.

[124]See G. H. Aldrich, Prospects for US ratification of Protocol I, *American Journal of International Law*, 1991, p. 56, who points out that hydro-electric power stations are not themselves dams or dykes, but 'other military objectives located in the vicinity' thereof.

[125]See Middle East Watch, *Needless Deaths*, p. 156.

[126]T. P. Keenan Jr., Die Operation Wüstensturm aus der Sicht des aktiven Rechtsberaters, *Humanitäres Völkerrecht Informationsschriften*, January–July 1991, p. 36. A US air force officer later told the author that the statue was not removed from the target list; it just had a lower priority than other targets.

[127]See, e.g., p. 159.

[128]DOD Report, p. 95.

hardened aircraft shelters, coastal defence positions, surface-to-air missile batteries, supply depots, naval vessels, artillery positions and concentrations of armour.[129]

The British Army in the Gulf was not presented with the dilemma of how to deal with mixed targets. The plan for the 1st (British) Armoured Division was to defeat Iraq's tactical reserves in the area between the southern flank of the VII US Corps and the Iraq–Saudi Arabia border. This involved ensuring that Iraqi forces did not attack the flanks of the VII US Corps by destroying armour and artillery in that area. In fact, all of the objectives actually attacked were of a purely military nature.[130] As Best comments, referring to the desert war of 1940– 42 and the absence of civilians, the principles of restraint and discrimination are observed 'not badly when men had will and space to observe them'.[131]

Allied targeting has been criticized by some commentators[132] in particular:

1 Food and grain warehouses, a dairy factory, flour mills and water treatment facilities.
2 The electricity system.
3 Civilian vehicles on highways and Bedouin tents.
4 The oil sector.

They are correct with regard to food facilities not being military objectives unless used exclusively by the armed forces or in direct support of military action,[133] but there is no evidence that any of these facilities was deliberately made the object of attack. Indeed, Parks comments that factories producing textiles, foodstuffs, cement and household goods 'were *not* attacked *unless* they also were of value to Saddam Hussein's defence of Kuwait or his CBW (chemical and bacteriological warfare) programmes through dual use for military and civilian purposes'.[134] Some damage to such factories may have been caused by Iraqi surface-to-air missiles and anti-aircraft munitions.[135] Shotwell refers to the effect of sanctions as well as air strikes on the morale of Iraqi troops during the Gulf war of 1991 when increasing numbers of Iraqi soldiers reported dwindling rations of food: some units were allocating only one piece of bread per day per soldier.[136] There is evidence that the Iraqi regime used civilian installations as a cover for military activities. For example, UN inspectors discovered chemical

[129]Hine, Despatch, p. G42.
[130]N. Pearce, *The Shield and the Sabre*, HMSO, 1992, pp. 90–121.
[131]Best, *Law and War*, p. 60.
[132]Middle East Watch, *Needless Deaths*, pp. 160 ff.; C. Jochnick and R. Normand, The legitimation of violence: a critical history of the laws of war, *Harvard International Law Journal*, 1994, p. 402. For a different perspective, see Best, *Law and War*, p. 384.
[133]See Protocol I, Art. 54, para. 3.
[134]W. H. Parks, in a letter dated 22 December 1994 to the author.
[135]G. Waters, *Gulf Lesson One: The Value of Air Power*, Air Power Studies Centre, 1992, p. 170.
[136]C. B. Shotwell, Food and the use of force, *Military Law and Law of War Review*, 1991, at p. 372.

bomb production equipment while inspecting a sugar factory in Iraq.[137] The most publicized incident in the allied bombing campaign was the attack on the al-Amariyah (or al Firdos) bunker in Baghdad. This was a command and control centre in which, unbeknown to the allies, civilians had been allowed to take refuge.[138]

The modern military machine relies very heavily on electrical power, especially for command, control, communications and air defence systems. Take away that power and the enemy is severely handicapped and may be rendered blind and leaderless and vulnerable to air attack. The suggestion by Jochnick and Normand[139] that repeated attacks are not necessary where a war is going to be short is unrealistic. It was known that Iraq possessed very powerful armed forces with a nuclear, chemical and bacteriological capability, it was not known how long it would take to fulfil the UN mandate,[140] and the allies were fully entitled to take no risks in that respect. In these circumstances, power sources become military objectives. Electrical power is fundamental to the functioning of many industries, especially armaments and other war material. In the case of Iraq, it was most urgent for the allies to neutralize Iraq's air defence and, more particularly, its nuclear, bacteriological and chemical warfare capability and its Scud missile system, and keep them neutralized by repeated attacks to prevent repair. However, steps were taken, for example, by adopting a policy of attacking switching stations rather than generating stations, to enable repair of the electricity system after the war.[141]

Of course, the civilian population will be badly affected too. Integrated electrical grids are such that electricity used to power air defence computers or a biological weapons factory cannot be separated from that used to power electrical pumps for the water supply and to light homes. So the rule of proportionality

---

[137]DOD Report, p. 613.

[138]*Ibid.*, p. 615. See also Best, *Law and War*, p. 327; T. A. Keaney E. A. and Cohen, *Gulf War Air Power Survey, Summary Report*, US Government Printing Office, 1993, pp. 69, 249. Ignorance of the presence of civilians means that there could be no war crime because of a lack of intent. If, however, their presence had been known, it would have been a question of applying the customary law rule of proportionality (the importance of the target compared to estimated civilian casualties, see Chapter 1). As Green, *Contemporary Law*, p. 125, points out, Protocol I did not apply to the conflict.

[139]Jochnick and Normand Legitimation of violence, p. 404.

[140]The comment by Michael Howard in November 1990 that the war could be 'a bloody and prolonged business' (On balance, Bush must go to war, *The Times*, 5 November 1990) probably reflected the views of many at the time. Even as late as 24 December 1990 military planners acknowledged that the war could last six months, see *The Times* of that day.

[141]The author is indebted to W. H. Parks for his assistance in dealing with these criticisms and for referring him to Keaney and Cohen, *Gulf War Air Power Survey, Summary Report*; D. J. Kuehl, Air power v. electricity: electric power as a target for strategic air operations, *Journal for Strategic Studies*, 1995; and various other authorities. He makes the valid point that in considering the post-war state of Iraq it is necessary to bear in mind the continuing UN sanctions and Saddam Hussein's failure to channel his resources into alleviating the conditions of the civilian population and refers in this respect to A. Dowty, Sanctioning Iraq: the limits of the new world order, *Washington Quarterly*, 1994.

applies.[142] It is estimated that ultimately allied air attacks rendered 88 per cent of Iraqi electrical-generating capacity unavailable[143] but that by mid-1992 capacity was back to 90 per cent of the pre-war level.[144] In this connection it is of interest that Middle East Watch cite a Harvard University group which visited Iraq in April and May 1991 who found that electricity was then supplied at 23 per cent of the pre-war figure. This may have been enough to support the needs of the civilian population and of agriculture, but not industry, and may be regarded as proportionate. This is probably what General Schwarzkopf had in mind when, according to Middle East Watch, he said that some electrical power must be left for the civilians.[145] The writer would reject the allegation that repeated bombing of previously disabled electrical facilities served no military purpose. The purpose obviously is to prevent repair and keep the facility out of action. The fact that the allies did not bomb electrical facilities in Kuwait is really irrelevant.[146]

Civilian vehicles carrying military supplies for the benefit of the Iraqi armed forces would have been military objectives. The view of the author is that civilian vehicles carrying Iraqi oil to Jordan would not. Some of the latter were attacked by mistake, being taken for mobile Scud launchers. Some suffered incidental damage as a result of attacks on military vehicles using the same road.[147] It also appears that many of the objects attacked in the Scud launch areas were 'decoys, vehicles such as tanker trucks that had infra-red and radar signatures impossible to distinguish from those of mobile launchers'.[148] Jochnick and Normand's criticism of allied attacks on Iraqi oil facilities is effectively answered by Keaney and Cohen, who state that during the war allied air attacks rendered 90 per cent of Iraq's petroleum-refining capacity inoperative but that by October 1992 it had returned to two-thirds of its pre-war level. Again, planners did not know how long the war would last and it was prudent to limit Iraq's ability to wage a protracted ground campaign.[149]

Legal opinion is divided on whether, in conflicts to which Protocol I does not apply, damaging civilian morale is a lawful aim of war,[150] but there seems to be no reason why that cannot lawfully be a by-product of attacks on legitimate military objectives. Remarks such as 'it is important that people understand that a war is going on'[151] must be seen in this context.

---

[142]See Chapter 1. Middle East Watch, *Needless Deaths*, seem to accept that it is a question of proportionality rather than targeting.
[143]Not 96 per cent, as alleged by Jochnick and Normand, The legitimation of violence, p. 404.
[144]Keaney and Cohen, *Gulf War*, pp. 73–5.
[145]Middle East Watch, p. 175.
[146]See Jochnick and Normand, The legitimation of violence, pp. 404–5.
[147]See DOD Report, p. 627.
[148]Keaney and Cohen, *Gulf War*, p. 83.
[149]*Ibid.*, pp. 76–7.
[150]See, e.g., Oppenheim, *International Law*, at pp. 528–9; Blix, Area bombardment, at pp. 44 ff.
[151]Quoted by J. Campbell, Rings of disaster, *London Evening Standard*, 3 July 1991.

Kosovo 1999

Targets attacked during the NATO bombing campaign were very similar to those attacked during the Gulf war of 1991.[152] There were three phases: air-defence systems and command and control bunkers; military targets below 44 degrees north latitude; and 'punishment' targets north of the 44th parallel, including targets in Belgrade.[153] Attacks on bridges received a lot of media attention when, as in two cases, these were carried out as a train[154] and a bus[155] respectively were crossing them, resulting in unfortunate, and perhaps avoidable, civilian casualties. As the author has written about the railway bridge case:

The case was examined by the committee of experts appointed by the Prosecutor of the International Criminal Tribunal for the former Yugoslavia (ICTY). Their report[156] indicates that the committee considered the bridge to be a legitimate target and, though having reservations about the second missile, decided that the case should not be investigated by the prosecutor. They must have considered the first missile strike to be a legitimate action against a military objective, the inference being that any civilian casualties of that strike were not disproportionate, and that the firing of the second missile was an error of judgement in the heat of the moment. It seems clear to me that the air-crew were concentrating on hitting the bridge but did not reach classroom levels of perfection in the agony of the moment. Errors of judgement such as this are not the stuff of criminal prosecutions.[157]

It seems that the policy objective of stopping ethnic cleansing made some US air commanders think that attacking Belgrade's power stations and government ministries would be more likely to succeed than attacking the Serbian Third Army in Kosovo.[158]

There seemed to be a tendency to attack targets associated with the regime of President Milošević as well as more traditional military objectives, for example, the headquarters of the ruling socialist party, Milošević's villa and a tobacco factory at Vranje. It may be that the first two were involved with the command and control of Serb forces in Kosovo and the last may have been a dual-use facility. However, reports of attacks on the foreign ministry and police

---

[152]See United States, *Kosovo/Operation Allied Force After-Action Report*, 31 January 2000 (US Kosovo Report), pp. 9, 57, 67, 883, 92, A-7, A-8 and A-10.

[153]P. C. Strickland, USAF aerospace-power doctrine, decisive or coercive? *Air Power Review*, spring 2001, p. 17.

[154]This was the attack on the Grdelica railway bridge on 12 April 1999.

[155]This was the attack on a bridge at Lužane on 1 May 1999.

[156]Final Report to the Prosecutor by the Committee Established to Review the NATO Bombing Campaign Against the Federal Republic of Yugoslavia (ICTY Report), para. 62, 39 ILM 1257 (2000) at p. 1275.

[157]A. P. V. Rogers, What is a legitimate military target?, in R. Burchill, N. White and J. Morris (eds.), *Peace, Security and Law: Essays in Honour of Hilaire McCoubrey*, Cambridge University Press, 2004.

[158]*Ibid.*

headquarters on 1 May 1999[159] raise questions about the legitimacy of such targets. The justification for attacks on the Ministry of Interior and police headquarters appears to be that they were responsible for directing the 'ethnic cleansing' campaign in Kosovo.

Apart from the Chinese Embassy in Belgrade, which was hit by mistake because out-of-date maps were used, most media attention was paid to the attack on the Serbian state television and radio station in Belgrade on 23 April 1999. This is dealt with later in this chapter (pp. 82–3). The attack also formed part of a case against the European NATO states before the European Court of Human Rights, but the court declined to exercise jurisdiction on the grounds that the European Convention on Human Rights does not apply extra-territorially in the absence of effective control of territory and its inhabitants abroad.[160] That meant, in effect, that the NATO states concerned could not be responsible for implementing the convention from the air!

A reappraisal of the definition of military objectives?

Some United States authors, notably Dunlap,[161] consider that the definition of 'military objective' is too narrow and that conflicts could be brought to a conclusion more swiftly and with less loss of human life if economic targets could be attacked. It seems that during the Kosovo campaign, plans for a computer-based strike on Milošević's personal bank accounts were abandoned for legal reasons, presumably because it could not be established that the funds were being used to support the military effort. Some consider that to hit an enemy financially is more ethical than bombing him and that it is strange that civilian leaders who serve as commanders-in-chief of their armed forces are legitimate targets, though not their personal property.[162]

Dunlap would exclude from the target-list objects that are genuinely indispensable to the survival of the non-combatant population. Almost everything else of any value would be a potential target. According to him, that would include:

[159]*The Times*, 2 May 1999.

[160]See the court's decision on admissibility of 19 December 2001 in the case of *Banković and Others* v. *Belgium and Others*. The convention would probably apply extra-territorially in cases of belligerent occupation.

[161]J. Dunlap Jr., The end of innocence: rethinking noncombatancy in the post-Kosovo era, *Strategic Review*, Summer 2000, 9. Even the US Joint Chiefs of Staff's targeting manual, *Joint Doctrine for Targeting* (Joint Publication 3–60) of 17 January 2002, at p. A–3, includes 'economic targets that indirectly but effectively support and sustain the adversary's warfighting capability'. The concept of indirect but effective support seems to be espoused by Green, *Contemporary Law*, p. 191. It is difficult to see that such an approach would be compatible with the definition of a military objective in Protocol I, Art. 52, to which, of course, the US is not a party. It is probably a matter of degree – how indirect?

[162]Dunlap, End of innocence, p. 13.

a. Banks and financial institutions; resorts, entertainment, sports and recreational facilities; factories, plants, stores, and shops that produce, sell, or distribute luxury products; together with their associated logistics systems. He considers that reducing the middle and upper classes to a subsistence level would induce them to put pressure on the government to concede.
b. Cultural, educational and historical objects that provide 'support – to include psychological sustenance – to the malignant ideology that stimulates the behaviour the use of force is intended to stop'.
c. Government offices and buildings even if they do not directly support military activities.   '
d. The personal property of the 'sentient, adult population'.[163]

The reason for excluding attacks intended solely to deny the civilian population water, power and other indispensable necessities of life is because, in addition to ethical and legal concerns, such strikes can be militarily counter-productive. 'Whatever tolerance the American public may have for the destruction of property, it does not appear to extend to acts that kill non-combatants, even unintentionally.'[164]

Dunlap suggests a new definition or understanding of the notion of 'military objective' without the current nexus to a contribution to a specific military action and explicitly including those civilian objects whose loss weakens the nation's collective will to continue the conflict.[165]

Of course, one has to see this proposal within the perspective in which it is put forward, namely, the difficulties in dealing with the regimes in Iraq and the former Yugoslavia.[166] It may not be relevant to more traditional forms of armed conflict or, indeed, to internal armed conflict. Furthermore, it is written from the point of view of the air force and of trying to achieve results on the basis of air power alone.

Even if it were feasible to renegotiate the definition of 'military objective', it does not follow that this would lead to fewer civilian casualties than current attacks on military objectives. The system would not work against a poor country. It is unlikely that wars can be won by air power alone, especially against a resolute enemy prepared to sit it out. Leaving aside the question of whether cyber-war in itself is an armed conflict governed by the law of war (since this would call for a chapter in its own right), it seems that cyber-war is not necessarily the answer, since only states dependent on high technology are at risk and, anyway, a return to low technology is always possible and an alternative low-technology back-up essential.

---

[163] *Ibid.*, p. 14.
[164] *Ibid.*, p. 15.
[165] *Ibid.*, p. 17.
[166] 'When societies propagate evil, democracies must be prepared to visit upon them force so staggering it will produce fundamental change. The force needed to do so – whether delivered via traditional kinetic bombing or imposed by way of a newly-developed cyber-technique – is not symbolic or incrementally administered, but rather massive, relentless, and profoundly shattering' (*ibid.*, p. 17).

Afghanistan 2001

It is too early to analyse the coalition campaign in Afghanistan as, at the time of writing,[167] information from official sources is limited. It seems that similar targets were selected for attack to those in previous conflicts: air defences, ammunition and vehicle storage depots, military bases and training facilities, fielded Taliban forces, the Taliban and al-Qa'ida leadership, the Taliban defence ministry in Kabul and terrorist training compounds.[168] Electric power was targeted, as in the case of a hydro-electric power station close to a dam.[169] Targets about which questions might legitimately be asked include the house of Mullah Omar,[170] an office of al-Jezeera television[171] and Ariana civil aircraft at Kabul airport.[172] Until more is known, one can only speculate as to the reason for these attacks if, indeed, they took place. Perhaps the house of Mullah Omar was a place from which military operations were conducted; the office of al-Jezeera suffered incidental damage as the result of an attack elsewhere; and the civil aircraft were destroyed as an incidental effect of attacks against the airfield or military targets there, although there were reports that these aircraft were being used for transporting members of al-Qa'ida and their weapons – in which case they would be legitimate targets.

The United States Department of Defence has issued instructions dated 30 April 2003 for its military commissions for the trial of al-Qa'ida suspects.[173] Instruction No. 2 contains the following definition: '"Military objectives" are those potential targets during an armed conflict which, by their nature, location, purpose or use, effectively contribute to the opposing force's war-fighting or war-sustaining capability and whose total or partial destruction, capture or neutralization would constitute a military advantage to the attacker under the circumstances at the time of the attack.'[174] This gives a clear indication of the current United States thinking on what constitutes a military objective. It will be noted that the definition, although borrowing language from Protocol I,[175] to

---

[167]30 June 2003.

[168]C. Finn, The employment of air power in Afghanistan and beyond, *Air Power Review*, winter 2002, p. 1.

[169]According to *The Independent* of 8 November 2001, US forces bombed a power station near a dam in southern Afghanistan, presumably the Kajaki dam, which retains 1.85 million cubic metres of water, on 1 November. The power station was reported to supply electricity to 500,000 people, several hospitals and a textile factory. Presumably the dam was not damaged in the attack, so the incidental effects of the attack would fall to be considered under the rule of proportionality.

[170]According to a report in *The Independent* of 17 October 2001, this resulted in the death of Mullah Omar's stepfather and nephew. This attack was confirmed by Finn, Air power, citing General Franks.

[171]*The Independent*, 14 November 2001.

[172]*The Independent*, 20 November 2001.

[173]These may be seen on www.nimj.org.

[174]Art. 5D.

[175]According to Art. 3B of Instruction 2, no conclusion should be drawn from the similarity of language in other articulations of law.

which the US is not a party, departs from the protocol in significant respects. This is evident if the US and protocol versions are superimposed on each other (common language is in bold, protocol language in ordinary type and US language in italics):

[In so far as objects are concerned,] **military objectives are** [limited to] **those** [*potential targets during an armed conflict*] **which by their nature, location, purpose or use** [make an effective contribution to military action][*effectively contribute to the opposing force's war-fighting or war-sustaining capability*] **and whose total or partial destruction, capture or neutralization** [,in the circumstances ruling at the time, offers a definite][*would constitute a*] **military advantage** [*to the attacker under the circumstances at the time of the attack*].

This effect of the United States' definition is to widen considerably the range of targets that might be attacked, including some of the targets that are problematic under Protocol I, especially economic, leadership and propaganda targets, though it probably would not extend to all the targets advocated by Dunlap. There are dangers in widening the definition of military objectives since others can take advantage of that too. Perhaps the use of the words 'during an armed conflict' are intended to exclude claims that the New York twin towers were legitimate targets,[176] but that would presuppose that the 'war on terrorism' started after that attack and not with earlier terrorist attacks in Kenya, Yemen and elsewhere.

Iraq 2003

At the date of writing,[177] there is a lack of reliable information about targets selected by coalition forces in the war against Iraq. Unlike the campaigns in Kosovo and Afghanistan, ground troops were deployed very early in the campaign. Media reports indicate that, apart from enemy armed forces, tanks and artillery, targets included air-defence systems,[178] missile batteries,[179] communications towers,[180] bridges,[181] fuel depots,[182] the headquarters of Special Security, the Republican Guard headquarters in Baghdad, the Rashid Barracks, Baghdad's international airport,[183] the information ministry, the Baath party offices, the office

[176]Osama bin Laden is reported as saying that the twin towers were legitimate targets as they were supporting US economic power, *The Independent*, 12 November 2001.

[177]30 June 2003.

[178]S. Payne, Tornadoes lead blitz on Baghdad, in *The Daily Telegraph*, *War on Saddam*, London, Robinson, 2003, p. 25.

[179]BBC News online, 26 March 2003; *The Independent*, 28 March 2003.

[180]BBC News online, 28 March 2003; *The Independent*, 29 March 2003.

[181]BBC News online, 24 March 2003.

[182]BBC News online, 30 March 2003.

[183]B. Rooney, First strike, in *War on Saddam*, pp. 37, 39. It seems that the capture of the airport was an important aim of the US military plan and that the attacks were limited to destroying the military defences of the airport.

of Tariq Aziz,[184] presidential palaces and bunkers,[185] the planning ministry,[186] and, on two occasions, locations where Saddam Hussein was thought to be.[187] Presumably the justification for targeting the ministries and leadership sites is that they were inextricably linked to the conduct of Iraqi military operations. A college of literature in Basra that formed an objective for British forces seems, at first sight, to be a civilian object, but it became a military objective because it was a stronghold of Feedayeen militia.[188] There have been the usual complaints about the use of depleted uranium rounds and cluster munitions but, in the author's opinion, subject to the rule of proportionality, these are legitimate weapons for use against military targets. There were cases of civilian deaths in marketplaces and journalists at the Hotel Palestine were killed in the fighting, but it is not clear at this stage how these deaths were caused.

Television stations as targets

The attack on the television station in Belgrade on 23 April 1999 attracted criticism.[189] It was apparently selected for attack as it was part of an integrated communications network that was used for both military and civilians purposes[190] but also as 'media responsible for broadcasting propaganda.'[191] Human Rights Watch, in a letter to the NATO Secretary-General, commented that it was not 'being used to incite violence (akin to Radio Milles Collines during the Rwandan genocide), which might have justified [its] destruction. At worst, as far as we know, the Yugoslav government was using [it] to issue propaganda supportive of its war effort' and that stopping that propaganda would not offer the concrete and direct military advantage necessary for a legitimate target.[192] The prosecutor of the International Criminal Tribunal for the former Yugoslavia appointed a committee of experts to prepare a report on various incidents in the Kosovo conflict. The experts came to the conclusion that the attack on the television station could be justified on the basis that it formed part of a general attack on the Yugoslav military command, control and communications network but that a justification based on propaganda was more debatable.[193]

---

[184] BBC News online, 20 and 29 March 2003.
[185] BBC News online, 21 and 31 March 2003; *The Independent*, 1 April 2003.
[186] BBC TV news, 10 p.m., 11 April 2003.
[187] Smith and Rooney, in *War on Saddam*, at pp. 14, 15, 21, 154.
[188] Bentham, *War on Saddam*, p. 146.
[189] See United Kingdom, Foreign Affairs Committee, Fourth Report, *Kosovo*, vol. 1, London, The Stationery Office, 23 May 2000, para. 152, which asked for the legal justification for attacks on broadcasting stations; the response of the Secretary of State, Cm 4825 dated August 2000, does not give a justification, it merely refers to the report by the ICTY committee of experts. See also the Human Rights Watch Report, *The Crisis in Kosovo* (HRW Kosovo Report) p. 12.
[190] ICTY report, para. 72.
[191] United States, *Kosovo Report*, p. 8.
[192] HRW Kosovo Report, p. 12.
[193] See ICTY report, paras. 71–9.

Despite the concerns expressed about the television station in Belgrade, the main television station in Baghdad was hit by cruise missiles in March 2003 because, according to press reports, the building was part of Iraq's military command and control system.[194] The state radio and television station in Basra was hit the next day, effectively isolating Basra from communications with the capital, Baghdad.[195]

Attacks on a media station may be permissible, therefore, subject to the rule of proportionality, if it helps the enemy in its military operations, for example, if it is integrated into the military communications system;[196] possibly if it is used to incite violence;[197] but not if it merely broadcasts news, even of doubtful validity, to the population.

Conclusions

Taking into account the practice of states and past attempts at codification, the following examples of military objectives are tentatively given. It is important to stress that:

1 The list is by no means exhaustive.
2 The mere fact that an object, such as a bridge or a communications installation, is in the list does not mean that it is necessarily a military objective. It must make an effective contribution to military action and its neutralization must offer a definite military advantage.[198]
3 When attacking these targets the proportionality rule must be respected and the natural environment protected against widespread, long-term and severe damage.

Examples of military objectives

1 Military personnel, and persons who take part in the fighting without being members of the armed forces.[199]
2 Military facilities, military equipment, including military vehicles, weapons, munitions and stores of fuel,[200] military works, including defensive works

---

[194]C. Milmo, Allied commanders open battle for the airwaves, *The Independent*, 27 March 2003.
[195]BBC news online, 27 March 2003.
[196]According to the US *Joint Doctrine for Targeting*, p. 13, radio or television transmitters may be legitimate targets if used by the enemy's government to support military operations.
[197]The case of Radio Milles Collines has already been mentioned (p. 82). A. Dworkin, Iraqi television: a legitimate target, on www.crimesofwar.org, asks whether it would be legitimate to attack a television station where Saddam Hussein was shown in military uniform, exhorting his supporters to rise up and 'slit the throats' of US troops.
[198]Protocol I, Art. 52(2).
[199]ICRC *Commentary*, p. 632.
[200]See Bothe *et al.*, *New Rules*, p. 323.

and fortifications,[201] military depots and establishments, including defence
and military supply ministries.[202]

3   Works producing or developing military supplies and other supplies of military
    value, including metallurgical, engineering and chemical industries supporting
    the war effort.[203]

4   Areas of land of military significance such as hills, defiles and bridgeheads. [204]

5   Railways, ports, airfields, bridges, roads, tunnels and canals used for troop
    movement or military logistic purposes.[205]

6   Oil and other power installations.

7   Communications installations, including broadcasting, television, telephone
    and telegraph facilities, used for military communications.[206]

Objects protected from attack

It follows that attacks on certain types of targets are *prohibited*. These include:

1   cities, towns and villages as such;[207]

2   buildings used by civilians such as houses, schools, museums, places of
    worship, shops, markets, agricultural and other buildings without military
    significance;

3   agriculture, foodstuffs and food storage, distribution and supply; water sources
    and water supply;[208]

4   cultural property;

5   central and local government buildings (except those that are military-
    related);

6   civilian transportation, such as passenger trains, ferries and civil aircraft,[209]
    buses, trams and private cars, not being used for military purposes.

---

[201] *Ibid.*, p. 323.

[202] See ICRC *Commentary*, p. 632.

[203] *Ibid.*

[204] The United Kingdom made a statement on ratification of Protocol I to the effect that an area
of land could be a military objective. A similar statement was made on ratification by Canada,
Germany, Italy, the Netherlands, New Zealand and Spain, see Roberts and Guelff, *Documents*,
pp. 499–512.

[205] See ICRC *Commentary*, p. 632.

[206] *Ibid.* Fleck, *Handbook*, includes as military objectives (at para. 443): 'Economic objectives
which make an effective contribution to military action (transport facilities, industrial plants etc.)'.

[207] That means that the morale of the civilian population may not be used as a justification, see
Doswald-Beck, The value of the 1977 protocols, p. 155.

[208] Food, food-producing areas and water are specifically dealt with in Art. 54 of Protocol I. This
prohibition does not include sustenance solely for members of the armed forces or objects used in
direct support of military action.

[209] Subject to the special rules on naval and air warfare, see, e.g., L. Doswald-Beck (ed.), *San
Remo Manual on International Law applicable to Armed Conflicts at Sea*, Cambridge University
Press, 1995.

7   civilian industrial, commercial and financial institutions not directly supporting the war effort;

8   zones under special protection,[210] specially protected installations, such as
dams, dykes and nuclear electrical-generating stations,[211] and installations and
transports relating to medical services,[212] prisoners of war and civil defence.

Objects in categories 2, 3, 4, 5 and 6 lose their protection if they are used for
military purposes. There are special provisions relating to military activity in
connection with zones and installations under special protection.

---

[210]Hague Regulations 1907, Art. 25; see Wounded Convention, Art. 23; Civilian Convention,
Arts. 14 and 15; Protocol I, Arts. 59 and 60.
[211]Protocol I, Art. 56.
[212]Such as hospitals and ambulances.

4

Precautions in attack

Until Protocol I,[1] there was no specific treaty provision dealing with the duty to take care to restrict the incidental damage caused by attacks. Even after Protocol I, some of the authors of books and articles dealing with methods of warfare ignored the question of precautions altogether.[2] That such a duty existed may be inferred from the principles of customary law and from some of the treaty texts, but its precise scope was unclear. This chapter will be devoted to trying to discern the relevant customary and treaty law and to examining and explaining the rules of Protocol I on the subject.

It seems a well-established principle of customary law that destruction of and damage to enemy property for the purpose of offence or defence is lawful, whether on the battlefield, in preparation for battle, in manoeuvring or reconnoitring, or in the transportation of military supplies, provided it is imperatively demanded by the necessities of war.[3] The reference to military necessity obviously requires an evaluation by the military commander contemplating such damage or destruction of whether it is really necessary and that implies a duty of care not to cause unnecessary damage or destruction. That duty must also imply the need to take precautions to avoid unnecessary damage, but failure to do so probably would not in itself have been a basis for criminal responsibility under customary law, unless, if as a result of such failure, unnecessary damage had been caused.

The Hague Regulations

The Hague Regulations introduced the following prohibitions, which, to some extent, require precautions to be taken.

---

[1] Art. 57.

[2] E.g. I. Detter, *The Law of War*, Cambridge University Press, 1st edn, 1987, 2nd edn, 2000; or L. C. Green, The new law of armed conflict, *Canadian Yearbook of International Law*, vol. XV, 1977.

[3] L. Oppenheim, *International Law*, vol. 2, 7th edn by H. Lauterpacht, Longman, 1952, at pp. 413–14.

1 To destroy or seize enemy property unless imperative military necessity so demands.[4]
2 To attack or bombard, by any means whatever,[5] undefended towns, villages, dwellings or buildings.[6]

They also introduced the following precautionary rules:

1 The requirement for the officer commanding an attacking force to do all in his power to give warnings of an impending bombardment, except in cases of assault.[7] Some commentators of the time considered that the duty to give warnings was the rule where the place threatened contained non-combatants.[8]
2 The requirement to take all necessary steps in sieges and bombardments to spare, as far as possible, buildings dedicated to art, science, or charitable purposes, historic monuments, hospitals, and places where the sick and wounded are being collected, provided they are not being used for military purposes.[9]

Destruction or damage

The first of the above prohibitions was the subject of various war crimes trials after the Second World War[10] but these cases were concerned about whether there was any military need to cause the damage done, not about the duty to take precautions.

Non-combatants

It has been said that, as hostilities are to be directed against the enemy armed forces, 'non-combatants are not to be deliberately or carelessly subjected to attack. This principle underlies the Hague Regulations concerning sieges and bombardments'.[11] The use of the word 'carelessly' indicates a duty to take some care.

Warnings

The warning is to enable non-combatants to leave or for them and their property to be moved to a place of safety;[12] the attacking commander cannot be held

---

[4]Art. 23(g).

[5]These words were added at the Second Hague Conference to cover bombardment by aircraft, T. E. Holland, *The Laws of War on Land*, Clarendon Press, 1908, p. 46; Oppenheim, *International Law*, p. 418; J. Stone, *Legal Controls of International Armed Conflict*, Stevens, 1954, at p. 621.

[6]Art. 25.

[7]Art. 26.

[8]See, e.g. J. R. Baker and H. G. Crocker, *The Laws of Land Warfare*, US Department of State, 1919, p. 205.

[9]Art. 27.

[10]*Lingenfelder* trial, IX WCR 67; *Szabados* trial, IX WCR 59; *Holstein* trial, VIII WCR 29; *High Command* trial XII, WCR 93; *List* trial, VIII WCR 66.

[11]H. Wheaton, *International Law*, 7th English edn by A. B. Keith, Stevens, 1944, at p. 215.

[12]Wheaton, *International Law*, p. 216; Oppenheim, *International Law*, p. 420; Stone, *Legal Controls*, p. 622.

responsible for death, injury or loss if this does not happen. No period of notice between warning and attack is laid down or is apparent in practice,[13] but clearly it has to be sufficient to allow civilians to take shelter. Warning is not required in case of assault, even if the assault is preceded or accompanied by a bombardment.[14] Further, a strict requirement to give warning is not imposed, since an officer is only required to 'do all in his power' to give a warning.[15] Clearly, he is not required to give a warning if he does not have the means to do so and, sometimes, military necessity[16] will preclude the giving of warnings. Stone adds that warnings will rarely be possible in cases of aerial bombardment because of the risk of loss of attacking aircraft and that it was not the practice to do so during the Second World War.[17] Greenspan agrees, saying that military exigencies and the necessity for surprise do not usually allow of prior warning in aerial bombardment.[18]

Assault

'Assault' refers to a surprise attack.[19] One author gives examples of cases where warnings were or were not given and of cases where civilians were not allowed by the attacking commander to leave, principally where it was decided to starve a town into submission rather than carry it by bombardment or assault.[20] According to Lauterpacht, assault, siege or bombardment on the battlefield is not prohibited; the rules only impinge on assaults, bombardments and sieges outside the battlefield.[21] Presumably by battlefield he meant areas that are not populated by civilians. Lauterpacht also expressed the view that undefended places may not be assaulted.[22]

Bombardment

According to the editor of Wheaton, there was 'no rule of law forbidding bombardment merely for destructive ends, and not as a measure to reduce a fortified place' but he criticized the long-range artillery bombardment of a town on the basis that the attackers would not be able to comply with the rule on

---

[13]Wheaton, *International Law*, p. 216.
[14]Oppenheim, *International Law*, p. 419.
[15]*Ibid.*, p. 420. The author refers to 'do all he can', which is slightly different.
[16]*C'est-à-dire quand la nécessité militaire ne le permet pas*, K. Obradovic, La protection de la population civile dans les conflits armés internationaux, in A. Cassese (ed.), *The New Humanitarian Law of Armed Conflict*, Naples, 1979.
[17]Stone, *Legal Controls*, p. 622.
[18]M. Greenspan, *The Modern Law of Land Warfare*, University of California Press, 1959, p. 339.
[19]Holland, *Laws of War*, p. 46.
[20]Wheaton, *International Law*, p. 216.
[21]Oppenheim, *International Law*, pp. 414–18.
[22]*Ibid.*, p. 418.

protected buildings.[23] He goes on to say that if hospitals are deliberately set up in parts of the town that are of vital importance for the assailants to shell, the responsibility for damage to them and injury to the inmates must fall on the defenders. At first sight, all this seems curious, but it must be subject to the qualification that the need to do so is one of imperative military necessity, that undefended places are not to be bombarded and that warnings are to be given except in cases of assault[24] and, of course, there could be no objection to the bombardment of enemy military positions and installations outside populated areas. Lauterpacht states that there is no rule of law that bombardment must be restricted to fortifications and also that bombardment of private and public property is lawful as a means of 'impressing on the authorities the advisability of surrender'.[25] This statement, too, must be subject to the prohibition on attacks on undefended places and the requirement to protect certain installations.

Stone draws a distinction between:

1 The combat zone where, he says, subject to the undefended places rule, liberty to bombard the whole area is quite plain, not restricted to enemy forces or installations, nor restrained by the presence of civilians in villages or towns usable for military purposes.
2 The hinterlands of belligerent controlled territory where the only common ground is that military objectives may be attacked.[26]

Necessary steps

Here a positive duty is placed on an attacking commander to take precautions to prevent damage to certain installations and a duty is also placed on the defenders to indicate those installations with signs. It has even been suggested that the signs must be visible from the point at which the besieging artillery carries out the bombardment.[27] While that might have been the case at the time of the Napoleonic wars, it cannot have been right by the time of the First World War when artillery was capable of engaging targets at a distance of several miles and no sign would have been visible.[28] It might, of course, have been visible to the artillery commander through the medium of reconnaissance aircraft. It would be totally impracticable to require the defenders to erect signs that would be visible at long ranges. It would seem, therefore, in those cases that some onus

---

[23]That is, Art. 27 of the Hague Regulations; see Wheaton, *International Law*, pp. 216–17.
[24]Arts. 25 and 26 of the Hague Regulations.
[25]Oppenheim, *International Law*, p. 421.
[26]Stone, *Legal Controls*, pp. 620–1; see also Greenspan, *Modern Law*, p. 333.
[27]Oppenheim, *International Law*, p. 421.
[28]For the difficulties of identifying the Red Cross emblem at a distance, see G. C. Cauderay, Visibility of the distinctive emblem on medical establishments, units and transports, *International Review of the Red Cross*, No. 277, July–August 1990.

rests on the attacking commander to ascertain by reconnaissance and intelligence reports whether certain installations are protected.

Precautions

Apart from the duty to give warnings and to take care to spare certain installations, there was no more general provision of the Hague Regulations requiring a commander to take precautions in attack. This omission may be contrasted with another treaty negotiated at the same time, the Naval Bombardment Convention. Article 2 lists various military objectives that may be bombarded, provides that in certain circumstances they may be attacked without notice and imposes a duty on the attacking commander to take 'all due measures in order that the town may suffer as little harm as possible'. This is clearly a requirement to aim fire at the military objectives and to reduce incidental damage as much as possible. According to Kalshoven, it is possible to deduce from the older treaties, including the 1899 and 1907 Hague treaties, certain unwritten rules: the duty to identify a target prior to attack, a prohibition on area bombardment and the rule of proportionality.[29]

Air Warfare Rules

Although not legally binding on states, the Air Warfare Rules are a useful guide to contemporary thinking about the state of customary law and have been described as of persuasive authority in the context of land warfare.[30] They emphasize the need for directing attacks against military objectives and give a rather restricted definition of military objectives. It has been suggested that this definition of a military objective completely abandons the 1907 distinction between open towns and defended towns,[31] a distinction which is somewhat artificial in the context of air warfare, where targets hundreds of miles from the opposing ground forces are attacked. The rules prohibit indiscriminate bombing and make a concession to target area bombing by permitting the bombardment of populated areas in the immediate vicinity of land force operations provided the military concentration is sufficiently important to justify the resulting danger to the civilian population.[32] However, there is no specific provision imposing a duty on the attacking commander to take precautions, only what can be inferred from the foregoing.

---

[29]F. Kalshoven and L. Zegveld, *Constraints on the Waging of War*, 3rd edn, ICRC, 2001, at p. 46.

[30]Greenspan, *Modern Law*, p. 334.

[31]C. Rousseau, *Le Droit des conflits armés*, Pedone, 1983, p. 362.

[32]Art. 24(3) and (4), an attempt to reduce the customary rule of proportionality to writing.

Greco-German Mixed Arbitral Tribunal

The tribunal was set up under the Peace Treaty of Versailles of 1919 to deal with claims arising out of the First World War. Two cases dealt with by the tribunal concerned precautions in air attack.

In *Coenca Brothers* v. *Germany*[33] Germany was held liable to pay damages for the destruction of coffee during an air raid made without warning on Salonica in 1916. The tribunal recalled the generally recognized principle of international law that civilian life and property should, so far as possible, be respected, and applied Art. 26 of the Hague Regulations by analogy.[34] According to Schwarzenberger, the tribunal was influenced in its decision by the fact that bombs were dropped from the considerable height of 3,000 m on a dark night when the lights of Salonica were switched off so that it was 'impossible to direct the bombs with the accuracy required to spare the private dwelling houses and the commercial establishments'.[35]

In the case of *Kiriadolou* v. *Germany*[36] the tribunal was concerned with the death of a civilian in an air raid on Bucharest in 1916 and applied by analogy not only Art. 26 of the Hague Regulations but also Art. 6 of the Hague Naval Bombardment Convention.

Schwarzenberger[37] considers that the decisions command respect as lonely attempts to uphold the standard of civilization against wartime sovereignty at its most virulent and destructive.[38]

It does seem that the tribunals, and for that matter Schwarzenberger, seem obsessed with Art. 26 of the Hague Regulations and the need to give warning. That seems to the author to be something of a side issue. More important is the reference in both cases to the failure of the bombers to take precautions to attack military objectives in a discriminate manner.

Second World War practice

The problem with unwritten or unratified rules is that opinions may vary as to their scope[39] and, worse, they tend to be ignored. There was not much evidence

---

[33]*Annual Digest*, 1927–28, Case No. 389.

[34]Requiring 'the authorities' to be warned of impending bombardments.

[35]G. Schwarzenberger, *International Law*, vol. 2, Stevens, 1968, p. 145.

[36]*Annual Digest*, 1929–30, Case No. 301.

[37]Schwarzenberger, *International Law*, p. 146, comments that 'the widespread resort to aerial bombardment without regard for the criteria laid down in Arts. 25 and 26 of the Hague Regulations during the First World War and, even more so, the Second World War has encouraged a critical, if not disparaging, attitude towards these decisions'.

[38]*Ibid.*, p. 149.

[39]Blix, quoting Spetzler, says that there is a pressing need to dispel doubts through codification (H. Blix, Area bombardment: rules and reasons, *British Yearbook of International Law*, 1978, p. 38).

of compliance with these rules or of precautions being taken in attack in the Italy–Ethiopia war of 1935–6, the Spanish civil war or the Sino-Japanese war.[40]

Air warfare

As has been noted above, the prohibition on the bombardment of undefended places also applied to bombardment from the air. As early as 1914 one author stated that it was forbidden to drop bombs on undefended towns or villages.[41] But apart from this, there were no rules in place affecting aerial bombardment on the outbreak of war in 1939. A resolution of the League of Nations Assembly in 1938 called for a prohibition of the intentional bombing of civilian populations, specified that only identifiable military objectives should be aimed at from the air and suggested that care be exercised to avoid the bombing by negligence of the civilian population.[42] Stone comments that this resolution did not seek to prohibit damage incidental to attacks on military objectives and adds that, although it had no binding force, it was close to the views of the British government at the time as evidenced by their reaction to Guernica and the Japanese attacks in China.[43] It was also based on a statement of the British Prime Minister on 21 June 1938.[44] It is also remarkably close to the provisions now to be found in Protocol I.

At the beginning of the Second World War, both sides declared an intention to spare the civilian population, subject to reciprocity. In the early stages of the war there were indications that bombs were only dropped if individual military objectives could be identified,[45] but as time went on practice did not conform to those declarations. A combination of various factors – the changing balance of air power and the capabilities of aircraft, an escalatory spiral of retaliation and reprisal, the use of target area bombing techniques against scattered and camouflaged objectives in populated areas,[46] a gradual extension of the concept of military objectives, the need to protect aircraft from anti-aircraft defences and the lack of sophisticated means of guiding bombs on to the target – led by 1943 to little discernible evidence of precautions being taken to protect civilians from attacks.[47]

[40]See Rousseau, *Droit des conflits armés*, p. 363.

[41]T. Barclay, *The Law and Usage of War*, Constable, 1914, p. 1.

[42]D. Schindler, and J. Toman, *The Laws of Armed Conflicts*, 3rd edn, Martinus Nijhoff, 1988, p. 222.

[43]Stone, *Legal Controls*, p. 625.

[44]Schindler and Toman, *Laws*, p. 221; Rousseau, *Droit des conflits armés*, p. 363.

[45]Stone, *Legal Controls*, pp. 625–6; and the Hague Air Warfare Rules seem to have had some influence on preventing indiscriminate bombardment (Blix, Area bombardment, p. 47).

[46]Greenspan, *Modern Law*, p. 335.

[47]Obradovic, Protection de la population, comments, at p. 140, that 'il y a des cas, comme par exemple le siège de Varsovie en 1939, ou on bombarde une ville sans discrimination, à savoir sans tenir compte des précautions exigées par l'art. 27 du Réglement de la Haye'.

These practices tended to obscure the clear line of customary law and The Hague. Best has described it more graphically: 'The Second World War acted like an earthquake on the international law of war and left some of it in ruins'.[48] Afterwards international lawyers, especially Anglo-American lawyers, struggled to rationalize the practices of the war and invented terms such as 'quasi-combatants'[49] or the 'workforce of the military objective',[50] but these terms did not take account of the many civilians who could not be termed quasi-combatants unless one regarded then as the victims of incidental damage caused by target area bombing of an area containing scattered military objectives.[51]

Monte Cassino

During the allied operations in Italy in 1943 various assurances were given by the allies that they would respect churches and religious institutions, provided they were not used for military purposes,[52] and the Benedictine abbey at Monte Cassino was included in the list of buildings to be protected. The German embassy at the Vatican gave an assurance that the abbey would not be used by German troops. On 29 December 1943, Eisenhower issued an order to all commanders drawing attention to the importance of cultural monuments in Italy, but saying that if there were a choice between buildings and men's lives, the buildings would have to go. However, he added that in many cases, monuments could be spared without any detriment to operational needs.[53]

The German forces included the ridge on which the abbey stood in their defensive plans, but gave instructions that the abbey itself was not to be used. When the allied attack began in January 1944, attempts to outflank Monte Cassino failed and a plan to conduct a wider, outflanking manoeuvre was abandoned because of a lack of mules to carry supplies for the maintenance of the troops involved. Attention then turned to a possible aerial bombardment of the abbey and its surroundings before an infantry attack.[54]

Alexander gave clearance for the bombing of the abbey 'if there is any reasonable probability that the building is being used for military purposes'. Although evidence has since come to light that the German forces were not using the abbey, intelligence reports received by the allies at the time included the reported capture of German soldiers from caves below the abbey foundations,

---

[48]G. Best, World War Two and the law of war, *Review of International Studies*, 1981. More soberly, Rousseau expressed it thus: 'la régression ne pouvait être plus complète' (Rousseau, *Droit des conflits armés*, p. 367).

[49]J. M. Spaight, Non-combatants and air attack (1938) 9 *Air Law Review*, p. 372.

[50]Stone, *Legal Controls*, p. 628.

[51]Oppenheim, *International Law*, p. 527.

[52]This reflected Art. 27 of the Hague Regulations.

[53]J. H. Green, The destruction of the abbey of Monte Cassino, *British Army Review*, December 1988, at p. 30.

[54]*Ibid.*, pp. 34–5.

reports of machine guns, aerials, telescopes and troop movements seen at the abbey (one from an Italian civilian that was probably highly exaggerated), and a report from an enemy prisoner of war that German troops were in 'the abbey on hill 468' (the abbey was actually on hill 516). Other intelligence reports, however, indicated no evidence of German presence or defences at the abbey.[55]

Nevertheless, it was decided to bombard the abbey. The decision was based on the intelligence reports and on supposition: the abbey made such a perfect observation point that surely no army could have refrained from using it. Other factors were that the walls of the abbey would provide shelter to troops outside it, the risk could not be run that the abbey might be used by the enemy for shelter once the infantry assault had been launched, and bombardment of the abbey would boost the morale of the attackers.[56] On 15 February 1944 the abbey was bombed and shelled,[57] leaving it a ruin and causing the death of an estimated 300 to 400 civilian refugees. But no Germans were killed.[58]

There is little doubt that the abbey was a military objective in the sense of being a dominating feature whose use to the enemy it was intended to deny. It is not clear whether the presence of the civilian refugees was known to the allies, but their deaths may not have been disproportionate to the value of the objective. As for precautions, unsuccessful efforts were made to bypass Monte Cassino or capture it by infantry attack and the bombardment itself seems to have been limited to the objective.

Events from 1945 to 1977

Warnings of aerial bombardment were sometimes given by the UN forces during the Korean war of 1950 to 1953.[59]

Fleck, writing in 1966, expressed the view that precautions to be taken in attack were left, in the main, to individual commanders, but that basic principles existed from which rules could be inferred: careful choice of targets, prior warning of the threatened civilian population, particular precautions in the carrying out of the attack and, finally, a duty to preserve proportionality between civilian damage and military success.[60] Fleck proceeds to analyse these duties in turn.

First, while emphasizing the duty to identify the object to be attacked, and excluding exceptions to this duty based on military necessity, on self-defence or on the basis of the overall military character of the area to be hit, does not say

---

[55]*Ibid.*, pp. 35–6.
[56]*Ibid.*, p. 36. See also G. Best, *Law and War*, p. 275.
[57]Green, Monte Cassino, p. 36, provides the statistics: 442 tons of bombs and 226 artillery shells.
[58]*Ibid.*, p. 36.
[59]Greenspan, *Modern Law*, p. 340.
[60]D. Fleck, Die rechtlichen Garantien des Verbots von unmittelbaren Kampfhandlungen gegen Zivilpersonen, *Military Law and Law of War Review*, 1966, p. 91.

of what this duty consists except roundly to condemn the target area bombing method.[61]

Second, although examples could be given of warnings of air attacks,[62] and while the provisions of Art. 26 of the Hague Regulations have no place in air warfare,[63] the attacker is under an obligation to consider whether the circumstances of a particular case permit a warning to be given.[64] Fleck considers that the rule on warnings is only of marginal importance even though it is the one express, rather than implied, rule of customary and treaty law having any application in connection with precautions in attack.

Third, precautions to be taken in attack involve a choice of the methods, means and strength of the attacking forces and a limitation of the measures of attack to the object to be attacked. Fleck suggests that particular care is required in attacking from the air military objectives in residential areas and moving objects and that attack by means of guns rather than bombs is to be preferred in those situations; and that railway lines should be bombed close to the military installations they serve rather than in the vicinity of residential areas.[65]

Fourth, customary law imposes a general duty on a military commander to balance military success against the danger to civilians; the armed forces therefore have a duty to develop standards for applying the proportionality principle when attacking military objectives.[66]

In their report to the Conference of Government Experts in 1971,[67] the ICRC said that the need for precautions in attack 'has been affirmed by publicists for a long time, but without being expressed in a very precise manner in the provisions of international law in force'. The report may be summarized, in almost the same language as that used by Fleck, as follows. No express rules existed prior to Protocol I, apart from the rules on warnings, and the need to take precautions could only be inferred from customary law and treaty language,

---

[61]*Ibid.*, pp. 91–6.

[62]In this connection, perhaps, air superiority places a greater onus on the attacker to give warnings.

[63]Art. 26 requires that the 'officer in command of an attacking force must, before commencing a bombardment, except in cases of assault, do all in his power to warn the authorities'. Instructions in conformity with the regulations were to be issued to the 'armed land forces'. At that time separate air forces probably did not exist but it is not clear to what extent the regulations were intended to cover bombardment from the air. The subsequent draft Air Warfare Rules of 1923 did not deal with the question of warnings. The following passage in Green's review of the first edition of this book in the summer 1997 issue of the *Naval War College Review*, at p. 133, is not, therefore, understood: 'Rogers states that "the provisions of Article 26, regarding warning before attack against places where civilian inhabit have no place in air warfare". He then states that Article 57 "of Protocol I endeavours to repair the harm done to international law by the practices of the Second World War and brings us back to the standards suggested in the Air Warfare Rules" of 1923, which never became part of the law, and in fact were in line with the principles to be found in Article 26'.

[64]Fleck, Die rechtlichen Garantien, pp. 97–8.

[65]*Ibid.*, pp. 98–9.

[66]*Ibid.*, p. 100.

[67]Report to the Conference of Government Experts, III – *Protection of the Civilian Population against the Dangers of Hostilities*, ICRC, 1971, at p. 75.

especially the principles of proportionality, identification of the target (or the rule of distinction), warning and the choice of methods and means. Like Fleck, a majority of the experts consulted by the ICRC felt that the one principle that was enshrined in treaty language, that of warning, had fallen into disuse.[68]

Current law

Precautions in attack

Art. 57 of Protocol I endeavours to repair the damage to international law done by the practices of the Second World War and brings us back to the standards suggested in the Air Warfare Rules. According to Blix, the key elements are identification of the target with some certainty, directing the attack to that target and using methods and means that will hit the target with some degree of likelihood.[69] The protocol lays down for the first time in writing the duties of commanders, military planners and others responsible for military operations to ensure that the risk of loss of life among civilians and damage to civilian property is kept to an absolute minimum. The rules may be paraphrased as follows.

In the conduct of military operations, constant care must be taken to spare the civilian population,[70] civilians[71] and civilian objects.[72] According to the ICRC,[73] the conduct of military operations includes movement at well as attack, so a tank driver who unnecessarily drives his tank through a civilian house, demolishing the house in the process, would be caught by this provision. An attack may not be necessary if the overall military aim can be achieved in another way, for example, by manoeuvre.

When planning or deciding on an *attack*,[74] *feasible precautions* must be taken to ensure that military objectives[75] are what they purport to be,[76] and to avoid and minimize incidental damage or loss to civilians.[77] Obradovic goes too far when he says 'le devoir d'être absolument sûr qu'il s'agit d'un objectif militaire'.[78] The French text of the protocol is the same as the English, i.e. 'faire tout ce qui est pratiquement possible pour verifier que les objectifs à attacquer sont . . . des

---

[68]Fleck, Die rechtlichen Garantien, p. 81.
[69]Blix, Area bombardment, p. 48.
[70]For definition, see Protocol I, Art. 50 para. 2.
[71]For definition, see Protocol I, Art. 50 para. 1.
[72]For definition, see Protocol I, Art. 52, para. 1 and Art. 57, para. 1.
[73]ICRC *Commentary*, para. 2191.
[74]For definition, see Protocol I, Art. 49, para. 1.
[75]For definition, see Protocol I, Art. 52, para. 2. For a full discussion of the concept of military objectives, see Chapter 3. It must be remembered that in cases of doubt, objects are to be presumed civilian: Protocol I, Art. 52, para. 3.
[76]Protocol I, Art. 57, para. 2(a)(i).
[77]Protocol I, Art. 57, para. 2(a)(ii).
[78]Obradovic, Protection de la population, p. 154.

objectifs militaires'. No commander could ever be absolutely sure that an objective to be attacked was a military objective unless he inspected it himself which, of course, is quite impracticable. Mistakes based on faulty intelligence can be made.

Where an attack may be expected to cause incidental loss or damage to civilians or civilian objects which would be excessive in relation to the *concrete and direct* military advantage anticipated, the attack must not be carried out.[79] This is the proportionality rule.

An attack must be cancelled or suspended if it becomes apparent that the proportionality rule will be violated, or that the target is not a military objective or that it is subject to special protection.[80]

Effective advance *warning* of attacks that may affect the civilian population must be given, *unless circumstances do not permit.*[81]

Where there is a choice of targets offering the same military advantage, the attack that is expected to cause the least incidental damage is to be chosen.[82]

Article 57 has been criticized as employing wording that allows 'wide and at times varying interpretations of the inferred standard' and as likely to confuse a commander in determining whether he has done everything feasible in identifying the target, in taking all feasible precautions for the safety of civilians, whether the proportionality rule has been complied with and whether the attack should be broken off, judgements which might be subjective and open to challenge by others, including subordinates.[83]

It seems to the writer that a lot of these points are matters that will need to be dealt with in military manuals or by legal advisers when military operations are being planned. In military manuals the rules can be stated relatively simply, perhaps with explanatory examples.

Usually, compliance with the requirements of the law is assured by issuing troops with rules of engagement which indicate the level of force that may be applied in dealing with given eventualities. They can also include further restraints dictated by political considerations, or even military reasons such as economy of effort, to coordinate an attack or for the safety of friendly forces.[84]

---

[79]Protocol I, Art. 57, para. 2(a)(iii).

[80]Protocol I, Art. 57, para. 2(b), for example, a nuclear power station protected under Protocol I, Art. 56.

[81]Protocol I, Art. 57, para. 2(c).

[82]Protocol I, Art. 57, para. 3. C. J. Greenwood, Customary international law and the first Geneva protocol of 1977 in the Gulf conflict, in P. J. Rowe (ed.), *The Gulf War 1990–91 in International and English Law*, Routledge, 1993, p. 83, considers that this provision may have gone beyond customary law.

[83]D. Craig, Should Australia ratify the 1977 Protocol I addendums to the 1949 Geneva Conventions?, *Defence Force Journal*, May–June 1989.

[84]See the interesting article by G. R. Phillips, Rules of engagement: a primer, in the *Army Lawyer*, July 1993, p. 4.

'Attack' and 'feasible'

The definition of attack is dealt with in Chapter 1.

Obviously, a military commander cannot always establish with certainty that the object to be attacked is a military objective. One version of the original ICRC draft article, which laid down such an absolute standard,[85] was rejected by the CDDH as unreasonable. The feasibility test is a fine balance because the commander will not wish to take precautions to such an extent as to reduce his chances of military success. On the other hand, military considerations cannot be overriding so as to render the protection for civilians useless. According to the ICRC, some delegations at the CDDH expressed the understanding that feasible means 'that which is practicable or practically possible, taking into account all the circumstances at the time of the attack, including those relevant to the success of military operations'. But the ICRC commentator felt that such statements were too broad because they seemed to neglect humanitarian considerations.[86]

There were similar discussions at the conference where the Weapons Convention was negotiated. These ended in consensus that feasible precautions 'are those which are practicable or practically possible taking into account all circumstances ruling at the time, including humanitarian and military considerations'.[87] Various statements on ratification of Protocol I, including that of the United Kingdom, are identical.[88]

Some consider that 'feasible' imposes a higher standard than customary law, which required only reasonable precautions.[89]

Precautions

Precautions include the type of weapons used and their means of delivery,[90] as well as factors such as the time of attack. For example, an attack on a factory at night, when it is known that civilian workers are not there, would be a sensible precaution.[91]

---

[85]Draft Additional Protocols to the Geneva Conventions of August 12, 1949, ICRC, June 1973, Art. 50, para. 1(a).

[86]ICRC *Commentary*, para. 2198.

[87]Protocol II to the Weapons Convention, Art. 3, para. 4 (or Art. 3, para. 10, of the amended version of 1996).

[88]See A. Roberts and R. Guelff, *Documents on the Laws of War*, 3rd edn, Oxford University Press, 2000, p. 510.

[89]E.g. D. L. Infeld, Precision guided missiles demonstrated their pinpoint accuracy in Desert Storm; but is a country obligated to use precision technology to minimize collateral civilian injury and damage? *George Washington Journal of International Law and Economics*, vol. 26, 1992, p. 118.

[90]See the discussion of the 1986 Libyan air strike in W. H. Parks, Air war and the law of war, *32 Air Force Law Review*, 1990, p. 155.

[91]ICRC *Commentary*, para. 2200; United States, *Conduct of the Persian Gulf War*, Department of Defence final report to Congress, April 1992 (DOD Report), p. 100.

Fighting in a town is always difficult, costly in lives and incidental damage. Tanks can be more easily attacked by the defenders.[92] The answer, sometimes, may be to bypass the town, leaving a blocking force to prevent enemy movement, or encircle it, cutting off the enemy's supply routes. Walzer refers to reports during the Korean war of artillery and air strikes being called up to assist advancing troops held up by automatic fire, observing that the strikes often did not work and that in the end the enemy position would have to be outflanked by an infantry patrol, with much less risk to the civilian population.[93] That is an example of an alternative method of warfare which proved not only more effective militarily, at some risk to the patrol, but also less likely to cause incidental damage.

'Concrete and direct'

According to the ICRC, 'concrete and direct' was intended to indicate that the advantage sought must be 'substantial' as opposed to 'hardly perceptible' and 'close' in time as opposed to 'long term'.[94] Neither of these explanations seems to accord with ordinary English usage. It is noteworthy, therefore, that Solf's explanation is that 'concrete' means 'specific' or 'perceptible' (or even 'definite') rather than 'general' and that 'direct' means 'without intervening condition of agency'.[95] This seems a sensible explanation of the term.

Warning

The requirement to give warnings of attacks is an echo of the Hague Regulations.[96] Carnahan comments that the protocol finally eliminates a conflict between Art. 26 of the Hague Regulations, which required a warning in all cases except assault, and the Hague Naval Bombardment Convention, which only provided that a warning should be given when circumstances permit, and imposes a single standard.[97] A similar provision appears in the Mines Protocol to the Weapons Convention, which provides that effective advance warning is to be given 'of any delivery or dropping of remotely delivered mines which may affect the civilian population, unless the circumstances do not permit'.[98] There is also a requirement, in respect of mines other than remotely delivered mines used in

---

[92]As the Russian Army found in its attempts to invade the Chechen capital in January 1995.

[93]M. Walzer, *Just and Unjust Wars*, 2nd edn, Basic Books, 1992, pp. 154–5.

[94]ICRC, *Commentary*, para. 2209.

[95]M. Bothe, K. J. Partsch and W. Solf, *New Rules for the Victims of Armed Conflicts*, Martinus Nijhoff, 1982, p. 365.

[96]Art. 26 of the Hague Regulations.

[97]B. M. Carnahan, Protecting civilians under the draft Geneva protocol, 18 *Air Force Law Review*, 1976, p. 62.

[98]Art. 5, para. 2, or Art. 6, para. 4 of the amended version of 1996. The latter also introduces a general obligation to give effective advance warning of any emplacement of mines that may affect the civilian population, unless circumstances do not permit, see Art. 3, para. 10.

populated areas which are not placed on or in the close vicinity of a military objective under the control of an adverse party, to take measures for the protection of civilians, and these include the issuing of warnings.[99]

It has been suggested that this provision of Protocol I is more restrictive than Art. 26 of the Hague Regulations[100] but it is very difficult, comparing the two texts, to discern any major differences between then, except for the requirement of Protocol I that the warning must be *effective* and that the warning can be given direct to the population rather than to the authorities, although a warning to the authorities would probably also suffice for the purposes of Protocol I, provided it were effective.[101] On the other hand, it has also been suggested that Protocol I is less stringent than Art. 26 of the Hague Regulations, which required warnings except in cases of assault.[102] It is, therefore, difficult to reconcile the two texts,[103] unless Protocol I is seen as an authoritative interpretation of the Hague warning requirements.[104]

Warnings include radio and television broadcasts as well as the dropping of leaflets.[105] 'Effective' in this context is not defined and must be a matter of common sense. Obviously, a broadcast in a language that the population does not understand would not be effective. A warning to the authorities hundreds of miles away and cut off from the place of the proposed attack might also be considered ineffective.

'Unless circumstances do not permit'

The words 'unless circumstances do not permit', rather like 'except in cases of assault' allow the commander a measure of discretion. The latter exception was intended to preserve the element of surprise that might be essential to an attack. The former formula will also cover the need to protect surprise, but the wording seems to be of wider application. Solf[106] compares Protocol I with the Hague

---

[99]Art. 4, para. 2(b).

[100]Obradovic, Protection de la population, p. 154. The Hague text is 'before commencing a bombardment, except in cases of assault, do all in his power to warn the authorities', whereas the protocol text is 'effective advance warning shall be given of attacks which may affect the civilian population, unless circumstances do not permit'.

[101]Carnahan comments that the protocol is a more accurate reflection of state practice than the Hague Regulations (B. M. Carnahan, Additional Protocol I: A military view, *Akron Law Review*, vol. 19, no. 4). Green, *Contemporary Law of Armed Conflict*, p. 156, says that before the atomic bombing of Hiroshima the Japanese authorities were warned that named towns would be heavily bombarded and that civilians should be evacuated, and that warnings were occasionally given in the European theatre.

[102]Carnahan, Protecting civilians, p. 62.

[103]Having regard to Art. 49, para. of Protocol I, which states that the rules of Protocol I are additional to other rules of international law relating to the protection of civilians from hostilities.

[104]Carnahan, Protecting civilians, p. 62.

[105]For a description of the use of leaflets by Israel in the Lebanon in 1982, see Parks, Air war, p. 165.

[106]Bothe *et al.*, *New Rules*, p. 367.

Naval Bombardment Convention,[107] points out that there is a conflict between the Hague Regulations, with the very narrow exception for cases of assault, and the Naval Bombardment Convention, which gives the naval commander a wider discretion, and concludes that Protocol I[108] is an attempt to bring these conflicting provisions together.

But when, apart from the need to preserve surprise, would circumstances not permit a warning to be given? Carnahan gives an example of Japanese soldiers dressed as women engaged in moonlight by US marines in Okinawa in the Second World War. Fire was opened on suspicion and no warning was given because that would have been too dangerous. The suspicion proved to be correct, but Carnahan comments that had the commander followed the rules as laid down in Protocol I, the presumption of civilian status would have prevailed.[109] It might be said in reply that it would not have been feasible in the circumstances to verify the status of the suspected Japanese soldiers nor would the circumstances have permitted a warning to be given. Walzer gives an example, which is the antithesis of the Okinawa case. It relates to the bombing of 'dug-outs', or cellars, during the First World War in a village where it was known that there were civilians in some of the cellars. In one case two soldiers shouted down to make sure there were no civilians and, receiving no reply, were about to pull the pins out of their hand grenades when a young civilian woman came up the cellar stairs. She had been too frightened to answer the warning shouts. Walzer comments that the soldiers had accepted a certain risk in shouting warnings because if there had been enemy soldiers in the cellar they might have scrambled out, firing as they came.[110]

Sieges

Attacks and bombardments are not the only way of trying to achieve the submission of the enemy. Where enemy forces are surrounded, the surrounding forces may decide to force the surrender of the enemy, and reduce the casualties it would sustain in an attack, by besieging the enemy forces, that is, cutting off all supplies and communications to the besieged locality. Siege has long been recognized as a legitimate method of warfare.[111] There are historical examples of humanity being shown. During the South African War of 1899–1902, Roberts refused a request for an armistice to allow the besieged Boers to bury their dead

---

[107] Art. 6 of which provides that 'if the military situation permits, the commander of the attacking naval force, before commencing the bombardment, must do his utmost to warn the authorities'.

[108] Art. 57, para. 2(c).

[109] Carnahan, Additional Protocol I, p. 544.

[110] Walzer, *Just and Unjust Wars*, p. 152.

[111] See Y. Dinstein, Siege warfare and the starvation of civilians, in A. J. M. Delissen and G. J. Tania (eds.), *Humanitarian Law of Armed Conflict, Challenges Ahead*, Martinus Nijhoff, 1991, p. 146.

because he thought it would give time for other Boer forces to come to their rescue. Cronje accused him of unkindness and invited him to bombard away. But when Roberts learned of the presence of women and children in the laager, he offered them safe conduct. Cronje refused, as he refused an offer to send in doctors and medical supplies unless they remained in the laager, but the Boers did not fire on thirsty men filling their water bottles from the river.[112] Siege has recently been practised in the Bosnian war, including the siege of the capital, Sarajevo.

Under customary law a besieging commander was permitted to drive escaping civilians back into the besieged area to increase the pressure on the defending commander to surrender.[113] It is likely, however, that this rule of customary law has been rendered obsolete by Protocol I.[114] In fact, the besieging commander would be better advised to allow all civilians and the wounded and sick to leave the besieged area.[115] He would then legitimately be able to prevent all supplies from reaching the enemy forces and bombardment and assault would be considerable eased. If the civilians elected to stay put, however, as Dinstein has pointed out,[116] that would put the besieging commander in a difficult position, because Protocol I[117] prohibits the starvation of civilians as a method of warfare, whatever the motive. Dinstein concludes that, in short, Protocol I prohibits siege warfare if civilians are affected but feels that such an injunction is untenable in practice, since no other method has been devised for bringing about the capture of defended towns.

The author considers that, on a close analysis of Protocol I, the situation is not for a number of reasons as gloomy for the besieging commander as Dinstein suggests. First, starvation of civilians is not a grave breach of Protocol I.[118] Second, a clear intention would need to be expressed in a treaty to abolish such a well-established practice.[119] Third, the besieging commander would not need to violate Art. 54, para. 2 of Protocol I. There would be no need to 'attack, destroy or render useless' food supplies. He would simply prevent those supplies from getting through to the besieged area by turning them back. Fourth, the provisions of Art. 54, para. 3 of Protocol I do not operate independently of those of Art. 54, para. 2. Fifth, the besieging commander would not violate Art. 54, para. 1 of Protocol I if he guaranteed the safe passage of civilians (and the

---

[112]A. J. Smithers, *The Man who Disobeyed*, Leo Cooper, 1970.

[113]The High Command Trial, 11 *Trials of War Criminals before the Nuremberg Military Tribunals*, Washington, 1950, at pp. 462, 563; *Manual of Military Law*, paras. 292, 296.

[114]Art. 51, paras. 2 and 7 and Art. 54, para. 1. See also, Bothe *et al.*, *New Rules*, p. 338.

[115]The suggestion by Best, *Law and War*, p. 258, to the contrary is not followed.

[116]Dinstein, Siege warfare, pp. 149 ff.

[117]Art. 54, paras 2–3.

[118]Art. 85.

[119]Bothe *et al.*, *New Rules*, p. 336, indicate that the intention was to prevent the destruction of foodstuffs, etc. Neither this commentary nor the ICRC *Commentary* (p. 652) refers to the practice of siege warfare.

wounded and sick) out of the besieged area. Sixth, given the terms of Art. 51, para. 7, last sentence and Art. 58 of Protocol I, the besieged commander could not refuse such an offer. Seventh, the relief actions referred to in Art. 70 of Protocol I can only take place with the agreement of the parties concerned.[120]

It is submitted that the interests of humanity are better served if the besieging commander proceeds as suggested above rather than by attempting to take the besieged town by bombardment and assault. If the commander of the besieged town refuses to allow the evacuation of civilians and the wounded and sick, the blame for their subsequent starvation must rest squarely on his shoulders.

The Gulf war 1991

Allied bombing campaign

It is evident that the allies intended to carry out their bombing strictly in accordance with the law of war and that military commanders gave orders to that effect. The principles of distinction and proportionality were observed at all times by the coalition forces. There were many examples of such restraint. Attacks were to be directed against military objectives, civilian casualties were to be kept to a minimum, religious and cultural sites were to be avoided as were water and sewage systems. Aircraft commanders knew that if they could not hit the designated target, they were to return to base with a full bomb load and frequently did so when they were hindered by bad weather or anti-aircraft fire. A British battle group were given permission to delay an attack on a logistic location until first light because they thought they saw a hospital tent and wanted to avoid unnecessary casualties. Dams were excluded from the target list because it was thought that breaching them would cause excessive civilian casualties. Royal Air Force (RAF) pilots aborted several attacks on targets in populated areas because they were worried about the effects on the civilian population. The RAF twice refused to bomb targets assigned to them because the risk of incidental damage was too high. In attacking a bridge, the line of attack was chosen so as to avoid collateral damage and civilian casualties.

Allied bombing caused incidental losses among the civilian population and damage to civilian homes in Iraq. This can be explained in a number of ways. Sometimes allied bombers missed their targets, were provided with faulty intelligence, attacked what had been a military target that had subsequently been moved or had genuine difficulty preventing collateral damage to buildings in close proximity to the target. Some damage was caused by the failure of guidance systems. Some cruise missiles were deflected from the target by defensive fire. Lessons can be learned from the experience. Human Rights Watch criticized

---

[120]Bothe *et al.*, *New Rules*, p. 434, indicate that there may be refusal for valid and compelling reasons, including imperative considerations of military necessity.

some coalition attacks on bridges, a factory and an oil-storage depot on the basis that the attacks were carried out during daylight hours when civilians were present and that night-time attacks would have caused fewer casualties. These are, clearly, factors that a commander has to consider and, of course, the type of weapons available to him, some of which might be less accurate at night, as well as the urgency of the need to attack the target in question. There was also criticism of the attack on the al-Amariyah bunker on the basis that it was sheltering civilians but if, as the United States authorities claimed, the bunker was being used as a command and control centre in which civilians took shelter, it could be said that it was a military objective and that the civilian deaths were not disproportionate. Some have also complained about the bombing of Basra by B-52 bombers because, although the port of Basra and the Republican Guard units stationed in the town were legitimate military objectives, the type of weapon used was less discriminate and likely to cause greater incidental loss in a populated area. Again, the commander always has to consider the type of target and its location, the likelihood of incidental damage, the type of weapons available and the urgency of situation, among other factors, in making his decisions.[121] Some people ask whether the law of war requires states to acquire precision-guided weapons or, if they have them in their arsenal, to use them exclusively. The answer is no on both counts. So long as weapons are not prohibited, states can use the weapons that are available to them. As for those states that have sophisticated weapons in stock, commanders must always be guided, in their choice of weapons, by the factors outlined above, particularly the need to target military objectives and to observe the rule of proportionality when considering the incidental effects of those attacks. Commanders who act in a responsible and professional way have nothing to be worried about.

This conflict showed some very sophisticated weaponry in use, some of it, like the Patriot missile, for the first time. Although of the main protagonists only Syria was a party to Geneva Protocol I of 1977,[122] early media reports indicated great efforts by the coalition forces to take precautions in attack to ensure that military objectives were hit and that incidental damage was reduced to a minimum. It was reported that of eighty-four American Tomahawk cruise missiles launched on the first day of the war, eighty hit their targets.[123] RAF Tornado aircraft sustained heavy losses attacking Iraqi airfields by dropping JP 233 bombs from a low altitude above the target.[124] According to Infeld, 8.8 per cent of the

---

[121]These criticisms are discussed by F. Smyth, Gulf war, in R. Gutman and D. Rieff (eds.) *Crimes of War*, New York, W. W. Norton & Company, 1999, at p. 162.

[122]Iraq, the United States, France and the United Kingdom were not.

[123]*The Times*, 22 January 1991. By the end of the war, 288 had been fired (DOD Report, p. 222 of the draft version of the report).

[124]P. Hine, Despatch by the joint commander of Operation Granby, second supplement to the *London Gazette*, 28 June 1991, p. G42; United Kingdom, *Preliminary Lessons of Operation Granby*, House of Commons Defence Committee Tenth Report, HMSO, 1991, p. xxi.

bombs or missiles delivered in the war were precision-guided missiles. They had an accuracy of 90 per cent compared with the rate of 25 per cent for conventional free-fall bombs and were used for attacking targets in heavily populated areas.[125] By contrast, Iraqi Scud missiles were notoriously inaccurate,[126] reminiscent of the V1 rockets of the Second World War, and landed, when not shot down, for the most part in residential areas.[127] Of the 81 launched, many landed in civilian areas, causing civilian casualties. Only one hit a military target, a barracks in Dharan, killing twenty-eight American troops.[128] Customary law requires belligerents to distinguish between civilian objects and military objectives and if a weapon is so inaccurate that it can only be aimed at an area the size of a town and not at a specific military objective, its use must be unlawful.

The accuracy of coalition air attacks was apparent from television footage shown at press briefings at the headquarters of the coalition commander, General Schwarzkopf, and from media reports: precision attacks using 'smart' bombs against military installations; the destruction of bridges on the road from Baghdad to Basra or in Baghdad itself;[129] or the precision attack on a fuel storage dump, leaving a neighbouring oil refinery unscathed.[130] Bombing by B52 aircraft, which by the nature of the means of delivery, was likely to have been less accurate, was directed to a large part at Iraqi republican guard positions, obvious military objectives and unlikely to have been in populated areas.[131] Sometimes targets were not attacked because of the danger to civilians. The British air commander, Air Vice-Marshal Wrattan, had the power of veto of particular targets, which he used twice when severe collateral damage could have resulted from a weapons-system malfunction.[132] Aircrew ordered to attack targets in populous areas were directed not to do so if they lacked positive identification of their targets.[133]

Infeld warns us that smart weapons are not a universal panacea. Laser-guided weapons are susceptible to deflection by heavy rain, thick cloud or fog or by smoke and other obscurants used by the defenders or by evading action taken by an attacking pilot. They are also extremely expensive. Smart bombs cost between $50,000 and $100,000 each and a Tomahawk cruise missile costs $1.35 million.[134]

[125]Infeld, Precision guided missiles, pp. 127–8.

[126]According to R. Gutman and D. Kuttab, Indiscriminate attacks, in Gutman and Rieff (eds.), *Crimes of War*, W. W. Norton & Co, 1999, the margin of error was at least 2,000 yards – over a mile!

[127]*The Times*, 23 January 1991.

[128]T. Post and others, the Secret History of the War, *Newsweek*, 18 March 1991, p. 24.

[129]See *The Times*, 31 January 1991 or *The Daily Telegraph*, 7 February 1991.

[130]*The Times*, 5 February 1991 where General Horner, the US air commander, was reported to have said that 'these high tech systems take war to a whole new level of efficiency'.

[131]*The Times*, 4 February 1991.

[132]Defence Committee Report, p. xi.

[133]DOD Report, p. 612.

[134]See Infeld, Precision guided missiles, pp. 126–33.

Despite the efforts of coalition commanders, some incidental injury and damage was caused.[135] On the bare information available from media reports,[136] it cannot be said that these incidents would have been violations of Art. 57 of Protocol I had it applied.

Where orders are given to attack targets from a preselected list, there is a reasonably good prospect, faulty intelligence apart, of only military objectives being hit and of the best weapons system being chosen for that particular target, so that incidental damage will be reduced as much as possible. It is when orders are given for 'search and destroy' missions, which enable pilots to strike at opportunity targets, that central control diminishes and a greater responsibility is placed on the shoulders of individuals. Accepting at face value for the sake of legal analysis a press report of a pilot whose attack on an army lorry and a busload of soldiers also killed a small boy in a civilian car,[137] this could not be said to have violated the proportionality principle. The same report refers to civilians having been killed in missile attacks on bridges. This raises an interesting point about long-range attacks. Even if cruise missiles accurately strike a military objective, the missile firer has no way of knowing whether there are civilians in the danger area, unlike the pilot who is guiding his missile on to the target by means of a television camera.

In fact, the allied bombing campaign can be seen as a good example of the application in practice of the principles of Art. 57 of Protocol I.[138] Even critics admit that 'one claim has survived the tarnished aftermath of the Gulf war intact – namely, that the coalition used modern military technology to comply with the fundamental legal requirement to distinguish between civilians and combatants more effectively than any belligerent in any past war'.[139]

Kosovo 1999

Air-war targeting[140]

The NATO military planners of the air campaign took care to ensure that targets were military objects and that they were continuously assessed to avoid collateral

[135] *Ibid.*

[136] E.g. *The Times*, 4 February 1991.

[137] *The Times*, 8 February 1991.

[138] See Greenwood, Gulf Conflict, p. 83 ff.

[139] C. Jochnick and R. Normand, The legitimation of violence: a critical history of the laws of war, *Harvard International Law Journal*, 1994, p. 387.

[140] For further reading, see the Human Rights Watch report (Internet); ICTY, Final Report to the Prosecutor by the Committee Established to Review the NATO Bombing Campaign, 39 (2000) *International Legal Materials* 1257 (ICTY report); *International Review of the Red Cross*, vol. 82, no. 837, March 2000; Krieger (ed.), *The Kosovo Conflict and International Law* (2001); UK Foreign Affairs Committee 4th Report (HC 28-I), 23 May 2000; US Department of Defence, *Kosovo/Operation Allied Force After-Action Report*, 31 January 2000 (Internet).

damage.[141] In fact, there were no aircrew losses and the proportion of about 500 civilian deaths to around 10,000 strike sorties flown[142] seems to be well within legal parameters, although this will be no comfort to those injured or to the relatives of those killed. Despite the care taken, several cases of incidental damage did occur.[143] In one case, that of the Chinese Embassy in Belgrade, the wrong building was attacked in error. The cluster bombs that fell on Niš on 7 May 1999 were aimed at the airfield but missed their target.

One incident, in particular, remains in the memory. On 14 April, a pilot, apparently looking for opportunity targets, attacked what he thought was the lead vehicle of a column of military vehicles. This occurred near Djakovica and, according to Serb reports, sixty-four civilians were killed, including three Serb policemen who were escorting the convoy. The NATO spokesman expressed regret about the incident the following day at the daily press briefing.[144]

This incident raises questions about why Serb policemen were escorting a convoy of refugees in this area but it also raises questions about the legal requirement on an attacker to identify the target as a military objective before he launches an attack.

NATO was criticized for its policy of carrying out attacks such as this at an altitude of 15,000 feet, where aircraft were out of range of some anti-aircraft weapons but where visual identification of targets was more difficult.

Humanitarian considerations require a pilot to get close to the target to identify it properly; military considerations require the pilot to fly at a safe height to reduce risk from anti-aircraft fire.[145] This is a dilemma that cannot be resolved easily.

The law does not demand that there be no casualties in armed conflict. However, the law, political expediency and public sentiment combine to demand that casualties, whether among members of the armed forces or among the civilian population, should be reduced to the maximum extent that the exigencies of armed conflict will allow. An important element of this endeavour is verification of the target because attacking the wrong target is likely to lead to unnecessary casualties. Target verification requires reasonable care to be exercised. The precise

---

[141]Mr Jamie Shea, the NATO spokesman, at the NATO press briefing on 26 March 1999.

[142]C. Finn, The broader implications of the increasing use of precision weapons, *Air Power Review*, spring 2001, p. 35.

[143]These are set out in some detail in A. P. V. Rogers, What is a legitimate military target?, in R. Burchill, N. White and J. Morris (eds.), *Peace, Security and Law: Essays in Honour of Hilaire McCoubrey*, Cambridge University Press, 2004.

[144]See the summary of the NATO press briefing of 15 April 1999 on the NATO website. According to para. 70 of the ICTY report: 'While this incident is one where it appears the aircrews could have benefited from lower altitude scrutiny of the target at an early stage, the committee is of the opinion that neither the aircrew nor their commanders displayed the degree of recklessness in failing to take precautionary measures which would sustain criminal charges.'

[145]P. S. Meilinger, Winged defence, answering the critics of air power, *Air Power Review*, winter 2002, 41 at p. 59, thinks this accident could have been avoided if the aircraft had flown at lower altitude, but asks at what point does the risk of misidentifying the target override the risk of losing the plane and its crew.

degree of care required depends on the circumstances, especially the time available for making a decision. In the event of doubt about the nature of the target, an attack should not be carried out, with a possible exception where failure to prosecute the attack would put attacking forces in immediate danger.[146] An incident such as that at Djakovica also puts the responsible commander on notice that there is a potential problem with his targeting procedures and requires him to review them. He cannot carry on as before. To do so would probably make him criminally liable if the same thing happened again.

Afghanistan 2001

At the time of writing,[147] it is too early to say much about the Afghanistan conflict of 2001 as there is little reliable information in the public domain; work on the United States after-action report has only just started.

The allied air campaign followed much the same pattern as that in Kosovo, with military equipment and training camps, air defences, communications, power plants and media installations being targeted. There were similar problems of incidental deaths and damage, including civilian casualties,[148] damage to the ICRC compound in Kabul, damage to a 'hospital' or 'senior citizens' residence' at Herat, hit when a bomb aimed at a nearby military vehicle compound missed its target and an incident at Karam when the wrong coordinates were programmed into a guided bomb.[149] These cases may have been exacerbated if, as some reports suggested, the Taliban were shielding tanks and military equipment in civilian areas and mosques. 'Friendly-fire' deaths, including those of Canadian soldiers in May 2002 or those in an Afghan wedding party on 1 July 2002, both cases where the pilot thought himself under attack,[150] are to be expected in this type of conflict but an interesting twist is the allegation that the attacks at Paktia and Karakak were based on false information planted by somebody with a score to settle.[151]

Iraq 2003

At the time of writing, there is little reliable information in the public domain about the conduct of hostilities by and against the coalition forces and the extent to which precautions in attack were taken. For the coalition forces, it was a

---

[146]Taken from A. P. V. Rogers, Zero-casualty warfare, in the March 2000 issue of the *International Review of the Red Cross*, p. 165, where this case was examined more fully.

[147]30 June 2003.

[148]A. H. Cordesman, *The Lessons of Afghanistan*, Washington, CSIS Press, 2002, p. 39.

[149]For the Karam incident, see C. Finn, The employment of air power in Afghanistan and beyond, *Air Power Review*, winter 2002, 1 at p. 4. He confirms the trend towards greater use of precision-guided munitions: 57 per cent in Afghanistan compared to 43 per cent in Kosovo and 7 per cent in the Gulf war of 1991.

[150]Cordesman, *Afghanistan*, p. 109.

[151]*Ibid.*, pp. 33, 53.

further refinement of the targeting skills that had been acquired in the previous air campaigns and, no doubt, the trend towards the greater use of precision weapons continued. There was an avowed intention to avoid damaging the Iraqi infrastructure. There is nothing in the media reports to suggest that proper precautions were not taken. As for ground operations, coalition troops were spared extensive fighting in urban areas that might have cost a lot of casualties, especially among civilians. British forces were careful not to launch a full-scale attack on Basra and, after some fighting outside Basra and some probing of the defences, were able to take the town with relatively small losses to their own troops and to civilians. The old town was captured by paratroopers on foot.[152] Press reports vary as to the number of civilians who died in Baghdad,[153] but it is too early to verify figures or to explain the circumstances. No doubt collateral damage was caused in the bombing[154] and the fighting[155] but at this stage there can be no suggestion that this was in any way disproportionate.

Legal responsibilities in practice

General principles

Despite the fears and stresses of battle,[156] a violation of Art. 57 of Protocol I may amount to a war crime. It will even amount to a grave breach of that Protocol if an attack is launched in the *knowledge* that it will cause excessive incidental damage contrary to Article 57 para. 2(a)(iii). It is, of course, a provision that applies to those who plan and decide upon attacks.

There may be a temptation to judge a commander after an attack is over and with the benefit of hindsight. To guard against these problems, some states have

---

[152]B. Rooney, *The Daily Telegraph, War on Saddam*, London, Robinson, 2003, p. 151.

[153]Writing about the first heavy attacks on targets in Baghdad, Rooney, *War on Saddam*, p. 42, stated that three civilians died. At the end of the war, the figure was put much higher, e.g., A. Gumbel, 1,700 civilians died as US took Baghdad, *The Independent*, 19 May 2003.

[154]Including damage to a Red Crescent maternity hospital, S. Nakhoul, Civilians killed in bombing near hospital, *The Independent*, 3 April 2003.

[155]Robert Fisk reported civilian deaths he claimed were due to cluster bombs in fighting near Hillah, *The Independent*, 2 and 3 April 2003. The author has not been able to verify this from official sources.

[156]Cordesman, *Afghanistan*, p. 111, gives us a flavour of the technicalities of targeting from the cockpit of an attack aircraft in the following passage: 'To execute a time-critical strike successfully, an aircraft must be equipped with the necessary munitions. JDAM [joint direct attack munition] and other satellite-guided munitions, for example, require more targeting time than laser-guided munitions, in part because a pilot must obtain specific GPS [global positioning system] coordinates, check their accuracy, and then input them into a computer before launching a satellite-guided bomb. Making successful use of laser-guided munitions, however, requires that pilots be able to spot and maintain a lock on a target from their aircraft. In many cases, the fighter aircraft on these missions were not equipped with adequate forward-looking infrared sensors, making it difficult for pilots to complete their task. Because the pilot and the wingman aboard the aircraft do not have the opportunity to study maps of a target given to them in mid-flight, the need for quality sensors is especially critical to the success of a time-critical strike. Even with accurate sensors and information from AWACS [airborne warning and control system] and other surveillance aircraft, pilots indicate they worry whether they are in fact striking the right target.'

made statements on ratification of which the Italian statement is typical: 'the Italian Government understands that military commanders and others responsible for planning, deciding upon or executing attacks necessarily have to reach decisions on the basis of their assessment of the information from all sources which is available to them at the relevant time'.[157] As Kalshoven has pointed out, the rule refers to the expected rather than the actual civilian loss and the anticipated rather than the actual military advantage.[158] In other words the test is subjective in the sense that in judging the commander's actions one must look at the situation as he saw it and in the light of the information that was available to him.

Even this understanding throws up other problems. What is meant by the information from all sources available to the commander? In one sense this is a useful qualification because a junior commander may have very little information apart from what he observes, radio reports and the orders he receives. At the other end of the scale, a commander-in-chief may have masses of information available to him, much of which he will not have seen but which will have been digested for him by his staff. He will also have access to information held by others, such as allied forces and national ministries. The problem is exacerbated by modern information technology. Wortley comments that there may be a higher standard for the attacker with the more sophisticated means of information-gathering.[159] How far does the commander-in-chief have to go in collating and assessing the available information before making a decision? Hampson asks the further questions: 'How strenuous must the efforts be to obtain intelligence?' and 'How regularly must it be updated?'[160] In what circumstances is the commander criminally responsible for the mistakes of his staff? What is the liability of his staff officers? There are further problems when, for example, an officer is given authority, within certain parameters, to attack opportunity targets. He may have to call for permission, but is the commander giving permission responsible if the officer does not give a truthful or accurate description of the target?

Kalshoven refers in this connection to the *Queenfish* case, where in 1945 the commander of a United States submarine torpedoed a Japanese ship that had been granted a safe conduct by the United States. Although information about the safe conduct had been received on board the submarine, the commander was unaware of it. But the court-martial found him guilty nevertheless because he was responsible for the inefficient internal procedures, which resulted in his not being informed.[161]

---

[157]Roberts and Guelff, *Documents*, p. 507.

[158]Kalshoven, Reaffirmation, p. 117.

[159]B. A. Wortley, Observations on the revision of the 1949 Geneva 'Red Cross Conventions', *British Yearbook of International and Comparative Law*, 1983, p. 153.

[160]F. J. Hampson, Means and methods of warfare in the conflict in the Gulf, in P. J. Rowe (ed.), *Gulf War*, p. 93.

[161]Kalshoven, Reaffirmation, p. 118, quoting US Naval War College, *International Law Studies*, 1966.

The test must be one of reasonableness and will depend to some extent on the amount of information readily available, the staff at hand to deal with it, whether that information raises questions that require further research of other sources of information. This must be what Kalshoven is referring to when he says that a commander may be responsible if, although information about the potentially indiscriminate nature of a projected attack is not available within his unit, it could have been made available but the commander neglected to take the necessary steps to acquire it – a requirement, he argues, of the obligation to verify that the target is a military objective.[162] Perhaps the most important factor of all is the time available for making the decision.

The question of the information available to a commander will also be relevant to the question of criminal intent for, and defences to, war crimes. An order to attack may seem perfectly reasonable and lawful to the officer with limited information who is ordered to carry out the attack, but not to a higher commander ordering the attack who has information that would indicate that, if the attack were carried out, there will be a serious breach of the proportionality rule. It would be unjust in such circumstances to hold the subordinate officer criminally responsible.

The view has been expressed elsewhere by the writer that any tribunal dealing with the matter would have to look at the situation as the soldier making the decision saw it before assessing his guilt.[163]

The situation could arise where the commander came to one conclusion on the information, but the tribunal trying him, even looking at the information available to him and as he saw it, come to a different conclusion. If the test is reasonableness, as suggested above, it is not entirely subjective. The court look at the situation as the commander saw it but then apply the standards of international law to that perceived situation. Kalshoven has described it thus: 'decisive is whether a normally alert attacker who is reasonably well informed and who, moreover, makes reasonable use of the information could have expected the excessive damage among the civilian population'.[164] One might describe such an attacker as the man in the Chobham tank! In a borderline case the tribunal might give the accused the benefit of the doubt.

Levels of responsibility

Those who plan or decide upon an attack seem to have more responsibilities than those who carry them out. The former must verify the target, minimize the risk of incidental damage and respect the rule of proportionality while the latter only have a responsibility to break off the attack if it turns out not to be a

[162]Kalshoven, Reaffirmation, p. 119.

[163]A. P. V. Rogers, Conduct of combat and risks run by the civilian population, *Military Law and Law of War Review*, 1982, p. 311. See the *Hostages Trial*, VIII WCR at p. 58.

[164]Kalshoven and Zegveld, *Constraints*, p. 109.

military objective or if the rule of proportionality would be breached. The ICRC, in introducing the text in the first place, stated that it was for the party concerned to decide upon the precise level of responsibility depending on the organization of its armed forces.[165]

Taken at face value, Art. 57, para. 2(a) would appear to apply to commanders at all levels. A platoon or company commander may be involved in planning and carrying out an attack on a specific objective within the overall framework of a directive from higher authority. Similarly, he may have to carry out defensive measures involving the use of the firepower available to him if his position is attacked by the enemy, sometimes without the time to consult higher authority. Kalshoven oversimplifies the matter when he states of the commander: 'in the event of a major operation this will be the commanding general with his staff; in the case of a minor action, say, of a few men on a patrol or a small group of guerrilla fighters it will be the leader (or the collective leadership) of the unit'.[166]

As was mentioned in Chapter 1, Switzerland made a reservation on ratification that the provisions of Art. 57, para. 2 of Protocol I create obligations only for commanding officers at the battalion or group level and above. Others have expressed the view less formally that the obligations apply to commanders at brigade level and higher[167] or even, as suggested by Austria, at high command level.[168] Kalshoven appears to provide some support for the Swiss position by saying that the provisions of the protocol 'are so intricate, both in language and in train of thought, that full implementation may probably be expected only at higher levels of command'. He points out that the small unit may be limited in the means of combat at its disposal and its capacity 'to evaluate all relevant aspects of the situation'.[169]

But these formulations may be too rigid. They look at the situation from the point of view of the commander. Suppose, however, a ground attack aircraft pilot is flying over the area of operations and attacking opportunity targets. Obviously, the tasking commander is under a responsibility to lay down certain parameters, but within those parameters, the pilot will have to make a decision to attack, and will be subject to the constraints of Art. 57.[170]

---

[165] W. J. Fenrick, The rule of proportionality and Protocol I in conventional warfare, *Military Law Review*, 1982, p. 107 (quoting Levie).

[166] Kalshoven and Zegveld, *Constraints*, at p. 107.

[167] See Rogers, Conduct of combat, p. 309. Fenrick, Proportionality, p. 108, considers that the proper level will not be below a divisional or equivalent headquarters.

[168] Fenrick, Proportionality, p. 108.

[169] Kalshoven and Zegveld, *Constraints*, p. 109. Solf, in Bothe *et al.*, *New Rules*, p. 366, supported this approach, saying that in a 'coordinated military operation, the relative importance of the military objective under attack in relation to the concrete and direct military advantage anticipated is not a matter that can be determined by individual tank leaders, the commanders of lower echelon combat units or individual attacking bomber aircraft ... they must assume that an appropriate assessment has been made ... Thus, in this situation, the decision to cancel will have to be made at the level at which the decision to initiate the attack was made.'

[170] See ICRC *Commentary*, para. 2220.

What of the responsibility of the officer under a duty to carry out the attack? As Kalshoven indicates, he may not have the weapons available to carry out the attack within the rule of proportionality[171] especially if unexpected factors, not taken into account in the plan of attack, arise. His responsibility must be to break off the attack and report back to higher authority or call up an attack using other means. Those carrying out attacks at long range would probably be unaware of a change of circumstances or new factors on the ground and would, no doubt, rely implicitly on what they had been told by the planners. Since the change or new factors would not 'have become apparent' to them, they would not be caught by Art. 57, para. 2(b) of the Protocol. This provision is more likely to affect those attacking at shorter ranges, who may well have a greater choice of means available to them.

Conclusions

The general requirement to take care obviously applies to everybody involved in military operations from the ministry of defence planning staff, through the commander in the field to the tank commander.

The requirement to take precautions in attack applies to military planners and commanders who give the orders for the execution of those plans.

The duty to suspend or cancel an attack applies not only to those ordering an attack, but also to those carrying them out. Pilots who, during the Gulf war of 1991, returned to base with full bomb racks because they were not able to identify the target[172] acted in accordance with this principle.

As Roberts has said, developments in military technology have made it far more likely that suitable precautions are now taken in attacks because the means have become available.[173]

The operator's responsibilities under Art. 57 may be summarized in military manuals on the following lines. He must:

1 When planning military operations always take into account the effect they will have on the civilian population and civilian objects, including the environment.
2 Do everything feasible to verify that the target is a military objective.

---

[171] Kalshoven and Zegveld, *Constraints*, p. 108.

[172] DOD Report, p. 612.

[173] A. Roberts, The laws of war and the Gulf conflict, *Oxford International Review*, vol. 2, no. 2, 1990–91, at p. 52, writing at the beginning of the Gulf war, said: 'there may be better prospects than in previous wars of the coalition partners focusing their air attack on military targets. The accuracy of their intelligence, the open nature of the terrain, and the huge improvements in the design of delivery systems, all make the restriction of the assault to military targets possible in a way that it was not in the Second World War.'

3   Take all feasible precautions to reduce incidental damage and loss. This will involve a careful choice of weapons as well as care in preparing the plans for carrying out the attack.

4   Observe the rule of proportionality. This requires a calculation of the likely casualties, both military and civilian, and damage compared with the expected military advantage. It is not clear whether there is a legal requirement to assess the risk and effect of weapons malfunctioning or human error[174] but the calculation does not include matters over which the attacker has no control, such as the effect of enemy action.[175] Obviously, factors such as air supremacy or availability of smart weapons will weigh heavily in favour of taking precautions to protect the civilian population.

5   Be ready to cancel or suspend an attack, if necessary. This also involves weighing military against humanitarian considerations.

6   Give warnings, unless the circumstances do not permit.

7   Consider carefully his choice of targets in terms of what offers the best military advantage with the least incidental loss or damage.

8   Ensure that target lists are kept constantly under review in the light of changing circumstances.[176]

The above guidelines are expressed in non-legal language in the check-list below.

Guidelines: offensive operations check-list

1   Is there a military purpose in carrying out the attack? If no, the attack must not be carried out. If yes ...

2   Is the target selected for attack a military objective in the sense that it is of tactical or strategic importance? If no, the attack must not be carried out. If yes ...

3   Is it feasible to give an effective advance warning? If yes, a warning should be given. In either case ...

4   What weapons or tactics are available for use in the attack and what are the advantages and disadvantages of each bearing in mind (a) achieving the military aim; and (b) incidental damage?

5   Is any likely incidental damage proportionate to the expected military gain? If not, the attack must be cancelled or re-planned so as to reduce incidental damage to a proportionate level. If yes ...

6   The attack may be carried out as planned, but ...

7   If in the course of executing the attack the circumstances change, the plan of attack will have to be changed accordingly.

---

[174]These matters were taken into account by allied planners during the Gulf war of 1991, see the evidence of Air Vice-Marshal Wrattan, Defence Committee Report, p. 38, q. 74.
[175]See Hampson, Gulf conflict, pp. 92–3.
[176]*Ibid.*, p. 94.

Explanation of guidelines

1 *Military purpose* This is, perhaps, the most important question for, if no military purpose it to be attained by the attack, it will be unlawful at the outset.

2 *Target selection* In the first place, it is necessary to do what is feasible to check that the target is actually a military objective. Feasible means what is practically possible taking into account the prevailing circumstances, including both military and humanitarian considerations. If there is a choice of targets, it is necessary to consider what offers the best military advantage (which includes taking account of own casualties and expenditure of resources) with the least incidental loss or damage. Where there is a choice of targets offering the same military advantage, the one whose attack would cause the least incidental damage is to be selected.[177] Then it is up to the commander to decide which military objectives should be attacked and in what order.

3 *Warning* The commander is under a responsibility in the case of any attack to consider the feasibility of giving a prior warning. Most rule-of-engagement cards for sentries or members of patrols require warnings to be given before fire is opened unless their lives would be put at risk by so doing. Obviously, attacks against combatant personnel are not normally preceded by a warning since the element of surprise is usually crucial to the successful outcome of an attack. However, if the civilian population is likely to be affected by an attack, the question of warnings must be considered. If the civilian population is friendly, it may be possible to get a warning to those likely to be affected; if they are hostile it may not be feasible to do so since the warning is likely to be passed to the enemy. Where one side has air or tactical supremacy, warning of proposed bombing may be possible without risk to the attacking aircrews.

The warning must be effective. Obviously, a broadcast in a language which the population does not understand would not be effective nor would a warning to authorities out of reach of a place that was cut off, or one whose terms were so vague as to be useless.

Warnings can be given by radio or television broadcasts or by the dropping of leaflets. Where territory is occupied by the enemy, the passing of warnings to the population by word of mouth would probably be safer.

4 *Weapons and tactics* The commander has to consider various factors when deciding what weapon or tactics to use, the object being to neutralize the military target with the least possible incidental damage or loss:

(a) the importance of the target and urgency of the situation;
(b) intelligence about the proposed target, i.e., what is it being, or will be, used for and when;
(c) what weapons are available, their range, accuracy and radius of effect;
(d) conditions affecting accuracy of targeting such as terrain, weather, night or day;

[177]Protocol I, Art. 57, para. 3.

(e)   factors affecting incidental loss or damage such as the proximity of civilians
       or civilian objects in the vicinity of the target or other protected objects or
       zones and whether they are inhabited, or the possible release of hazardous
       substances as a result of the attack;
(f)   the risks to his own troops posed by the various options open to him.

5 *Incidental damage*   The question here is: are any likely incidental effects
of the attack proportionate to the military gain expected? This rule of proportionality requires a calculation of the likely casualties, both military and civilian,
and damage compared with the specific military advantage expected from the
attack.[178] It should, in practice, include an assessment of the risk and effect of
weapons malfunctioning[179] or human error, but not matters over which the attacker
has no control, such as the effect of enemy actions.

Although they are not military objectives, civilians and civilian objects are
subject to the general dangers of war in the sense that attacks on military
personnel and military objectives may cause incidental damage. It may not be
possible to limit the radius of effect entirely to the objective to be attacked,
a weapon may not function properly or be deflected by defensive measures,
or a civilian object may be attacked by mistake because of faulty intelligence.
Similarly, civilians working in military objectives, though not themselves legitimate targets, are at risk if those objectives are attacked. Members of the armed forces
are not liable for such incidental damage, provided it is proportionate to the
military gain expected of the attack.

To understand the workings of the rule of proportionality, it is best to look at
a practical example. Suppose a commander identifies an empty enemy military
truck parked in a residential area of a town. The commander will have to consider the various factors listed above when deciding what weapon to use, then
decide how to neutralize the target with the least incidental damage. In the case
in question, the military target is of relatively low priority whereas the likelihood of incidental damage is high. This would indicate a decision either not
to attack the target at all or to use direct-fire weapons, such as aimed 30 mm
cannon rounds or an anti-tank missile, which combine a relatively high probability of hitting the target with reduced incidental effects, provided they can be
effectively deployed in the circumstances.

To take a variation of the first example, suppose that the enemy truck armed
is equipped with a mortar on the back and drives to a point in a residential area
from which it would be well placed to fire at your position. It would have been

---

[178]The US Air Force has set up procedures to calculate probable collateral damage, has different
modelling tools to get the best kill to minimum damage ratio and allows for an examination of the
proportionality of collateral damage, see Cordesman, *Afghanistan*, p. 113.

[179]The US Air Force has created planning data to predict malfunctions and errors and has
procedures, such as run-in restrictions, target acquisition/lock, rules of engagement, abort criteria
and pre-analysis planning of weapon–target match to mitigate these problems, Cordesman, *Afghanistan*, p. 113.

unlawful for the enemy deliberately to use a residential area as a shield but, subject to the rule of proportionality, permissible if there were a good military reason for locating the mortar there, such as that the position offered the best position for engaging targets. The factors in response to the enemy action are the same except that here the enemy truck is a higher priority target because, first, it is armed and, second, it poses an immediate threat. The option of taking no action, therefore, does not arise.

6 *Changing circumstances* Whether an object is a military objective will often depend on the prevailing circumstances at the time the attack is launched, so plans have to be continuously updated. The classic example of this need was the mistaken attack on the Chinese embassy in Belgrade based on out-of-date information. Plans have to be changed, if necessary, if the circumstances on which they were based change. In a static situation, a commander may draw up target lists, but those lists must be kept up to date in the light of changing circumstances.

Practicalities

Nothing is laid down in the law of war about how the commander should meet his responsibilities in practice.[180] Leaving aside the law of war, command, under normal military structures, implies power to direct the effort of the military organization under command in the most efficient way to achieve a military purpose and an accountability to higher military authority for what is done. By and large, commanders direct operations by issuing appropriate orders and ensuring, in broad terms, that those orders are complied with. That will mean adopting proper procedures, for example, staff procedures, periodic briefings or situation reports, so that they are aware of what is going on. They need to do so to be able to command effectively. Further, if they become aware that their orders are not being carried out properly, they will issue further orders or investigate the matter and deal with offenders.

Orders to subordinates about target selection
Orders may either be specific to the task to be performed or, if they relate to duties of a routine nature, may be standing orders. Orders may be given orally or in writing. Standing orders are usually in writing. Orders for opening fire are often issued in the form of a card to be carried in the pocket. There may be different cards for different types of weapons or duties. These orders are sometimes called rules of engagement (ROE). ROE can take the form of a series of

---

[180]This is left to national practices and procedures. The US forces have issued a comprehensive manual on targeting: Joint Chiefs of Staff, *Joint Doctrine for Targeting*, 17 January 2002 (Joint Publication 3–60). This goes into considerable detail about the responsibilities of commanders and their staffs and associated agencies. It contains, at Annex A, a brief synopsis of legal considerations in targeting.

permissions based on the commander's assessment of the threat or tactical situation. Within the level of permissions granted, the soldier may be expected to use his discretion to deal with the circumstances he faces. Nothing in his orders prevents a soldier, as a matter of law, from using necessary force in self-defence. The more advanced, sophisticated or deadly the weapon or weapons system, the more stringent one would expect the controls in orders or ROE to be and the higher the command level at which one would expect orders to fire to be given and those weapons to be controlled. For example, sniper rifles, medium or heavy machine guns, mortars and artillery pieces and tanks are likely to be controlled at least at company or battalion level.

Evaluating compliance with orders
Once a target has been engaged, nothing specific is laid down by the law of war as to the steps to be taken by the commander to ensure that those under his command have acted lawfully. It is a question of the responsibility of the commander for the actions of troops under his command, that is, to ensure that they act lawfully and to take steps to deal with those who commit offences. At the very least one would expect a commander, as a matter of normal military procedure, to receive regular reports or briefings from his own staff and from his immediate subordinates on the progress of military operations. If, as a result, he becomes aware that those under his command are acting unlawfully, he has the power, and the opportunity, to issue correcting orders and investigate and deal with any offences. He must also keep operational plans under review in the light of changing circumstances because Plan A, which was drawn up to deal with contingency X, will probably be useless if the commander has to meet contingency Y.

Responsibility for the activities of those not directly under command
The responsibilities of commanders are clear where there is a unified command structure but it is less clear when allied or other elements are operating in the same area without being placed under command.[181]

A commander has a responsibility for the actions of soldiers under his command but for the actions of others, it will depend on his command status, for example, whether he commands an area or district[182] and everybody in it, as is

---

[181]During the war in the former Yugoslavia from 1992–95, a group of mercenaries, including Japanese, Russians and even an American, who offered their services to the Bosnian-Serbs and called themselves the 'heroes', indulged in sniping from part of the line around Sarajevo which they held until they were forcibly removed from their positions by Bosnian-Serbs (M. Rose, *Fighting for Peace*, Harvill Press, London, 1998, p. 65).

[182]In the case of *Prosecutor* v. *Blaškić* 122 ILR 1, the accused had been appointed chief of the Central Bosnia Operative Zone, but the tribunal based his responsibility on effective control. It concluded that 'to achieve the political objectives to which he subscribed, General Blaškić used all the military forces on which he could rely, whatever the legal nexus subordinating them to him', see p. 226 of the report. In the case, for example, of the attack on Gaćice, Blaškić claimed that the forces involved were an independent unit acting on its own initiative (p. 174), but the tribunal found that he commanded the troops involved (p. 182).

the case when he is appointed to such a command or a state of martial law exists, or whether the persons concerned have been placed under his command. At the very least, however, he should be making complaints to the appropriate authorities about any unlawful activities. If he does not and tolerates them, it is possible to draw an inference that he was condoning or encouraging their actions. In principle, it makes no difference if the activities take place closer to the front-line save that it may be easier to draw an inference of military command responsibility in forward areas. Further, the commander may be putting the civilian population in the area under his control at greater risk of counter-attack if he does not control all military activity in that area, so carries a heavier burden of responsibility there, unless, of course, civilians have been evacuated from the area in question.

5

Precautions against the effects of attacks

The early law of war treaties and writings seem hardly to have addressed the problem of how to protect the civilian population from the effects of attacks. Prior warning of bombardments was perceived as giving the authorities of the besieged town an opportunity to evacuate non-combatants, especially women and children.[1] Although it was accepted that direct attacks on civilians were prohibited, it was recognized that civilians were at risk from attacks conducted against legitimate targets. But attention was mainly concentrated on regulating the conduct of the attackers. Very little thought was given to the responsibilities of the authorities of the place or country being attacked to ensure the safety of its civilian population.

By 1907 the only positive rule relating to precautions against the effects of attacks was the requirement to mark hospitals and religious edifices with distinctive signs.[2] An early, but nugatory, attempt to improve matters was the Draft Convention for the Protection of the Civilian Populations against the New Engines of War adopted by the International Law Association in 1938. This included quite detailed rules for setting up safety zones under the supervision of an independent controlling authority for the protection of a very limited section of the population: those under fifteen or over sixty, expectant or suckling mothers or persons too infirm to be able to carry out any war work. Such zones were to be immune from attack or bombardment.

Van Dongen,[3] echoing the ICRC, criticizes the draft convention on the grounds that it gives belligerents an excuse not to take any precautions for the protection of the civilian population outside these zones. This is not a very cogent argument given the clear requirement to take precautions outside safety zones in Arts. 2–5 of the draft convention. As is mentioned below, the concept of safety zones is retained in the modern law of war.[4]

---

[1]See, e.g., the Lieber Code, Art. 19.
[2]Hague Regulations, Art. 27.
[3]Y. Van Dongen, *The Protection of Civilian Populations in Time of Armed Conflicts*, Groningen University, 1991.
[4]Civilian Convention, Art. 14.

For the rest it was left to the good sense of the authorities of a place under attack to provide shelter for its citizens and, with the advent of aerial bombardment, air raid warning systems and air raid shelters were usually provided. Rousseau adds the practice of issuing gas masks and the possibility of evacuating part of the population to a neutral country, but underlines that effective plans would require enormous resources, especially in transport, which are more likely to be devoted to the military effort.[5] During the Second World War plans were also drawn up and executed to evacuate civilians, especially children, from towns or from the vicinity of military objectives. Children of foreign nationality can now be evacuated to a neutral country only in the limited circumstances laid down by Protocol I, Art. 78.

Current law

Precautions against the effects of attacks

The parties to a conflict are obliged by Art. 58 of Protocol I to the maximum extent *feasible* to:

1 *Remove civilians and civilian objects* from the vicinity of military objectives.
2 *Avoid* locating military objectives in *densely populated areas*.
3 *Protect civilians and civilian objects* from the dangers of military operations.

This provision, which involves longer-term planning,[6] seems primarily to be addressed to the civil authorities but the military authorities will also have a role to play, especially with regard to 2 and 3 above, or where the military authorities are effectively in control, as when opposing forces are in contact. As for 1, the military authorities might be asked to assist the civil authorities. Roberts warned the United Kingdom authorities that on ratification of Protocol I they would have to review their policy of leaving civil defence on a 'care and maintenance basis'.[7] The extent to which a state can be forced to comply with its obligations to its own citizens, an area in which international law has in the past, with the exception of human rights, been slow to intervene, is a moot point. According to Parks – who reminds readers that some states have made statements on signature or ratification that this provision is not to be regarded as a restriction on measures for the defence of their national territory – this provision is not obligatory.[8] Understandings of what is meant by 'to the maximum extent feasible' will vary. Systematic provision of shelters is expensive, although Switzerland introduced the requirement some years ago for certain new buildings to be equipped with

[5]C. Rousseau, *Le Droit des conflits armés*, Pedone, 1983, p. 82.
[6]L. Doswald-Beck, The value of the 1977 protocols, in M. A. Meyer, *Armed Conflict and the New Law*, British Institute of International and Comparative Law, 1989, p. 142.
[7]A. Roberts, Civil defence and international law, in Meyer, *Armed Conflict*, pp. 187, 193.
[8]W. H. Parks, Air war and the law of war, *32 Air Force Law Review*, 1990, p. 159.

shelters. Some states would argue that, with limited budgets, other priorities are more urgent and that, in any event, Protocol I only applies in armed conflicts and, therefore, that peacetime obligations are only to undertake the necessary planning for war. From the military point of view, however, it is obviously easier to wage war in the knowledge that one's own civilian population is adequately protected and that military resources do not have to be diverted from the conduct of military operations in order to support the civil authorities in protecting the civilian population.

Remove civilians and civilian objects

Although the first priority must be to avoid locating military objectives in populated areas, where that is not possible efforts have to be made to evacuate civilians and civilian objects from the vicinity of obvious military objectives.[9]

The first obligation seems a tall order, especially as regards immovable civilian objects, but even in respect of civilians who, compared with objects, are mobile, it may be difficult to apply in practice, since what may be a military objective today because of the prevailing circumstances may not be tomorrow because of a change of circumstances. Evacuation itself will cause hardship, especially if it is for an extended period, there is a shortage of housing and the weather makes tented accommodation unsuitable, and probably would only be undertaken when there is an immediate threat, for example, if the enemy had complied with its obligation to give warning of an impending attack on a military objective in a populated area,[10] though citizens might, as a general precaution, be advised to send their children away from industrial centres to relatives in areas thought to be remote from danger. Here the second obligation overlaps with the first.[11]

Measures are likely to be undertaken only in time of war but, bearing in mind, as Fleck has pointed out,[12] that they are likely to be carried out under great time pressure and against a background of panic, it is in the interests of the military authorities that civilians should be evacuated in a controlled and orderly way, otherwise the deployment of its armed forces may be adversely affected.[13] During long-range aerial bombardment civilians may stay put if adequate air raid warnings and shelters are available, but even so they may be tempted to move

---

[9]Any evacuation policy must, of course, be applied even-handedly and without discrimination, e.g., on racial or ethnic grounds.

[10]The question of warnings is discussed in Chapter 4.

[11]Evacuation within the borders of a state is governed by the law of that state, D. Fleck, Die rechtlichen Garantien des Verbots von unmittelbaren Kampfhandlungen gegen Zivilpersonen, *Military Law and Law of War Review*, 1966, p. 103. Evacuation into occupied or foreign territory is controlled by Art. 49 of the Civilian Convention and Art. 78 of Protocol I. In occupied territory the special provisions of Art. 49 of the Civilian Convention apply. In the case of children, the special provisions of Art. 78 of Protocol I must also be complied with.

[12]Fleck, Die rechtlichen garantien, p. 103.

[13]See also ICRC *Commentary*, para. 2248.

to relatives or friends in country areas. On the other hand, the approach of enemy ground forces is likely to result in panic and a serious refugee problem.[14] So evacuation plans must be drawn up in peacetime and resources earmarked to execute them. In Germany, for example, a whole range of emergency laws has been passed including those amending the Basic Law, covering business and finance, the supply of food and water, the building of shelters and the movement and location of the civilian population.[15] This obviously involves close co-operation between the civil and military authorities.

Avoid densely populated areas

Solf commented that there was a consensus at the Diplomatic Conference that 'to avoid placing military objectives in populated areas is a goal to be achieved if feasible which must, however, give way to military requirements if necessary'.[16]

There may be little that the authorities can do in any event, especially where the war industry is closely bound to the civilian population. If a bridge across a river is a military objective because it is on a route for the transport of military supplies, nearby civilian buildings[17] cannot be moved although clearly in danger if the bridge is attacked. Use of smart bombs, however, may mean that the other end or the centre of the bridge can be destroyed if that lessens the risk to civilian objects. In planning the location of new military installations, of course, the rule would have to be taken into account and mobile military units would have to take care about where to position themselves. Military units are frequently stationed in barracks in towns in peacetime. Because their location is likely to be known to an enemy, however, they may well deploy out of these locations in wartime if there is a possibility of their being attacked. But when deployed into the countryside, units are often based in villages where soldiers can be billeted in houses and vehicles put under cover in barns and use can be made of local power and water supplies.[18] It is submitted that these tactics have not been affected by Protocol I because it may not be feasible to do otherwise. Commanders will, nevertheless, have to ask themselves before locating troops in a populated area whether it would not be feasible to locate them somewhere else. So much depends on the circumstances at the time: the urgency or otherwise of the moment, the tactical situation, the level and density of the civilian population, the overall deployment or battle plans and many other factors.

---

[14]The conflict in Yugoslavia had by July 1992 led to 2,300,000 people fleeing the fighting: see *International Review of the Red Cross*, July–Aug 1992, p. 389.

[15]Fleck, Die rechtlichen Garantien, p. 103.

[16]Bothe, M., Partsch, K. J., and Solf, W., *New Rules for the Vicitims of Armed Conflicts*, Martinus Nijhoff, 1982, p. 372.

[17]Like the cathedral and museum next to the railway bridge over the Rhine at Cologne. Cologne cathedral is on the World Heritage List.

[18]This is the experience of the writer on exercises in Germany. See also Parks, Air war, p. 160.

The meaning of 'densely populated' is not defined. Interpretation is left to the good sense of the authorities concerned, whether military or civil.

As Fleck has pointed out,[19] this rule of Protocol I is partly a matter of planning in peacetime, since it should be possible when deciding on the location of headquarters, barracks and supply depots as well as armaments factories to ensure that these are located at a suitable distance from centres of population. But even if new headquarters are set up in the middle of nowhere, they will soon attract to the area an assembly of civilian bars and second-hand car salesrooms. Consideration should also be given to moving existing military installations away from populated areas, but it is unlikely, on grounds of cost, that this can be done on a systematic basis, though when the opportunity arises, it should be taken. Roberts[20] underlines the difficulty of moving such potential military objectives as Heathrow airport and the Ministry of Defence in London.[21] As he rightly says, though, more could be done in this matter, for example, a thorough review of potential military objectives to see what can be done about their relocation. To this might be added a legislative requirement for both the Crown and local government to consider the provisions of Art. 58 of Protocol I when concerned with the siting of potential military objectives and when drawing up development plans.

Fleck comments that the removal of potential military objectives from populated areas is to be preferred to attempts to camouflage them.[22] Attempts to camouflage military objectives by trying to make them look like something else can lead to accusations of bad faith and of trying to protect military objectives by locating them close to civilians.

The provisions of Art. 58 pose something of a dilemma, since moving military objectives out of populated areas may make them more readily identifiable by the enemy. Furthermore, if it is not possible to move a fixed installation in a populated area, the defenders will inevitably wish to camouflage it and this will increase the risk to civilians in the vicinity.[23]

Protect civilians

The last obligation covers a wide range of possibilities from the provision of shelters, fire-fighting, provision of equipment to protect civilians from nuclear,

---

[19]Fleck, Die rechtlichen Garantien, at p. 101.

[20]Roberts, Civil Defence, p. 195.

[21]However, the rustication of sections of the Ministry would be consistent with the requirements of Protocol I.

[22]Fleck, Die rechtlichen Garantien, p. 102.

[23]In this connection, the following passage in a newspaper report is salutary: 'In some cases the Iraqis have only themselves to blame for the loss of civilian life. Their policy of relocating staff from government offices to schools and other civilian buildings and of moving military hardware out of their barracks to better camouflaged wooded areas in the countryside near farms and villages frequently exposes non-combatants to attack' (R. Beeston, Civilian casualties take on a key role, *The Times*, 11 February 1991). Of course, if barracks are in towns, the danger to the civilian population is probably greater.

chemical or biological attack, the enforcement of blackout, an evacuation service, coordination of the emergency services and taking other adequate civil defence measures, a civil responsibility, to the broadcasting of warnings such as air raid warnings, a shared responsibility, and the fencing of minefields or the provision of military engineer support, a military responsibility.

Feasible

The word 'feasible' appears again here. It was included on the insistence of representatives of the densely populated countries, who felt that Art. 58 would adversely affect their ability to defend themselves, and of countries worried about the expense of complying with the provision.[24] Its meaning is also discussed in Chapter 4. There does not seem to be any significant difference between 'to the maximum extent feasible' used in Art. 58 and 'everything feasible' or 'all feasible precautions' used elsewhere in the Protocol.[25] Kalshoven comments that the words 'to the maximum extent feasible' merely reflect the fact that the obligations of Art. 58 'may be very difficult, if not impossible, to realize'.[26] Gasser sums up the obligation well by saying that 'the law does not expect the impossible, but it asks the commander or the staff officer to do what he can do'.[27]

The need for close co-operation between military and civil authorities is clearly vital with exchange of all necessary information. In Belgium, in all cases short of a state of siege (martial law), there is an interdepartmental committee responsible for coordinating the civilian and military efforts.[28]

Own territory

In some respects, despite the provisions of Art. 49, para. 2 of Protocol I, which applies the rules on attacks to all attacks in whatever territory, the rules of the Protocol are more relaxed in respect of a state's acts on its own territory. Switzerland anticipated difficulties, for geographical and population structure reasons, in evacuating its civilian population from heavily populated areas and in removing military objectives from residential areas. In addition, its infantry were dependent on the defence potential of populated areas and, although good protection was available to the population through civil defence measures, it was

---

[24]Bothe *et al.*, *New Rules*, pp. 372, 374.

[25]A. P. V. Rogers, Conduct of combat and risks run by the civilian population, *Military Law and Law of War Review*, 1982, p. 313.

[26]F. Kalshoven and L. Zegveld, *Constraints on the Waging of War*, 3rd edn, International Committee of the Red Cross, 2001, p. 110.

[27]H. P. Gasser, Some legal issues concerning ratification of the 1977 Geneva Protocols in Meyer, *Armed Conflict*, p. 88.

[28]A. de Smet, General Report on Civilian Support to the Armed Forces, at the Brussels Congress of the International Society for Military Law and the Law of War, 1991.

thought that Switzerland might be accused of violating Art. 58(a) and (b) of Protocol I. Relying on the words 'to the maximum extent feasible', and on the special circumstances of Swiss defence plans, Switzerland entered a reservation to Art. 58 in the following terms: 'Inasmuch as Article 58 contains the expression "to the maximum extent feasible", paragraphs (a) and (b) will be applied subject to the requirements of the defence of the national territory'.[29]

Failure by defenders; position of attackers

State practice suggests that the attackers are unlikely to be deterred from attacking military objectives sheltering in populated areas.[30]

Protection of the civilian population is not only a matter for the attackers, because the defenders share the responsibility for putting civilians in danger by using them in war production or by placing military objectives in their midst.[31] Art. 58 of Protocol I seems to be based on the assumption that a state will wish to protect its own civilian population and will, therefore, take steps to separate civilian and military activities. The United States Air Force pamphlet reinforces this assumption by saying that a party to the conflict which places its own citizens in danger by failing to separate civilian and military activities necessarily accepts collateral damage caused as a result of attacks on military objectives.[32] But this is an overoptimistic statement. What of the ruthless leader for whom protection of the civilian population is subordinate to his war aims?

At the beginning of the Iraq war of 2003, some were clearly worried about this problem.[33]

As is clear from such terms as 'to the maximum extent feasible', 'endeavour' and 'avoid', the requirements of Art. 58 of Protocol I are not absolute. A defender

---

[29]See Switzerland, *Botschaft über die Zusatzprotokolle zu den Genfer Abkommen*, Swiss Federal Council, 1981, p. 53.

[30]G. Schwarzenberger, The revision of the law of war, *British Yearbook of International Law*, 1952, at p. 367, wrote in connection with the Hague Air Warfare Rules: 'it assumed – incorrectly, as events proved – that governments would accept or act upon a rule which would make it possible for the belligerent to gain immunity for objectives of the highest military value by resorting to the device of placing them in centres of population outside the zone of military operations'.

[31]See M. Walzer, *Just and Unjust Wars*, 2nd edn, Basic Books, 1992, p. 158.

[32]United States, *International Law – The Conduct of Armed Conflict and Air Operations*, Department of the Air Force, Pamphlet 110-31, 1976. The US is not a party to Protocol I, so this statement is presumably based on the US Air Force view of customary law.

[33]A group of United States academic lawyers called for public affirmation of 'the legal obligations of defending military forces, as well as attackers, to take measures to protect civilians and minimize collateral damage during combat operations. These measures include prohibitions against the wilful co-location and commingling of military targets among civilians and civilian objects for the purpose of rendering legitimate military objectives "off-limits" to attacking forces for fear of causing collateral damage. They further include prohibitions against the use of human shields or hostages, whether voluntary or involuntary, and whether by attackers or defenders, in order to protect military objectives' (K. Anderson and others, A public call for international attention to legal obligations of defending forces as well as attacking forces to protect civilians in armed conflict, 19 March 2003, on www.crimesofwar.org).

might be tempted to ignore his obligations under this article to make things more difficult for the attacker. Why, he might ask, should I ease my opponent's task and lose the propaganda victory that I would achieve if my civilian population were attacked?[34] Sometimes a party to a conflict might provoke massive retaliation by the enemy so as to evoke sympathy from the world's media for the resultant losses among that party's civilians.[35]

During the Gulf war of 1991 it was alleged that Iraq pursued a deliberate policy of placing military objectives near protected objects, for example, near mosques, medical facilities and cultural property. Examples included dispersing military helicopters in residential areas, storing military supplies in mosques, schools and hospitals, including a cache of Silkworm missiles in a school in Kuwait City, placing fighter aircraft near the ancient temple of Ur and the discovery by United Nations inspectors of chemical weapon production equipment in a sugar factory in Iraq.[36] It was also alleged that Iraq used hostages, some of them civilians, as a 'human shield' to protect military objectives.[37] There was also some ambiguity in their approach. Using a facility for both military and civilian purposes such as the al-Amariyah bunker bombed by the allies on 13 February 1991 is to court disaster.[38]

According to the United States Department of Defence, Iraq also adopted a deliberate policy of not moving civilians away from military objectives, not evacuating civilians from Baghdad and providing air raid shelters for only a very small percentage of the population. The fact that they were capable of carrying out evacuation plans was demonstrated by the civil defence exercise carried out in the month preceding the allied air campaign, in which over one million civilians were evacuated from Baghdad.[39]

Such tactics might lead to deaths among the civilian population that would be disproportionate to the military gain achieved by the attackers. Are the attackers, therefore, relieved of their responsibilities because of the failure of the defenders to comply with their obligations?[40]

---

[34]Parks, Air war, p. 166, refers to his experience of deliberate attempts by the PLO to use the civilian population of Beirut as a shield against attacks by the Israeli forces.

[35]A graphic example of this in the Vietnam war is given by Parks, *ibid.*, p. 160.

[36]United States, *Conduct of the Persian Gulf War*, Department of Defence final report to Congress, April 1992 (DOD Report), p. 613.

[37]*Ibid.*

[38]*Ibid.*, p. 615 where it is stated that part of the bunker was a C2 centre (a command and control centre) and that, unbeknown to the allied authorities, it was also used as a shelter for civilians.

[39]*Ibid.*, pp. 614–15.

[40]It may be assumed that Anderson and the other American academic lawyers referred to above (n. 33) think that under customary law the answer to the question should be in the affirmative. They wrote: 'death or injury to human shields, whether Iraqi or non-Iraqi, who voluntarily take up positions at the site of legitimate military objectives does not constitute "civilian" collateral damage, because those voluntary human shields have assumed the risk of combat and, to that extent, have compromised their noncombatant immunity'. For further discussion of this problem, see Chapter 1, p. 21.

It may be inferred from Kalshoven that, under Protocol I, this question should be answered in the negative. He points out that the use of civilians to shield military objectives does not release the attacker from the requirement to take precautions in attack[41] and comments that 'the above precautions against the effects of attacks have not been introduced to facilitate military operations'.[42] The author agrees with Kalshoven, and with Schmitt[43] who says that 'the assumption of the risk of incidental injury by a civilian does not release an attacker from the obligation to perform proportionality calculations'. However, there is, inevitably, the question of the significance in those calculations that the military planners attach to likely civilian casualties in different situations. They, and the public, will be very concerned about civilians who happen to be in the vicinity of objects that have been selected for attack, but perhaps less so for civilians who aid the war effort by, for example, working in an armaments factory, and hardly at all for those who have volunteered to act as 'human shields'.

In the end, the matter may have to be determined by a war crimes tribunal. An attack that causes excessive loss of life to civilians may be a grave breach of Protocol I.[44] Failure to take precautions against the effects of attacks is not a grave breach. Nor is a failure by a party to distinguish at all times between civilian objects and military objectives,[45] an obligation that applies to defenders as well as attackers.[46] It seems that a state could almost with impunity carry out a policy of using the civilian population as a shield, [47] especially on foreign territory where its forces were deployed, and yet this would be no defence to an attacker charged with causing excessive loss of civilian life. At most it would amount to mitigation.

There was some evidence of the use of civilian cover in the Kosovo conflict. On 13 May 1999, NATO carried out an attack on a target at Koriša in which civilians were killed and injured. On 16 May, the BBC reported a survivor as saying that refugees who had been hiding in the hills were directed to that place by Serb police.[48] If the allegation is true that civilians were deliberately placed

---

[41]Protocol I, Art. 51, para. 8.

[42]F. Kalshoven, Reaffirmation and development of international humanitarian law, *Netherlands Yearbook of International Law*, 1978, p. 121.

[43]M. N. Schmitt, Book review: Law on the battlefield, US Air Force 8 (1998) *Journal of Legal Studies*, p. 255.

[44]Art. 85, para. 3 (b).

[45]Protocol I, Art. 48.

[46]Bothe *et al.*, *New Rules*, p. 282.

[47]In the opinion of the author, it would nevertheless be a war crime, being a serious violation of the law of war, and irrespective of whether the state had ratified Protocol I, though not carrying the stigma of a grave breach. It is of interest in this context that the United States Military Commission Instruction No. 2, para. 10, makes the use of protected property (including civilian property) as a shield a war crime.

[48]Allegations that people were used as human shields is raised but dismissed in the Amnesty International report of June 2000, entitled *NATO/Federal Republic of Yugoslavia, 'Collateral Damage' or Unlawful Killings?*.

close to a military site with a view to giving it immunity from attack, or in the event of attack, to hold NATO responsible for their deaths, a serious war crime has been committed.

This is an area where Protocol I fails to achieve an objective balance between the rights and duties of attackers and defenders and, perhaps, encourages the defenders to violate the law of war.[49] This is a point made with force by Parks,[50] who thinks that there was deliberate attempt to shift responsibility onto the shoulders of the attacker only; and in the Department of Defence report,[51] where it is stated that this problem is exacerbated by the presumption of civilian status in Art. 52, para. 3 of Protocol I and that media attention is likely to focus on the incidental loss and damage caused by the attacker rather than on the perfidious activities of the defender, a point that public relations staff and psychological warfare experts would do well to remember.[52] The justification by Adler of target area bombing on the basis that the enemy concealed and camouflaged its war industry and made no real attempt to separate military targets[53] might be inapplicable to parties to Protocol I[54] unless it could be argued that the targets were not 'clearly separated and distinct'.

Nevertheless, in the author's opinion, a tribunal considering whether a grave breach had been committed would be able to take into account, when assessing the criminal liability of the attacker in respect of any death or injury to civilians, the extent to which the defenders had flouted their obligations to separate military objectives from civilian objects and to take precautions to protect the civilian population. The tribunal would be entitled to take all the circumstances into account and attach such weight as it considers proper to such matters as the defender's: (a) use of civilians in war support activities; (b) failure to take precautions in defence; (c) deliberate use of civilians or civilian objects as a cover for military operations, including taking advantage of voluntary 'human shields'; or (d) use of hostages or involuntary 'human shields'.

It is submitted that the proportionality approach by tribunals should help to redress the balance which otherwise would be tilted in favour of the unscrupulous.

---

[49]For the opposite view, see M. N. Schmitt, Book review: law on the battlefield, p. 255, at p. 268. He considers that the law is not intended to balance the rights and duties of attackers and defenders and that fairness is not the issue. The author considers that some criticism of the drafters is justified as, in practice, perceived unfairness will not encourage compliance with the law.

[50]Parks, Air war, p. 163.

[51]At p. 616.

[52]Schmitt, Book review, p. 269, makes the point that 'the reality of media impact on warfare would probably convince most commanders to forego an attack which is arguably justified based on the other side's misconduct'. He is right. During the Iraq war of 2003, it was alleged by a British tank commander that he held back from firing at Fedayeen paramilitaries who were trying to out-flank him because they dragged some children with them while crossing the road in front of the tank: M. Bentham, Iraqi paramilitaries 'used children as human shields', *The Independent*, 2 April 2003.

[53]G. J. Adler, Targets in war: legal considerations, *Houston Law Review*, 1970, at p. 36.

[54]Since such attacks would amount to indiscriminate attacks: Art. 51, para. 5(a).

Civil defence

The provisions of Art. 58 of Protocol I overlap to quite an extent with those of the protocol dealing with civil defence.[55] Civil defence falls outside the scope of this work,[56] which is concerned with the law as it affects the military commander, but Art. 61 of Protocol I contains a list of civil defence measures that can be taken for the protection of the civilian population. The list is useful in indicating to the military commander where the responsibilities of the civil authorities towards the civilian population lie, namely in:

1 Warning.
2 Evacuation.
3 Management of shelters.[57]
4 Management of blackout measures.
5 Rescue.
6 Medical and religious services.
7 Fire-fighting.
8 Detection and marking of danger areas.
9 Decontamination.
10 Emergency accommodation and supplies.
11 Emergency assistance in restoring and maintaining order.
12 Emergency repair of public utilities.
13 Emergency disposal of the dead.
14 Assistance in preserving objects essential for survival.

The military authorities may be able to assist the civil authorities of their own, friendly or occupied territory with points 1, 2, 5, 8, 9, 10, 11, 12, 13 and 14 above by providing information, transport, medical personnel and facilities,[58] decontamination equipment, tents and rations, engineering equipment, support to police patrols and the facilities of the military burial service. Such assistance will depend on the tactical situation and availability of resources. The primary duty will, in any event, rest with the civil authorities. The appointment to the commander's staff of a civil liaison officer would be of immense benefit in ensuring that a party's obligations under Protocol I were complied with.

In a fluid battlefield, or where territory is still being fought over, it is unlikely that the military authorities will be able to assist except, possibly, in treating civilian wounded and, of course, there will be no or little contact with the civil authorities.

[55] Arts. 61–7.
[56] For a detailed treatment of this subject, see Roberts, Civil defence, p. 175.
[57] The civil authorities would also be responsible for the provision of shelters.
[58] Although Art. 15, para. 2 of Protocol I envisages help being supplied to the civilian medical services by a party to the conflict, where that help is provided by the military authorities, care must be taken to ensure that the protected status of these civilian services is not compromised; see Art. 13, para. 2 of Protocol I.

Zones

The provisions of Art. 58 of Protocol I cannot be viewed in isolation. There are other provisions designed to protect civilians and others from the effects of attacks. They may conveniently be grouped under the heading of zones. The underlying idea of providing sanctuary for civilians was put into practice to good effect in the Sino-Japanese conflict of 1937–8 when troops, munitions factories and military establishments were removed from Shanghai, Hankow and other cities.[59] There have been many examples since 1945 of zones being set up by agreement between the parties at the instigation of the United Nations or the International Committee of the Red Cross.[60] Recent examples include the safety zone in Port Stanley in the Falkland Islands in 1982, the safe havens for the Kurds in Iraq in 1991[61] and so-called 'safe havens' in Bosnia in 1993.[62] The latter were not successful, mainly because they were not properly demilitarized and they were not put under full UN control. As it was, the fall of Srebrenica was a severe blow to the credibility of the concept of 'safe havens'.[63]

The types of zones may be briefly listed as follows:[64]

1 Hospital zones and localities to protect the wounded and sick of the armed forces and medical personnel.[65]
2 Safety zones for wounded and sick civilians, old people, children, expectant mothers and mothers of small children.[66]
3 Neutralized zones. These are larger in scale than safety zones and possibly encompass whole towns. They are intended to protect the wounded and sick, both combatants and civilians, and also civilians who are taking no part in hostilities.[67]
4 Civilian hospitals are also immune from attack and may display the protective emblem.[68]

---

[59]See J. Stone, *Legal Controls of International Armed Conflict*, Stevens, 1954, p. 631. The Shanghai safety zone served as a refuge for 250,000 Chinese fleeing the fighting.

[60]See, e.g. Rousseau, *Le Droit des conflits armés*, p. 131.

[61]Under UN Security Council Resolution 688 of 5 April 1991.

[62]Other examples, taken from Y. Sandoz, *The establishment of safety zones for persons displaced within their country of origin*, ICRC, 1995, include: shelter for more than 2,000 civilians in three neutralized zones, being hotels in Nicosia, administered by the ICRC in 1974; a neutralized zone set up by the ICRC in the Le Phnom hotel in Phnom Penh during the final battle for that city in 1975 where around 2,000 foreign nationals were allowed to take refuge; several protected zones set up in Nicaragua in 1979 in refugee centres, churches, hospitals and embassies and a major zone near Managua airport, known as the 'Zona Franca', for civilians and for government troops who wished to lay down their arms.

[63]Several thousand Bosnian Muslim men were executed; see the Yugoslav Tribunal case of *Prosecutor* v. *Krstić*, 40 (2001) ILM 1346.

[64]A more detailed analysis can be found in L. C. Green, *The Contemporary Law of Armed Conflict*, Manchester University Press, 2nd edn, 2000, pp. 98–100.

[65]Wounded Convention, Art. 23.

[66]Civilian Convention, Art. 14.

[67]*Ibid.*, Art. 15.

[68]*Ibid.*, Art. 18.

5 Non-defended localities may be created where opposing forces are in contact. All combatants and movable military equipment must be evacuated. The locality may not be attacked, but may be occupied by the adverse party.[69]

6 Demilitarized zones. These are similar to non-defended localities but may not be occupied, so are likely to be set up in rear areas.[70]

Open or undefended towns

According to the Hague Regulations, attacks on or bombardment by any means whatsoever of undefended towns, villages, dwellings or buildings is prohibited.[71] Since these objects are undefended, they can be occupied by ground troops without opposition or casualties, rendering attack or bombardment unnecessary.

Some authors have reflected upon whether the presence of supplies of military value to the enemy or the presence of railway establishments, telegraphs or bridges in a town constituted sufficient excuse for bombarding it.[72] Again, the answer is probably in the negative if the town is open to occupation by troops. Of course, the situation is different in respect of military objectives such as munitions factories in undefended towns behind the enemy frontline, which cannot be occupied without opposition.

As long ago as 1920, Garner came to the conclusion that the distinction between defended and undefended places had no place in air bombardment.[73] Rousseau,[74] seems to be of the same opinion, expressing the view that by the time of the static First World War the concept of the open town had become archaic, that it was inappropriate in the context of aerial warfare and that the modern trend was to provide protection by means of zones of special protection. It may be inferred from the Tokyo district court decision of 1963 that the open-town concept only applies to towns capable of being occupied by enemy forces and does not apply to towns in rear areas.[75] This decision is consistent with military practice[76] and with naval practice, since the Naval Bombardment Convention permits the bombardment of military objectives in undefended towns.[77]

Writers may have fallen into the trap of thinking that the concept of the open town had fallen into disuse because the matter was not addressed in the Air

---

[69]Protocol I, Art. 59.

[70]*Ibid.*, Art. 60.

[71]Hague Regulations, Art. 25.

[72]See J. W. Garner, *International Law and the World War*, vol. I, Longman, 1920, p. 421; J. M. Spaight, *War Rights on Land,* Macmillan, 1911, p. 170.

[73]Garner, *International Law*, p. 469. The US Air Force seem to take the view that refugee camps are also capable of being open towns, see the US, *Commander's Handbook on the Law of Armed Conflict*, Department of the Air Force, Pamphlet 110-34, para. 3-6a.

[74]Rousseau, *Droit des conflits armés*, at p. 128.

[75]The *Shimoda* case, 1965, 32 *International Law Reports* 626, at p. 631.

[76]US, *Air Operations*, pp. 5–12; *Manual of Military Law*, para. 290. See also Doswald-Beck, The value of the 1977 protocols, p. 142.

[77]Art. 2.

Warfare Rules.[78] The reason why it was not addressed was probably that a town could not be occupied by air forces. In the words of Doswald-Beck, the 'notion of "defended" or "undefended" had no sense whatever for bombardments behind enemy lines'.[79] While there is no doubt that the addition in the Hague Regulations of the words 'by whatever means' was intended to include aerial bombardment, their inclusion seems to have left doubt in the minds of commentators whether it is possible to apply the concept of the open town to towns in the rear areas which were accessible to bombing from the air but not accessible to occupation by ground troops.[80] As the principle of the open town was based on the notion that, since such towns were open to unopposed occupation, bombardment was unnecessary, it ought to be evident that an open town cannot exist in rear areas.[81]

However, in a mobile war fought by ground forces the concept could still be usefully applied to allow towns to be occupied to prevent unnecessary damage. As Green has pointed out, however, if enemy troops hold a line in front of a city, it cannot be regarded as an undefended town, since it is not open to occupation.[82] It may be concluded that the provisions of the Hague Regulations about attacks on and bombardments of undefended places have been overtaken by the provisions of Protocol I on attacks, military objectives and precautions in attack. The only relevance now of the undefended-place concept is to allow the occupation of such places by advancing troops without a fight.

It is likely in future practice that, rather than relying on the Hague Regulations, parties to Protocol I will avail themselves of the provisions of that protocol dealing with non-defended localities.

---

[78]See, e.g., I. Detter, *The Law of War*, Cambridge University Press, 2nd edn, 2000, p. 278. It is true, however, that a vestige of the open-town concept appears in the Rules. As Doswald-Beck, The value of the 1977 protocols, p. 143, rightly indicates, they permitted the bombardment of towns only in the 'immediate neighbourhood of the operations of land forces'.

[79]Doswald-Beck, The value of the 1977 protocols, at p. 142.

[80]See, e.g., H. Lauterpacht, The problem of the revision of the law of war, *British Yearbook of International Law*, 1952, p. 366.

[81]See H. Blix, Area bombardment: rules and reasons, *British Yearbook of International Law*, 1978, p. 41. So Green's question about a place defended by anti-aircraft guns is probably academic; see Green, *Contemporary Law*, p. 101.

[82]Green, *Contemporary Law*, p. 100.

6

Cultural property

The protection of cultural property is based on the principle that it forms part of the common property of mankind.[1] Yet every conflict results in the destruction or loss of important cultural property. Sometimes this happens through ignorance or greed; sometimes it is the result of a deliberate policy of attacking the enemy's cultural heritage or that of a minority group. The siege of Dubrovnik during the Yugoslav war of 1991–95 directed attention to the vulnerability of cultural property during war. Dubrovnik was one of the most perfectly preserved walled cities in Europe and a world heritage site.[2] Yet, according to press reports, on 6 December 1991 it was hit by more than 500 rockets, which damaged 45 per cent of the buildings in the old city and destroyed 10 per cent. The fifteenth-century Rector's palace and St Saviour's church were badly damaged.[3] In more recent conflicts there has been no amelioration of the situation.

There are two main problems concerning protection of cultural property in war: damage to cultural monuments, for example by bombing as in the case of Dresden, and the looting of art treasures, as in the case of the Rosetta Stone which passed from Egypt through French to British hands and now rests in the British Museum.[4]

The German military instruction manual,[5] outlining the history of the protection of cultural property, gives numerous historical examples which amount to a sad litany of the destruction and looting of cultural property from antiquity through the Middle Ages, the Crusades and the Thirty Years War to the World Wars of

---

[1]C. Rousseau, *Le Droit des conflits armés*, Pedone, 1983, p. 132.

[2]P. J. Boylan, *Review of the Convention for the Protection of Cultural Property in the Event of Armed Conflict*, UNESCO, 1993, p. 19.

[3]M. Binney, Dubrovnik's scars laid bare, *The Times*, 8 February 1992. In a letter to *The Times* of 6 October 1993, P. Cormack and others drew attention to the destruction of mosques in Banja Luka and monasteries at Žitomislić and Sutjeska in Bosnia as well as important collections of manuscripts and works of art.

[4]H. McCoubrey, *International Humanitarian Law*, Dartmouth, 1990, p. 119.

[5]Germany, *Der Schutz von Kulturgut bei bewaffneten Konflikten*, ZDv 15/9, Ministry of Defence, July 1964, p. 35.

the twentieth century. Perhaps attitudes to the need to protect cultural property are now beginning to change. The plan of the army of the former German Democratic Republic for the invasion of West Berlin (Operation Centre, 1987) included plans to occupy and protect a number of sites of significant cultural heritage: the Egyptian Museum, Schloss Bellvue, Schloss Charlottenburg, the State Library, the National Gallery, the Museum of Antiquity and the Prussian Heritage Foundation.[6]

It was only after the Napoleonic Wars that a different perception started to develop: that cultural property was common property and, therefore, that it should not be transferred from one country to another. This principle was recognized at the Congress of Vienna in 1815.[7] After that commanders started to protect art treasures, as in the case of the French commander, Oudinot, in Rome in 1849.[8]

By the time of the Lieber Code, it was accepted that the protection previously reserved for churches extended to 'classical works of art, libraries and scientific collections' even if they were contained in fortified places being besieged or bombarded,[9] and at the Brussels Conference of 1874 a draft declaration was drawn up which protected 'buildings dedicated to art, science, or charitable purposes' provided they were not being used for military purposes. The drafters, perhaps encouraged by the adoption of the red-cross emblem in the first Geneva Convention of 1864, also envisaged the use of protective emblems communicated to the enemy beforehand.[10] This approach was reflected in the Oxford Manual, prepared by the Institute of International Law in 1880, on the laws and usages of war.[11]

Protected property

The Hague Regulations

The Hague Regulations require 'buildings dedicated to religion, art, science, or charitable purposes and historic monuments'[12] to be spared so far as possible during sieges and bombardments, provided they are not being used for military purposes.[13]

---

[6]A. D. Meek, Operation Centre, *British Army Review*, No. 107/1994.

[7]*Ibid.*, p. 9.

[8]Referred to by J. R. Baker, and H. G. Crocker, *The Laws of Land Warfare*, US Department of State, 1919, p. 211; H. Wheaton, *International Law*, 7th English edn by A. B. Keith, Stevens, 1944, p. 217.

[9]Art. 35.

[10]Art. 17.

[11]Art. 34.

[12]Historic monuments were included at the suggestion of the Greek delegation, see Baker and Crocker, *Laws of Land Warfare*, p. 209.

[13]Art. 27.

There is a duty on the besieged to indicate protected buildings by distinctive and visible signs, notified to the enemy beforehand.[14] Parks[15] points out that the language of the regulations is neutral and, therefore, places obligations for the protection of cultural property on both attackers and defenders. The defenders can, for example, place sandbags around statues or evacuate moveable cultural property such as the contents of libraries and art treasures.[16]

In occupied territory the Hague Regulations provide protection from seizure, destruction or damage for 'institutions dedicated to religion, charity and education, the arts and sciences as well as historic monuments and works of art and science'.[17]

Despite the provisions of the Hague Regulations and the efforts of the French and German cultural protection organizations,[18] there were many instances of the destruction of or damage to protected property during the First World War.[19] At Strasbourg, 400,000 volumes and 2,400 manuscripts in the library were destroyed by artillery fire.[20] At Rheims the cathedral was virtually destroyed by artillery fire. According to the German general headquarters, the cathedral was bombarded by light artillery after an observation post was discovered in one of the towers. This was denied by the French.[21] Similar claims and counter-claims were made in respect of the destruction of the Cloth Hall at Ypres, which dated back to 1304.[22] It has been suggested that allegations of the destruction of cultural property are often denied by the enemy or justified on the basis that it was being used for military purposes.[23] It is more likely, though, that such destruction is caused in the main incidental to attacks on military objectives, caused by mistake when the wrong target is attacked from a distance by artillery fire, or it is done at junior level by someone who is either ignorant or reckless of or indifferent to the protection of cultural property.

The Air Warfare Rules

The Air Warfare Rules[24] contain similar provisions to those of the Hague Regulations in the context of bombardment by aircraft. The basic Hague provision is extended to meet the special circumstances of air warfare by requiring: (1) Protective signs to be visible from the air and at night; (2) The use of a

---

[14]*Ibid.*

[15]W. H. Parks, Air war and the law of war, *32 Air Force Law Review*, 1990, p. 60.

[16]This was done in Leningrad in 1941, *ibid.*

[17]Art. 56. This differs from Art. 27 in protecting institutions rather than buildings and adding 'education' to the list.

[18]Germany, *Der Schutz*, p. 9.

[19]Wheaton, *International Law*, p. 217.

[20]See Baker and Crocker, *Law of Land Warfare*, p. 210.

[21]A full account of this incident is given in J. W. Garner, *International Law and the World War*, vol. 1, Longman, 1920, pp. 441 ff.

[22]*Ibid.*, p. 448.

[23]L. Oppenheim, *International Law*, vol. 2, 7th edn by H. Lauterpacht, Longman, 1952, p. 421.

[24]There were drafted by a Commission of Jurists but never put into treaty form.

protective emblem for buildings (other than military hospitals and the like protected by the red-cross emblem) of a 'large rectangular panel divided diagonally into two pointed triangular portions, one black and the other white'.[25]

The rules also envisage the setting up of published and marked neutralized zones around historic monuments and neutral inspection committees to ensure that these monuments and zones are not used for military purposes.[26]

Roerich Pact

Most states of the American continent are parties to the Roerich Pact of 1935. This confers a neutral status in peace and war on 'historic monuments, museums, scientific, artistic, educational and cultural institutions'.[27] They and their personnel are to be respected and protected. There is a protective flag.[28] States party are required to send to the Pan American Union[29] lists of the property to be protected under the pact.[30] It is not clear whether this is a prerequisite of protection. Property used for military purposes loses its protection.

Draft convention of 1939

A draft convention for the protection of historic buildings and works of art in time of war was prepared in 1939 under the auspices of the League of Nations. Although never implemented, the draft was evidently a forerunner of the Cultural Property Convention of 1954. Apart from the requirement to respect historic buildings and works of art and to punish people looting or damaging them, the draft provides for a protective emblem, special rules on refuges, special provision for notified monuments, an obligation not to use them for military purposes, shelter in another country and international commissions of inspection to ensure that no breaches occur. The draft was enhanced by draft implementing regulations.

Second World War practice

Things did not improve during the Second World War. Commenting that the city of London suffered severe losses in historic churches and other buildings, Boylan points out that since the accuracy of long-range night bombers at the time was plus or minus 5 kilometres, no part of the city was safe from attacks directed

[25]Art. 25.
[26]Art. 26.
[27]This differs from Art. 56 of the Hague Regulations by specifically mentioning museums, though these are probably covered by the Hague Regulations anyway.
[28]A red circle containing a triple sphere on a white background.
[29]The predecessor of the Organization of American States.
[30]Boylan, *Review*, p. 30, states that only Mexico has prepared such a list.

at the docks.[31] Even places like Peckham suffered badly from attacks directed at the docks. The British bombing of Lübeck resulted in reprisal attacks, known as the Baedeker raids, on English cathedral cities.[32] The allied bombing very late in the war of Nuremberg on 2 January 1945 and of Dresden on 13–14 February 1945[33] resulted in the destruction of irreplaceable cultural property.[34]

The bombing of towns like Dresden and Hamburg is very well documented, but they are only examples of the extensive damage of cultural centres in Germany during the war. Another example is that of Brunswick, which had aspirations to be the cultural capital of Lower Saxony. Brunswick had to endure forty bombing raids between August 1940 and March 1945. Of these the most severe were those that started in 1944 and culminated in the raid of 14–15 October 1944 when 90 per cent of the historic town centre was destroyed. This included the cathedral and most of the medieval churches, the ancient castle, the ducal palace, guild houses and no less than 800 timbered houses. A town whose appearance had hardly changed since the fifteenth century was reduced to ruins.[35]

On the other hand, examples can be given of care being taken to protect important cultural property, especially during the campaign in Italy in 1943–44. The allied commander-in-chief, General Eisenhower, sent out an order to all allied commanders requiring them to respect cultural monuments so far as war allowed, saying that he did not want military necessity to cloak slackness or indifference and requiring commanders to determine the location of cultural property through the allied military government.[36] From 1944 the allies had cultural advisers on their staff to assist in identifying property to be protected.[37] On 19 June 1944 all military installations were removed from Florence by order of the German authorities and the military transport was banned from the historic centre.[38]

The international military tribunal at Nuremberg dealt with the systematic plunder of works of art in occupied territory.[39] The only war crimes trial relating to cultural property seems to have been the case of *Lingenfelder*,[40] who was convicted by a French tribunal of the wanton destruction of public monuments.

[31]Boylan, *Review*, p. 35.

[32]*Ibid.*

[33]According to P. W. Gray, Dresden 1945 – just another raid, *Air Power Review*, spring 2001, p. 1, Dresden became a target because it contained an optical factory, a glass works, two plants producing radar components, an arsenal, a poison gas factory and marshalling yards. It was an important communications centre and troop concentration area. For Bomber Command, the aiming point was the centre of the old town, most of which was gutted as a result of the raid.

[34]Germany, *Der Schutz*, p. 10.

[35]R. Moderhack, *Braunschweig – das Bild der Stadt in 900 Jahren*, vol. 1, Städtisches Museum Braunschweig, 1985, pp. 101–3.

[36]See Parks, Air war, p. 61. For a discussion of the attack on Monte Cassino, see Chapter 4.

[37]Boylan, *Review*, p. 37.

[38]Germany, *Der Schutz*, para. 906.

[39]Trial of the Major War Criminals before the International Military Tribunal, Nuremberg, 1948, vol. XXII, p. 481 onwards.

[40]IX *War Crimes Reports* (WCR) 67. The *IG Farben* case (X WCR 1) was concerned with the plunder of public and private property.

Cultural property

Cultural Property Convention[41]

In the light of experience in the Second World War, attempts were made to improve the protection of cultural objects, hence the Hague Convention of 1954 for the Protection of Cultural Property in the Event of Armed Conflict (Cultural Property Convention). This places an equal obligation on defenders and attackers by requiring states party to refrain from uses of cultural property that would expose it to danger in armed conflict and to refrain from acts of hostility against cultural property.[42] The convention is supplemented by two protocols. The first, of 1954, deals with the prevention of the export of cultural property from occupied territory, its safeguarding and return. The second, of 1999, is more comprehensive and endeavours to improve the implementation of the convention.[43]

The United States, the United Kingdom and most English-speaking countries are not parties to the Cultural Property Convention.[44] Most continental European countries are parties to the convention and within the NATO framework British forces may be fighting on the territory of a contracting party and should understand the principles of the convention.[45]

Although the obligation to protect cultural property is a requirement of customary law, it is not true to say that the Cultural Property Convention is part of customary law.[46] It may well be that the requirement to respect cultural property (along with all civilian property) is a principle of customary law, but by no stretch of the imagination can all the detailed provisions of the Cultural Property Convention be regarded as customary law.

Scope of application

The Cultural Property Convention (CPC) contains an article, equivalent to common Art. 2 to the Geneva Conventions, which applies the convention to wars and armed conflicts between the high contracting parties and to the occupation of the territory of one party by the forces of another.[47] The provisions of the CPC that

---

[41]An important work on the Convention is J. Toman, *La protection des biens culturels en cas de conflit armé*, UNESCO, 1994.

[42]Art. 4, para. 1.

[43]At the time of writing, 30 June 2003, the protocol is not in force, as the twenty requisite ratifications have not been deposited.

[44]Although the United States is not a party because of objections by the Joint Chiefs of Staff, the US Army has included the convention in its doctrine and the details of the convention are taught in law of war courses (Parks, Air war, p. 59).

[45]The United Kingdom *Manual of Military Law*, HMSO, 1958, contains no narrative chapters dealing specifically with cultural property but does contain the text of the Cultural Property Convention (CPC).

[46]Boylan, *Review*, pp. 7, 104, misquotes the DOD Report, US, *Conduct of the Persian Gulf War*, Department of Defense final report to Congress, April 1992.

[47]Art. 18.

deal with the protection of cultural property must also be respected in civil war.[48] Parties are required to take measures in peacetime to protect cultural property against risks foreseeable in the event of an armed conflict.[49] That would include identifying property and preparing inventories, earmarking shelters, planning for the eventuality of fire or structural damage, allocating transport and personnel,[50] giving appropriate instructions in military regulations[51] designating an authority for safeguarding cultural property, and establishing a policy of non-defended localities or demilitarized zones for the protection of cultural property. Even after the end of hostilities, the parties to the First Cultural Property Protocol have a residual obligation to return cultural property removed from occupied territory.

Definition

Cultural property is defined as 'movable or immovable property of great importance to the cultural heritage of every people', and includes: 'monuments of architecture, art or history, whether religious or secular; archaeological sites; groups of buildings which, as a whole, are of historical or artistic interest; works of art; manuscripts, books and other objects of artistic, historical or archaeological interest; as well as scientific collections and important collections of books or archives or of reproductions of the property defined above'. The term also covers buildings in which such objects are collected and refuges intended to shelter such property during armed conflict.[52] It also extends to cultural centres,[53] being those containing a large amount of cultural property or the buildings housing it, and transports.

It is immediately apparent that the definition in the CPC is both wider and narrower in scope than that of the Hague Regulations. While the categories of property are wider, they do not include charitable and educational institutions (unless of historic, etc., importance). Furthermore, the property must be of significance going beyond national boundaries. It must be property of great importance to the cultural heritage of every people. This may involve delicate decisions about whether, for example, an original manuscript by a minor composer, say, Spohr, was of great importance to the cultural heritage of every people, perhaps not. The situation would be different if it were an original manuscript by one of the great composers, say, Schubert.

---

[48]Art. 19. The provisions in questions are those set out in Art. 4.

[49]Art. 3.

[50]Germany, *Der Schutz*, p. 31.

[51]Art. 7, para. 1; Second Cultural Property Protocol 1999 (2HP), Art. 5.

[52]Art. 1.

[53]According to Rousseau, *Le Droit des conflits armés*, p. 133, this would include the historic parts of certain towns such as Florence, Venice, Ghent, Cambridge and Carcassonne. As the United Kingdom is not a party to the CPC, Cambridge can be included only as an indication of the sort of cultural centres that are covered by the convention. Curiously, the historic centres of Cambridge and Oxford are not on the World Heritage List.

Basic protection

The scope of basic protection is to be found in Art. 4, where the parties agree to refrain from:

1 Using cultural property, its immediate surroundings and appliances for its protection for purposes that are likely to expose it to damage in the event of armed conflict.
2 Acts of hostility directed against cultural property.
3 Reprisals against cultural property, even if the enemy has unlawfully attacked cultural property.

Furthermore:

4 The parties are obliged to prevent theft, pillage, misappropriation and acts of vandalism against cultural property[54] and undertake to respect cultural property in their own territory and in the territory of another party, especially in occupied territory.[55]

The prohibition on reprisals is, presumably, based on the notion that cultural property is the common heritage of mankind and must be preserved at all costs. It is a prohibition that cannot be waived on grounds of military necessity. Military necessity can never justify recourse to reprisals, since reprisals are not actions taken in the conduct of military operations, they are actions taken to redress violations of the law of war. In any event, Art. 4, para. 2, of the CPC, which allows waiver of protection of cultural property, only refers to the general protection of that property under Art. 4, para. 1, not to the protection from reprisals in Art. 4, para. 4.[56]

Cultural property normally displays the single, blue and white shield protective emblem.[57] According to Carcione[58] protective emblems are not displayed on Italian cultural monuments, unlike those in Belgium.[59]

Special protection

The parties to the CPC agree in respect of specially protected property to refrain from: (1) Any act of hostility directed against such property; and (2) Any use of such property or its surroundings for military purposes.[60]

---

[54]Germany, *Der Schutz*, p. 17 refers to the vandalism involved in the breaking of the vases in a valuable collection at Schloß Stolpe by Soviet troops in May 1945.

[55]For occupied territory, see Art. 5.

[56]See also F. J. Hampson, Belligerent reprisals and the 1977 Protocols, (1988) 37 *International and Comparative Law Quarterly* at p. 826.

[57]Art. 17, para. 2.

[58]M. M. Carcione, Protection des biens culturels en cas de conflit armé, International Institute of Humanitarian Law, September 1991 (sixteenth Round Table).

[59]Or, as the author has seen, in Austria and Germany.

[60]Art. 9.

Contrasting ordinary and special protection reveals certain anomalies in the drafting of the convention. In the case of specially protected property there is no mention of appliances for the protection of cultural property, of reprisals or of protection from theft and so on. It can only be assumed that the larger category includes the smaller and that the provisions of Art. 4 apply to all cultural property.[61] If that construction is correct, there seems little point in having a separate article dealing with the immunity of specially protected property.

Specially protected property falls into one of three categories:

1   Refuges for sheltering cultural property such as the Oberrieder Stollen in the Breisgau district of the Black Forest.[62]
2   Centres containing monuments. The Vatican City has been so registered, but it is the only one.[63]
3   Immovable cultural property of very great importance. No property in this category has been registered.[64]

Transport of cultural property may, in certain circumstances, also be entitled to special protection.[65]

Specially protected property bears a triple, blue and white shield protective emblem and is registered in an international register of cultural property under special protection. It has to be at an adequate distance from potential military objectives,[66] unless it is in a bombproof shelter, and must not be used for military purposes.[67] A cultural centre is deemed to be used for military purposes if it is used for the movement, even transit, of military personnel or supplies, activities directly concerned with military operations, stationing of military personnel or the production of war material. The guarding of cultural property by specially appointed 'armed custodians' or by ordinary police officers does not amount to military use.[68] The position of the armed custodian who kills a member of an occupying force who is smashing priceless vases is rather awkward. It is submitted

---

[61]That is the position taken in Germany, *Der Schutz,* p. 20.

[62]Germany, *Der Schutz,* para. 912. The Netherlands and Austria have registered such shelters (Boylan, *Review,* p. 77).

[63]Carcione, Protection de biens culturels. An application by Cambodia to register Angkor Wat was suspended because of objections from countries that did not recognize the regime in Cambodia (Boylan, *Review,* pp. 79–80). The UNESCO website, visited on 1 July 2003, contains a document entitled 'International Register of Cultural Property under Special Protection', dated August 1997, which states: 'To date, cultural sites in 4 States (Austria, Germany, the Holy See and the Netherlands) have been entered in the Register at the request of those States (a total number of five refuges as well as the whole of the Vatican City State).

[64]Boylan, *Review,* p. 79. He complains, at p. 17, that this category does not include the world's great museums. They would be protected by the Hague Regulations and Protocol I in any event.

[65]CPC, Arts. 12 and 13.

[66]For example, large industrial centres, aerodromes, broadcasting stations, defence establishments, ports, important railway stations or main lines of communications (see Art. 8, para. 1(a)).

[67]Art. 8.

[68]Art. 8, para. 4.

that at a trial by the occupying power for murder, the tribunal would have to consider the circumstances, the heat of the moment and whether the custodian could reasonably have resorted to other methods to protect the property in his care. Unlike medical installations, which can be guarded by military personnel, it does seem that cultural property may not be guarded by military personnel, even if assigned to civil defence duties, since, according to Protocol I, Art. 61, guarding of cultural property is not a civil defence task.[69] Even when cultural property is close to a military objective, special protection can still be afforded if an undertaking is given not to use that objective.[70]

Boylan points out that some states are reluctant to register shelters as they regard this information as secret. He quotes the case of Vukovar where a shelter for cultural property was identified from official records and the contents removed to Belgrade.[71]

Enhanced protection

The Second Cultural Property Protocol introduces a new category of property placed under enhanced protection, provided:

a. it is cultural heritage of the greatest importance for humanity;
b. it is protected by adequate domestic legal and administrative measures recognizing its exceptional cultural and historic value and ensuring the highest level of protection;
c. it is not used for military purposes or to shield military sites and a declaration has been made by the party which has control over the cultural property, confirming it will not be so used.[72]

The protocol establishes an International Committee for the Protection of Cultural Property in the Event of Armed Conflict,[73] with the responsibility for maintaining a list of property under enhanced protection and to supervise the implementation of the protocol.[74] Applications by states for property to be included in the list are to be made to the committee. This can also be done by states at the committee's suggestion. The parties to the protocol have the right to make representations but the committee has the final decision.

The protocol also makes the following offences: attacking, extensive destruction or appropriation of, theft, pillage or misappropriation of, and acts of vandalism against, cultural property protected under the convention. For some reason it

---

[69]Art. 8, para. 3.
[70]Art. 8, para. 5. In the case of ports, railway stations and aerodromes, traffic is to be diverted elsewhere.
[71]Boylan, *Review*, p. 79.
[72]2HP, Art. 10.
[73]2HP, Art. 24.
[74]2HP, Art. 27.

makes only the use of cultural property, or its immediate surroundings, in support of military action an offence if it is property under enhanced protection.[75]

If property has both special and enhanced protection, only the provisions of enhanced protection apply.[76]

Waiver of protection

The protection of cultural property can be waived in the limited circumstances set out below. The rules on waiver apply to defenders or attackers and cover both attacks on cultural property and the use of cultural property for military purposes. The level at which the decision to waive protection may be taken depends on whether the cultural property is entitled to basic, special or enhanced protection.

Basic protection can be waived 'only in cases where military necessity imperatively requires' it by an officer commanding a force the equivalent of a battalion in size or larger, or a force smaller in size where the circumstances do not permit otherwise.[77] The meaning of 'officer commanding' in this context must be the person who gives the order for the attack upon or use of the cultural property in question.

In the ordinary course, fire should not be directed at protected property in any event. There is, however, no provision of the convention dealing with incidental damage. This must mean that while precautions must be taken to prevent incidental damage in the usual way, incidental damage to protected property is not a breach of the convention, subject to the rule of proportionality.[78] If, for example, enemy snipers are operating from protected property, it may be possible simply to bypass that property.[79] Imperative military necessity permitting waiver implies that there is no other way the military aim can feasibly be achieved than by attacking or using the protected property.[80] Attacks are only permissible if, and for so long as, the property is a military objective.[81] The German manual[82] gives two examples of imperative military necessity permitting the destruction or

---

[75]2HP, Art. 15.

[76]2HP, Art. 4(b).

[77]Art. 4, para. 2; 2HP, Art. 6.

[78]This interpretation is confirmed by 2HP, Art. 7. A commander waiving protection would still be bound by the provisions of Protocol I, e.g., Art. 51, para. 5(b).

[79]L. C. Green, in his review of the first edition of this book in the summer 1997 issue of the *Naval War College Review*, at p. 133, considers this unrealistic. He says that is more likely 'that a commander whose troops are under attack by such a sniper will conclude that the property in question is no longer protected and is a legitimate military objective'. A lot depends on the circumstances, but if bypassing the property is not a realistic option, the commander would still have to think carefully about the weapons and tactics to be used in dealing with the sniper, bearing in mind that extensive collateral damage may be caused to irreplaceable cultural property that is the heritage of all people.

[80]See 2HP, Art. 6.

[81]2HP, Arts. 6 and 13.

[82]Germany, *Der Schutz*, p. 16.

military use of cultural property: a cultural bridge which is the only means of access across a river for enemy forces; and an artillery position close to cultural property if that is the only position from which an enemy stronghold dominating the battlefield can be attacked. In cases of attacks on cultural property, an effective warning is to be given whenever circumstances permit.[83]

Special protection can be waived in 'exceptional cases of unavoidable military necessity' by an officer commanding a force the equivalent in size of a division, or larger.[84] Whenever circumstances permit, the enemy is to be informed a reasonable time in advance of the decision to withdraw immunity.[85] While this provision applies to both attackers and defenders, it is difficult to imagine cases where attacking commanders would admit that circumstances permit warnings to be given, at least not where the element of surprise is an important factor in the success of the attack. In one case, though, prior notification has to be given, and that is where immunity is to be withdrawn because of the violation of the protection of cultural property by the enemy.[86] This is most likely to occur where the enemy uses specially protected property for military purposes. Although at first sight a decision to waive the immunity of very important cultural property can be made at a relatively low level of command, in practice it is likely that approval at government level will be needed because of the requirement to report in writing to the commissioner-general for cultural property why immunity is being withdrawn.[87] It is submitted that there is no difference between imperative and unavoidable military necessity.

Rousseau refers to the insistence of the 'Anglo-Saxon' states that there should be this reservation for military necessity, which was passed by twenty-two votes to eight with eight abstentions.[88] Carcione[89] goes further and says that the threat by the 'Anglo-Saxon' states not to ratify the convention unless provision were made for military necessity turned out to be a pretext.

Whenever circumstances permit, the enemy must be notified of the intention to withdraw immunity from specially protected property and a written report giving the reasons for doing so must be delivered to the commissioner-general for cultural property.

Property under *enhanced protection* may be attacked only 'if, and for as long as, the property has, by its use, become a military objective' and if ordered at

[83] 2HP, Art. 6(d).

[84] Art. 11, para. 2. Parks, Air war, p. 62, reminds us that this is a lower level than that at which the decision to bomb Monte Cassino was taken.

[85] Art. 11, para. 2.

[86] Art. 11, para. 1.

[87] Art. 11, para. 3.

[88] Rousseau, *Le Droit des conflits armés*, p. 133; Alexandrow refers to the unwillingness of the United States, Great Britain and 'other imperialist states' to provide radical solutions for the protection of cultural property (E. Alexandrow, *International Legal Protection of Cultural Property*, Sofia Press, 1979, p. 57).

[89] Carcione, Protection de biens culturels.

the highest operational level of command'.[90] However, a lot of conditions are attached. The attack must be the only feasible way of terminating its use as a military objective, all feasible precautions must be taken to avoid, or at least minimize, damage to the property, effective advance warning must be issued to the opposing forces requiring the termination of military use and a reasonable time given to them to redress the situation.[91] In the case of property under enhanced protection, no waiver for military use is permitted. This is a rather curious omission. Thus if a cultural bridge under enhanced protection is the only crossing over a river, force A would not be allowed to conduct a tactical withdrawal across the bridge; but enemy force B might, after due warning once the first retreating soldier had set foot on the bridge and after a short time for compliance, be entitled to destroy the bridge to prevent them doing so!

Precautions in attack

Military commanders and military planners, as well as those who execute plans and orders, are, of course, under an obligation to take precautions in attack to verify that the target is a military objective and to minimize incidental damage to civilian objects (see Chapter 4). It is important that cultural property is included in these precautions.[92]

Precautions in defence

The CPC, like the Hague Regulations, imposes a duty on defenders, as well as attackers. They must, so far as possible, remove movable cultural property from the vicinity of military objectives or provide adequate *in situ* protection, avoid locating military objectives near cultural property,[93] avoid siting shelters for specially protected cultural property near potential military targets,[94] avoid the use of cultural property and its surroundings for military purposes[95] and may unilaterally declare a waiver of use for military purposes of what might otherwise be military objectives in the vicinity.[96] Of course, effective protection of cultural property involves much more than compliance with the treaty obligations. It requires comprehensive listing of property, coordination between ministries, local government and the armed forces, plans for protection of cultural property

---

[90]2HP, Art. 13. The second requirement can be waived if circumstances do not permit owing to requirements of immediate self-defence. It is not clear what immediate self-defence means. Presumably it does not include obtaining a tactical advantage over the enemy.

[91]2HP, Art. 13. In the case of the last two conditions, these can be waived if circumstances do not permit owing to requirements of immediate self-defence.

[92]For parties to 2HP, there is a specific requirement to do so, see Art. 7.

[93]2HP, Art. 8.

[94]Art. 8.

[95]Art. 4. That would preclude the placing of military aircraft near to cultural property.

[96]Art. 8, para. 5.

in peacetime including establishing refuges, duplicating important archives and the protection of electronic data.[97] Some of these requirements are provided for in the Second Cultural Property Protocol, which requires states in peacetime to prepare inventories, plan emergency measures to protect against fire or structural collapse, plan for removal of property or protection *in situ* and designate authorities responsible for safeguarding cultural property.[98]

Occupation

In addition to the other rules for the protection of cultural property, when occupying enemy territory, the occupying forces are obliged to support the authorities of the occupied territory in protecting cultural property and provide assistance where those authorities are unable to take measures to preserve cultural property. There is even an obligation on parties to the convention to remind recognized resistance movements of their obligation to respect cultural property.[99] The German Manual refers to textbook action by Israeli forces when they occupied Sinai in 1956–7 in assisting in the running of the monastery of St Katharine, looking after visitors, providing the monks with food and investigating an attempted breaking into the treasury of the monastery church.[100] The First Cultural Property Protocol requires parties, on pain of payment of an indemnity, to prevent the exportation of cultural property from territory they occupy.[101] Other parties are required to preserve and return at the end of hostilities property so exported. It may not be retained as war reparations. The Second Cultural Property Protocol places further obligations on the occupying power with regard to the export, removal or transfer of ownership of cultural property, archaeological excavation of, and alterations to, or change of use of, cultural property.[102]

Transports

The CPC and Cultural Property Regulations contain detailed provisions for the transport of cultural property. Basically there are two possibilities:[103]

---

[97] See Boylan, *Review*, p. 72.

[98] 2HP, Art. 5.

[99] Art. 5.

[100] Germany, *Der Schutz*, p. 21. The suggestion by Boylan, *Review*, p. 58, that the authorities in the various parts of the former Yugoslavia should control the various fighting factions would only apply in the case of occupation of territory.

[101] First Cultural Property Protocol 1954, Art. 1. The Hague Regulations and Protocol I do not contain a corresponding provision, but the expropriation and export of cultural property may still be a war crime and any 'consent' obtained by threats a nullity, see the *IG Farben* and *Krupp* trials, X WCR 1 and 69 abstracted at XV WCR 125–30.

[102] 2HP, Art. 9.

[103] And it matters not whether the property transported is under ordinary or special protection (Germany, *Der Schutz*, p. 23).

1 Special protection where specific arrangements have been made with the commissioner-general for cultural property.[104] In that case the distinctive emblem is to be displayed, attacks against such transports are prohibited and there is no waiver for military necessity.

2 Urgent cases where there is not time to make these arrangements. Notification should, so far as possible, be made to opposing parties and the distinctive emblem may be displayed within, but not outside,[105] the territory of the state arranging the movement. Other states are required to take 'so far as possible, the necessary precautions to avoid acts of hostilities directed against the transport ... displaying the distinctive emblem'.[106]

The distinctive emblem to be displayed in the case of all transports is that applicable to immovable cultural property under special protection.[107] That makes it difficult to distinguish transports under special protection and transports in urgent cases.[108]

Personnel

Persons engaged in the protection of cultural property have a status rather like that of military medical personnel: they must be respected and if they fall into the hands of the enemy they must be allowed to continue their cultural duties if the property for which they are responsible also falls into enemy hands.[109] They will, of course, be protected by the Prisoner of War Convention, if they are members of the armed forces, or by the Civilian Convention, if they are civilians. They carry a special identity card and wear a special armband.[110]

Protective emblem

The protective emblem is a blue and white shield displayed singly for property under ordinary protection and cultural personnel, or as a group of three shields (the triple emblem) for immovable property under special protection, transports and refuges.[111] No special emblem is specified for property under enhanced protection.

[104]Art. 12; and Art. 17 of the Cultural Property Regulations. The latter sets out the detailed provisions for the application to the commissioner and the movement of property.

[105]Art. 31, para. 1, states that transport conveying cultural property to the territory of another country may not display the distinctive emblem unless immunity has been expressly granted to it. This seems to be a reference to the special immunity under Art. 12.

[106]Art. 13, para. 2.

[107]That is the triple emblem, see below, Arts. 16–17.

[108]Germany, *Der Schutz*, p. 25.

[109]Art. 15.

[110]Reg. 21 of the Cultural Property Regulations.

[111]Art. 17.

Carcione[112] criticizes the regime of the convention in that it is left to the discretion of the parties to the convention whether to display the protective emblem (except in the case of specially protected property) and then only during armed conflicts. This leads to insufficient knowledge of the emblem. Further confusion is caused by the fact that different emblems are prescribed by the Hague Regulations and the Roerich Pact. He feels that the display of the emblem on specially protected property in peacetime should be mandatory, and that display[113] of the emblem on property under basic protection should be actively encouraged.[114] This would be an aid to recognition of the emblem.

Supervision

It is envisaged that the convention will be applied with the assistance of the protecting powers and of UNESCO.[115] Parties are to nominate to the director-general of UNESCO persons qualified to act as commissioner-general for cultural property. Once an armed conflict occurs, a commissioner-general is to be accredited to each party to the conflict by agreement between the recipient party and the protecting powers. In the absence of agreement, the president of the International Court of Justice may arbitrate. If there is no protecting power, the commissioner-general exercises its functions. The parties to the conflict are also to appoint representatives for cultural property who act as a liaison between the commissioner-general and the authorities of the state appointing him[116] and the protecting powers are to appoint delegates.[117]

This elaborate structure seems to suffer from the weakness that, for its efficacy, it depends on the efforts of the protecting powers. So far as the author is aware, no protecting powers have been appointed for any purposes in recent conflicts,[118] certainly not by the United Kingdom during the Gulf war of 1991. It is not clear what is to happen in the absence of protecting powers, especially where the parties to the conflict, as is likely, have broken off diplomatic relations and are not in communication with each other. Perhaps the director-general of UNESCO could lend his good offices in persuading the parties to accept his proposals for commissioners-general.[119]

Unlike the Geneva Conventions, which depend to a large extent on the activities of the ICRC and the national red-cross societies to ensure compliance by the

---

[112]Carcione, Protection de biens culturels.

[113]It must be capable of being seen to afford protection.

[114]Boylan, *Review*, p. 85, is of the same opinion.

[115]Arts. 22–3.

[116]Germany, *Der Schutz*, p. 28.

[117]Cultural Property Regulations, Regs. 1–6.

[118]Boylan, *Review*, p. 85, mentions the absence of protecting powers in the Iran–Iraq conflict of the 1980s and the Yugoslav conflict of 1991–95.

[119]Boylan, *Review*, p. 87, also complains about serious problems of appointing commissioners-general where there are no protecting powers.

parties, the CPC gives only a minor role to an outside supervision agency.[120] The parties may turn to UNESCO for assistance but UNESCO is not given a positive role in the protection of cultural property,[121] save for making proposals,[122] or in the dissemination of information about the convention.[123] Reports are submitted to UNESCO by parties about the steps they have taken to comply with the convention[124] and UNESCO may, and must if one-fifth of the parties so request, convene meetings of the parties to discuss implementation of and amendments to the convention.[125]

Almost in despair, Carcione called for a 'Red Cross for cultural property'.[126] The precedent of the ICRC seems to indicate that states are more willing to deal with a non-governmental body because this does not necessarily mean official recognition that a particular state of affairs exists. In the first edition of this book it was suggested that it would be counter-productive to have a multiplicity of bodies active in the same field; that UNESCO already has a leading role and that it might be better to strengthen its position than introduce something new. However, parties to the Second Cultural Property Protocol have accepted the role of the Committee for the Protection of Cultural Property, whose tasks include developing guidelines for the implementation of the protocol, to deal with the lists of property under enhanced protection and to monitor and supervise the implementation of the protocol.[127]

Enforcement

It is left to the parties to introduce penal legislation to punish breaches of the convention.[128] Reprisals against cultural property are prohibited.[129]

Measures for compliance

It is instructive to see what measures states party have taken to implement the Cultural Property Convention. Under Art. 26, parties are required to submit a report of such measures to UNESCO every four years.[130]

---

[120]Carcione, Protection de biens culturels.

[121]Art. 23.

[122]According to Boylan, *Review*, p. 88, the director-general of UNESCO has intervened to good effect on several occasions in relation to Cyprus (1972) and Tyre (1980) and, more recently, Dubrovnik.

[123]Art. 25.

[124]Art. 26.

[125]Art. 27.

[126]Although the International Committee of the Blue Shield has since been established, and is mentioned in the Second Cultural Property Protocol, it is not given a supervisory role.

[127]2HP, Art. 27.

[128]Art. 28; 2HP, Art. 15(2).

[129]Art. 4, para. 4.

[130]Submission of reports has been somewhat erratic. Some states have submitted regular reports; others have submitted none (Boylan, *Review*, p. 89).

An example is that of Germany.[131] The convention entered into force for Germany on 11 November 1967 and the text was published in the *Federal Law Gazette*. A German translation of the text was distributed to the competent federal, state and local authorities, schools, universities, museums, art galleries, churches and the press in 1966 and again in 1973. The text was also published in military regulations, reinforced by leaflets and posters and the inclusion of the subject in military training programmes and the production in 1964 of a training pamphlet and other training aids. In 1975 the Federal Ministry of the Interior published a first list of cultural property worthy of protection and a map has been produced showing all important immovable cultural property in Germany. A commissioner-general for cultural property has been appointed and steps have been taken to include the following offences in criminal law:

1 Damaging and pillaging of cultural property.[132]
2 Misuse of and damage to the protective emblem.
3 Obstruction, violence, insults and threats to those responsible for the protection of cultural property.

The Netherlands has comprehensive arrangements for the protection of cultural property in place in peacetime, including inter-ministerial co-operation and the listing of cultural property. Of interest to the armed forces in this respect is the appointment of army reserve officers as cultural protection officers whose role is to prevent damage to or theft of cultural property or its use for military purposes.[133]

Sending and receiving states

What is the position of the troops of a sending state that is not party to the CPC on the territory of a receiving state that is a party? That is the situation in respect of British troops assigned to NATO on German soil. Under Art. II of the NATO Status of Forces Agreement,[134] it is the duty of the force 'to respect the laws of the receiving state'. In Germany the CPC is part of German law following ratification and approval by the federal parliament. It cannot, of course, be

---

[131] Report of the Federal Republic of Germany concerning the execution of the Cultural Property Convention, Bonn, September 1977, published in *Military Law and Law of War Review*, 1978, vol. 4, p. 718.

[132] In implementation of the Rome Statute of 1998 for the International Criminal Court, Germany has introduced an International Criminal Code (*Völkerstrafgesetzbuch*), which came into force on 30 June 2002. Para. 9 of the code deals with looting and destruction of cultural property (see R. Pienkny, Der Schutz von Kulturgütern bei bewaffneten Konflickten im Lichte jüngster völkerrechtlicher Entwicklungen, *Humanitäres Völkerrechts – Informationsschriften*, 1/2003, p. 27).

[133] Boylan, *Review*, p. 68.

[134] Agreement regarding the Status of Forces of Parties to the North Atlantic Treaty, London, 1951, UK Treaty Series No. 3 (1955), Cmd. 9363 (HMSO).

binding on states not party, but the duty to respect German law does place an obligation on the troops of the sending state to respect the principles of the CPC when planning military deployments and operations on German soil. It would be incumbent on them to respect any lists of cultural property supplied by the German authorities.

Discussion

Carcione contrasts the differences in definition between the broad concept of cultural property in the preamble, the main definition in Art. 1, which speaks of property of 'great importance', and Art. 8, dealing with special protection, which refers to property of 'very great importance', and considers that these differences may give rise to difficulties of interpretation on the part of military commanders. This is especially true of property under ordinary protection where the display of the protective emblem is not mandatory.

Carcione is also very critical of the language of the convention. He points out that Art. 8, para. 1 uses terms which give rise to fine shades of interpretation such as: cultural property 'of very great importance', 'important' military object-ives and, in his words, the almost grotesque railway station of 'relative import-ance'. Then the articles permitting derogation on grounds of military necessity are different. Art. 4 (property under ordinary protection) speaks of 'military necessity' while Art. 11 (property under special protection) speaks of 'exceptional cases of unavoidable military necessity'. It seems absurd to have shades of military necessity. He is of the opinion that the special rules of the convention do not affect the normal application of the principle of military necessity. This must be because of the rather cavalier manner in which the term is used in the CPC. It should not affect the way the term is understood outside the context of the CPC. Carcione thinks that much is left to the good sense and linguistic skills of commanders. He wonders whether the movement of military units or supplies in the vicinity of specially protected property would amount to a violation of Art. 9, which requires the high contracting parties to refrain from using the property or its surroundings for military purposes. This is because Art. 8, para. 3, specifically states that movement of military personnel or material through a cultural centre would be regarded as using it for military purposes. The answer would depend on whether one applied a strict construction of the text, or tried to implement the spirit of the convention. A further curiosity, according to Carcione, is Art. 8, para. 2, which makes a violation of the protection of specially protected property the standard by which it is decided whether protection can be afforded!

The main advantage of the CPC is not so much the protection it affords, which can be waived by officers at a relatively low level, but the discipline it imposes on states in peacetime with regard to the identification, marking, registration and siting of cultural property.

Cultural property and places of worship

Protocol I

Protocol I also prohibits acts of hostility against, or use in support of the military effort of, or reprisals against, 'historical monuments, works of art or places of worship which constitute the cultural or spiritual heritage of peoples'.[135] That means property of international rather than national or local importance. In one sense Protocol I is stricter than the Hague Regulations. It prohibits acts of hostility against cultural property while the earlier rule was more exhortatory in requiring steps to be taken, so far as possible, to spare cultural objects. On the other hand, Protocol I only applies to a limited class of objects: those constituting the cultural or spiritual heritage of peoples.[136]

Protocol I, while prohibiting use of cultural property in support of the military effort, is also stricter in not repeating the principle of customary law, confirmed in the CPC, that protected property used for military purposes loses its immunity. It is not clear whether that was thought so obvious as not to require stating or whether a conscious decision was made to afford protection to cultural property at all times. The summary records throw no light on this matter, apart from an oblique reference by Brigadier-General Wolfe of Canada to the corresponding provision of draft Protocol II where he said (in reported speech): 'to the extent that the Hague Convention provided certain exceptions, his delegation interpreted that reference as giving those exceptions validity in the Protocol'.[137] Some states decided to put the matter beyond doubt by making statements on ratification on the lines of the statement by Italy that 'if and so long as the objectives [*sic*] protected by Article 53 are unlawfully used for military purposes, they will thereby lose protection'.[138] Commentators would avoid confusing people if they stopped saying 'objective' when they mean 'object' and, as so often in the media during the Gulf war of 1991, 'civilian target' when 'civilian object' is meant.[139]

---

[135] Protocol I, Art. 53.

[136] See F. Kalshoven, Reaffirmation and development of international humanitarian law, *Netherlands Yearbook of International Law*, 1978, p. 124. The Swiss understanding is that the protocol applies to property of considerable historical value and of international importance. The report of the Swiss Federal Council, *Botschaft über die Zusatzprotokolle zu den Genfer Abkommen*, 1981, put it as follows: *Es handelt sich folglich um Objekte mit erheblichem, historischem Wert, deren Bedeutung über den lokalen oder nationalen Rahmen hinausgeht.*

[137] Official Records of the CDDH, vol. XV, Swiss Federal Political Department, 1978, p. 110.

[138] See A. Roberts, and R. Guelff, *Documents on the Laws of War*, 3rd edn, Oxford University Press, 2000, p. 507. The former legal adviser to the Directorate at the ICRC commented that 'so long as it remains clear that the limits set by articles 48 *et seq* of Protocol I remain applicable, in particular the rule of proportionality, it is difficult to object to the Dutch and Italian reservation' (H. P. Gasser, Some legal issues concerning ratification of the 1977 Geneva Protocols, in M. A. Meyer (ed.), *Armed Conflict and the New Law*, British Institute of International and Comparative Law, 1989, p. 91).

[139] The UK statement on ratification reads, more correctly, 'if the objects protected by this Article are unlawfully used for military purposes they will thereby lose their protection from attacks directed against such unlawful military uses' (see Roberts and Guelff, *Documents*, p. 511).

Further, Protocol I does away with the derogation for military necessity to found in the CPC. This is surprising given the insistence of the English-speaking states on the inclusion of such a derogation in the CPC. Was it an oversight, or have the attitudes of those states changed?[140] The answer may be that there is no need to attack cultural objects, unless they are used by the enemy for military purposes. In the words of Parks,[141] the 'burden essentially shifted entirely to the attacker despite clear evidence that many nations in the intervening years regularly used hospitals, cultural objects, civilian objects and the civilian population to shield lawful targets from attack'.

Protocol I does not specify any protective emblems for cultural property.[142] However, making clearly recognized cultural property the object of an attack is a grave breach of Protocol I if the property is subject to special protection (for example, under the auspices of a competent international organization), extensive destruction is caused and the object is not in the immediate proximity of a military objective.[143]

If a monument or work of art is marked with the protective emblem under the CPC, that must be regarded as *prima facie* evidence that it may also be protected under the Hague Regulations or under Protocol I and puts a military commander on notice. It would be useful for military planners to be given details of property listed under the World Heritage Convention of 1972.[144]

However, the precise nature of the property that is protected defies analysis.[145] The Hague Regulations,[146] at least in sieges and bombardment, cover in very general language 'buildings dedicated to religion, art, science' and 'historic monuments' provided they are not used for military purposes. The CPC[147] deals with property 'of great importance to the cultural heritage of every people'. Protocol I[148] protects 'historic monuments, works of art or places of worship which constitute the cultural or spiritual heritage of peoples'. It is not clear whether 'works of art' includes scientific collections or libraries, but it is submitted that 'historic monuments' would cover cultural or archaeological sites. Detter[149] refers to the discussions at the CDDH as to whether all churches were protected under Protocol I or only those which constitute the cultural heritage of peoples and concludes, rather obviously, that Protocol I implies the more limited protection.[150]

---

[140]Again, the summary records of the CDDH, vols. XIV and XV, do not provide illumination.

[141]Parks, Air war, p. 62.

[142]Kalshoven, Reaffirmation, p. 125.

[143]Protocol I, Arts. 53 and 85 para. 4(d).

[144]As at 3 July 2003, 754 sites and monuments had been listed (http://whc.unesco.org/heritage.htm).

[145]Boylan, *Review*, p. 50, also complains that there are considerable variations in the wording used for identical categories of property in twelve UNESCO texts.

[146]Art. 27.

[147]Art. 1.

[148]Art. 53.

[149]I. Detter, *The Law of War*, 2nd edn, Cambridge University Press, 2000, p. 295.

[150]See also M. Bothe, K. J. Partsch and W. Solf, *New Rules for the Victims of Armed Conflicts*, Martinus Nijhoff, 1982, p. 332.

Nevertheless, the more general protection of churches is provided by the Hague Regulations, which reflect customary international law.[151] The result may be that St Nicholas's Church, Shepperton, would have the limited protection in sieges and bombardments of the Hague Regulations while Westminster Abbey[152] would have the more general protection of Protocol I.

Reprisals against the important cultural property protected by Protocol I are prohibited. That is not to say that reprisals may be taken against other cultural property because Protocol I prohibits reprisals against civilian objects.[153]

Discussion

It seems at first sight that an officer who takes advantage of the CPC and withdraws protection would be caught by Protocol I.[154] However, Solf considers that since Protocol I is expressed to be without prejudice to the CPC and all other relevant instruments, 'it must be inferred that loss of . . . protection . . . is an appropriate defensive [*sic*] measure . . . if the protected property is used to support the military effort' provided, of course, that it satisfies the test of a military objective.[155] The suggestion is made by the ICRC that 'in case of a contradiction between [Protocol I] and a rule of the [Cultural Property] Convention, the latter is applicable'.[156] Does this mean that the protection of Protocol I goes no further than the CPC? That would be a surprising result given the clear language of the former. Here the ICRC seem contradictory in stating that the obligation under Protocol I is 'stricter than that imposed by the . . . Hague Convention since it does not provide for any derogation even where military necessity imperatively requires such a waiver'.[157] Even allowing for the fairly elastic interpretation of international agreements, the following statement of the ICRC seems strange at first sight: 'when parties to the Protocol are also parties to the [Cultural Property] Convention . . . , these derogations continue to apply . . . If one of them is a party to the Protocol and not to the [Cultural Property] Convention, no derogation is possible'. Can it be that the obligations of a party to Protocol I vary according to whether or not it is also a party to the CPC? This may be explained by the contractual nature of international agreements and the provisions of Art. 30 of the Vienna Convention on the Law of Treaties.[158]

Another important difference between Protocol I and the CPC is the omission in the former of the loss of protection where cultural property is used by the enemy for military purposes, the classic example being the cathedral tower

[151]*Ibid.*, p. 329. See the Trials of the Major War Criminals, vol. XXII, p. 497.
[152]This is on the World Heritage List.
[153]Arts. 52, para. 1 and 53, sub-para. (c).
[154]Art. 53.
[155]Bothe *et al.*, *New Rules*, pp. 332–3.
[156]ICRC *Commentary*, para. 2046.
[157]*Ibid.*, para. 2072.
[158]See paras. 2 and 4 of that article.

being used as an observation post. The United Kingdom made a statement on ratification of Protocol I that if cultural objects are 'unlawfully used for military purposes they will thereby lose protection from attacks directed against such unlawful military uses'. Similar statements were made on ratification by Canada, Ireland, Italy and the Netherlands.[159] It seems that the ICRC are of the opinion that the United Kingdom approach is admissible,[160] although there is nothing in the text of Protocol I that would appear to support it, so it must be based on the context of the negotiations. On the other hand, Germany seems prepared to accept the restrictions appearing on the face of Protocol I, since no statement on this point was made on ratification, yet the German Manual[161] states that 'cultural property which the enemy uses for military purposes shall also be spared so far as possible'. It may be that the German forces are expected to be fighting on their own territory so the German perspective may be different from that of the United Kingdom, whose forces have traditionally fought on the territory of other states.

Finally, Solf considers that the property qualifying for protection under Protocol I is substantially the same as that qualifying for special protection under the CPC[162] and that the words 'acts of hostility' rather than 'attacks' would include demolition of a cultural object,[163] for example, by defenders wanting to clear a field of fire.

The cultural bridge referred to earlier in this chapter poses something of a conundrum for the defenders who cannot attack it until the enemy uses it. So how do they deny the enemy access across the river? One answer might be to lay charges and put up warning signs, but only blow up the bridge if the enemy actually starts to cross it.

ICC Statute

The 1998 Rome Statute of the International Criminal Court (ICC Statute) makes the following a war crime within the jurisdiction of the court whether committed in an international or an internal armed conflict:[164] 'Intentionally directing attacks against buildings dedicated to religion, education, art, scientific or charitable purposes, historic monuments ... provided they are not military objectives.' Although this text closely follows that of the Hague Regulations 1907, there are some differences. The word 'education' has been included and 'provided they are not military objectives' has been substituted for 'provided they are not being

---

[159]Roberts and Guelff, *Documents*, pp. 499–512.
[160]ICRC *Commentary*, paras. 2072 and 2079.
[161]Germany, *Der Schutz*, para. 906.
[162]Bothe *et al.*, *New Rules*, p. 333.
[163]*Ibid.*
[164]ICC Statute, Art. 8, para. 2(b)(ix) and (e)(iv).

used at the time for military purposes'. In addition, the emphasis in the ICC Statute is on preventing attacks, whereas in the Hague Regulations it is on sparing such buildings in sieges and bombardments.

The ICC Statute also makes pillaging a war crime[165] within the jurisdiction of the court, so this would enable the punishment of looters of cultural property. The statute does not, unfortunately, include an offence of misuse of cultural property for military purposes or the use of cultural property to shield military action.

Iraq

Iraq contains some of the earliest monuments of civilization, including the cities of Ur, Babylon, Nineveh and Uruk. The mounds that remain of ancient cities are features in the desert that might, if they were not cultural sites, be regarded as military objectives in giving forces a vantage point. There was evidence to suggest that in the Gulf war of 1991 Iraq had adopted a policy of placing military objectives close to archaeological sites to protect the former from attack.[166] One account refers to the allied bombing of Iraqi military aircraft shelters at Tallil air base in southern Iraq and in camouflaged positions on roads near the base. They were all destroyed by precision attacks although they were in sight of the ziggurat of Ur, an important cultural monument.[167] But it is clear that the allies had target lists[168] and that although Iraqi aircraft, command posts and troops had been placed near civilian areas, including schools and religious sites, the allies would avoid bombing anything of religious significance. A photograph in *The Independent*[169] above an article by Geoffrey Best shows damage to a structure close to a mosque, which is intact.

Although the allied target lists for the bombing campaign were restricted to military objectives and, therefore, excluded cultural property, it is alleged that the lists did include two items of a cultural nature, though probably not amounting to cultural property in the sense of the common heritage of mankind, one being a statue of Saddam Hussein in Baghdad and the other an Iraqi war memorial, and that both were removed from the list by the United States Secretary of Defence.[170] The writer has not been able to verify this allegation from officially

---

[165]ICC Statute, Art. 8, para. 2(b)(xvi) and (e)(v).

[166]DOD Report, p. 615. See also, G. Hill, Conflict threatens ancient sites, *The Times*, 28 February 1991.

[167]B. Brown and D. Shukman, *All Necessary Means*, BBC Books, 1991, at p. 53.

[168]DOD Report, p. 100. See also M. Evans, Freedom of the sky, *The Times*, 5 February 1991; Brown and Shukman, *All Necessary Means*, p. 16.

[169]4 February 1991.

[170]T. Matthews *et al.*, The Secret History of the War, *Newsweek*, 18 March 1991, p. 20. A US Air Force officer later told the author that the statue had not been removed from the list; it was not a sufficiently high priority. In the end, the statue was demolished by Iraqis, with some help from a US armoured vehicle, BBC news online, 10 April 2003.

published sources, but if taken as a hypothetical question the removal of such items from the target list would seem correct.

The United States Department of Defence report to Congress[171] contains information about the steps taken by the allies to protect cultural property. Lists were drawn up of historical, archaeological and religious installations in Iraq and Kuwait that were not to be targeted. Analysts were also asked to look at a six-mile radius around listed targets for schools, hospitals and mosques that would necessitate special care in planning. The weapon system, munitions, time of attack and direction of attack, desired impact point and level of effort were carefully planned factors.[172]

No doubt, similar steps were taken in 2003 to protect Iraq's cultural heritage from attacks by coalition forces. While one might query the military need for destroying statues and pictures of Saddam Hussein, these objects were hardly cultural property. The same might be said of the presidential palaces. Despite their connection with the former regime in Iraq, however, it seems a pity to attack, unless strictly militarily necessary, or allow vandalism or looting in, buildings that have been constructed at great cost and that could, perhaps, be put to a different, and better, use.

The main problem in 2003 was of looting and vandalism. There was an unfortunate period, before coalition troops were able to establish effective control in Baghdad, when cultural property was looted and destroyed. According to early media reports, the Iraqi National Museum was stripped of priceless artefacts up to 7,000 years old and the National Library and Archive, a collection of Ottoman historical documents, set on fire.[173] However, it may turn out that the initial alarm was unjustified as many items were taken to places of safety.[174]

There is a legal loophole in the transition period between war fighting and effective occupation. During war fighting, the duties of the armed forces are,

---

[171]DOD Report, p. 100.

[172]See also On International Policies and Procedures regarding the Protection of Nature and Cultural Resources during Times of War, 19 January 1993, published as an appendix to the *Review* of Boylan, p. 201.

[173]See A. Gumbel and D. Keys, US blamed for failure to stop sacking of museum, *The Independent*, 14 April 2003; R. Fisk, Library books . . . set ablaze, *The Independent*, 15 April 2003.

[174]An initial investigation was carried out by the British historian, Dan Cruickshank, who reported that, at that stage, 33 major artefacts and up to 2,000 smaller items were missing from the museum. He exonerated US forces from the charge of failing to protect the museum on the basis that the evidence pointed towards the use by Iraqi soldiers of the museum grounds as well as its interior, including some storerooms, thereby compromising its protected status (Dan Cruickshank and the Raiders of the Lost Art, BBC 2 television broadcast on 8 June 2003 at 9 p.m.). According to a report by G. Shaw of the British Library dated 1 May 2003, the worst affected libraries were the National Library of Iraq, the National Archive of Iraq, the al-Awqaf Library, the Central Library of the University of Baghdad, the Library of Baytal Hikma in Baghdad, the Central Library of the University of Mosul and the Library of the Mosul Museum. The report indicated that the National Library also suffered from its proximity to the Iraqi Defence Ministry building and that the Library of the Mosul Museum suffered bomb damage. However, some material was evacuated before the war started. The collection of the Library of the Iraqi Museum and its Islamic manuscripts were protected by evacuation to a bunker.

broadly, not to attack cultural property, to protect it from incidental damage, not to use it for military purposes and not to loot it. Once an occupation becomes effective,[175] the occupying power has a general duty to maintain law and order. The Hague Regulations provide that the occupant 'shall take all the measures in his power to restore, and ensure, as far as possible, public order and safety . . .'.[176] That would include the prevention of looting but the qualifications of 'in his power' and 'as far as possible' indicate that this is not an absolute requirement; it does depend on the occupying power having the time, with other pressing commitments, and the resources to deal with public order. War-fighting troops are generally not best armed and equipped for such duties.

In the case of Iraq, there was some criticism in the media of shortcomings in the allied operational plan to foresee and provide for the eventuality of looting. The CPC and Protocol I did not, formally, apply as the United States and the United Kingdom were not parties to the former and the United States and Iraq were not parties to the latter. That left only the very limited protection for cultural property offered by the Hague Regulations. Looting in the period of anarchy between war fighting and the establishment of an occupation regime is foreseeable but the author, and probably others too, was surprised by the extent of the phenomenon in this case and by the fact that museums and even hospitals were looted and damaged.[177] It is to be hoped that, in the 'lessons learned' exercise that follows the operation, this will be noted for the future. It seems that, in a situation where ground troops take over enemy territory, they need to be closely followed by military police or *gendarmerie* units staffed, trained and equipped to deal with police, crowd control and key point protection duties.

Conclusions

The rules for the protection of cultural property are quite complicated and seem, at first sight, to be redundant because civilian property is immune from direct attack in any event. Nor is cultural property any less likely than other civilian property to be damaged as a side effect of attacks on military objectives in the vicinity. If movable, it may, of course, be attractive to the looter, but looting is prohibited anyway.

What seems more important is a ban on the use of cultural property for military purposes so that there is no need to attack it, and this is provided by

[175]Hague Regulations, Art. 42.

[176]Hague Regulations, Art. 43.

[177]In a letter to *The Independent*, published on 5 March 2003, Dr Harriet Crawford, British School of Archaeology in Iraq, and other leading experts from Oxford and Cambridge Universities, drew attention to the dangers to archaeological sites posed by bombing but they were also far-sighted enough to warn of the consequences of internal political and social destabilization, following any intervention, on Iraq's mosques, churches, desert forts, bridges and khans as well as the treasures in Iraq's museums.

Protocol I, though there may be *rare* cases where it is essential to use such property for military purposes. The protection of the CPC can be waived relatively easily. The definition of cultural property defies analysis and there is, perhaps, a case for harmonizing the various treaty provisions dealing with cultural property since different treaties provide different protection for different property.

The advantage of the special rules on cultural property is in making attacking commanders more aware of its existence, particularly if it is marked, or contained in a published list that is available to him. Much more responsibility is, however, placed on the authorities of the defending state to compile and publish lists, to register property under special protection, to mark property, to establish refuges and arrange transfer of cultural property in good time to these refuges and to have a policy of non-defended localities or demilitarized zones. This is a substantial undertaking, which requires a lot of peacetime planning and preparation and allocation of personnel and money. Like civil defence, however, it is unlikely to be allocated sufficient priority in the competition for resources.

The tendency of states not to appoint protecting powers undermines the efficacy of the CPC, and the director-general of UNESCO may have to fill the vacuum by persuading the parties to the conflict to accept his proposals for commissioners-general and by becoming active in trying to protect cultural property in wartime.

Should a state not party to the CPC be contemplating ratification of Protocol I, and wish to take advantage of the derogations permitted by the convention, it might wish to ratify the convention first or enter an appropriate reservation on ratification of the protocol. A statement on ratification of Protocol I to the effect that cultural property loses its protection if it is used for military purposes would, in any event, be advisable.[178]

---

[178]The UK made such a statement when ratifying Protocol I (see Roberts and Guelff, *Documents*, p. 511).

7

Environmental protection

We are profligate with the natural environment. Often an intervention for short-term gain can upset the natural balances and cause long-term problems for which artificial solutions must be sought. As Mahmood Abdulraheem so poignantly writes,[1] the reduction of the Iraqi marshes has deprived the area of a giant kidney that acts as a self-sustaining water treatment facility. Perhaps this inexorable peacetime assault on the environment is more damaging than the sharp but relatively short shocks caused by conventional warfare.[2] Nevertheless, experts are concerned about the environmental consequences of attacks on targets like oil refineries, petrochemical plants, chemical and fertilizer factories and pharmaceutical plants.[3]

Although the law of war has been mainly concerned with the protection of human life,[4] various principles of customary law can work towards the protection of the environment.[5] First, the principle that military operations are to be directed against the enemy armed forces[6] and military objectives. Second, that

[1] M. Abdulraheem, War-related damage to the marine environment in the ROPME sea area, in J. E. Austin and C. E. Bruch, *The Environmental Consequences of War*, Cambridge University Press, 2000, at p. 351.

[2] Austin and Bruch, *Environmental Consequences*, p. 5, point out that war can occasionally benefit the environment by putting a stop to this activity, allowing regeneration of forests and fish stocks.

[3] R. Falk, Evaluating the adequacy of existing international law standards, in Austin and Bruch, *Environmental Consequences*, p. 149.

[4] It has been described as 'anthropocentric in scope and focus' by the Office of the Judge Advocate General, Canadian Forces, in a Note on the Current Law of Armed Conflict relevant to the Environment in Conventional Conflicts, Ottawa Conference of Experts, July 1991 (Ottawa Conference). P. Painchaud, in Environmental Weapons and the Gulf War, Ottawa Conference, makes the point that in the case of various attacks on dams, dykes and irrigation systems in the Sino-Japanese war, the Second World War and the Korean war the military planners did not consider the environmental consequences.

[5] The environment referred to in this chapter is the natural environment, not the human environment referred to by A. Roberts, Failures in protecting the environment, in P. J. Rowe, *The Gulf War 1990–91 in International and English Law*, Routledge, 1993, p. 121, though it includes areas cultivated by humans.

[6] The preamble to the St Petersburg Declaration of 1868.

any damage or destruction caused in war must be dictated by military necessity[7] and not by some other motive, for example, revenge or lust for destruction. There must be some reasonable connection between the destruction of property and the overcoming of the enemy forces.[8] Third, that the damage or destruction must be proportionate to the military gain sought.[9]

Writers once thought it permissible for a belligerent to attain the object of war by laying waste to a country and destroying food and provender to prevent the enemy from subsisting there. But it was thought wrong to carry out devastation if it was motivated by hate and passion.[10] Those writers seem to have accepted devastation by way of legitimate reprisals; to create a barrier in one's own[11] or allied territory[12] against invasion; or to harass an invading force.[13] Even the devastation of enemy-held territory was regarded as legitimate[14] if it was done to deny the area to enemy forces.[15] It followed, therefore, that General Rendulic, who laid waste to large areas of Northern Norway to impede an expected Soviet army advance, was acquitted by a United States war crimes tribunal.[16]

Despite the practice of states over the centuries of inflicting damage on the environment in war,[17] including the many historical examples of a 'scorched

---

[7]Hague Regulations 1907, Art. 23(g). This also applies, by virtue of Art. 53 of the Civilian Convention, to destruction caused by an occupying power; and if that destruction is not militarily necessary and is extensive, those responsible commit grave breaches of the Convention, see Art. 147. The occupying power is only the administrator and usufructuary of property in occupied territory, Hague Regulations, Art. 55.

[8]The *Hostages* trial, VIII *War Crimes Reports* (WCR) 66.

[9]According to Bothe, increased awareness in the world of environmental problems must have an impact on the proportionality rule, M. Bothe, The Protection of the Environment in Time of Armed Conflict, Ottawa Conference. Bothe also mentions that the 'dictates of public conscience' in the Martens preamble to Hague Convention No. IV of 1907 will include environmental concerns. Roberts, Environment, p. 116 also mentions the principle of humanity as being relevant.

[10]As in the French devastation of the Palatinate in 1674 and 1689.

[11]Compare the actions of Peter the Great in Russian territory in 1709. This right in national territory is still recognized by Protocol I, Art. 54, para. 5.

[12]As in the devastation in front of the lines of Torres Vedras in Portugal by Wellington.

[13]As in the burning of Moscow in 1812.

[14]As in the case of the Shenandoah valley during the American civil war.

[15]For a more detailed study of early writers and military practice, see G. Best, *Humanity in Warfare*, Methuen, 1983, pp. 65–6 and 206–7. See also I. Doswald-Beck, The value of the 1977 protocols, in M. A. Meyer, *Armed Conflict and the New Law*, British Institute of International and Comparative Law, 1989, p. 160.

[16]The *Hostages* trial, VIII WCR 34, 69. It is questionable whether, had Protocol I applied, a tribunal would have come to the same conclusion.

[17]McCoubrey speaks of the ancient Roman practice of putting salt on the fields of the enemy to render them infertile, H. McCoubrey, *International Humanitarian Law*, Dartmouth, 1990, p. 162. M. Saalfeld, Umweltschutz in bewaffneten Konflikten, *Humanitäres Völkerrecht Informationsschriften*, 1992, No. 1, p. 15, refers to various mentions in the Bible of such practices, e.g., 'and that the whole land thereof is brimstone, and salt, and burning, that it is not sown, nor beareth, nor any grass groweth therein' (Deut. 29:23), but also points to historical examples of orders of military leaders prohibiting destruction of crops, e.g., the biblical injunction in sieges not to cut down fruit trees for use for military purposes 'for the tree of the field is man's life' (Deut. 20:19).

earth' policy mentioned above, early law of war treaties were concerned more with the protection of human beings than with the protection of objects or of the environment.[18] Even though the artillery barrages of the First World War and the bombing of the Second World War caused severe environmental damage, it was not until defoliants,[19] daisy-cutter bombs and Rome ploughs were used and until consideration was given to the possibility of causing precipitation to flood enemy supply routes in Vietnam that attention was paid to techniques in war that were specifically aimed at the environment.[20] Worldwide concern for the environment was expressed in the World Charter for Nature,[21] which provides that:

5. Nature shall be secured against degradation caused by warfare or other hostile activities . . .
20. Military activities damaging nature shall be avoided.

It is arguable that both these concerns are covered by the provisions of Protocol I, Art. 57 (precautions in attack), which protects civilian objects from attack and from incidental damage, and Arts. 35 and 55 (protection of the environment). Although not a binding treaty obligation, one would expect states that had voted in favour of the World Charter for Nature to issue internal instructions, perhaps in military manuals, or laws to ensure compliance.[22] But it is not a simple matter and there are delicate judgements to be made.[23] The need to protect the lives of combatants needs to be balanced against the protection of the environment; any health hazards to the civilian population caused by the use of chemical herbicides will have to be taken into account; and the extent of the damage to the environment and its capacity to regenerate need to be considered.

[18] See Saalfeld, Umweltschutz, for a review of the limited environmental protection provisions in customary and early treaty law.

[19] Aldrich points out that so far as he was aware defoliants were deliberately used in South Vietnam and Laos only where the consent of the governments had been obtained (G. H. Aldrich, Prospects for US ratification of Protocol I, *American Journal of International Law*, 1991, p. 14).

[20] See P. J. Rowe, *Defence: the Legal Implications*, Brassey, 1987, at pp. 116–17; F. Kalshoven and L. Zegveld, *Constraints on the Waging of War*, 3rd edn, International Committee of the Red Cross, 2000, p. 92; McCoubrey, *Humanitarian Law*, p. 163, refers to the possibility of 'cloud-seeding' being considered during the Vietnam war.

[21] UN General Assembly Resn. (1982) 22 *International Legal Materials* (ILM) 455.

[22] N. A. Robinson, Draft articles with commentary on a Convention securing Nature from Warfare or other Hostile Activities, paper for the Ottawa Conference, speculates that, because this resolution was a 'soft law' instrument, Iraq, which had voted in favour, felt free to breach this principle. Szasz defines 'soft law' as norms which are not, strictly speaking, binding on states but which may nevertheless influence their actions: P. C. Szasz, Study of Proposals for Improvements to Existing Legal Instruments relating to the Environment and Armed Conflicts, Ottawa Conference. L. C. Green, The Environment and the Law of Conventional Warfare, Ottawa Conference, is of the opinion that the International Law Commission's Art. 19 (on criminal liability for breach of environmental obligations) in its draft Declaration on State Responsibility lacks any legal significance. Roberts, Environment, p. 111, refers to other treaties and bilateral agreements that have an impact on environmental issues in wartime.

[23] McCoubrey, *Humanitarian Law*, pp. 162–3.

Current law

Property Protection

There are various rules that provide, in effect, that property is not to be damaged unless military necessity so requires.[24] These can indirectly help to protect the environment.

Environmental protection

There are three treaty provisions dealing directly with the protection of the environment during armed conflicts. First, the Convention on the Prohibition of Military and Any Other Hostile Use of Environmental Modification Techniques, 1977 (ENMOD Convention); second, Art. 35, para. 3 of Protocol I; and third, Art. 55 of Protocol I. There is also a prohibition, in Protocol III to the Weapons Convention,[25] of incendiary attacks on forests or other kinds of plant cover, unless they are used to 'cover, conceal or camouflage combatants or other military objectives, or are themselves military objectives'.[26]

ENMOD Convention

Art. I.1 is an undertaking by states party: 'not to engage in military or any other hostile use of environmental modification techniques having widespread, long-lasting or severe effects as a means of destruction, damage or injury to any other State Party'. Westing refers to this as a ban on actions carried out with the deliberate intent to manipulate the environment for hostile purposes but suggests that it ought to include reasonable expectation since such a deliberate intent is difficult to establish in the absence of an admission by the perpetrator.[27]

It is worth mentioning here that non-hostile uses of environmental modification techniques are not caught by the convention.[28]

Art. II defines such techniques as those 'for changing – through the deliberate manipulation of natural processes – the dynamics, composition or structure of the Earth, including its biota, lithosphere, hydrosphere and atmosphere, or of outer space'.

---

[24]Hague Regulations, Reg. 23(g). This is reinforced by the provisions of Regs. 22 (means of injuring the enemy are not unlimited) and 25 (no attacks on undefended places) as well as the Martens clause in the preamble. The same principles apply in occupied territory under Reg. 55 of the Hague Regulations and Art. 53 of the Civilian Convention. By virtue of Art. 147 of the Civilian Convention, extensive and wanton destruction of property can amount to a grave breach and a war crime.

[25]Art. 2, para. 4.

[26]For area of land as military objective, see Chapter 3.

[27]A. H. Westing, The Environmental Modification Conference of 1991, *Humanitäres Völkerrecht Informationsschriften*, 1992, p. 71.

[28]J. Goldblat, Legal protection of the environment against the effects of military activities, *Bulletin of Peace Proposals*, vol. 22, no. 4 (1991), p. 5; Robinson, Draft Articles.

In submitting the text of the treaty[29] to the UN General Assembly, the UN Conference of the Committee on Disarmament also submitted a set of understandings. The first relates to the meaning of the terms 'widespread, long-lasting or severe' and defined them as follows:

1   Widespread: encompassing an area on the scale of several hundred square kilometres.
2   Long-lasting: lasting for a period of months, or approximately a season.
3   Severe: involving serious or significant disruption or harm to human life, natural and economic resources or other assets.

The understanding was expressly said to be exclusively for the ENMOD Convention and was without prejudice to the interpretation of similar terms in any other international agreement.

Another understanding included a list of examples of phenomena that could be caused by environmental modification techniques: 'earthquakes, tsunamis,[30] an upset in the ecological balance of a region; changes in weather patterns (clouds, precipitation, cyclones of various types, and tornadic storms); changes in climate patterns; changes in ocean currents; changes in the state of the ozone layer; and changes in the state of the ionosphere'. McCoubrey refers to the problems for allied air operations of ash and gritty particles released by the natural eruption of Mount Vesuvius in 1944 and speculated as to the military effects that could be caused by bombing volcanoes.[31]

Some commentators seem to think that the convention has a wider scope than seems apparent on a reading of Articles I and II. One speaks of deliberate[32] destruction of a forest to deprive the enemy of shelter[33] as being caught by the convention. It is difficult to follow the logic of this argument, since the convention only deals with 'deliberate human manipulation of the natural processes, as distinct from conventional acts of warfare which might result in adverse effects on the environment'[34] except in cases of such extensive destruction of, for example, the tropical rain forest as to cause a climatic change and to lead to the inference that that change was intended. Westing[35] is nearer the mark when he

[29]1108 UNTS 151–78. See also A. Roberts and R. Guelff, *Documents on the Laws of War*, 3rd edn, Oxford University Press, 2000, p. 407.

[30]Tidal waves.

[31]H. McCoubrey and N. D. White, *International Law and Armed Conflict*, Dartmouth, 1992, p. 263.

[32]Rather than incidental, say, to a severe bombardment.

[33]Szasz, Study of Proposals. This may be a reference to the statement made in 1976 by the US negotiator that such use is prohibited only if it upsets the ecological balance of a region, see J. Goldblat, The ENMOD Convention: a critical review, *Humanitäres Völkerrecht Informationsschriften*, 1993, No. 2, p. 82. In fact, Szasz expresses doubt later in his paper about whether Iraq's deliberate spillage of oil and setting on fire of oil wells, if not done for the purpose of deliberately damaging the environment, would have been a violation of the Convention if carried out by a party to it.

[34]Goldblat, ENMOD Convention, p. 81.

[35]A. H. Westing, The environmental modification conference of 1991, *Humanitäres Völkerrecht Informationsschriften*, 1992, p. 71.

says that an environmentally devastating attack with nuclear weapons would not readily fall within the purview of the ENMOD Convention since the ensuing environmental modification might well be presented as unintended collateral effects. This is the nub of the problem. It will be difficult to prove that nuclear weapons were used for the purpose of environmental modification rather than for the simple destruction of the targets at which they were aimed.

The environmental protection of the ENMOD Convention applies to all states party, and not just the states in conflict. It extends to the environment at large.[36] Although Art. I.1 specifically refers to destruction, damage or injury to any other state party, this can still be caused by manipulation of the environment at large.

Szasz raises but leaves open the question of whether the essential terms of the ENMOD Convention have already become part of customary international law.[37]

As Goldblat has pointed out, one of the greatest difficulties with a convention that does not impose an absolute ban is verification – establishing that the environmental changes were due to human activity and that they were brought about by deliberate, hostile intent.[38] The procedures laid down in the convention for a consultative committee of experts and for referring complaints to the UN Security Council[39] are intended to alleviate this problem.

A review conference took place in 1992 to assess the convention in the light of the Gulf war of 1990–91 and was attended by forty states party, but little of substance emerged save for the understanding that under certain conditions the use of herbicides could be equated with environmental modification techniques prohibited under Art. II of the Convention.[40]

Protocol I

Although it comes into operation only during armed conflicts, occupation and liberation wars involving states party, within those situations Art. 35, para. 3 of Protocol I seems also to protect the environment at large and not merely the territories of the parties to the conflict.

Art. 35, para. 3 of Protocol I, which is in the part dealing with methods and means of warfare, prohibits the employment of 'methods and means of warfare which are intended, or may be expected, to cause widespread, long-term and severe damage to the natural environment'.

---

[36] Szasz, Study of proposals.

[37] *Ibid.*

[38] Goldblat, ENMOD Convention, p. 83.

[39] Art. V.

[40] A. Bouvier, Protection of the Natural Environment in time of Armed Conflict, 1991, *International Review of the Red Cross*, p. 563.

Art. 55 of Protocol I,[41] which is in the part dealing with the protection of the civilian population against the effects of hostilities,[42] requires care to be taken in warfare 'to protect the natural environment against widespread, long-term and severe damage'. It repeats the prohibition on methods and means in Art. 35 para. 3 but with the additional qualification 'and thereby to prejudice the health or survival of the population'.[43] It also prohibits *attacks*[44] against the environment by way of reprisals.

It is important to emphasize the point made by Bothe,[45] that Arts. 35 and 55 only come into play once the military planner has surmounted two hurdles: first, that the object to be attacked is a military objective and, second, that the rule of proportionality will not be violated.[46] After that he must have regard to the specific rules on environmental protection. It is likely, though, that if the environmental damage is going to be widespread, long-term and severe, the military planner may well fall at the second hurdle in any event.[47]

Kalshoven has criticized the vague formulation of Protocol I and suggested that express prohibitions would have been more useful.[48] This is a dilemma always faced by those negotiating law-of-war treaties. If the treaty imposes a specific ban, states will find other ways of achieving the same result. If the language is more general, so as to catch all foreseeable means, states will argue about its scope of application and the intentions of the negotiators.

Representatives of the ICRC have suggested that these articles prohibit not only attacks on the environment as such but also making use of the environment as a tool of warfare.[49] Although one normally looks to the ENMOD Convention

[41]Not of the 'Geneva convention' as suggested by A. Taylor MP, Hansard (Commons), 15 March 1991, col. 1381.

[42]And, therefore, applies only in the limited circumstances laid down in Art. 49, para. 3, i.e. affecting the civilian population on land.

[43]Kalshoven considers that as only long-term damage is envisaged, 'health' and 'survival' have to be interpreted in the sense of future health or survival (Kalshoven, Reaffirmation and development of international humanitarian law, *Netherlands Yearbook of International Law*, 1978, p. 130). M. Bothe, K. J. Partsch and W. Solf, *New Rules for the Victims of Armed Conflicts*, Martinus Nijhoff, 1982, p. 346, point out that the committee report states that 'population' is not preceded by the usual qualification 'civilian' because it is the whole population that is protected, irrespective of combatant status and 'health' was included because, even if the population survived, it might suffer from, e.g., congenital defects.

[44]'Attack' means an act of violence against the adversary, see Chapter 1, and is a narrower concept than methods and means of warfare.

[45]Bothe, Protection.

[46]As to the difficulty of making proportionality calculations in respect of potential environmental damage, se M. N. Schmitt, War and the environment: fault lines in the prescriptive landscape, in Austin and Bruch, *Environmental Consequences*, at pp. 111–16.

[47]Fleck seems to be of the view that legal protection of the environment is based on proportionality rather than on an absolute ecological standard (D. Fleck, Environment: legal and policy perspectives, in H. Fox and M. A. Meyer (eds.), *Effecting Compliance*, British Institute of International and Comparative Law, 1993, p. 147).

[48]F. Kalshoven and L. Zegveld, *Constraints on the Waging of War*, 3rd edn, ICRC, 2001, p. 92.

[49]A. Bouvier and H. P. Gasser, Protection of the natural environment in time of armed conflict, Ottawa Conference.

when thinking about the manipulation of the environment for hostile purposes, the ICRC may be right about the effect of Protocol I. However, before Protocol I applied it would have to be established that there was a risk of environmental damage by such manipulation.

It is not specifically a grave breach of the Protocol to violate Arts. 35 and 55. But, an indiscriminate attack launched in the knowledge that it would cause excessive damage to the environment would be a grave breach.[50]

The treatment of the same subject in two different articles and in slightly different terms seems to have been the result of an attempt to accommodate different approaches to the problem suggested by delegates to the CDDH.[51] It was decided to leave the matter in two separate articles because Art. 55 deals with the protection of the civilian population while Art. 35 deals with the prohibition of unnecessary injury and has a wider scope, including transnational damage. The United Kingdom protested that there was no need for environmental provisions in Art. 35 since they were found, in the context of civilian protection, in Art. 55 and that the ultimate purpose of protecting the environment was to protect the civilians living in it. The logic of this dissenting view seems very compelling.[52] Both provisions contain the words 'which are intended or may be expected'. They seem to introduce an objective element into the test of whether the articles have been breached. Strangely, it does not even seem to be necessary to prove that actual damage has been caused, although, if it has, that would be evidence from which intent or expectation could be inferred. On the wording of the articles, it is not clear whether 'or may be expected' means may be expected by the attacker or may be expected by an objective onlooker.[53]

Another difference between the scope of Art. 35 and that of Art. 55 is that the former relates to all methods or means of warfare, whether on land, at sea or in the air, whereas Art. 55 is in the part dealing with the protection of the civilian population, civilians and civilian objects on land against the effects of hostilities.[54] Art. 55 extends to a state's territorial waters, but only Art. 35 applies to damage on the high seas.[55]

[50]Art. 85, para. 3(b).

[51]Bothe *et al.*, *New Rules*, p. 345.

[52]See ICRC, *Commentary*, paras. 1449 and 1459.

[53]Kalshoven, Reaffirmation, p. 130, refers to the concept of 'objective expectation'. Bothe *et al.*, *New Rules*, p. 347, refer to 'objectively foreseeable collateral effects'.

[54]Art. 49, para. 2. Kalshoven and Zegveld, *Constraints*, p. 111, point out that Art. 55 is intended to prevent consequential prejudice to the health or survival of the population.

[55]M. Bothe, at a meeting of the Committee for the Protection of Human Life in Armed Conflict at the twelfth Congress of the International Society for Military Law and the Law of War, Brussels, May 1991. However, Rauch considers that the provisions of Section I, Part IV of Protocol I cover the collateral effects on land of operations against enemy warships and merchant ships (E. Rauch, *The Protocols Additional to the Geneva Conventions . . . and the Convention on the Law of the Sea: Repercussions in the Law of Naval Warfare*, Institute of International Law, Kiel, Duncker & Humblot, 1984, pp. 60, 141). S. Witteler, Der Krieg im Golf und seine Auswirkungen auf die natürliche Umwelt, *Humanitäres Völkerrecht Informationsschriften*, January–July 1991, p. 53, comments that Art. 35, being wider in scope, allows a more broadly based assessment of environmental damage to be made, such as the entire Iraqi oil-letting episode during the Gulf war of 1991.

Protocol I has been criticized on the grounds that it antedates the modern environmental law of peace in which the environment is protected even in the absence of proved specific damage (the principle of precaution which is absent from the protocol).[56] However, it must be said that the words 'or may be expected' do incorporate a precautionary element, though less far-reaching than the Montreal Protocol.[57]

It has been pointed out that it is strange that the protection of the natural environment in Arts. 35 and 55 of Protocol I is absolute, not being subject to any considerations of military necessity or proportionality, and is therefore more rigid than the protection of human life. Of course, it is only methods or means of warfare that cause, or may be expected to cause, widespread, long-term and severe damage to the natural environment that are forbidden.[58] This takes account of national defence interests for it allows less severe environmental damage to be caused if it is militarily necessary. Reference has been made to military plans to burn oil installations in a harbour since this would deny the use of both the harbour and the oil to a potential enemy and although there would be environmental damage, it would not be on an international scale.[59] It is noteworthy that the word 'attack' is not to be found in Arts. 35 and 55, but only the words 'use' or 'employ'. The word 'use' has in the past been found in treaties that impose a complete ban. The view has been expressed that perhaps the natural environment is more important than human life because human life depends on the environment for its very existence.[60] On the other hand, the Protocol I provisions are really aimed at unconventional methods of warfare such as herbicides specifically designed to damage the environment and, therefore, will only affect high-level planners and decision-makers rather than those at lower levels carrying out attacks with conventional weaponry.[61]

Relationship between the ENMOD Convention and Protocol I

Bothe puts the differences between the two instruments most succinctly by saying that in the case of the convention, the environment is the weapon and, in the case of Protocol I, the environment is the victim.[62] Rowe gives the classic example of a technique caught by the ENMOD Convention as an attempt to

---

[56]M. Bothe, The protection of the environment in time of armed conflict, *German Yearbook of International Law (GYIL)* 34 (1991), at p. 57.

[57]Protocol on Substances that Deplete the Ozone Layer, Montreal, 1987.

[58]This is a reference to the natural environment as a whole and not to a local site of nature. In the words of Witteler, Der Krieg im Golf, p. 51, '*die natürliche Umwelt in Sinne eines grösseren ökologischen Gesamtsystems*'.

[59]S. B. Magnusson, *Brussels Congress*, 1991.

[60]A. P. V. Rogers, Military necessity and the rule of proportionality, *Military Law and Law of War Review*, vol. 1/2, 1980, Addendum.

[61]Kalshoven, Reaffirmation, p. 130. He adds that even in the case of the higher-level planners, the 'widespread, long-term and severe' principles apply. See also, Bothe *et al.*, *New Rules*, p. 348.

[62]Bothe, *Brussels Congress,* 1991. See also the ICRC Commentary at para. 1450.

modify the weather so as to cause a drought.[63] However, causing a drought by destroying reservoirs would not be a breach of the convention. Furthermore, the convention applies to damage to another state while Protocol I applies to any environmental damage,[64] so would apply to damage in a state's own territory, on the high seas or, for example, in Antarctica.

The ENMOD Convention seems to be of an absolute nature. If the environmental consequences occur, the convention applies even if those consequences were neither intended nor foreseen.[65] On the other hand, in the case of Protocol I, the consequences must have been intended or foreseen, but the damage need not necessarily have occurred. Even if it does occur, liability does not arise if it could not have been foreseen.[66] Finally, the ENMOD Convention applies to any hostile uses of environmental modification techniques, whereas Protocol I applies only in declared wars, armed conflicts and hostile occupations of enemy territory.[67]

It is unfortunate that similar terminology is used in both the ENMOD Convention and Protocol I. The former speaks of 'widespread, long *lasting or* severe' damage while the latter refers to 'widespread, long-*term and* severe' damage. But the terms are interpreted differently in the two instruments. It is immediately apparent that the terms are disjunctive in the ENMOD Convention and conjunctive in Protocol I; in the former case, the convention applies if any of the criteria are satisfied, while in the latter, they must all be satisfied. The understanding relating to the ENMOD Convention is set out above but there is no equivalent understanding with regard to Protocol I. Witteler[68] comments that the threshold cannot be so low as to prevent normal military activity nor so high as not to prevent the most conspicuous cases of environmental damage but that it is impossible to lay down any fixed standards such as the area affected, the proportion of territory or of an environmentally sensitive area affected.

According to those who negotiated Protocol I, 'long-term' was understood to relate to a period of decades and was not intended to include damage on the scale of the battlefield damage suffered in France in the First World War or to battlefield damage incidental to conventional warfare.[69] Only the expression 'long-term' was explained in the report of the negotiating committee.[70] One can only

---

[63]Rowe, *Defence*, p. 117.
[64]ICRC, *Commentary*, para. 1452.
[65]Szasz, Study of proposals.
[66]*Ibid.*
[67]*Ibid.*, see Art. 1, para. 3 of the Protocol.
[68]Witteler, Der Kreig im Golf, p. 51.
[69]See para. 27 of the Report of Committee III, *Official Records of the Diplomatic Conference on the Reaffirmation and Development of International Humanitarian Law applicable in Armed Conflict*, Geneva (1974–77), Berne 1978, vol. XV, p. 269.
[70]Bothe *et al.*, *New Rules*, p. 346.

assume that it was considered that the other terms did not need explanation. An examination of the various commentaries on Protocol I leads one to infer that 'severe' means prejudicing the continued survival of the civilian population or involving the risk of major health problems and that 'widespread' means more than the standard of several hundred square kilometres considered in connection with the ENMOD Convention. Antoine's suggestion that widespread means *less* than the standard laid down by the ENMOD understanding seems inconsistent with the generally accepted interpretations of long-term and severe; perhaps he means *less stringent*.[71] Witteler[72] makes much of the difference in the size of states, saying that damage that would obliterate Luxembourg would hardly be noticed in Russia, but it seems to the author that this is only a factor to be taken into account since severe environmental damage is of concern to all humans. Witteler also makes the interesting point that since Art. 55 of Protocol I is not concerned with individual attacks,[73] the cumulative effect on the environment of individual attacks may amount to a breach of the article.[74]

A comparison of the ENMOD Convention with the environmental articles of Protocol I highlights the point made by Painchaud that a distinction is necessary between the deliberate manipulation of the environment for military purposes and the environmental consequences of military operations. He points out that the destruction of a chemical factory can have two objects: to weaken the industrial potential of the enemy or to create pollution that will curtail the enemy's freedom of movement. It is difficult to follow his argument that the second tactic is an attempt to manipulate the environment. It is certainly not manipulation in the sense of the ENMOD Convention.[75] He goes on to suggest that environmental weapons should be placed in two categories: first-degree weapons, which use the environment as an immediate instrument, and second-degree weapons, which make use of an intermediate instrument to act on the environment. To these might be added third-degree weapons: those that, though not intended to do so, have environmental consequences.

Other provisions of Protocol I

Indispensable objects
It is prohibited to attack agricultural areas, crops, drinking water or irrigation installations for the purpose of denying them for their sustenance value to the

---

[71] See P. Antoine, International humanitarian law and the protection of the environment in time of armed conflict, *International Review of the Red Cross*, 1992, p. 526.
[72] Witteler, Der Krieg im Golf, p. 51.
[73] He presumably means parts of an attack.
[74] Witteler, Der Krieg im Golf, p. 52.
[75] Painchaud, Environmental weapons.

adverse party unless they are used solely as sustenance for the enemy armed forces or in direct support of military action.[76] An example of crops being used in direct support of military action is where, for example, a wheat field is used as cover by advancing infantry.

It has been suggested that the right to carry out a scorched earth policy on national territory under national control as a defence against invasion is still preserved.[77] Kalshoven refers to a Netherlands Law of 1896, which allows the authorities to inundate parts of Netherlands territory to impede an invasion. Although this would damage crops, it would not be done to deny them for their sustenance value and so there would be no breach of Protocol I.[78]

Dangerous forces

One commentator observes that exceptions to the provisions of Art. 56 of Protocol I may be made in several important instances on grounds of military necessity and that the required justification is bound to be subjective, leaving the military commander much room for discretion.[79] Goldblat says that the commander is required to balance such unquantifiable notions as human suffering and the demands of war and that responsibility is passed to commanders to decide, in the heat of battle, what is lawful.

Of course, the scope of Art. 56 is limited to dams, dykes and nuclear electrical generating stations and there is no international legal instrument protecting facilities containing other dangerous materials such as chemical works[80] or oil installations.[81] Furthermore, the article is concerned with loss of human life so that the environment is only indirectly protected and it would be possible to conceive of a situation in sparsely populated territory where loss of water through the destruction of a dam could have severe ecological consequences. Regret has been expressed that environmental concerns have not been reflected in the 'grave breach' provisions of Protocol I.[82] But, of course, deliberately indiscriminate attacks and attacks on works containing dangerous forces in the knowledge that there will be excessive collateral damage are grave breaches of Protocol I[83] and may encompass environmental damage.

[76]Protocol I, Art. 54.

[77]Canada, Note on the Current Law of Armed Conflict relevant to the Environment in Conventional Conflicts, paper by the Office of the Judge Advocate General for the Ottawa Conference, referring to Protocol I, Art. 54, para. 5.

[78]Kalshoven and Zegveld, *Constraints*, p. 105.

[79]Goldblat, Legal Protection, p. 3.

[80]Szasz, Study of proposals; or factories containing toxic substances (Goldblat, in an intervention at the Ottawa Conference).

[81]Kalshoven, in an intervention at the Ottawa Conference, said that a proposal at the Diplomatic Conference to include oil installations in Art. 56 was defeated.

[82]Bothe, Ottawa Conference; Bothe, *GYIL*, p. 58.

[83]Art. 85, para. 3(b) and (c).

Particular weapons[84]

Conventional weapons

The environmental provisions examined above were not intended to cover damage ordinarily caused by conventional means and methods of warfare.[85]

Mines and other remnants of war

According to the ICRC,[86] unexploded mines are a serious and constant threat to the environment. Other commentators have referred to the UN General Assembly resolution on the remnants of war[87] and stress that such remnants may constitute a significant environmental degradation.[88] This argument is not always valid. Unexploded munitions cannot damage the environment unless they contain toxic chemicals or heavy metals.[89] They may make areas inaccessible or unusable, but this may even encourage the growth of the natural vegetation. Clearance of mines now tends to be addressed in cease-fire arrangements.[90]

The Mines Protocol of 1980 to the Weapons Convention contributes to environmental protection by prohibiting indiscriminate use of mines, restricting the use of remotely delivered mines and requiring the recording of certain minefields.[91] The Amended Mines Protocol of 1996 adds to this protection, in particular, in relation to the requirement to record mines, to fit self-deactivation devices to remotely delivered mines and in the clearance of minefields. Finally, parties to the Ottawa Convention of 1997, undertake never to use, develop,

[84]Bouvier and Gasser, Natural environment, point out that Art. 36 of Protocol I, which requires parties introducing new weapons to ensure their compatibility with the requirements of international law, also requires those parties to ensure compatibility with the environmental standards laid down by Protocol I.

[85]ICRC, *Commentary*, para. 1454; Bothe *et al.*, *New Rules*, p. 348; Doswald-Beck, The value of the 1977 protocols, p. 162.

[86]ICRC, *Commentary*, para. 1443. The ICRC take the view that problems arising from the material remnants of war are also covered by Arts. 35 and 55, *Commentary*, para. 1455. This concern is reflected in Goldblat, Legal protection, who talks about incidental damage being caused to cropland by mines and refers to the damage to the environment caused by the remnants of war, particularly the chemical component of some munitions.

[87]A/RES/37/215 of 20 December 1982.

[88]Szasz, Study of proposals, who expresses the view that the resolution remains at best hortatory and cannot even be categorized as *de lege ferenda*.

[89]See A. R. G. Price, *Possible Environmental Threats from the Current War in the Gulf*, Greenpeace, 2 February 1991, p. 14.

[90]UN Security Council Resn. 686 of 2 March 1991 called upon Iraq to provide information and assistance in identifying Iraqi mines, booby-traps and other explosives and chemical and biological weapons in Kuwait and the parts of Iraq temporarily occupied by allied forces.

[91]For a more detailed treatment of the subject, see A. P. V. Rogers, A commentary on the Protocol on Prohibitions or Restrictions on the Use of Mines etc., *Military Law and Law of War Review*, 1987; Mines, booby-Traps and other devices, 1990, *International Review of the Red Cross*; The Mines Protocol: Negotiating History, ICRC Report on a Symposium on Anti-personnel Mines, Montreux, 21–23 April 1993.

acquire, stockpile, retain or transfer anti-personnel mines, or assist, encourage or induce such activity, and undertake to destroy existing stocks.[92]

The question of explosive remnants of war is being discussed in a group of governmental experts of the states party to the Weapons Convention and it is to be hoped that a legally binding instrument dealing with the post-conflict clearance of unexploded ordnance and warnings to civilians will be negotiated as a result. The first meeting of the experts took place in March 2003.

Nuclear weapons

The use of nuclear weapons may have environmental consequences.[93] However, negotiations at the CDDH were based on an ICRC draft, which specifically stated that it was not intended to deal with the problem of nuclear weapons.[94] It was only on this basis that the nuclear powers were prepared to enter into negotiations. The United Kingdom and the United States made declaratory statements on signature that the rules established by Protocol I are not intended to have any effect on, and do not regulate or prohibit, the use of nuclear weapons. Statements to the same effect were made on ratification by Belgium, Canada, Italy, the Netherlands, Germany, Spain, the United Kingdom and, possibly, Ireland.[95] The effect is that environmental damage caused by nuclear weapons is not covered by Protocol I at all.[96]

In its advisory opinion of 1996, the International Court of Justice, having concluded that there was in international law no specific authorization or prohibition of the use of nuclear weapons, considered that any such use should be compatible with the requirements of the law of armed conflict, expressed some

---

[92]Convention on the Prohibition of the Use, Stockpiling, Production and Transfer of Anti-Personnel Mines and on Their Destruction, 36 ILM (1997) 1507, Art. 1.

[93]See, e.g., Rowe, *Defence*, p. 117; Rauch, *The Protocols*, p. 143. For the long-term effects of plutonium, see V. S. Sidel, The impact of military preparedness and militarism, in Austin and Bruch, *Environmental Consequences*, at pp. 435–7.

[94]The ICRC, in the introduction to their June 1973 version of the Draft Additional Protocols to the Geneva Conventions of August 12, 1949, stated: 'Problems relating to atomic, bacteriological and chemical warfare are subjects of international agreements or negotiations by governments, and in submitting these draft Additional Protocols the ICRC does not intend to broach those problems. It should be borne in mind that the Red Cross as a whole, at several International Red Cross Conferences, has clearly made known its condemnation of weapons of mass destruction and has urged governments to reach agreements for banning their use.'

[95]See Roberts and Guelff, *Documents*, pp. 499–512. The Irish statement is that 'nuclear weapons, even if not directly governed by Additional Protocol I, remain subject to the existing rules of international law'.

[96]Kalshoven and Zegveld, *Constraints*, p. 111, said that the drafting history of Protocol I shows that any new rules embodied in the Protocol were not written with a view to the potential use of nuclear weapons and that Arts. 35 para. 3 and 55 are obvious examples of new rules. Those who argue that Protocol I applies to nuclear weapons, e.g. Rauch, *The Protocols*, p. 71, and Witteler, Der Krieg im Golf, p. 50, seem to ignore the essentially contractual nature of the basis of the relationship between states party.

scepticism as to whether that could be achieved[97] and left open the question of whether their use might be justified in 'an extreme circumstance of self-defence, in which the very survival of a State would be at stake'.[98] On the specific issue of environmental damage, the court found that: 'While the existing international law relating to the protection and safeguarding of the environment does not specifically prohibit the use of nuclear weapons, it indicates important environmental factors that are properly to be taken into account in the context of the implementation of the principles and rules of law applicable in armed conflict.'[99] States are still being encouraged by the international community to reach agreement 'on the elimination and complete destruction of such weapons'.[100]

Incendiary weapons

It is prohibited to make forests or other kinds of plant cover the object of attack by incendiary weapons unless they are used to cover, conceal or camouflage combatants or other military objectives or are themselves military objectives.[101]

Chemical and biological weapons

These are weapons that could have environmental effects and are, subject to the 'no first use' reservations with regard to chemical weapons, prohibited.[102] The precise definition of a chemical weapon in customary law is somewhat obscure. Rowe has suggested that chemical herbicides can be brought within the regime of the 1925 Geneva Gas Protocol, particularly in the light of the interpretation given it by the United Nations General Assembly in 1969.[103] The operative part of the resolution declares as contrary to international law, in particular the Gas Protocol, the use in international armed conflicts of 'any chemical agents of warfare – chemical substances, whether gaseous, liquid or solid – which might be employed because of their direct toxic effects on man, animals or plants'. It

---

[97]However, it did not express a view on the possible legitimacy of use of tactical nuclear weapons nor was it prepared to say that nuclear weapons were by their nature illegal by virtue of the principle of humanity, see 110 ILR 1, at p. 212.

[98]*Ibid.*, at p. 216.

[99]*Ibid.*, at p. 193.

[100]Principle 26 of the Declaration of the UN Stockholm Conference of 1972. Green, The Environment, points out that the Stockholm conference did not deal with harm to the environment caused by conventional weapons or by the remnants of war and that the Declaration is not a legally binding document.

[101]Art. 4, para. 4, of Protocol III to the Weapons Convention of 1980. Kalshoven, Reaffirmation, p. 157, says that the exceptions deprive the paragraph of virtually every practical significance.

[102]Geneva Gas Protocol of 1925 and Bacteriological Weapons Convention of 1972. According to Goldblat, Legal Protection, p. 5, the Gas Protocol also protects plants. In so far as the Gas Protocol bans any use of chemical and bacteriological weapons, this must be true.

[103]Rowe, *Defence*, p. 117. The resolution is No. 2603 A(XXIV) of 16 December 1969.

will be noted that the United Kingdom abstained in the voting, so, as a 'soft law' instrument, its relevance for the UK is limited. In any event, General Assembly resolutions are not law, nor is the Assembly a court or legal body having power to interpret the law. A UN resolution could, depending on the voting pattern, be *some* evidence of the views of the international community. Possession of biological and chemical weapons is, in any event, prohibited by the Biological Weapons Convention of 1972 and the Chemical Weapons Convention of 1993. The latter, which also prohibits use, now contains, for the first time, a definition of chemical weapons. The Rome Statute of the International Criminal Court of 1998 makes the employment of 'asphyxiating, poisonous or other gases, and all analogous liquids, materials and devices', language taken from the 1925 Gas Protocol, a war crime.

Szasz is doubtful whether chemical and bacteriological weapons should be included in any study of the environmental effects of war since chemical weapons only have short-term effects in a given area and that only in the event that bacteriological weapons create a persistent epidemic could their effect be categorized as environmental.[104] Such might be the case if, for example, land that had been used for biological experiments were declared unfit for human habitation or agriculture for a lengthy period.

Fuel-air explosive

Apparently, this was used in the Gulf war of 1991 for the clearance of minefields,[105] which is perfectly legitimate. A new form of fuel-air explosive was used against al-Qa'ida and Taliban targets near Gardez, Afghanistan, on 2 March 2002. This produces a long-duration, high-temperature pulse that can kill people and damage vehicles.[106] The author has no information about the environmental effects of such weapons.

Depleted uranium

Depleted uranium is used in the penetrating rods of armour-piercing shells because of a penetrative capability that is not matched by any of the alternatives.[107] It does emit alpha and beta particles and gamma rays and, being a heavy metal, is a source of chemical toxicity. However, the skin and clothing provide protection from the particles, the amount of gamma radiation is very low and it is

---

[104] Szasz, Study of proposals.

[105] Hansard (Commons), 2 May 1991 at col. 484 and 17 June 1991 at col. 16.

[106] A. H. Cordesman, *The Lessons of Afghanistan*, Washington, CSIS Press, 2002, p. 48.

[107] S. Osborne, Faculty of Engineering and Applied Science, University of Southampton, in a letter to *The Independent* published on 25 April 2003.

unlikely that sufficient quantities could be taken into the body to cause toxicity problems. Health risks are considered by United States Department of Defence experts to be negligible and posed only by the inhalation or ingestion of large amount of particles after a fire or explosion or, possibly, by fragments being lodged in the body.[108] The United Nations Environment Programme's Post-Conflict Assessment Unit has carried out three assessments of the impact of depleted uranium in the Balkans, most recently, in Bosnia–Hercegovina, in respect of weapons used in 1994–95. The most recent report is of interest because it is concerned with the longer-term effects of depleted uranium weapons. The unit found that contamination levels are very low and do not present immediate radioactive or toxic risk for the environment or human health. Ground contamination occurs at low levels within a radius of one to two metres from penetrator impact points. Penetrators have corroded by 25 per cent in seven years and will corrode completely in twenty-five to thirty years after impact. Corroding depleted uranium can penetrate the soil and groundwater. Air contamination can be caused by the suspension of depleted uranium particles from penetrators or contamination points due to wind or human actions. The unit recommends the collection and proper disposal of penetrators, covering contaminated points with asphalt or clean soil, regularly monitoring groundwater and using alternative water sources.[109] It seems, therefore, that the severity of depleted uranium contamination does not reach the threshold laid down in Protocol I.

Effect on neutral states

Article 1 of the Hague Neutrality Convention of 1907 provides that the territory of neutral powers is inviolable. Bothe considers that this is sufficiently wide to cover environmental damage, points out that during the Second World War compensation was paid to Switzerland for collateral damage caused on Swiss territory from attacks on targets in neighbouring Germany and concludes that the normal peacetime rules relating to transfrontier pollution apply.[110]

[108] See www.gulflink.osd.mil/faq_17apr.htm.

[109] See the Unit's press release on http://postconflict.unep.ch/actbihdu.htm, where the full report can also be found.

[110] Bothe, Ottawa Conference. See also, Bothe, *GYIL*, pp. 59–60; and Bouvier, Natural environment, p. 568. Some authors, e.g., G. Plant, Environmental damage and the law of war, in H. Fox and M. A. Meyer (eds.), *Effecting Compliance*, British Institute of International and Comparative Law, 1993, p. 163, refer in this connection to principle 21 of the 1972 Stockholm Declaration (confirmed in UN General Assembly Resn. 2996) that each state has a responsibility to ensure that activities under its jurisdiction or control do not cause damage to the environment of other states or areas beyond national jurisdiction. But this is only a 'soft law' instrument. Green, Ottawa Conference, said it could be ignored and Kalshoven, Reaffirmation, said it had been incorporated, so far as possible, in Protocol I, Arts. 35 and 55.

Iraq

Oil pollution

Environmental concerns certainly affected allied military planning in the Gulf war of 1991. It is reported that the allies decided not to attack four Iraqi super-tankers inside the Gulf that were contravening United Nations Security Council resolution 665 because of the environmental consequences of so doing.[111] This was being more environmentally conscious than the law requires, since there is nothing in international law to prevent a party to an armed conflict attacking and sinking enemy supertankers or nuclear submarines.[112]

In January 1991 Iraq opened the oil valves of the Sea Island Terminal in Kuwait and the Mina al-Bakr terminal in Iraq causing massive oil spills into the Persian Gulf,[113] and perhaps even more on land in Kuwait, and, in February 1991, Iraq sabotaged hundreds[114] of Kuwaiti oil wells, setting over 500 on fire, causing huge daily emissions of sulphur dioxide, nitrous oxide and carbon dioxide.[115] So much smoke resulted that Kuwait City was in darkness for two days out of every three. The oil fires deposited soot on five-eighths of Kuwait. It was estimated that the environmental damage to Kuwait would take ten to twenty years to repair. The smoke plume extended over Iran, Afghanistan, Pakistan and India, black rain fell 600 miles away in Turkey and blackened snow fell in the Himalayas.[116] The large amounts of sulphur caused rain to be highly acidic and the smoke reduced daytime temperatures but also reduced night-time cooling. It was estimated that the main fall-out effects would be within 2,000 km.[117] UNESCO described the oil fires as the largest environmental catastrophe since Chernobyl.[118]

[111]G. van Hegelsom, *Brussels Congress*, 1991.

[112]H. P. Gasser, Some legal issues concerning ratification of the 1977 Geneva protocols, in M. A. Meyer (ed.), *Armed Conflict and the New Law*, British Institute of International and Comparative Law, 1989, pp. 91–2. For the contrary view, see Rauch, *The Protocols*, pp. 143–51, who also deals with offshore oil installations at pp. 151–3.

[113]Estimates seem to vary. The DOD Report (United States, *Conduct of the Persian Gulf War*, Department of Defence final report to Congress, April 1992), p. 624, mentions 7 to 9 million barrels; the Greenpeace report mentions 11 million barrels on pp. 1 and 11 and 6 to 8 million barrels on p. 3 (Price, *Environmental Threats*); and J. Guthrie, Ottawa Conference, 1991, spoke of 5 to 6 million barrels of which Saudi Arabia recovered about 1 million and 70 per cent of which evaporated.

[114]The DOD Report, p. 624, mentions 590 damaged or destroyed well heads of which 508 were set on fire and eighty two damaged to allow oil to flow freely.

[115]One estimate was of 40,000, 3,000 and 500,000 tonnes respectively each day (Robinson, Draft Articles). The Parliamentary Under Secretary of State for the Environment, T. Baldry MP, mentioned a Kuwaiti estimate of a rate of burn of 5 million to 6 million barrels a day, which, he said, would be 'more severe and widespread' than had previously been feared, Hansard (Commons), 15 March 1991, col. 1387.

[116]Robinson, Draft Articles, who gives a very graphic account of the pollution effects; and Guthrie, Ottawa Conference.

[117]Study by the Parliamentary Office of Science and Technology, quoted in Hansard (Commons), 15 March 1991, col. 1388.

[118]Paper entitled Basis and objectives of the meeting of experts on the use of the environment as a tool of conventional warfare, presented by B. Mawhinney, Ottawa Conference.

While predictions of a 'nuclear winter' appear to have been exaggerated, there seems little doubt that the atmosphere in the region was dangerously polluted, involving damage to agriculture and risks to the health of the local population, particularly in increased lung cancer.[119] It seems that if the ENMOD Convention applied, it would cover the damage done to the atmosphere.[120] Although the oil spillage was the world's largest, a combination of the Gulf's high salinity and the hot sun in the region caused the bulk of the oil to evaporate,[121] so the actual damage may not have been so severe or long-term as may first have been feared.[122] However, Iraq is not a party to the convention, though as a signatory it is obliged to refrain from acts that would defeat the object and purpose of the convention,[123] It is doubtful whether the breach by one party of one provision of many in a convention could be said to defeat its object and purpose, and it is arguable, in any event, whether the techniques adopted were those envisaged by the convention.[124]

There was speculation that Iraq had done all this to impede naval and military operations by the allied forces. However, some commentators consider that Iraq's action in respect of the Kuwaiti oil wells was an act of revenge rather than an act dictated by military necessity,[125] and done systematically rather than inadvertently and was wholly out of proportion to any military gain.[126] Others suggested that it was deliberately done to contaminate Saudi Arabian desalination plants,[127] or to deny the allies the fruits of victory.[128]

The Iraqi actions seem to have violated Art. 23(g) of the Hague Regulations, which prohibits the destruction of enemy property unless imperatively demanded by the necessities of war. A similar provision, applicable in occupied territory,

---

[119]Painchaud, Environmental weapons. As to the potential environmental problems in the Gulf, see Price, Environmental threats. E. Nicholson MP stated that 'the incomplete combustion of oil-producing carcinogens may cause cancer', Hansard (Commons), 15 March 1991, col. 1346.

[120]Goldblat, Legal protection, p. 4.

[121]*The Times*, 8 May 1991; Guthrie, Ottawa Conference.

[122]The ENMOD Convention did not apply in the Gulf war. If it had, one would still have had to look at the damage actually done.

[123]Vienna Convention on the Law of Treaties 1969, Art. 18.

[124]Goldblat, in an intervention at the Ottawa Conference, said that setting oil on fire was analogous to releasing volcanic energy through an explosion. However, that still does not amount to manipulation of natural processes as envisaged by Art. II of the ENMOD Convention.

[125]G. Plant, Elements of a new convention on the protection of the environment in time of armed conflict, Ottawa Conference; Painchaud, Environmental weapons. Goldblat, Legal protection, points out that, even if Protocol I had applied in the Gulf war, it would not have helped Iraq, since Arts. 35 and 55 allow no exception on grounds of military necessity, such as to repel a marine invasion. Kalshoven, in an intervention at the Ottawa Conference, described Iraq's actions as wanton destruction of property. His views seemed to be shared by many delegates except, perhaps, Green who pointed out the defences available to Iraq, and Sur who emphasized that the conference was not a court and had no access to the evidence.

[126]Robinson, Draft Articles, who described what happened as the largest single human-induced air and oil pollution event.

[127]J. Arnold MP, Hansard (Commons), 15 March 1991, col. 1365.

[128]Roberts, Environment, p. 147.

appears in Art. 53 of the Civilian Convention and the damage in Kuwait would certainly appear to fall into the category of 'extensive' so as to amount to a grave breach of that convention.[129]

It has been suggested[130] that, even in the case of a charge based on Art. 23(g) of the Hague Regulations or Art. 53 of the Civilian Convention, a plea of military necessity might have been based on the need to prevent or hamper an allied advance into Kuwait, as in the case of General Rendulic. However, had it been desired to produce smoke as an obscurant, that could have been done without completely destroying oil wells.[131] Alternatively, Iraq could argue that the oil wells were legitimate military objectives because it was essential to deny their use to enemy mechanized forces.[132] Any tribunal would, therefore, have to look at the reasons for the destruction of the oil wells and the oil spillages to ascertain whether it was done to deny use of installations or areas to the enemy or to blind 'spy' satellites or whether it was simply an act of wanton destruction or of revenge against Kuwait and the allies.[133] In examining Iraq's motives they would, no doubt, take account of the fact that before hostilities started Saddam Hussein was threatening to cause environmental damage.[134] That would indicate environmental terrorism rather than a resort to military necessity. A tribunal would also have to consider the question of proportionality. That would include an examination of the methods used to determine whether the military aim could have been achieved in less devastating ways.

Also to be considered is the principle that a state is under a duty to pay compensation for damage caused by violations of the law of armed conflict.[135] This principle was applied in the case of Iraq following the Gulf conflict by Security Council Resolution 687,[136] which confirms Iraq's liability to pay compensation for damage caused as a result of the invasion and occupation of Kuwait, including environmental damage and the depletion of natural resources.

---

[129]Art. 147.

[130]Goldblat, Legal protection, p. 4.

[131]For example, by opening the valves and setting light to them (W. H. Parks in an intervention at the Ottawa Conference).

[132]Green, Environment. As O. Bring pointed out in an intervention at the Ottawa Conference, however, Iraq would have to show that it was militarily necessary to attack the oil installations.

[133]F. J. Hampson, Liability for war crimes, in Rowe (ed.), *Gulf War*, p. 254. The DOD Report, p. 626, confirms that oil spillages and smoke did not hamper allied operations at all.

[134]See, e.g., *The Independent*, 24 September 1990.

[135]Hague Convention IV of 1907 concerning the laws and customs of war on land, Art. 3. The convention is considered to reflect customary international law. Szasz, Study of proposals, refers in this connection to the work of the International Law Commission in codifying the responsibility of states for acts prohibited by international law, including a provision on responsibility for massive pollution of the atmosphere or the sea. However, damage caused in the course of military activities is excluded from the commission's considerations.

[136]S/RES/687(1991) of 3 April 1991, para. 16. See also H. Fox, Reparations and state responsibility, in Rowe (ed.), *Gulf War*, p. 261. The failure of the Security Council to spell out precisely which legal obligations Iraq had violated is criticized by C. D. Stone, The environment in wartime: an overview, in Austin and Bruch, *Environmental Consequences*, pp. 27–30.

'Environmental damage' would include the costs of cleaning up the damage and 'depletion of natural resources' would include compensation for oil spilt or burnt off. The Security Council purported to be acting under chapter VII of the UN Charter (action with respect to threats to the peace, breaches of the peace, and acts of aggression), so they were acting under the *jus ad bellum* rather than under the Hague principles. At all events, Resolution 687 was accepted by Iraq as a condition of the cease-fire.[137]

The allied response to Iraq's actions was prompt. On 24 January 1991 Iraq started releasing oil into the Gulf. The United States Department of Defence immediately established an oil spill taskforce and on 27 January US air strikes against oil manifolds upstream of the al-Ahmadi terminal stopped the flow of oil into the Gulf. On the same day, US teams of experts were sent to Saudi Arabia to provide technical assistance and booms were supplied.[138] The United Kingdom also provided anti-pollution equipment, which was flown to the Gulf on 28–30 January.[139] These actions helped local efforts to limit the damage and went beyond the requirements of Protocol I, to which the United States and United Kingdom were not even parties. In fact there is no obligation of the law of armed conflict to limit environmental damage caused by the enemy's actions.[140] Roberts is, nevertheless critical of what he perceives as the allied lack of effective response to Iraq's environmental threats.[141] Apart from clearer statements that such acts are unlawful, which Roberts acknowledges might have achieved nothing, it is difficult to see what else might have been done, short of reprisal action which might have made things even worse.

It is of interest to speculate whether, had Iraq been a party to Protocol I[142] as well as Kuwait, the environmental damage would have fallen within the 'widespread, long-term and severe' criteria of Arts. 35 and 55. It seems likely that the widespread and severe tests would be satisfied, but what of long-term?[143] That

---

[137]Fox, Reparations, p. 264.

[138]*The Conduct of the Persian Gulf Campaign*, US Department of Defence Interim Report to Congress, July 1991 (DOD Interim Report).

[139]Hansard (Commons), 15 March 1991, col. 1334.

[140]Except, possibly, Art. 58(c) of Protocol I, which refers to precautions to protect civilians from the dangers resulting from military operations, see Chapter 5.

[141]Roberts, Environment, p. 148.

[142]The ENMOD Convention did not apply as Iraq was not a party. Even if it had, it is extremely doubtful whether Iraq's actions would have violated the convention, as it was not a deliberate manipulation of the natural processes. For the opposing arguments, see Roberts, Environment, p. 138 and Plant, Environmental damage, at p. 168.

[143]Rauch, *The Protocols*, p. 147, studies the *Amoco Cadiz* disaster, which caused an oil slick 100 km long and 10 km wide, deposited 64,000 metric tons of oil ashore and polluted 200–300 km of coastline. He also examines the case of the leaking oil well in the Nowruz field off the coast of Iran in 1983 when an estimated 5,000 barrels of oil a day leaked into the Persian Gulf. He concludes that the damage in both cases was 'widespread' within the meaning of Protocol I, reaches no conclusion as to the 'long-term and severe' criteria, but considers that the element of objective expectation suffices to render such methods and means of warfare unlawful.

test does not seem to be satisfied.[144] The report, prepared before the event, by the Meteorological Office estimated that the only possible long-term effect would be the impact of carbon dioxide on global warming and that this would be almost negligible;[145] that the effect on the Asian monsoon would be within normal annual fluctuations.[146] McCoubrey, however, refers to the increased incidence of respiratory disease due to ozone-laden smog caused by the oil fires.[147]

Allied planners, on the other hand, were very concerned to reduce the environmental impact of their attacks. For example, they attacked oil refineries producing petrol that had immediate military use but avoided attacks on Iraq's long-term oil production capability.[148]

Roberts tends to damn with faint praise the allied efforts to reduce environmental damage,[149] saying that their actions were 'less wanton and gratuitous than the Iraqi oil crimes in Kuwait, and that some, but only some, significant efforts were made to avoid or reduce certain kinds of environmental damage'. He is obviously referring to all kinds of damage caused by the allied bombing, not just damage to the natural environment, but it is not clear what evidence he relies on for his stance. Plant disagrees with Roberts in characterizing the damage to Iraqi civil and industrial infrastructure as an 'environmental' question.[150]

Roberts's statement is surprising given the lengths that the allies went to in identifying targets and selecting appropriate methods and means of attack.[151] In the words of Aldrich,[152] 'there had probably never previously been in the Twentieth Century a conflict in which attacks were made with the accuracy of those by the Coalition forces'.

During the Iraq war of 2003, the coalition planners were concerned to prevent the burning of Iraqi oil wells, so one of the early tasks of ground troops was to secure the oil installations and protect them from sabotage. In this they were largely successful.[153] While there may have been a degree of self-interest in this

---

[144]See Plant, Environmental damage, p. 169. Even Witteler, Der Krieg im Golf, p. 52, who argues for a more restrictive interpretation of these terms, considers that there would not have been a breach of Art. 55. Saalfeld, Umweltschutz, p. 31, comes to the same conclusion and complains that the provisions of Protocol I do not do enough to protect the environment. See also A. K. Biswas, Scientific assessment of long-term environmental consequences, in Austin and Bruch, *Environmental Consequences*, pp. 312–14.

[145]Quoted by T. Dayell MP, Hansard (Commons), 15 March 1991, col. 1337.

[146]Quoted by R. G. Hughes MP, Hansard (Commons), 15 March 1991, col. 1374.

[147]McCoubrey and White, *International Law*, p. 236.

[148]DOD Report, p. 97.

[149]Roberts, Environment, p. 141.

[150]Plant, Environmental damage, p. 161.

[151]In his review of the first edition of this book, Roberts commented that: (a) this air campaign was indeed unusually, even admirably, discriminate; and (b) he discussed the damage caused by the bombing, and the literature about it, more fully in an article published in *International Security*, winter 1993/94 issue.

[152]In a letter dated 6 April 1993 to the author.

[153]Press reports indicated that half a dozen well heads were set on fire by Iraqi troops or workers, and they were not booby-trapped: see T. Judd, 'I thought wells would have been rigged to go off', *The Independent*, 24 March 2003.

action, it certainly prevented a recurrence of the environmental damage caused by the burning of the Kuwaiti oil wells in 1991.

Nuclear facilities

In attacking Iraqi nuclear chemical and nuclear facilities in 1991, precautions were taken to prevent the escape of dangerous forces.[154] It is of interest to note that the United States air force attacks on the Iraqi nuclear power stations did not create a risk of radioactive contamination.[155]

Goldblat[156] criticizes the bombing on the grounds that a military necessity could not be shown. He says that Iraq's reactors were not large enough to produce the quantities of plutonium needed for nuclear weapons and they were not used in 'regular, significant and direct support of military operations'.[157] But there were intelligence reports that Iraq was developing nuclear weapons[158] and, if so, that would certainly have justified the attacks. Evidence has since emerged, through the visits of United Nations inspectors, that Iraq was doing so.[159] Attacks on power stations[160] are justified if they are military objectives. The only difference in the case of nuclear power stations is the risk of radioactive contamination. If a power station can be attacked in such a way that there is no such risk, the attack is lawful. Even if radioactive material escapes, it would then be a question of proportionality:[161] how severe the pollution caused and its effects on the civilian population and the environment.

Diverting rivers

The *Manual of Military Law* makes the bold statement, without quoting any authority, that there is no rule 'to prevent measures being taken to dry up springs and to divert rivers and aqueducts'.[162]

Following the invasion of Kuwait by Iraqi forces in August 1990, it was at first estimated that an attack to free Kuwait would cost in excess of 100,000

---

[154]Mr Lennox-Boyd in a written parliamentary answer, Hansard (Commons), 26 June 1991, col. 487.

[155]Painchaud, Environmental Weapons, quoting *Le Devoir*, 1991. See also the evidence of the UK Secretary of State in *Preliminary Lessons of Operation Granby*, House of Commons Defence Committee 10th Report, HMSO, 1991, p. 11.

[156]Goldblat, Legal protection, p. 2.

[157]These words are taken from Geneva Protocol I of 1977, Art. 56, which did not apply in the Gulf conflict.

[158]DOD Report, p. 97.

[159]See, e.g., Douglas Hurd, the UK Foreign Secretary, in *The Times*, 2 August 1991.

[160]According to Gasser, the installations attacked in Iraq were research installations, not power stations: H-P. Gasser, *Humanitäres Völkerrecht Informationsschriften*, January–July 1991, p. 32.

[161]This is recognized in Protocol I, Art. 56, para. 1, which speaks of 'consequent *severe* losses among the civilian population'.

[162]At p. 42.

casualties. Newspaper reports indicated that some experts had suggested an alternative –[163] turning off Iraq's water supply – since, with the completion of the Ataturk dam in Turkey in January 1991, 328 of the 400 cubic metres of water discharged every second by the rivers Tigris and Euphrates could have been siphoned off before it reached Iraq.[164] The question arises whether this would have been lawful.

Applying the Manual, the answer would be in the affirmative. But would the answer still be the same today? Had the ENMOD Convention, to which the United States and United Kingdom are parties, applied, it might have been violated, bearing in mind Iraq's dependence on the two rivers for its water supply, though there would be an argument about whether the threshold of Art. II of the Convention had been crossed.[165] But the convention did not apply because Iraq was not a party.[166] Had Protocol I applied to the Gulf war, it is questionable whether there would have been a violation of Arts. 35 and 55, given the regenerative capacity of the desert, but there may well have been a breach of Art. 54 since it could hardly be argued that the action had not been intended to starve the civilian population.

Painchaud[167] speculates about the reasons why the allies did not make use of this method of warfare: did they fear chemical or bacteriological retaliation, did they hold back for legal reasons, was Turkey opposed,[168] were the allies afraid of public opinion? He thinks the answer was a combination of these factors. It could have been kept in reserve for possible reprisal purposes had Iraq used chemical or bacteriological warfare, but it was confirmed in Parliament that the allies never envisaged the use of environmental techniques.[169]

Depleted uranium

It can be assumed that there will be similar findings in respect of the use of depleted uranium weapons in the Iraq war of 2003 to those in the case of the Balkans. The United Kingdom authorities are reported to have helped in the removal of depleted uranium in Kosovo and to have offered, on moral rather than legal grounds, to do the same in Iraq, by providing funds and making available records of where the ammunition had been used.[170]

[163]*Evening Standard*, 15 November 1990.

[164]Painchaud, Environmental weapons, considers that if Iraq's water supply had been cut off in this way, Iraq would have been able to sustain its population and armed forces for only a few days.

[165]South Korea, on accession to the convention, made a statement that it included 'any technique for deliberately changing the natural state of rivers' (Roberts and Guelff, *Documents*, p. 417).

[166]DOD Report, p. 606.

[167]Painchaud, Environmental weapons.

[168]Pazarci, in an intervention at the Ottawa Conference, said that Turkey would not use its waterways as a weapon of war.

[169]Lennox-Boyd, Hansard (Commons), 26 June 1991, col. 487. It was agreed between the allies in advance that water supplies would not be attacked: see Defence Committee Report, p. 10.

[170]A. Kirby, UK to aid Iraq DU removal, BBC news online, 23 April 2003.

Evaluation

Various experts have examined the current state of the law and the environmental effects of recent conflicts to conclude that the environmental consequences of, for example, the use of 'agent orange' in Vietnam, the Kuwait oil fires in the Gulf war of 1991 or the NATO attack on the Pancevo oil refinery during the Kosovo conflict of 1999, though serious enough, did not perhaps reach the high prohibitive thresholds that have been laid down in the treaties because of the reluctance of states to accept standards that they might find difficult to apply in wartime. The result is that states do not know what is expected of them, much being left to the good sense of decision-makers.

Conclusions

The following conclusions may be reached about the law as it currently stands:

1 Natural processes must not be deliberately manipulated for hostile purposes if that would have widespread, long-lasting or severe effects.
2 The environment as such may not be attacked.
3 In the conduct of military operations, care must be taken to spare the environment.
4 Damage may not be inflicted unless it is militarily necessary.
5 When attacking a military objective, methods or means should be chosen which, commensurate with military success, cause the least environmental damage.
6 Any environmental damage caused must be proportionate to the military objective to be attained.
7 It is prohibited to employ methods or means of warfare that are intended, or may be expected, to cause widespread, long-term and severe damage to the environment and thereby prejudice the health or survival of the population.

In addition, there are other rules that protect the environment, for example the protection of forests from incendiary attack, the rules on dangerous forces and the protection of objects that are indispensable to the survival of the civilian population.[171]

The threshold for the applicability of the environmental provisions in warfare is very high. It is unlikely that military commanders would be involved in environmental manipulation. As for Protocol I, even the severe pollution caused in the Gulf war of 1991 does not seem to have fallen within the widespread, long-term and severe criterion.

---

[171] A complete list appears in the ICRC Report, *Protection of the Environment in Time of Armed Conflict* (Report for the Forty-eighth Session of the UN General Assembly), ICRC, 1993.

The future

There is no doubt that there has been greater interest in recent years in environmental protection and that political leaders ignore this interest at their peril.[172] Modern developments have had both negative and positive effects. Precision weapons can be used to strike targets with a reduced risk of environmental damage; but on the other hand, the increase in the number of nuclear power stations, chemical facilities and dams has increased the risk of attacks that might have environmental consequences. Some commentators consider that customary law now requires the avoidance of unnecessary damage to the environment.[173] While that formulation may be disputed, it is clear that, under the customary law rule of proportionality, military commanders must take into account the consequences for the civilian population when planning attacks and that would include the effect on the population of environmental damage.[174]

There have been calls for what might be described as a fifth Geneva Convention, or Ecocide Convention,[175] to protect the environment, with some peacetime principles,[176] such as the precautionary principle,[177] responsibility for damage caused to the environment outside the limits of national jurisdiction, impact assessments,[178] and the duty to warn of transboundary escapes, being applied in wartime and a 'protecting power' for the environment modelled on the ICRC[179] and protective emblems being established.[180] Some consider that breaches of Arts. 35 and 55 of Protocol I should be grave breaches.[181] One useful suggestion is that environmentally sensitive areas should be declared non-defended

[172] As Painchaud, Environmental weapons, puts it, 'the use of environmental weapons is proving to be more and more costly from a political point of view'.

[173] B. Mawhinney's conclusions at the Ottawa Conference.

[174] Parks, in an intervention at the Ottawa Conference, said that in planning the ground and air campaign to liberate Kuwait, great care was taken to protect the environment and that any attack on the environment is a two-edged sword. See also, Bothe, *GYIL*, p. 58.

[175] R. Falk, The environmental law of war: an introduction, in G. Plant (ed.), *Environmental Protection and the Law of War*, Belhaven, 1992, at p. 94.

[176] The author shares the opinion of Green, The Environment, that the law of war is *lex specialis* and, to the extent to which it conflicts with the *lex generalis*, it prevails. Others like Kiss expressed the view at the Ottawa Conference, that the peacetime rules for the protection of the environment, like those for the protection of human rights (subject to derogations), are not suspended in wartime.

[177] See Bothe, *GYIL*; ICRC Report to UN General Assembly, p. 21.

[178] See the authorities quoted by Szasz, Study of proposals. In the case of the European Union, the requirement for impact assessments is laid down in Council Directive 85/337: see P. Sands and D. Alexander, Assessing the impact, *New Law Journal*, 1 November 1991, p. 1487.

[179] Bothe, *GYIL*, p. 62, considers that the ICRC could take the lead by clearing the way for organizations expert in dealing with pollution problems to combat the environmental hazards occurring as a consequence of military activity.

[180] G. Plant, Elements. S. Hughes, MP, made a similar point in Parliament, Hansard (Commons), 15 March 1991, col. 1357. Szasz, Study of proposals, considers that such a body could have norm-making, monitoring and dispute-resolving functions.

[181] ICRC Report to UN General Assembly, p. 21.

localities.[182] This might work in respect of small areas or those containing no objects of military significance. In the case, for example, of areas containing offshore oil installations, however, the coastal state might be reluctant to declare them undefended. Falk complains that existing law is deficient in being based on customary principles, sweeping generalizations and vaguely defined terms, with too much subjectivity and loopholes and a lack of means of implementation.[183] There have also been calls for objective criteria for assessing what amounts to 'widespread, long-term and severe damage' and a suggestion that the ICRC might evaluate the matter.[184] There is growing concern in the world that states should be made responsible for removing the remnants of war and clearing up environmental damage caused by war. It is for consideration whether, when troops are lent to another country to assist in its defence, responsibility for dealing with remnants of war and environmental damage should be dealt with in the treaty or memorandum of understanding governing the deployment of troops. Fleck calls for an updating of standards for the legal protection of the environment in line with the dictates of public conscience, and an examination of the rules on criminal responsibility, internal armed conflicts and neutrality.[185] Plant demands a lowering of the threshold of environmental harm in Protocol I, an extension of Art. 56 of Protocol I to severe damage to the natural environment, an extension of the Weapons Convention to fuel-air explosives, the special protection of environmentally sensitive areas and the institution of a Green Cross type of organization.[186] Some experts make suggestions about measures for the better protection of the environment: specially protected areas, models for better verification, liability determination, damage assessment, remedial and criminal enforcement.

Green[187] doubts the utility of negotiating yet another treaty and suggests that the International Law Commission might be charged by the United Nations Security Council with drafting principles of customary law for the protection of the environment which could be made binding by a resolution of the Council.

Anyway, as noted above, there is already a respectable body of treaty law which, whether directly or indirectly, protects the environment. It may be that energy would be better directed in encouraging states to adhere to those

[182]Goldblat, Legal protection, p. 6; Bouvier, Protection, p. 577; Antoine, Environment, p. 532. See Protocol I, Arts. 59 and 60. The differences between the two articles are briefly explained in Chapter 5.

[183]Falk, Environmental law of war, p. 93. His criticisms are shared by Roberts, Environment, p. 125.

[184]M. Saalfeld and H. P. Gasser, *Brussels Congress*, 1991; Bothe, *GYIL*, p. 58. Indeed, the ICRC studied these matters at meetings of experts in 1992 and 1993: see ICRC Report to UN General Assembly.

[185]Fleck, Environment, pp. 148–9.

[186]Plant, Environmental damage, pp. 172–4.

[187]Green, The environment.

instruments,[188] and reflecting them, and any 'soft law' instruments to which they had subscribed, in national law and military manuals,[189] rather than in negotiating new, and in some cases somewhat fanciful, texts.

[188]This was the feeling of many delegates to the Ottawa Conference, and at the London Conference entitled a 'Fifth Geneva Convention on the Protection of the Environment in Time of Armed Conflict', June 1991 (see the rapporteur's executive summary), was the thrust of the resolution of the Sixth Committee of the UN General Assembly (A/C.6/47/L.2/Rev.1), and seems to be the view of Roberts, Environment, p. 152; Fleck, Environment, p. 152; A. Bouvier, Recent studies on the environment in time of armed conflict, 1992, *International Review of the Red Cross*, p. 577; the ICRC, Report to UN General Assembly, p. 24; and McCoubrey, see McCoubrey and White, *International Law*, p. 237.

[189]Fleck refers to the steps taken in this regard in the German manual, *Humanitäres Völkerrecht in bewaffneten Konflikten, Handbuch*, Bundesministerium der Verteidigung, 1992: Fleck, Environment, p. 154.

8

Command responsibility

Commanders are responsible for the orders they give and so if the orders are unlawful they share responsibility in law with those who carry out the orders.[1]

Quite apart from his (or her) responsibility to conduct military operations under national and international rules and regulations, a commander may also be criminally liable if war crimes are committed by him or those under his command. It is this liability, known as command responsibility, that will be addressed in this chapter. Even if he does not order his subordinates to commit unlawful acts, a commander is liable if he knew, or ought to have known, of them and failed to take steps to prevent them.[2]

For the purposes of this chapter, a commander may be defined as a soldier having either direct authority over a body of troops or authority over a geographical area in which troops are stationed.[3] Depending on the circumstances, a commander can be a corporal commanding a section, a major appointed commandant of a prisoner-of-war camp, a colonel commanding a military district in occupied territory or a general commanding a combined military taskforce.

The war crimes trials

The following principles of command responsibility are drawn from the decisions of tribunals in the war crimes trials that followed the Second World War.

Liability is clear if the commander commits a war crime himself or orders the commission of a war crime, but very often his responsibility will be less sharply defined because he will be remote from the scene of the crime or from those who have committed it.

---

[1]The *Dostler* trial, I *War Crimes Reports* (WCR) 22. General Dostler was found guilty of having ordered the illegal shooting of fifteen prisoners of war.
[2]The *Yamashita* trial, IV WCR 35 as confirmed by Protocol I, Art. 86, para. 2.
[3]See Queen's Regulations for the Army, HMSO, 1975, para. 2.001.

The commander has always been held responsible for the outcome of the orders he gives[4] but the concept of a superior's responsibility for the acts of his subordinates where those acts do not flow from that superior's orders is a comparatively recent development of the law of war.[5] It started with the trial of General Yamashita after the Second World War and has found confirmation in Protocol I,[6] which provides that a superior is responsible for the offences of his subordinates if he knew, or ought to have known, of them and failed to take steps to prevent them.

Exception for detail

Criminal responsibility does not automatically attach to the commander for all acts of his subordinates. The court in the *Von Leeb* case said that: 'a high commander cannot keep completely informed of the details of military operations of subordinates and most assuredly not of every administrative measure. He has the right to assume that details entrusted to responsible subordinates will be legally executed'.[7] There must be an unlawful act by the commander or a failure to supervise his subordinates constituting a dereliction of duty on his part.

Assumption of legality of orders not obviously unlawful

Within certain limitations, a commander is entitled to assume that orders issued by his superiors and the state he serves are issued in conformity with international law.

A commander may be required to pass on for execution by his subordinates an order from a superior commander. Sometimes this order may be issued without consultation with the intermediate commander; sometimes it is passed on by the intermediate commander's staff as a matter of routine without the personal knowledge or involvement of the intermediate commander. The court in the *Von Leeb* case also dealt with this situation and said that, within certain limitations, a commander is entitled to assume that orders issued by his superiors and the state which he serves are issued in conformity with international law. 'He cannot be held criminally responsible for a mere error of judgment as to disputable legal questions.' To be held criminally responsible, the intermediate commander 'must have passed the order to the chain of command and the order must be one that is criminal upon its face, or one which he is shown to have known was criminal'.[8]

---

[4]T. Meron, Henry the Fifth and the law of war, *American Journal of International Law*, 1992, pp. 16–21.

[5]Cassese comes to the same conclusion, see A. Cassese, *Violence and Law in the Modern Age*, Polity, 1988, p. 84.

[6]Art. 86, para. 2.

[7]*High Command* trial, XII WCR 76.

[8]*Ibid.*, p. 74.

This is not confirmation of the availability of the defence of superior orders; the defence is based on the lack of *mens rea* (criminal intent).

General von Falkenhorst, who had been commander-in-chief of German forces in Norway during the Second World War, was charged with causing the killing of allied military personnel by passing to his subordinates Hitler's commando order. The first paragraph of the order stated that the allies had been using prohibited methods of warfare and that the 'brutal and treacherous' commandos were under orders to kill 'defenceless prisoners'. The order required quarter to be refused to all commandos, whether captured in uniform or not, and directed the court-martial of officers who failed to instruct their troops accordingly or who acted contrary to its provisions. The defence was that von Falkenhorst 'took this measure as a reprisal' and that he was not able to verify the facts set forth by Hitler. The accused was found guilty and it is probable that his rank and position placed a higher standard on him than would have been imposed on a subordinate commander. Because Norway was often the scene of commando raids, he could have ascertained that the commandos did adhere to the laws and customs of war and this would have eliminated any basis for the claim of reprisals. Furthermore, under the Geneva Prisoner of War Convention of 1929, then in force, reprisals against prisoners of war were prohibited.

Duty to prevent crimes

Commanders have a duty to prevent crimes being committed by their subordinates. That may engage the criminal responsibility of the commander if he fails to carry out that duty or has condoned offences. General Yamashita, the Japanese military commander of the Philippines during the Second World War, was found guilty by a United States military commission of unlawfully disregarding and failing to discharge his duty as commander to control the operations of members of his command, permitting them to commit brutal atrocities and other high crimes, thereby violating the law of war.[9] On his petition to the United States Supreme Court, that court held that he had an affirmative duty to take such measures as were in his power and appropriate in the circumstances to protect prisoners of war and the civilian population.[10] While not disagreeing with this principle, Walzer[11] is critical of the findings in the *Yamashita* case because the circumstances were such that he was unable to exercise effective control over the troops under his command. This notion formed the basis of the scathing dissenting judgment of Mr Justice Murphy.[12] The latter, rightly in the opinion of the author, criticized the legal basis cited by the Supreme Court[13] for holding a

[9]The *Yamashita* trial, IV WCR 3.
[10]*Ibid.*, pp. 43–4.
[11]M. Walzer, *Just and Unjust Wars*, 2nd edn, Basic Books, 1992, pp. 319–22.
[12]IV, WCR 51.
[13]*Ibid.*, p. 43.

commander responsible for controlling his subordinates, but it is submitted that there should be no difficulty in accepting the general principle that an officer, by the nature of his appointment, carries some responsibility for the acts of his subordinates and it is right that a military tribunal should assess the level of that responsibility in the particular circumstances of the case. The following questions arise about the commander's duty:

1 Is the commander liable for not taking steps in advance to prevent the commission of offences?
2 To what extent is knowledge of the commission of offences required as a basis for liability for not intervening to stop offences?
3 What is the extent of the duty to enquire whether offences are being committed?
4 Is there a difference between the duty as a commander and liability for war crimes committed by others?

Duty to take steps

Responsibility may arise if war crimes were committed as a result of the commander's failure to discharge his duties either deliberately or by culpably or wilfully disregarding them, not caring whether this resulted in the commission of war crimes or not,[14] for example, if the commander had reasonable grounds for suspecting that men under his command were going to commit war crimes and failed to do anything about it.[15]

Knowledge

Proof of knowledge, actual or inferred, is necessary.[16] Although General Sawada was away on duty when prisoners of war were denied that status, he did subsequently ratify the death sentences that had been imposed upon them.[17] On the other hand, General Hisakasu's responsibility did not arise because he was away on duty until after the execution of the victim.[18]

If knowledge cannot be proved by direct evidence, it can be inferred from the surrounding circumstances, for example, the widespread nature, severity or notoriety of offences,[19] the prevailing state of discipline, and the participation in offences of officers in the command chain between the commander and troops committing offences.[20] The repeated occurrence of offences by troops under one

---

[14] The *Baba Masao* trial, abstracted in XV WCR 69.
[15] The trial of *Schonfeld and others*, abstracted at XV WCR 69.
[16] The *Seeger* trial, IV WCR 88.
[17] V WCR 4.
[18] V WCR 79.
[19] The *Yamashita* trial, IV WCR 1.
[20] The *Rauer* trial, IV WCR 85.

command may amount to *prima facie* evidence of the responsibility of the commander for those offences.[21] The commander will be liable for offences committed during his temporary absence from duty if they arise out of a general prescribed policy he has formulated.[22] But knowledge will not be inferred if the offences are not of sufficient magnitude or duration to constitute notice to the accused.[23] Milch was acquitted because of lack of proof that he had guilty knowledge,[24] but this may have been due to the fact that he was charged with being 'a principal in, accessory to, ordered, abetted, took a consenting party in and was connected with' plans for certain offences.

The leading case on the question of knowledge is the *Yamashita* trial.[25] There was no doubt that widespread atrocities had been committed in the area of his command, but Yamashita claimed that he was unaware of them, since communications were bad and he was totally preoccupied in dealing with the conduct of the military campaign. The case is unsatisfactory in that, while there was *some* evidence that the accused knew of some war crimes, the prosecution case seems to have been based on imputed knowledge. In its judgment, the commission did not specifically state the basis for its finding. That it was based on imputed knowledge may be inferred from the following passage:

It is absurd, however, to consider a commander a murderer or a rapist because one of his soldiers commits a murder or rape. Nevertheless, where murder and rape and vicious, revengeful actions are widespread offences, and there is no effective attempt by a commander to discover and control the criminal acts, such a commander may be held responsible, even criminally liable, for the lawless acts of his troops, depending upon their nature and the circumstances surrounding them.[26]

Later on the commission concluded: that 'during the period in question you failed to provide effective control of your troops as was required by the circumstances'.[27] One is driven to the conclusion that the commission found as a matter of fact that, despite his protestations to the contrary, Yamashita did know of the atrocities.

Ignorance of reports

Want of knowledge of the contents of a report made for a commander is not a defence, since failure to acquaint himself with the contents of reports made for his special benefit is a dereliction of duty.[28] Again, much depends on the circumstances of the case. If the commander is busy conducting a military

---

[21] IV WCR 85.
[22] The *Hostages* trial, abstracted at XV WCR 76.
[23] The *Pohl* trial, VII WCR 63–4.
[24] IV WCR 88.
[25] IV WCR 1.
[26] IV WCR 35.
[27] *Ibid.*
[28] The *Hostages* trial, VIII WCR 71, quoted with approval in the *High Command* trial, XII WCR 112.

operation, he may simply not have the time to read all reports, even those made for him personally. He may have to put some on one side until time becomes available. But, if he does so, that will require him at least to enquire as to the subject matter of those reports so that he can decide on their priority. If he is told that a report deals with, say, the massacre of civilians by troops under his command, he is put under a duty to do something about it. He cannot simply turn a blind eye to it. He must give appropriate orders to his staff.

Cases where commander put on notice

There are also cases where, because of the circumstances, the commander should have been put on notice that war crimes were being committed and his failure to do anything about it gives rise to criminal liability on his part.[29]

A duty to enquire arises when a commander is put on notice or ought, in the circumstances, to have been put on notice.[30] Tschentscher was acquitted because the activities of his subordinates were not of sufficient magnitude or duration to constitute notice.[31] Commanders also have a duty to establish proper procedures to ensure that war crimes are not committed and to ensure that those procedures work efficiently. Otherwise they are only liable if they know crimes are being committed and fail to take steps to prevent them, or are at fault in having failed to acquire such knowledge.[32]

Practical examples of the commander's duties relating to the handling of prisoners of war would include ensuring that proper procedures were instituted and instructions issued, personnel and material made available, occurrences reported, enquiries conducted and periodic inspections carried out. During the Gulf war of 1991, the United Kingdom established a special prisoner-of-war guard force consisting of three infantry battalions advised by a military lawyer. The responsibility for prisoners of war does not end when they are transferred to another nation under Art. 12 of the Prisoner of War Convention, so the UK set up a prisoner-of-war monitoring team, which included a military lawyer, to monitor the treatment of prisoners of war handed over to allies.

After the Second World War, Major Rauer was charged in respect of three separate killings by troops under his command of a total of twelve allied airmen. He was acquitted of the first set of killings but convicted of the other two, presumably on the basis that, although he had not given the orders for the killings, he created a climate in which it was known by his subordinates that they would not be punished for killing prisoners of war. He took no steps to investigate the killings and accepted at face value assurances that prisoners of

---

[29] The *Rauer* trial, IV WCR 113.
[30] The *Yamashita* trial, IV WCR 94–5; The *Doctors'* trial, VII WCR 63; the *Pohl* trial, VII WCR 63.
[31] The *Pohl* trial, VII WCR 63.
[32] The *Tokyo* trial, abstracted at XV WCR 73.

war had been killed while attempting to escape. The court may have thought that he had been put on notice after the first set of killings.[33]

Proof of knowledge, summary

It follows from the above that there are various ways of proving the commander's knowledge:

(a)   that he actually knew (admission or documentary or witness evidence); or
(b)   that he must have known (evidence of notoriety); or
(c)   that he ought to have known (serious nature of offence plus evidence of a dereliction of duty on the part of the commander or of his being put on notice).

Offences by persons not under command

A commander may also be liable for war crimes committed in an area under his control by persons not under his command.[34] Thus commanders of occupied territory were held responsible for crimes committed by the *Einsatzgruppen* of the Security Police and *Sicherheitsdienst* (SD) of which they had knowledge and neglected to suppress[35] and for crimes committed in occupied territory without their consent or approval by *Schutzstaffeln* (SS) units under the direct command of Heinrich Himmler.[36] At first sight this decision seems somewhat harsh but it is based on the proposition that the commander derives his authority over occupied territory under international law and this does not take into account national regulations or chains of command. He has certain responsibilities, which he cannot set aside or ignore by reason of the activities of his own state within his area. He is the instrument by which the occupation exists.[37] In the *von Manstein* trial[38] the accused was acquitted of having 'ordered, authorized and permitted' mass murders of civilians by paramilitary and police detachments operating in his area of command, but he was found guilty of violating Arts. 43 and 46 of the Hague Regulations by failing in his duty as a military commander to ensure public order and safety and to respect family honour and individual rights. This finding turned on the precise degree of subordination of the taskforce police units to the accused in his capacity as commander in chief, and his actual knowledge of their role and activities.[39] Cassese[40] draws some interesting parallels

---

[33]The *Rauer* trial, IV WCR 113.
[34]*High Command* trial XII WCR 74 ff.
[35]*Ibid.*
[36]The *Hostages* trial, VIII WCR 69–70.
[37]*High Command* trial, XII WCR 77.
[38]*Annual Digest*, 1949, Case No. 192.
[39]United Kingdom, *Manual of Military Law*, Part III, HMSO, 1958, p. 178.
[40]Cassese, *Violence and Law*, p. 84.

between the war crimes trials and the massacres in the Sebra and Shatila camps in 1982.[41] He considers that since Israeli troops wielded effective power over the Philangist troops, once they knew the slaughter had started, they were under a duty to stop it and, afterwards, to seek out and punish those responsible.

Duty/liability

There is a very fine distinction between complicity in war crimes committed by others on the one hand and an omission to act, which may itself amount to a war crime, on the other.[42] In the *Milch* trial, one of the questions considered by the tribunal was 'did he fail to act, thereby becoming *particeps criminis* and accessory to' the offences.[43]

Hampson has summarized the position of the commander as follows:

It could be argued that a commander should only be responsible where the facts were of sufficient notoriety or involved breaches on such a scale that alleged ignorance of the violations must, in effect, have been wilful. At the other end of the spectrum, a commander could be held responsible for failing to institute effective mechanisms to prevent violations and to ensure that any possible breach was reported to him.[44]

It seems that Hampson's above statement covers both aspects. The first sentence deals with complicity in the breaches complained of. The second sentence does not deal with complicity in war crimes committed by others but in breach of duty by the commander. As Hampson[45] indicates, the duty of the commander in this respect may be inferred from the requirement of the Geneva Conventions for states to take measures necessary for the suppression of all acts contrary to the provisions of the conventions.

In borderline cases it may be best to charge the commander in respect of his dereliction of duty rather than as a party to war crimes committed by others.

It is suggested that the commander also has a duty to bring to trial those under his command who have committed grave breaches of the Geneva Conventions or other serious war crimes.[46] This duty can be inferred from the duty placed on

---

[41] See the Kahan Report, 22 (1983) International Legal Materials, p. 473.

[42] Greenwood puts this duty thus: 'a commander has a duty to ensure that forces under his command behave in accordance with the laws of armed conflict and may be convicted of a war crime if he fails to restrain them from unlawful behaviour' (C. J. Greenwood, *Command and the Laws of Armed Conflict*, Strategic and Combat Studies Institute, The Army Staff College, Camberley, 1993, p. 35).

[43] IV WCR 90.

[44] F. J. Hampson, Liability for war crimes, in P. J. Rowe (ed.), *The Gulf War 1990–91 in International and English Law*, Routledge, 1993, p. 245.

[45] Hampson, Liability, p. 245.

[46] Alleged killings of prisoners of war by British troops during the Falklands war of 1982 were referred to the Crown Prosecution Service which instructed the Metropolitan Police Commissioner to investigate: see, e.g., *The Times*, 20 August 1992 and 9 November 1993, but the Director of Public Prosecutions decided not to mount a prosecution.

states by the Geneva Conventions 'to search for persons alleged to have committed grave breaches and to bring them to justice'.[47]

Evidence

The evidential provisions at the war crimes trials were relaxed, especially with regard to the admission of hearsay evidence. Rowe refers to the difficulties in a wartime situation of obtaining sufficient admissible evidence to secure a conviction but points out that exclusion of evidence that may be unreliable ensures that the accused receives a fair trial.[48] For example, at the war crimes trials, membership of a group was *prima facie* evidence of responsibility for the activities of that group.[49] It is questionable whether such provisions would be acceptable today. Protocol I[50] provides that no one shall be convicted of an offence except on the basis of individual penal responsibility. The War Crimes Act of 1991 contains no provisions for the relaxation of the law of evidence in trials to which the Act relates.

Staff officers

For the purposes of this chapter, a staff officer may be defined as an officer on the staff of a commander who assists the commander in carrying out his duties.[51]

A staff officer is not guilty of a war crime by reason only of his knowledge of illegal acts or of the outcome of his commander's orders which he approved from the point of view of form and issued on his commander's behalf.[52] Unlike a commander, a staff officer cannot normally be found guilty of a war crime for failure to act because he does not have any command responsibility.[53] There is an implication in the war crimes reports[54] that a staff officer is not liable for failing to pass to his commander information about war crimes on the grounds that a staff officer's duty to pass information to his superiors stems from national regulations rather than international law.

[47]Greenwood, *Command*, p. 34. See, e.g., Art. 146 of the Civilian Convention. The duty is now confirmed in Protocol I, Art. 87, para. 3.

[48]P. J. Rowe, in his memorandum to the Foreign Affairs Select Committee, Third Report from the Foreign Affairs Committee, *The Expanding Role of the UN and its Implications for UK Policy*, Appendix to the Minutes of Evidence, 1993, p. 313.

[49]See Art. 8(ii) of the British Royal Warrant of 14 June 1945 with regulations for the trial of war criminals, published in the *Manual of Military Law*, p. 347.

[50]Art. 75, para 4(b).

[51]For more information about the British army staff structure, see Queen's Regulations for the Army, Chapter 4.

[52]The *Hostages* trial, VIII WCR 34–92.

[53]The *High Command* trial, XII WCR at p. 81.

[54]XV WCR 77-8.

There must, therefore, be some personal involvement on the staff officer's part, such as when he issues orders on his own behalf,[55] drafts them himself[56] or influences policy,[57] or events –[58] for example, where he presents a policy paper which is adopted by the commander, or, it is suggested, where he deliberately conceals offences committed by others by failing to bring them to his commander's notice. It will be for a tribunal to decide, depending on the facts of the case, whether a staff officer is liable as an accessory.

The responsibility of staff officers was considered more recently by the Ministry of Defence in its examination of material in its possession relating to Kurt Waldheim when he was a junior staff officer at headquarters Army Group E in the Balkans during the Second World War. While it seems in one or two cases that he was aware of the existence of captured commandos and of their intended fate, known as special treatment,[59] there was no evidence of any complicity on his part in the matter sufficient to form the basis for war crimes responsibility.[60]

Protocol I

Protocol I reinforces the grave breach provisions of the Geneva Conventions by introducing grave breach provisions of its own.[61] One example is wilfully, in violation of Art. 51, para. 2 of Protocol I,[62] making individual civilians or the civilian population the object of attack and thereby causing death or serious injury to body or health. Clearly, this applies to those who carry out the attack, but what of their military superiors? On the basis of general legal principles, the criminal responsibility of the commander who orders such an attack or otherwise takes an active part in encouraging or acquiescing in it is implied.

The Commander as a party to war crimes committed by his subordinates
(Protocol I, Art. 86, para. 2)

Basic rule
A commander becomes liable for a breach[63] committed by a subordinate if he knew, or had information which should have enabled him to conclude in the

---

[55]XII WCR 81–2 and the *Woehler* trial XII WCR 113–18.

[56]The *High Command* trial, XII WCR at p. 118.

[57]*Tokyo* trial abstracted in XV WCR 78.

[58]The *Isayama* trial, V WCR 60.

[59]*Sonderbehandlung*.

[60]United Kingdom, *Review of the results of investigations . . . and the involvement . . . of Lieutenant Waldheim*, HMSO, 1989.

[61]Art. 85.

[62]Which provides that the civilian population as such, as well as individual civilians, shall not be the object of attack. Acts or threats of violence the primary purpose of which is to spread terror among the civilian population are also prohibited.

[63]This provision is not limited to grave breaches, ICRC *Commentary*, p. 1012.

circumstances at the time, that his subordinate was committing or was going to commit such a breach and did not take all feasible measures within his power to prevent or repress[64] the breach.[65]

Protocol I thus deals specifically with the problem addressed in the *Yamashita* case of the commander who has knowledge, express or implied, of breaches of the law of war and does nothing.

Partsch is critical of this provision because it is unbalanced: it deals with the responsibility of the commander, but the corresponding responsibility of the subordinate who receives an unlawful order is not dealt with.[66] He also criticizes the failure to set out clearly the three conditions for the commander's responsibility laid down in the *Yamashita* case: that he knew of the breach, that he had the power to prevent it, that he did nothing to do so.[67] He accepts that the second condition is included in the words 'all feasible measures in his power' but considers that the first condition has been extended by inclusion of the words 'had information which should have enabled him to conclude in the circumstances at the time'. However, this may have been an attempt at the CDDH to articulate the thought processes of the tribunal in the *Yamashita* trial, which was faced with a denial of knowledge yet had evidence which led it to believe that he must have known.

Problems of interpretation arise when the English and French texts of this passage are compared:

Had information which should have enabled them to conclude in the circumstances at the time.

Possédaient des informations leur permettant de conclure, dans les circonstances du moment.

At first sight the use of the words 'should have' in the English text seems to introduce an element that is not present in the French version and various authorities suggest that the French text should prevail.[68] But both texts seem to

---

[64] According to Partsch, 'repress' means action under penal law; 'suppress' means other action, e.g., disciplinary measures (M. Bothe, K. J. Partsch and W. Solf, *New Rules for the Victims of Armed Conflicts*, Martinus Nijhoff, 1982, p. 524).

[65] Art. 86 para. 2.

[66] Bothe *et al.*, *New Rules*, p. 524.

[67] Rowe considers that where a commander 'fails to take steps that he might take to prevent an offence taking place (without ordering that the offences be committed), he may also be liable' and refers to Smith and Hogan, *Criminal Law*, 7th edn, 1992, p. 132, where the authors state: 'where [the defendant] has a right to control the actions of another and he deliberately refrains from exercising it, his inactivity may be a positive encouragement to the other to perform an illegal act, and therefore an aiding and abetting [of the offence committed]': see P. J. Rowe, Response from the United Kingdom Group of the International Society for Military Law and the Law of War to the questionnaire of the society's criminology commission, 1994. The work of the criminology commission is summarized in 1995 *Military Law and Law of War Review*, p. 175.

[68] Bothe *et al.*, *New Rules*, p. 525; ICRC, *Commentary*, p. 1013.

lead to the same result, since in either case the tribunal will have to decide whether the information was such that knowledge can be inferred.

Relevant factors

De Preux[69] lists some of the factors that a tribunal might take into account in deciding whether constructive knowledge of the superior could be established: the tactical situation, the level of training and instruction of subordinate officers and their troops (particularly on the Geneva Conventions and Protocols and the handling of prisoners of war) and their character traits, the means of attack allocated or available in an area densely populated by civilians or lack of medical services. He adds that a commander cannot absolve himself from responsibility by invoking temporary absence as an excuse or by pleading ignorance of reports addressed to him. Here one has to be careful because no one is to be convicted of a war crime except on the basis of individual penal respons- ibility.[70] A tribunal has to look at all the circumstances before it can find constructive knowledge. A temporary absence is one of the factors that it would take into account. The fact that a report is addressed to a commander does not mean that he sees it or is even aware of its existence. It is frequently the case in practice that a report addressed to the commander is first seen by the chief of staff, who decides whether the commander needs to be made aware of it or not. The chief of staff may well pass it to another staff officer for action. Again, the tribunal would have to look at the circumstances before coming to any conclusion. It might be more inclined to find against a commander if it con- cluded that he was deliberately turning a blind eye to reports or information about war crimes committed by those under his command, especially where those offences were widespread and a matter of public notoriety.

De Preux[71] also refers to the difficulty of establishing *mens rea* in cases of failure to act, particularly in cases of negligence, points out that the Geneva Con- ventions do not contain any provision qualifying negligent conduct as criminal, recalls that one delegation at the CDDH thought that the words 'should have' implied responsibility incurred by negligence and concludes that negligence is not necessarily criminal: 'it must be so serious that it is tantamount to malicious intent'. In English criminal law the level of negligence required to constitute an offence depends on the nature of the offence. A relatively small amount of negligence will suffice for driving without *due* care and attention; yet gross negligence is required for manslaughter.[72] In military law, negligence has to be blameworthy and deserving of punishment.[73]

---

[69]ICRC *Commentary*, pp. 1013–14.
[70]Protocol I, Art. 75, para. 4(b).
[71]ICRC *Commentary*, pp. 1011–12.
[72]*R.* v. *Prentice and Others* [1993] 4 All ER 935.
[73]*Manual of Military Law*, Part I, HMSO London, 1972 (reprinted 1992), pp. 311, 350.

The author does not share the view of de Preux[74] that the concept of the superior 'should be seen in terms of a hierarchy encompassing the concept of control'. If so, there would be no need for 'persons under his control' to be specifically included in the text of Art. 87, para. 3 of Protocol I. Since the two texts are different, and deal with different situations, they must have been intended to impose different liabilities.

It is debatable whether Art. 86, para. 2 of Protocol I has affected the liability of staff officers in respect of failure to act. It is of interest that the term 'commander' is not used in this provision, but the word 'superiors'. It is certainly arguable that 'superiors' encompasses staff officers at a superior headquarters. They would indeed be well placed to do something about suppressing breaches by issuing appropriate orders or instructions, if it lay within their competence to do so, or passing the matter to another staff division or to the commander with appropriate recommendations if it did not.

Duty of commanders to deal with breaches (Protocol I, Art. 87, para. 3)

Apart from being liable to be considered a party to war crimes committed by his subordinates, a commander is in any event under a general duty to maintain discipline, and that includes a duty to take action in respect of war crimes committed, or about to be committed, by his subordinates or by other persons under his control.[75] Protocol I is curiously drafted in that when dealing with the suppression of breaches it does not place any direct responsibility on commanders.[76] It places the responsibility on the high contracting parties and the parties to the conflict to ensure that commanders prevent breaches, train their subordinates and take action against offenders.[77]

Partsch is critical of the drafting of Art. 87, para. 3 of Protocol I, saying that it does not conform to Art. 86, para. 2.[78] However, the use of the word 'aware' may have been an attempt by the drafters to cover both actual and constructive knowledge, so that one could argue that both paragraphs are consistent.

Although Partsch suggests[79] that Art. 87, para. 2 of Protocol I goes no further than Art. 83 of the Protocol,[80] it does make it clear that the responsibility for

---

[74]ICRC, *Commentary*, p. 1013.

[75]The *Yamashita* trial, IV WCR 1.

[76]Unlike, e.g., Art. 57, para. 2a, which states that 'those who plan or decide upon an attack shall . . .' or Art. 85, dealing with grave breaches which, again, is based on personal liability.

[77]Art. 87. This provision of Protocol I depends for its effectiveness on the introduction by the parties of implementing legislation or regulations. The German Manual places a positive obligation on the disciplinary superior to act when he learns of a breach of international humanitarian law: see Germany, *Humanitäres Völkerrecht in bewaffneten Konflikten – Handbuch*, Bundesministerium der Verteidigung, 1992, para. 1213.

[78]Bothe *et al.*, *New Rules*, p. 529. Art. 86, para. 2 deals with the legal responsibility of the commander if he fails to act to deal with breaches.

[79]Bothe *et al.*, *New Rules*, p. 529.

[80]Which deals with dissemination.

instructing others in the law of war is not limited to those who are involved in running formal courses.

Prevent, suppress and report

Commanders are to prevent and, where necessary, suppress and report to the competent authorities breaches of the Geneva Conventions and Protocol I.[81]

This applies in relation to 'members of the armed forces under their command and other persons under their control'.

Members of the armed forces under command include not only those who are regularly under command but also those who are placed under command temporarily[82] and, within a sector of occupied territory for which a commander is responsible, persons under their control include the population of that sector and even troops operating in the sector that are not directly subordinate to him.[83]

Training

Commanders are to make 'members of the armed forces under their command' aware of their obligations under the Conventions and Protocol.[84]

This applies commensurate with the commander's level of responsibility. The law of war is becoming very complicated. One cannot really expect every soldier and officer to know every article and every nuance of the Geneva Conventions and Protocols, let alone the other conventions and writings. It suffices if they understand the general principles of the law of war and then receive training or instructions specifically related to their mission. Legal advisers should be on hand[85] to advise commanders about appropriate levels of instruction.

Penal or disciplinary action

If aware that persons are going to commit or have committed breaches of the conventions or Protocol I, a commander is to initiate such steps as are necessary to prevent those breaches and, where appropriate, initiate penal or disciplinary action against the violators.[86] This applies in relation to 'subordinates or other persons under his control'.

If the offence were not a grave breach but some other serious war crime, the issue would arise as to the appropriate charge. An example might be a soldier who altered his ammunition to produce a dum-dum round. The answer would depend on the legal system being applied. Under British military law, a soldier can be charged under the appropriate section of the Army Act 1955, for example, s. 30 (looting), s. 34 (disobeying a lawful command), s. 36 (disobeying standing

---

[81]Art. 87, para. 1.
[82]ICRC, *Commentary*, p. 1019.
[83]*Ibid.*, p. 1020; the *List* trial VIII WCR 69–71.
[84]Art. 87, para. 2.
[85]Protocol I, Art. 82.
[86]Art. 87, para. 3.

orders), s. 44 (damaging public property), s. 63 (offences against the civilian population), s. 64 (scandalous conduct), s. 66 (disgraceful conduct) and s. 69 (prejudicial conduct). Under the Royal Warrant of 14 June 1945, authorized officers may convene military courts to try persons who are within the limits of their command for war crimes.[87]

It is submitted that even if the state, or party to the conflict, to which the commander belongs fails to issue the appropriate instructions, the tests enunciated in the war crimes trials would still apply to him.

Practicalities

The important thing is that commanders are alert to the implications of the law of war and take them into consideration, seeking expert advice where necessary, when issuing orders or instructions and take steps to prevent or report breaches of which they become aware, including instituting formal disciplinary action when necessary.

The level at which a commander's responsibility arises will depend on the circumstances. A corporal commanding a section would be responsible for ensuring that the soldiers under his command acted in accordance with the law of war by issuing appropriate orders and instructions and reporting offenders to officers having disciplinary powers. Although he could not be expected to carry out formal law-of-war training, he might, depending on the circumstances, be under a duty to remind his soldiers about the aspects of their law-of-war training that were relevant to the tactical situation in which they found themselves.

Mental element[88]

A person is only guilty of a war crime if he commits it with intent and knowledge.[89]

Before a war crime or a grave breach of the Geneva Conventions or Additional Protocol I can be established, it must be proved that the accused not only did the act complained of but also that he intended the consequences of his act. This intent is usually referred to as *mens rea*, criminal intent or basic intent.

If, for example, a commander did not intend the consequences of his attack on a military target because the civilian casualties were due to a weapons malfunction or to faulty target intelligence, he would not be guilty of an offence. He would lack the criminal intent despite the consequences of his actions. Or if, for example, a soldier is ordered to take a group of women and children from

---

[87]For a more extensive discussion of the Royal warrant, see A. P. V. Rogers, War crimes trials under the Royal Warrant, 39 (1990) *International and Comparative Law Quarterly* 780.

[88]This passage was published in similar form as A. P. V. Rogers, Wilfulness, in R. Gutman and D. Rieff (eds.), *Crimes of War*, W. W. Norton & Company, 1999, p. 383.

[89]This is confirmed by Art. 30 of the 1998 Rome Statute of the International Criminal Court (ICC Statute).

a battlefield village under armed guard to a town well away from the fighting and there hand them over to the garrison commander, yet it later transpired that they were being held as hostages to protect the military headquarters in that town from attack, his defence might be that he had no criminal intent since he was unaware that the civilians were being taken hostage and thought that they were being brought to a place of safety.

Very often the required intent is specified in the grave breach provision of a treaty as being wilfulness, as in '*wilful* killing, torture or inhuman treatment' or '*wilfully* . . . making the civilian population or individual civilians the object of attack'. Or it may take the form of wantonness, as in 'extensive destruction . . . of property, not justified by military necessity and carried out unlawfully and *wantonly*'.

The words wilful and wanton necessarily encompass the intentional or deliberate but go beyond that to include cases of recklessness. Criminal liability is not limited to positive acts. It can arise in the event of a failure to act when there is a duty to do so and the failure is either with intent that the consequences should follow or is due to recklessness about those consequences.

In their Commentary on the Additional Protocols, the International Committee of the Red Cross explain wilfulness as follows:

– *wilfully*: the accused must have acted consciously and with intent, i.e. with his mind on the act and its consequences and willing them . . . ; this encompasses the concepts of 'wrongful intent' or 'recklessness', viz., the attitude of an agent who, without being certain of a particular result, accepts the possibility of it happening; on the other hand, ordinary negligence or lack of foresight is not covered, i.e., when a man acts without having his mind on the act or its consequences.[90]

Negligence, which is not sufficient to render the act a grave breach, may still suffice for disciplinary action under national military law.

Recent developments

Some enlightenment of questions of command responsibility can be derived from the Statute of the International Criminal Tribunals for the former Yugoslavia (ICTY Statute) and the ICC Statute.

ICTY Statute

Article 7 of the tribunal's statute, reflecting customary law, deals with failure to act as follows:

[90]ICRC *Commentary*, para. 3474.

the fact that any of the acts ... was committed by a subordinate does not relieve his superior of criminal responsibility if he knew or had reason to know that the subordinate was about to commit such acts or had done so and the superior failed to take the necessary and reasonable measures to prevent such acts or to punish the perpetrators thereof.

In the *Čelebići* case, the tribunal was concerned with matters of command responsibility. One issue was whether command responsibility could arise when the superior had not been formally appointed as a matter of law. This was against the background of the break-up of the former Yugoslavia, self-proclaimed governments and *de facto* armies and subordinate paramilitary groups with hastily organized command structures.

The trial chamber held that, while a position of command is a necessary precondition for the imposition of command responsibility, this cannot be determined by reference to formal status alone, it is a question of the 'actual possession, or non-possession, of powers of control over the actions of subordinates'.[91] The appeals chamber agreed, saying that: 'as long as a superior has effective control over subordinates, to the extent that he can prevent them from committing crimes or punish them after they committed the crimes, he would be held responsible for the commission of the crimes if he failed to exercise such abilities of control'.[92] The appeals tribunal was also asked to determine whether the words 'had reason to know' in Art. 7 of the statute meant that a commander could also be held liable if he is seriously negligent in his duty to obtain the relevant information. They concluded that was not the case under customary international law nor under Protocol I and that 'a superior will be criminally responsible through the principle of superior responsibility only if information was available to him which would have put him on notice of offences committed by subordinates'.[93] It is submitted that this is correct. Otherwise the commander's position would be too remote from the actual offences to engage his responsibility for *those* offences, though his failure to put proper procedures in place for collecting and assessing information might contravene national military regulations or standards. One might add that 'relevant information' refers not only to offences that have been committed but also to information that puts the commander on notice that offences are about to be committed.

The appeals chamber also decided that the correct standard to apply in deciding whether the superior to subordinate relationship entailed command responsibility was one of effective control over the subordinate, which requires the possession of material abilities to prevent subordinates or to punish subordinate

---

[91]*Prosecutor* v. *Delalić*, Case No. IT-96-21-T, trial judgment of 16 November 1998, para. 370.
[92]40 (2001) ILM 630, 669 (para. 198).
[93]*Ibid.*, para. 241. In the light of this, the passage in the *Blaškić* case referring to the commander's negligence can probably be ignored: see *Prosecutor* v. *Blaškić*, 122 ILR 1, at p. 182 (para. 562).

offenders.[94] Substantial influence as a means of control does not suffice, so the position of staff officers probably remains unaltered by the tribunal's jurisprudence. The fact that a person is a deputy commander does not necessarily dispose of the issue; it is necessary to look for evidence of *actual* authority or control.[95]

In many armies, officers and soldiers are required to obey the orders of soldiers or officers of higher rank. Does an officer, therefore, become liable under the doctrine of command responsibility if he sees a soldier not under his command on the point of committing a war crime but fails to order him to desist? The answer, on the basis of the *Čelebići* case, is no. But if his failure to intervene was intended to facilitate the commission of the offence, there would then be the question of his criminal liability as someone assisting in the commission of an offence. Even without that intent, if it was a matter of ineptitude on the part of the officer concerned, it should be possible to deal with him for dereliction of duty under national military regulations.

ICC Statute

The effective-control test is confirmed in the ICC Statute, which deals with command responsibility as follows:[96]

A military commander . . . shall be criminally responsible for crimes . . . committed by forces under his or her effective command or control, or effective authority and control as the case may be, as a result of his or her failure to exercise control properly over such forces, where:

    (a)   That military commander . . . either knew or, owing to the circumstances at the time, should have known that the forces were committing or about to commit such crimes; and

    (b)   That military commander . . . failed to take all necessary and reasonable measures within his or her power to prevent or suppress their commission or to submit the matter to the competent authorities for investigation and prosecution.

The statute deals with the question of intent by specifying that an accused person is only to be convicted if his offence were committed 'with intent and knowledge'. An accused has intent if, in relation to conduct, he 'means to engage in the conduct' and, in relation to a consequence, he 'means to cause that consequence or is aware that it will occur in the ordinary course of events'. Knowledge means 'awareness that a circumstance exists or a consequence will occur in the ordinary course of events'.[97]

---

[94]*Ibid.*, para. 266.
[95]*Ibid.*, para. 306.
[96]Art. 28(a). Art. 28(b) deals with superior responsibilities outside the military command structure.
[97]Art. 30.

Conclusions

The following is an attempt to distil the rules relating to command responsibility in the context of the conduct of combat into a few short paragraphs.

A commander will be criminally responsible if he participates in the commission of a war crime himself, particularly if he orders or facilitates its commission.

But even if he does not participate directly, the fact that a breach was committed by a subordinate will not absolve a superior from responsibility if he knew or ought to have known that it was being committed and did nothing to prevent it or bring the offender to justice.[98]

It is unlikely that a senior commander would himself carry out an individual attack though he may have been involved in its planning and so be responsible for the outcome. His responsibility is more likely to be engaged either because he orders the attack or because it is carried out by troops under his command by virtue of authority expressly or implicitly delegated to them.

Actual knowledge may be difficult to prove, but can be inferred from the surrounding circumstances, especially if war crimes by those under command are so widespread as to be notorious, for example, when soldiers under command carry out sustained and frequent unlawful attacks,[99] but any presumption to that effect would be rebuttable and if the tactical situation is hectic it may not be possible for the commander to concern himself with the detail of every individual attack. In assessing the commander's responsibility, therefore, full account must be taken of the difficulties under which he was operating at the relevant time. The closer a commander is in the chain of command to those who commit offences, the more likely is knowledge going to be inferred.

Liability may also attach to a commander even if he did not actually know about the acts of subordinates but ought to have known about them and his failure in this respect constituted a dereliction of duty on his part, for example, if he is put on notice but fails to do anything about it. This would include failure to try and punish offenders or report offences to the appropriate authorities. Failure to punish war crimes committed by those under his command can make a commander party to those crimes if by consistently failing to take action over a period of time he creates a climate of disregard for the law of war. Even where failure to take action over a period of time does not make the commander a party to the actual crimes committed, failure to take action may itself amount to a war crime if the case is sufficiently serious to warrant it.

Sometimes an intermediate commander is bypassed and orders are passed direct from a senior commander to a subordinate unit. The responsibility of the

[98]Protocol I, Art. 86.
[99]W. J. Fenrick, Attacking the enemy civilians as a punishable offence, *Duke Journal of International and Comparative Law*, 1997, p. 563.

intermediate commander would be engaged if he knowingly passed on the orders or if he adopted them in some other way.

Evidence in support of charges against commanders would include not only evidence of command structures, the room for discretion of subordinate commanders, the rights and responsibilities of commanders and subordinates under relevant military law but also the actual practice of the conduct of military operations and the extent to which violations were brought to the attention of commanders and the effect of protests. In considering the responsibility of commanders of regular forces for the activities of irregular armed groups operating in their areas, the extent to which those activities had been encouraged, condoned, tolerated, disowned or prevented by the commander would be relevant. The following list of factors that a tribunal might wish to take into account to infer the commander's responsibility has been suggested:[100] the number, type and scope of illegal acts; the number and type of troops and logistics involved; the geographical location and widespread occurrence of the acts; the tactical tempo of operations; the *modus operandi* of similar illegal acts; the officers and staff involved; and the location of the commander at the time.

A tribunal considering the commander's responsibility would have to look at the situation as the commander saw it in the light of his knowledge of the situation and of the relevant information actually or reasonably available to him and of the characteristics of the available weapons, the way they are to be used, the importance of the military target and the likely incidental effects of any attack. In considering the responsibility of military commanders with regard to attacks, the attack as a whole, or that part for which he is responsible in the context of the attack as a whole, should be examined, not merely isolated of particular parts of the attack and it must be remembered that military commanders are obliged to make decisions on the basis of their assessment of the information which is available to them at the relevant time, not on the basis of the information or situation as it subsequently emerged.

Military discipline and superior orders[101]

Military effectiveness depends on the prompt and unquestioning obedience of orders to such an extent that soldiers are prepared to put their lives at risk in executing those orders. During military operations decisions, actions and instructions often have to be instantaneous and do not allow time for discussion or

---

[100]W. J. Fenrick and A. J. van Veen, in Annex VI.B of the Final Report of the United Nations Commission of Experts established pursuant to UN Security Council Resolution 780 (1992), at p. 36.

[101]This part of this book deals only with superior orders under *international* law. For a more detailed discussion of this problem, see A. P. V. Rogers, The defence of superior orders in international law, 1991 *Military Law Journal*, p. 17.

attention by committees. It is vital to the cohesion and control of a military force in dangerous and intolerable circumstances that commanders should be able to give orders and require their subordinates to carry them out.[102] In return for this unswerving obedience the soldier needs the protection of the law so that he does not afterwards risk his neck for having obeyed an order that later turns out to be unlawful.

Until the 1920s obedience to orders was usually regarded as a complete defence to a charge.[103] If anybody had to accept responsibility for the outcome of orders it must be he who gave them.

But the decisions of the German supreme court after the First World War in the hospital ship cases[104] indicated otherwise: that the defence of superior orders would provide no justification where the act was manifestly and indisputably contrary to international law.

During the Second World War, the rule was understood in the same way by the allies: the accused could not escape punishment for complying with an order that was manifestly illegal and thereby committing acts which both violated the unchallenged rules of warfare and outraged the general sentiment of humanity.[105]

Article 8 of the Nuremberg Charter seemed even stricter, providing only that superior orders might be considered in mitigation of punishment. However, in its judgment the International Military Tribunal (IMT) said that the true test was not the existence of the order but whether a moral choice was, in fact, possible.[106] The International Law Commission (ILC) also referred to moral choice when codifying the Nuremberg principles.[107] Perhaps the crimes dealt with by the IMT were so obviously illegal that the finer points of the defence did not fall to be considered.

National war crimes tribunals, on the other hand, seem to have allowed a little more latitude.[108] The United States tribunal in the *Einsatzgruppen* case indicated that the defence of duress might be available in suitable cases[109] and also raised manifest illegality in the following passage: 'If the nature of the ordered act is

---

[102]G. J. Cartledge, *The Soldier's Dilemma: When to Use Force in Australia*, Australian Government Publishing Service, 1992, pp. 174–5. In many military systems, disobedience to lawful orders is a punishable offence.

[103]E.g., United Kingdom, *Manual of Military Law*, 7th edn, HMSO, 1929, p. 83.

[104]*Annual Digest* 1923–24, Case Nos. 231, 235.

[105]E.g., United Kingdom, Amendment 34 to the *Manual of Military Law*, 7th edn, HMSO, 1944.

[106]Trial of the Major War Criminals before the IMT, Nuremberg, 1948, vol. XXII, p. 497. For more about the Nuremberg trials, see R. K. Woetzel, *The Nuremberg Trials in International Law*, Stevens, 1962.

[107]D. Schindler and J. Toman, *The Laws of Armed Conflicts*, 3rd edn, Martinus Nijhoff, 1988, p. 923.

[108]A useful discussion of the defence of superior orders in these cases is at XV WCR pp. 157–60.

[109]As did the other tribunal referred to in XV WCR 170 ff. The defence of duress was also considered in *Prosecutor* v. *Erdemović*, 111 ILR 298, and is confirmed in the ICC Statute, Art. 31(d).

manifestly beyond the scope of the superior's authority, the subordinate may not plead ignorance to [*sic*] the criminality of the order'.[110] In the *High Command* trial, the court held that, as orders relating to prisoner-of-war labour were not criminal on their face, it was a matter that a field commander had the right to assume was properly determined by higher authority.[111] On the other hand, a plea by von Falkenhorst that he had passed on Hitler's commando order as a reprisal and had no means of verifying the facts set out in the order was not accepted by a British military court, presumably on the basis that von Falkenhorst could have verified the facts in his command area.[112] In any case, the Geneva Conventions of 1929 prohibited reprisals against prisoners of war.

The question of manifest illegality is well dealt with in the following passage: 'The true test in practice is whether an order, illegal under international law, on which an accused has acted was or must be presumed to have been known to him to be so illegal or was so obviously illegal ... or should have been recognized by him as being so illegal.'[113] To the author, this seems a clear reference to establishing *mens rea*.

On the whole, modern theorists have rejected superior orders as a complete defence but are divided into two camps: those, epitomized by Dinstein, who consider that superior orders are no defence at all and those, represented by Green, who say that superior orders ought to be a defence if the orders are not manifestly illegal.[114]

Those who negotiated Protocol I were not able to agree on any text dealing with the defence of superior orders.[115] During the negotiations a text was put forward by the ICRC which provided that superior orders were no defence to an accused if 'in the circumstances at the time, he should have reasonably known that he was committing a grave breach ... and that he had the possibility of refusing to obey the order'.[116] Several delegations opposed this text on the basis that it created special rules for grave breaches while war crimes remained regulated by customary law, and the text did not receive approval by the necessary

---

[110]*US* v. *Ohlendorf*, No. 9, Trials of War Criminals before the Nuremberg Military Tribunals under Control Council Law No. 10, vol. IV, pp. 470–1.

[111]XII WCR 88–9.

[112]XI WCR 18, at p. 26. See also, M. H. F. Clarke, The status of guerrillas and irregular forces, unpublished, 1976.

[113]XV WCR 158.

[114]Y. Dinstein, *The Defence of Obedience to Superior Orders in International Law*, Leyden, 1965 and L. C. Green, *Superior Orders in National and International Law*, Sijthoff, 1976. In his article, Superior orders and the Geneva conventions and protocols, in H. Fox and M. A. Meyer (eds.), *Effecting Compliance*, British Institute of International and Comparative Law, 1993, Green refers to 'obvious' illegality. McCoubrey seems to be a follower of the Green school. Referring to the IMT and war crimes tribunal judgments, he states the position thus: 'superior orders may protect a subordinate from criminal responsibility but only if he or she neither knew nor ought to have known, upon the basis of normal professional competence, them to have been unlawful' (H. McCoubrey and N. D. White, *International Law and Armed Conflict*, Dartmouth, 1992, p. 341).

[115]F. Kalshoven and L. Zegveld, *Constraints on the Waging of War*, 3rd edn, ICRC, 2001, p. 150.

[116]This formulation seems to cover both manifest illegality and duress.

two-thirds majority, so was not adopted, leaving the matter to be governed by customary law.[117]

Soldiers[118] have a duty to obey lawful orders and a duty not to comply with unlawful orders. The fact that a soldier acted on the basis of orders from a superior will not generally relieve him from personal responsibility if, as a result, he commits a war crime. When tried for a war crime, the orders he received may be relevant in establishing *mens rea*[119] or to defences such as mistake of fact[120] or duress.[121] In any event, superior orders will normally be taken into account in mitigation of punishment. Prior to the ICC Statute, there was some weight of academic authority in favour of allowing a limited exception to the principle that ignorance of the law is no excuse[122] in cases where a soldier has acted in good faith on the basis of superior orders in circumstances where the law is not clear or controversial, but such cases are going to be rare.[123] It is to be hoped that in those cases the accused will not be prosecuted or, if prosecuted, given the benefit of any doubt by the court.

Of course, the court in any trial would determine the law. If a superior has made a mistake of law, this will not affect his liability and therefore the liability of the soldier. The soldier's act is illegal, so there is no defence.[124] If prosecuted, the soldier could only be given the benefit of the doubt by the court's exercising its inherent right not to convict if it thought that to do so would not be in the interests of justice.

It is argued by the authors of the United States Army pamphlet on international law[125] that there should be an exception to the *ignorantia juris* principle in international law because international law 'does not in some cases possess either the exactness or the degree of publicity which pertains to municipal law'. However, in the case there quoted of *Flick*[126] the plea of ignorance of local law was allowed only in mitigation of punishment and the *Scuttled U-boats*[127] case,

---

[117]Green, Superior orders and the Geneva conventions and protocols, pp. 196–7.

[118]Whatever their rank.

[119]See ICC Statute, Art. 30.

[120]See ICC Statute, Art. 32.

[121]See ICC Statute, Art. 31(d).

[122]H. McCoubrey, *The idea of War Crimes and Crimes against the Peace since 1945*, University of Nottingham Research Papers in Law, June 1992, No. 2, p. 25, says that the root of the *ignorantia juris* principle lies in knowledge and application not of one but two, municipal and public international, legal systems.

[123]Because it is only the most serious and obvious war crimes that are likely to be tried.

[124]Unless it negates *mens rea*, see ICC Statute, Art. 32(2), but then the defence would be one of lack of *mens rea*.

[125]United States, *International Law*, vol. II, Department of the Army, Pamphlet 27–161–2, 1962, p. 246. McCoubrey makes the same point: 'potentially a conflict between two systems of law is involved, the detailed resolution of which lies beyond the reasonably expected competence of the average soldier or indeed junior officer' (McCoubrey and White, *International Law and Armed Conflict*, p. 342).

[126]IX WCR 1.

[127]I WCR 55.

also referred to, seemed to turn on issues of fact (knowledge of the surrender) rather than on the question of knowledge of the law (the terms of the act of surrender).

Many military men – understandably given the importance of orders in the military context – cling tenaciously to the manifest illegality test. They will find academic support too. McCoubrey states that 'It would thus be strongly arguable that the defence of superior orders, with the strict "ought to know" qualification, survived 1945 and remains a feature of modern law'.[128] Cartledge[129] considers that both *mens rea* and manifest illegality are important. He refers to various national manuals and court rulings to the effect that the prosecution must show that either the accused knew that the order was unlawful or could reasonably be expected to have known it. He says that there is a parallel with some military offences such as insubordination, which require the prosecution to prove that the accused knew or ought to have known that the complainant was his superior officer.

But perhaps *mens rea* and manifest illegality are the same thing or, at least, lead to the same result. This can only be demonstrated by examples.

Example 1 The accused is ordered to and does bomb a building, which the military planners have decided is a military aircraft factory. It later turns out to be a musical instruments factory, which has been reduced to smouldering rubble, twanging strings and squeaking trumpets.

Here there is no war crime: there is neither *mens rea* nor manifest illegality.

Example 2 The accused is ordered to and does shoot and kill a man passing by who is dressed in civilian clothes. He is an enemy guerrilla commander.

Here there is no war crime because the person attacked is a legitimate target. The questions of *mens rea* and manifest illegality do not arise.

Example 3 Against a background of enemy guerrilla operations the accused is ordered to shoot and kill a man passing by who is dressed in civilian clothes on the grounds that he is an enemy guerrilla commander. In that belief the soldier complies with the order. It turns out that the man is an innocent civilian.

Although at first sight a man appearing to be a civilian ought not to be attacked, the soldier would say that he had no *mens rea* for a war crime because he had no reason to believe the facts to be other than as stated in the order. He would, no doubt, also claim that the order, in its context, was not manifestly unlawful.

Example 4 A soldier is ordered to and does use riot control gas to clear an enemy trench. He is prosecuted for violating the Geneva Gas Protocol of 1925.[130] He claims in his defence that the protocol does not include riot control agents, but the tribunal finds against him on this point of law.

---

[128] McCoubrey, *War Crimes*, p. 25.

[129] Cartledge, *The Soldier's Dilemma*, pp. 176–84.

[130] Of course, the situation would be different if the states party to the conflict were parties to the Chemical Weapons Convention of 1993, which prohibits the use of riot control agents as a method of warfare.

In this case, the fact that he was ordered to use gas is irrelevant to the issue of criminal responsibility, so questions of *mens rea* and manifest illegality do not arise. Ignorance of the law is no excuse. However, it is to be hoped that the tribunal would make allowance for the fact that the law on this point is the subject of controversy and either acquit or award only a nominal punishment.

Example 5 A long-range patrol ambushes a group of enemy soldiers and in the exchange of fire kills all its members except one who is wounded. A soldier is ordered to kill the wounded man because the patrol cannot take him with them and if he is left behind he might endanger the patrol by reporting its existence.

The order is illegal so the soldier carrying it out would be liable to be prosecuted for a grave breach of Protocol I.[131] Here, it is submitted, neither the *mens rea* nor manifest illegality test is going to help the defence.

Example 6 Prior to an infantry assault, the artillery commander is ordered by the divisional commander to, and does, destroy a village, which is an enemy guerrilla stronghold. The village is devastated as a result and most civilians living there are killed or injured, but none of the guerrillas, since they are in protected positions.

It might be alleged that this attack was indiscriminate and that those involved were criminally liable.[132]

Both the artillery commander and the commanding officer of the artillery regiment involved in the bombardment would have been involved in the planning of the attack so cannot rely on superior orders, but what of battery and troop commanders? They would probably realize that they were firing at areas in a village but might say that on the basis of the orders they had received and the information in their possession they had no reason to believe that the targets that had been identified for them were not military targets and carried out the orders they had received, so it would be a question of *mens rea* rather than manifest illegality. In this context, issues such as recklessness might be considered by the tribunal.

It is difficult to think of an example of a case where applying the *mens rea* and manifest illegality tests would lead to different results except, possibly, those where the law is unclear or controversial (Example 4). Schmitt, however, considers that 'relying on courts to come to the right result as a matter of "grace" rather than law ... is a reliance that is fragile at best'.[133]

As late as 1991, the International Law Commission, in its draft code of crimes against the peace and security of mankind, which included 'exceptionally serious

---

[131]Protocol I, Arts. 41 and 85, para. 3(e).

[132]W. J. Fenrick, The rule of proportionality and Protocol I in conventional warfare, *Military Law Review*, 1982, p. 115, suggests the following test: 'in all but the most blatant cases of indiscriminate attacks, subordinates would be entitled to assume that their superiors had carried out the attack precautions specified in Art. 57 of Protocol I and, as a result, they could not be held personally liable for any violation which occurred as a result of superior orders'.

[133]M. N. Schmitt, Book review: law on the battlefield, US Air Force 8 (1998) *Journal of Legal Studies*, 255, at pp. 272–3.

war crimes', made no reference to manifest illegality in their draft article on superior orders,[134] which read as follows: 'The fact that an individual charged with a crime against the peace and security of mankind acted pursuant to an order of a Government or a superior does not relieve him of criminal responsibility if, in the circumstances at the time, it was possible for him not to comply with that order'. This seems close to the formula adopted by the Commission when codifying the Nuremberg principles and does not include the manifest illegality test.[135]

Prior to the ICC Statute, the author was in serious doubt about whether manifest illegality was a legitimate consideration. The Nuremberg Charter as well as the International Law Commission's draft seemed to point against it. The statutes of the Yugoslav and Rwanda tribunals reflected the strict Nuremberg approach: 'the fact that an accused person acted pursuant to an order of a Government or of a superior shall not relieve him of criminal responsibility, but may be considered in mitigation of punishment . . .'.[136]

However, for parties to the ICC Statute, the debate about manifest illegality has become academic because the statute contains a specific provision on the defence of superior orders, as follows:[137]

1. The fact that a crime within the jurisdiction of the Court has been committed by a person pursuant to an order of a Government or of a superior, whether military or civilian, shall not relieve that person of criminal responsibility unless:
   (a) The person was under a legal obligation to obey orders of the Government or the superior in question;
   (b) The person did not know that the order was unlawful; and
   (c) The order was not manifestly unlawful.
2. For the purposes of this article, orders to commit genocide or crimes against humanity are manifestly unlawful.

It will be noted that the manifest-illegality test does not apply to genocide and crimes against humanity, presumably on the basis that they are obviously illegal, but it can be applied in the case of war crimes where the law is not clear or is unsettled.

---

[134] UN Doc. A/46/405.

[135] H. S. Levie, The rise and fall of an internationally codified denial of the defence of superior orders, *Military Law and Law of War Review*, 1991, at p. 204, makes the interesting point that because of the failure of any international body to draft a provision on superior orders, that defence will be available to somebody charged with a violation of the law of war. Green, Superior orders and the Geneva conventions and protocols, in Fox and Meyer, *Effecting Compliance*, comments that, if adopted, the ILC draft provides a limited defence of superior orders in the case of exceptionally serious war crimes but that in the case of grave breaches and other war crimes, the matter is governed by customary law.

[136] Arts. 9(4) and 6(4) respectively.

[137] ICC Statute, Art. 33.

9

The conduct of hostilities in internal armed conflicts

The purpose of this chapter is to supplement the standard works on the law of internal armed conflicts[1] by concentrating on the law relating to the conduct of hostilities in such conflicts. It is evident from any review of state practice[2] that the parties to an internal armed conflict tend to pay little attention to the principles of civilian immunity, targeting and proportionality dealt with in the earlier chapters of this book. That may be partly due to the fact that international treaties have very little to say on the subject.

Treaty law relating to internal armed conflicts is much less developed than that relating to international armed conflicts, particularly in respect of the rules governing the conduct of hostilities.[3] The main reason for this is that states consider that there is no place for the international law of armed conflict in what they consider to be an internal problem, governed by domestic law. It was only when the situation amounted, to all intents and purposes, to a full-scale armed conflict that belligerency was recognized and a broad application of the law of armed conflict followed. Nevertheless, states have accepted a limited application of international law in internal armed conflicts. This covers mainly the protection of the victims of such conflicts but hardly at all the conduct of hostilities.

---

[1] There were some collections of essays in the 1970s, which looked at the legal lessons to be drawn from various civil wars, such as R. A. Falk (ed.), *The International Law of Civil War*, Baltimore, Johns Hopkins Press, 1971; E. Luard, *The International Regulation of Civil Wars*, London, Thames & Hudson, 1972; or J. N. Moore, *Law and Civil War in the Modern World*, Baltimore, Johns Hopkins University Press, 1974. A more recent work that concentrates more on the legal regime applicable to internal armed conflicts is L. Moir, *The Law of Internal Armed Conflict*, Cambridge University Press, 2002.

[2] E.g., Moir, *The Law of Internal Armed Conflict*, pp. 67–88 and 120–32. In Kosovo, prior to the NATO intervention in March 1999, there were reports of mass executions, random killings, so-called 'ethnic cleansing', rape camps and use of forced labour, but not about the conduct of military operations as between the Serb authorities and the Kosovo Liberation Army (KLA).

[3] The United Kingdom, *Manual of Military Law* Part III, London, HMSO, 1958, devoted only paragraphs 8, 9 and 131 to 'armed conflicts not of an international character' and the United States Army Field Manual, *The Law of Land Warfare*, Washington, US Government Printing Office, 1956 (US Manual) only paragraph 11. The reasons for this are summarized by H. J. Taubenfeld, The laws of war in civil wars, in Moore, *Law and Civil War*, at p. 503.

The most important difference between an international and an internal armed conflict is that, in the latter case, the domestic law of the state where the conflict takes place continues to govern the conduct of the parties, though it may not always be applied, especially by armed factions, or may not be enforceable because of a breakdown of law and order. In addition, domestic law may be considerably modified by the introduction by the state of emergency legislation or the imposition of martial law. Rebels or insurgents are unlikely to be able to uphold and enforce domestic law unless they control autonomous regions. International law, in the form of human rights law, may help to fill the vacuum, but human rights treaties permit some latitude to states, in time of war or other public emergency threatening the life of the nation, to take measures derogating from their obligations under those treaties.[4] The law of armed conflict may, therefore, provide a modicum of additional protection.

The extent to which it does so will depend on the nature of the conflict. If the state remains in control and domestic law continues to be enforced through the courts, there may be a case for arguing that it is not an armed conflict at all but an internal security problem. It is when, owing to internal violence, that control has ceased in a significant part of the state or when the normal apparatus of domestic law has broken down that an armed conflict may be said to exist. That is why the United Kingdom government has consistently argued, and rightly in the author's opinion, that the situation that has existed in Northern Ireland since 1969 is not an armed conflict. On the other hand there may be an armed conflict in the following scenarios, if:

(a)   a rebel movement is trying either to overthrow the government or to establish its own autonomous region and, in either case, controls significant areas of territory;
(b)   a federal state starts to break up into its constituent parts and there is an armed contention between central government forces and local militias; or
(c)   there is a complete breakdown of law and order in a significant area of territory over which the government has no control and which is either controlled by an armed faction or is fought over by armed factions.

The situation was most complicated in Bosnia, with both internal and international armed conflicts taking place at the same time.[5]

---

[4]See, e.g., Art. 15 of the European Convention on Human Rights of 1950. However, it should be noted that there can be no derogation in respect of fundamental human rights – the right to life (except deaths resulting from lawful acts of war), the prohibition of torture, the prohibition of slavery and the principle of no punishment without law.

[5]C. J. Greenwood, War crimes proceedings before the International Criminal Tribunal for the former Yugoslavia, *Military Law Journal*, 1997, p. 18, put it thus: 'there were hostilities between the Bosnian Government and Bosnian Serbs, between the Bosnian Government and the Bosnian Croats, between the Bosnian Croats and the Bosnian Serbs, between the Bosnian Government and dissident Muslims in the Bihać enclave, between Bosnian Government forces and Croatian Government forces and between both of these and the forces of the Federal Yugoslav Army ... In addition, UNPROFOR forces and NATO air force units became involved in often very heavy fighting, especially during the summer of 1995.'

Law applicable

The law is to be found in certain basic principles of customary law,[6] including principles enunciated in the Hague Regulations of 1907,[7] in common Art. 3 to the Geneva Conventions of 1949 and in Additional Protocol II of 1977 (Protocol II). In addition, certain treaties have been extended to apply to internal armed conflicts, notably the basic protection of the Hague Cultural Property Convention of 1954, the Amended Protocol II of 1996 on mines,[8] the Ottawa Convention of 1997 on anti-personnel mines and the Second Hague Cultural Property Protocol of 1999. Furthermore, the Rome Statue of the International Criminal Court of 1998 (ICC Statute) contains a list of acts that, if committed in an internal armed conflict, amount to war crimes.

This body of law can, in many cases, provide protection equivalent to that provided for in international armed conflicts. However, for the law to apply, there must be an armed conflict. That term is not defined. It is not always easy to distinguish between internal security operations, governed by domestic law and human rights law, and internal armed conflict, governed by domestic law, human rights law and the law of armed conflict. This distinction is recognized by Protocol II, which does not apply in internal disturbances and tensions, such as riots and isolated and sporadic acts of violence.[9]

Agreements can be reached between the parties to an internal conflict to apply other provisions of the law of armed conflict and the International Committee of the Red Cross tries to persuade parties to adopt a broader application of the law.[10] Zegveld discusses the interesting question of why, as a matter of law, the provisions of common Art. 3, or Protocol II, bind armed opposition groups that, of course, have not ratified the treaties in question.[11] Perhaps the answer lies in the fact that law of war obligations are binding on individuals as well as

---

[6]The US Manual, para. 11, states that customary law only applies upon recognition of the rebels as belligerents. However, this view is obsolete. The applicability of customary law to internal armed conflicts was not doubted in the discussions at the Diplomatic Conference at which Protocol II was negotiated, see Y. Sandoz, C. Swinarski, and B. Zimmerman, with J. Pictet, *Commentary on the Additional Protocols of 8 June 1977 to the Geneva Conventions of 12 August 1949*, Geneva, Martinus Nijhoff, 1987 (ICRC *Commentary*), para. 4776.

[7]The Commission of Experts whose work preceded the setting up of the Yugoslav tribunal doubted whether there was any customary law applicable to internal armed conflicts which were not rooted in Common Article 3 to the Geneva Conventions of 1949, Additional Protocol II of 1977 and Art. 19 of the Hague Cultural Property Convention of 1954, see UN Doc. S/1994/774 at para. 52. However, the tribunal itself has been less cautious.

[8]The whole of the Conventional Weapons Convention was applied to internal armed conflicts in December 2001 by an amendment to Art. 1 – not in force at the time of writing (30 June 2003).

[9]Protocol II, Art. 1, para. 2.

[10]A special agreement to supplement Common Article 3 was entered into in Bosnia on 22 May 1992 and this replaced an earlier memorandum of understanding of 27 November 1991. The texts of both agreements are set out in M. Sassòli and A. Bouvier, *How does Law Protect in War?* Geneva, International Committee of the Red Cross, 1999, pp. 1109–16.

[11]L. Zegveld, *The Accountability of Armed Opposition Groups in International Law*, Cambridge University Press, 2002, pp. 14–18.

states and are, therefore, equally binding on members of armed opposition groups.[12]

When is there an armed conflict?

The law of armed conflict applies once the situation reaches the intensity of an armed conflict. This may be the case if the government has recognized the insurgents as belligerents, or the parties have agreed to apply the law of armed conflict or if the United Nations Security Council has so determined. Other factors pointing towards the existence of an armed conflict include whether the insurgents possess organized armed forces, control territory and ensure respect for the law of armed conflict.[13]

The existence of an armed conflict does not necessarily mean that there is an armed contention between the state and an insurgent faction. There can be an armed conflict between factions within a state. Some light has been thrown on these issues by the important ruling on jurisdiction of the Appeals Chamber of the International Criminal Tribunal for the Former Yugoslavia (the Yugoslav tribunal) in the *Tadić* case.[14] The chamber adopted the following definition of armed conflict:

an armed conflict exists whenever there is a resort to armed force between States or protracted armed violence between governmental authorities and organized armed groups within a State. International humanitarian law[15] applies from the initiation of such armed conflicts and extends beyond the cessation of hostilities until a general conclusion of peace is reached; or, in the case of internal conflicts, a peaceful settlement is achieved. Until that moment, international humanitarian law continues to apply in the whole territory of the warring States or, in the case of internal conflicts, the whole territory under the control of a party, whether or not actual combat takes place there.

This is not a bad working definition. It distinguishes internal from international armed conflicts on the basis of protraction, organization of dissident forces and territorial control but omits that other essential feature, reflected in Art. 1, para.

---

[12]In *Prosecutor* v. *Furundžija*, 121 *International Law Reports* (ILR) 213, the Yugoslav tribunal dealt with a person who was the commander of a special unit of the HVO military police, the HVO being a self-proclaimed entity of the Bosnian Croats in Bosnia. See also *Prosecutor* v. *Aleksovski*, Case No. IT-95-14/1, judgment of 15 June 1999, where the accused was the leader of an armed opposition group.

[13]J. Pictet, *Commentary on the I Geneva Convention for the Amelioration of the Condition of the Wounded and Sick in Armed Forces in the Field*, Geneva, International Committee of the Red Cross, 1952 (Pictet, *Commentary* I) p. 49.

[14]*Prosecutor* v. *Tadić*, 105 ILR 419, at p. 488. The definition was applied by the trial chamber, see 112 ILR 1, at p. 179 (para. 561).

[15]Another term for the law of war.

2, of Protocol II, of the requisite threshold of violence.[16] An interesting feature of the definition is the geographical aspect. The chamber rejected Tadić's ingenious argument that there was no armed conflict in the region of Prijedor where his offences were alleged to have taken place because the forces concerned had taken control without any active opposition.

The chamber also had to deal with whether the conflict in question, i.e., the one involving Tadić, was internal or international. They rejected the notion that the whole of the conflict in Bosnia was international, preferring, and rightly in the author's opinion, a more analytical approach, looking at each conflict separately:

> To the extent that the conflicts had been limited to clashes between Bosnian Government forces and Bosnian Serb rebel forces in Bosnia-Herzegovina, as well as between the Croatian Government and Croatian Serb rebel forces in Krajina (Croatia), they had been internal (unless direct involvement of the Federal Republic of Yugoslavia (Serbia and Montenegro) could be proven).[17]

The distinction is important, as the body of law that applies to international armed conflicts is substantial whereas that applying to internal armed conflicts is slight. It is of interest, therefore, that in the *Rajić* case, the trial tribunal held that a conflict could become international if one of the warring factions was effectively controlled[18] by another state. So far neither the trial nor appeal chambers has ruled on the question of whether there was an armed conflict between, on the one hand, the states which provided troops to UNPROFOR and the NATO states which provided air strikes and reaction forces and, on the other hand, the Bosnian Serbs, though the indictment of Karadžić and Mladić for taking hostage UNPROFOR personnel is, perhaps, an indication that the prosecutor considers that there was not.[19]

Sometimes what starts as an internal armed conflict becomes 'internationalized' by the intervention of states in support of the parties. In that case, the whole of the law of armed conflict would apply, not just the rules applicable in

---

[16]However, the trial chamber seems to have considered 'protracted' as an element of intensity, see 112 ILR 179 (para. 562), but nevertheless went on to find that, in the context of the case, an armed conflict was going on of sufficient intensity for the application of Common Article 3 to the Geneva Conventions, see 112 ILR 1, 181 and 200 (paras. 568 and 607).

[17]105 ILR 490.

[18]*Prosecutor* v. *Rajić*, 108 ILR 141, 154 (paras. 22–32). The International Court of Justice in the case of Military and Paramilitary Activities in and against Nicaragua (*Nicaragua* v. *United States*) (Merits) (*Nicaragua* case), 76 ILR 349, 396 (para. 109), considered that the United States did not exercise such a degree of control as to enable the inference to be drawn that the contras acted on its behalf.

[19]The Geneva Prisoner of War Convention of 1949 does not specifically prohibit taking military personnel hostage, though to do so would be incompatible with prisoner-of-war status. However, the situation is different if it is an internal armed conflict, since Common Article 3 to the Geneva Conventions imposes a general prohibition on hostage-taking, or if Protocol I applies, see Art. 75, para. 2(c).

internal armed conflicts. That was the case in Yugoslavia, as its constituent parts gradually broke away in the period 1991–93. The Yugoslav tribunal has declined to categorize the conflict as a whole as internal or international, preferring to look in each case at the aspect of the conflict that formed the background to that case. This has resulted in some parts of the conflict as being regarded as internal and others as international. In the *Tadić* case, the appeals chamber concluded that the armed conflict it was concerned with was international because the Bosnian Serb armed forces were under the overall control of the authorities of the Federal Republic of Yugoslavia. Such control involved more than the financing and equipping of forces, but also participation in the planning and supervision of military operations.[20] In the *Blaškić* case, the trials chamber concluded that the acts attributed to the defendant occurred as part of an international armed conflict because the Republic of Croatia exercised total control over the Croatian Community of Hercegovina–Bosnia and the Croatian Defence Council (the HVO) and exercised general control over the Croatian political and military authorities in central Bosnia.[21] In the *Delalić* case,[22] the appeals chamber decided to follow the *Tadić* overall control test.[23]

Types of internal armed conflict

There continues to be a distinction in law between national liberation struggles, internal armed conflicts, and internal armed conflicts to which Protocol II of 1977 applies, because the applicable legal regime is different in each case.

National liberation struggles

These are the armed conflicts referred to in Art. 1, para. 4, of Additional Protocol I of 1977 (Protocol I). Provision for this type of armed conflict was made against background of struggles for independence from colonial rule and increasing international pressure to regard such struggles as internationalized. However, the authority representing the people concerned is required to lodge with the depositary a declaration of compliance with the Geneva Conventions and Protocol I. The author is not aware of any case where an Art. 96, para. 3, declaration was successfully made. Since these conflicts are treated as international armed conflicts, they will not be dealt with further in this chapter.

---

[20]124 ILR 61, 121 (para. 145). The appeals chamber declined to follow the 'effective control' test enunciated in the *Nicaragua* case, 76 ILR 349 (para. 115).

[21]*Prosecutor* v. *Blaškić*, 122 ILR 1, 225 (para. 744).

[22]The *Delalić* case, often referred to as the *Čelebići* case, concerned the treatment of detainees at the *Čelebići* camp near Konjić in central Bosnia in 1992.

[23]*Prosecutor* v. *Delalić* and Others, 40 (2001) ILM 630, 636 (para. 26).

Internal armed conflicts

These are internal armed conflicts between the armed forces of a state and one or more armed factions in that state, or internal armed conflicts between such factions.[24]

Recent examples include Kosovo before the NATO intervention in March 1999 and Somalia in 1993.

Protocol II conflicts

These are internal armed conflict between the armed forces of a state and an organized armed faction where the conflict has reached the level at which Protocol II comes into operation. According to the ICRC *Commentary*,[25] the criteria required of the insurgents – responsible command, territorial control and compliance with the protocol – restrict the applicability of the protocol to conflicts of a certain degree of intensity and that 'not all cases of internal armed conflict are covered as in the case of common Art. 3'. Pictet, in his commentary on the Geneva Conventions, mentions these and other criteria for the applicability of common Art. 3 but states that they are only indicative and not determinative.[26] So there may be internal armed conflicts governed by common Art. 3 (but not Protocol II), for example, where armed factions are fighting each other. There may be other internal armed conflicts governed by both instruments, for example, where there are sustained and concerted military operations between government forces and organized armed groups. A conflict may develop from one of low intensity to one of high intensity and thus cross the threshold for the applicability of Protocol II.

The conduct of hostilities in internal armed conflicts

Common Art. 3 does not deal directly with the conduct of hostilities. It seems, at first sight, only to protect the victims of such conflicts.[27] However, a close reading of the text of the article leads to the conclusion that it does more than that. For example, the principle of civilian immunity can be inferred from paragraph 1, which prohibits violence to the life of persons taking no active part in hostilities.

---

[24]Geneva Conventions 1949. Art. 3.

[25]ICRC *Commentary*, para. 4453.

[26]J. Pictet, *Commentary* on the IV Convention relating to the Protection of Civilian Persons in Time of War, Geneva, International Committee of the Red Cross, 1958, pp. 35–6.

[27]R. Higgins, in her article, International law and civil conflict, in Luard, *The International Regulation of Civil Wars*, includes a section headed 'The conduct of civil war hostilities', which sets out the text of common Article 3, described as 'a basic humanitarian code of conduct', but does not explain its impact, if any, on the conduct of hostilities.

Common Art. 3 does not stand alone. The jurisprudence of the Yugoslav tribunal indicates that some basic rules of international armed conflict law apply equally to internal armed conflicts.

In the *Tadić* (jurisdiction) case, the appeals chamber expressed the view, albeit *obiter dicta*, that:

It cannot be denied that customary rules have developed to govern internal strife. These rules ... cover such areas as protection of civilians from hostilities, in particular from indiscriminate attacks, protection of civilian objects, in particular cultural property, protection of all those who do not (or no longer) take active part in hostilities, as well as prohibition of means of warfare proscribed in international armed conflicts and ban of certain methods of conducting hostilities.[28]

This passage has been criticised by Greenwood[29] as going beyond the treaty rules contained in common Art. 3 and Protocol II, though he accepts that there 'is likely to be broad agreement that the law of internal conflicts includes principles regarding the protection of the civilian population'.

However, the *Tadić* case has been reinforced by the ICC Statue. Furthermore, the basic customary law principles of military necessity, humanity, distinction and proportionality,[30] dealt with in Chapter 1, provide guidelines, as do the Hague Regulations of 1907, generally considered to be reflective of customary law.[31] Taken together, these provide quite a body of international law that governs internal armed conflicts, which is binding on all states irrespective of whether they have ratified Additional Protocol II, the Second Hague Protocol or the various treaties dealing with weapons.

Enemy armed forces

Common Art. 3 does use terms relevant to the conduct of hostilities: 'persons taking no active part in the hostilities', 'members of the armed forces who have laid down their arms' and 'those placed *hors de combat*'. Protocol II uses similar

---

[28] 105 ILR 453, 520 (para. 127).

[29] C. Greenwood, International humanitarian law and the *Tadić* case, 7 (1996) *European Journal of International Law*, 265, at p. 278.

[30] Common Article 3 itself is rooted in the principle of humanity and there seems little argument that the law protects civilians in internal armed conflicts, hence the principle of distinction. Referring to UN General Assembly resolution 2444 (XXIII) recognizing, in all armed conflicts, the principles of civilian immunity and distinction, E. David, *Principes de Droit des Conflits Armés*, Brussels, Bruylant, 3rd edn 2002, p. 405, comments: '*le minimum minimorum de la rés. 2444 devrait en tout cas être considéré comme du droit positif applicable à tout conflit armé*'. Furthermore, Theodor Meron wrote in 1996, 'general principles first developed for international wars, such as proportionality and necessity, may be extended through customary law to civil wars: T. Meron, The continuing role of custom in the formation of international humanitarian law, 90 *American Journal of International Law*, 238, 244.

[31] However, their precise applicability to internal armed conflicts is far from clear, see *Tadić* (Jurisdiction), 105 ILR 418, 519; Moir, *The Law of Internal Armed Conflict*, pp. 146–7; Meron, The continuing role of custom, p. 243.

language: 'persons who do not take a direct part . . . in hostilities'.[32] It also refers to 'civilians' and 'civilian population',[33] 'dissident armed force or other organized armed groups' and 'responsible command'.[34] The use of such terms implies a distinction between fighters and civilians.

Neither instrument deals, specifically, with the question of combatant status. Nevertheless, in order to apply the law, it is necessary to be able to distinguish between those who take a direct part in the fighting and those who do not.

In some cases this will be easier than in others. During the conflict in Bosnia from 1992–95, most of the fighting was done by militias based on the previous territorial defence structure in Yugoslavia. There were identifiable armed units belonging to the Army of Republika Srpska (VRS), the HVO, the Muslim Army of Bosnia–Hercegovina (AbiH) and so forth, usually wearing uniform. In Kosovo in 1999, the contention was generally between the Serb special police units (MUP), a paramilitary organization, and the KLA, a group with some of the trappings of military structure and, at least before the camera, a camouflage pattern uniform with the KLA patch. On the other hand, in Somalia in 1992–93 there was a weak central government with large parts of the country controlled by so-called war lords with their own fighters whose appearance and actions indicated little formal training and structure. The same was true in Afghanistan before the coalition forces became involved in October 2001 and the Northern Alliance fighters were ranged against the Taliban forces. In these areas a recognizable uniform in the Western military sense was hard to discern. Of course, there is no requirement for such uniform so long as those involved in the fighting are distinguishable from the civilian population. That may be a matter of local custom and usage.

Many internal armed conflicts are characterized by guerrilla operations where insurgents operate under the cover of the civilian population or carry out attacks from within civilian crowds and so prefer to avoid distinguishing themselves from that population. Furthermore, they may be organized in a cellular structure to hinder outside penetration and identification of their membership. In these cases, convention with regard to the wearing of uniform is likely to be reversed: fighters may parade in uniform on ceremonial occasions or when they feel safe from attack but are likely to discard it when deployed on operations. The governmental forces may also feel vulnerable to ambush or sniping or bomb attack when in uniform or in military vehicles, so may be inclined to make increasing use of undercover operations. Guerrilla campaigns often see the use of bombs, such as car bombs, detonated by remote control or by a time switch, often in civilian areas. In recent years there has been the increasing use of suicide bombers: persons in civilian clothes who detonate their bombs in crowded places.

---

[32] Protocol II, Art. 4, para. 1.
[33] Protocol II, Part IV.
[34] Protocol II, Art. 1, para. 1.

All these factors undermine the protection that the law of armed conflict strives to provide. Much continues to be controlled by domestic law in any event. International legal obligations do not override domestic law unless there is a direct conflict between them. Human rights law, subject to any permissible derogations, continues to apply. Captured fighters may, subject to the above, be tried for the offences they have committed. The law of armed conflict does not allow for combatant or prisoner-of-war status in internal armed conflict unless either belligerency has been recognized or the parties have agreed, or decided, to accord that status or apply the law of armed conflict in full.

It can be inferred from common Art. 3 that, subject to anything that domestic law may provide, persons taking an active part in hostilities may be attacked. So the question arises: what is meant by taking an active part in hostilities? At one extreme, a person would be taking an active part in hostilities if he were actually taking part in an attack; at the other extreme he would not if he had been arrested and put up no further resistance.

In the *Tadić* case the trial chamber stated:

It is unnecessary to define exactly the line dividing those taking an active part in hostilities and those who are not so involved. It is sufficient to examine the relevant facts of each victim and to ascertain whether, in each individual's circumstances, that person was actively involved in hostilities at the relevant time. Violations of the rules contained in Common Article 3 are alleged to have been committed against persons who, on the evidence presented to this Trial Chamber, were captured or detained by Bosnian Serb forces, whether committed during the course of the armed take-over of the Kozarac area or while those persons were being rounded-up for transport to each of the camps in opstina Prijedor. Whatever their involvement in hostilities prior to that time, each of these classes of persons cannot be said to have been taking an active part in the hostilities. Even if they were members of the armed forces of the Government of the Republic of Bosnia and Herzegovina or otherwise engaging in hostile acts prior to capture, such persons would be considered 'members of armed forces' who are 'placed *hors de combat* by detention'. Consequently, these persons enjoy the protection of those rules of customary international humanitarian law applicable to armed conflicts, as contained in Article 3 of the Statute.[35]

But between taking part in an attack and being arrested there is wide spectrum. It seems from *Tadić* that a person may not be attacked simply because he belongs to an armed faction, though that would not preclude the use of necessary force to effect an arrest, but there is a case for arguing that he is taking an active part in hostilities if he is deploying to, or withdrawing from, the place of attack.[36] For a further discussion of this problem, see Chapter 2.

Although, in 1996, Greenwood was doubtful about the validity of the suggestion by the appeals chamber in the *Tadić* case that feigning civilian status in an internal

[35] 112 ILR 1, 203 (para. 616).
[36] See Moir, *The Law of Internal Armed Conflict*, p. 59.

conflict constitutes perfidy[37] it would, in the author's opinion, be a war crime to kill or wound an adversary who is *hors de combat* through surrender, and this would extend to capture, wounds or sickness;[38] to deny quarter;[39] or to make improper use of the flag of truce, the red-cross or red-crescent emblems or the flag or military insignia or uniform of the enemy.[40] Further, Art. 8, para. 2(e), of the ICC Statute makes the following acts war crimes in internal armed conflicts:

(ix)   Killing or wounding treacherously a combatant adversary;[41]

(x)   Declaring that no quarter will be given;[42]

Treachery would include killing by feigning civilian status. However, ruses of war would be permissible.[43]

Civilian immunity

It was not until the Additional Protocols of 1977 that the principle of civilian immunity was set out in treaty language, but, as explained in Chapter 1, it had been recognized long before 1977. Dr Francis Lieber wrote in 1863 that 'the unarmed citizen is to be spared in person, property, and honour as much as the exigencies of war will admit'.[44]

As mentioned above, the principle of civilian immunity can be inferred from paragraph 1 of common Art. 3, which prohibits violence to the life of persons taking no *active* part in hostilities.[45] This also prohibits the starvation of civilians[46] or the use of civilians as shields[47] as methods of combat.

---

[37]Greenwood, the *Tadić* case, p. 278.

[38]Hague Regulations 1907, Art. 23(c).

[39]This follows inescapably from Common Article 3, para. 1. Protocol II goes further and prohibits orders that there shall be no survivors, Art. 4, para. 1. Even in cases to which Protocol II does not apply, a commander who issues such an order would be criminally responsible as an aider and abettor if, as a result of the order, a captured fighter were summarily executed.

[40]Hague Regulations, Art. 23(f).

[41]See Hague Regulations, Art. 23(b).

[42]See Hague Regulations, Art, 23(d).

[43]Hague Regulations, Art. 24.

[44]Lieber Code 1863, Art. 22.

[45]W. A. Solf put it more cautiously in M. Bothe, K. J. Partsch and W. A. Solf, *New Rules for the Victims of Armed Conflicts*, The Hague, Martinus Nijhoff, 1982, at p. 667 as follows: 'It is arguable that the prohibition in Art. 3 common to the Conventions of "violence to life and person" against "persons taking no active part in the hostilities" is broad enough to include attacks against civilians in territory controlled by the adverse party in a non-international conflict'. Zegveld, *Accountability of Armed Opposition Groups*, p. 8, quoting Draper and others, counsels caution in citing Common Article 3 as authority for civilian immunity in the conduct of hostilities, since the article was never intended to cover that, but rather the protection of persons in detention.

[46]ICRC, *Commentary*, para. 4794. Zegveld, *Accountability of Armed Opposition Groups*, pp. 86–9, argues that armed opposition groups are legally bound not to prohibit or interfere with the delivery of humanitarian relief.

[47]Bothe *et al.*, *New Rules*, p. 678.

Protocol II deals with the matter as follows:

Art. 13. Protection of the civilian population

1. The civilian population and individual civilians shall enjoy general protection against the dangers arising from military operations. To give effect to this protection, the following rules shall be observed in all circumstances.

2. The civilian population as such, as well as individual civilians, shall not be the object of attack. Acts or threats of violence the primary purpose of which is to spread terror among the civilian population are prohibited.

3. Civilians shall enjoy the protection afforded by this part, unless and for such time as they take a *direct*[48] part in hostilities.

Loss of protection when civilians take a direct part in hostilities reflects customary law and the rules for international armed conflict.[49] Hostilities have been defined as 'acts of war that by their nature or purpose struck [*sic*] at the personnel and matériel of enemy armed forces' but this includes preparation for combat and returning from combat.[50] Taking a direct part in hostilities would not include 'supplying labour, transporting supplies, serving as messengers or disseminating propaganda'.[51] There does not seem to be any difference in meaning between taking a 'direct' part, or taking an 'active' part, in hostilities.

Art. 8, para. 2(e) of the ICC Statue makes the following acts in internal armed conflicts a war crime:

(i) Intentionally directing attacks against the civilian population as such or against individual civilians not taking direct part in hostilities.

In the *Blaškić* case,[52] the trial chamber declared that common Art. 3 represented customary international law, that the list of rules in that article was not a closed list, that Art. 3 of the Tribunal's statute subsumes, but is more broadly based than, common Art. 3 and that the Hague Regulations also form part of customary international law.[53] The court went on to say, in respect of the charges of unlawful attacks on civilians and civilian property, that: 'The parties to the conflict are obliged to attempt to distinguish between military targets and civilian persons or property. Targeting civilians or civilian property is an offence

---

[48] Emphasis supplied.

[49] See Protocol I, Art. 51, para. 3.

[50] ICRC *Commentary*, para. 4788. This passage seems to make more sense when read in the light of para. 1942, which refers to 'acts which by their nature and purpose are intended to cause actual harm to the personnel and equipment of the armed forces'. For a discussion of this issue in the context of international armed conflict, see Chapter 1.

[51] Bothe *et al.*, *New Rules*, p. 672. See also Chapter 1.

[52] The case was mainly concerned with the 'ethnic cleansing' of Bosnian Muslims by the armed forces of the Croatian Defence Council (the HVO).

[53] 122 ILR 1, 68–9 (paras. 166–8).

when not justified by military necessity.'[54] This should not be read as permitting the targeting of civilians or civilian when military necessity so dictates. It can only be a reference to cases where civilian immunity has been abandoned, for example, where a civilian takes a direct part in hostilities or where civilian property is being used for military purposes.

The trial chamber explained the matter better in the *Kupreškić* case:[55]

The protection of civilians in time of armed conflict, whether international or internal, is the bedrock of modern humanitarian law. The protections of civilians and civilian objects provided by modern international law may cease entirely or be reduced or suspended in three exceptional circumstances: (1) when civilians abuse their rights; (2) when, although the object of a military attack is comprised of military objectives, belligerents cannot avoid causing so-called collateral damage to civilians; and (3) at least according to some authorities, when civilians may legitimately be the object of reprisals.[56]

The tribunal has, in several cases, affirmed that attacks on civilians and civilian objects in internal armed are unlawful. In the *Martić* case[57] (Rule 61), the trial chamber decided: 'As regards customary law the rule that the civilian population as such, as well as individual civilians, shall not be the object of attack, is a fundamental rule of international humanitarian law applicable to all armed conflicts.'[58] The appeals chamber in the *Strugar* (jurisdiction) case decided that: 'The principles prohibiting attacks on civilians and unlawful attacks on civilian objects stated in Articles 51 and 52 of Additional Protocol I and Article 13 of Protocol II[59] are principles of customary international law. Customary international law establishes that a violation of these principles entails individual criminal responsibility.'[60] In the *Krstić* case,[61] the trial chamber considered that an armed conflict existed between Bosnia–Hercegovina and its armed forces, on the one hand, and the Republika Srpska and its armed forces, on the other. It did not categorize the conflict as international or internal but considered that the link to armed conflict was sufficient support for the charges

---

[54]*Ibid.*, 71 (para. 180). Although the case was based on the application of customary law, rather than Protocol I, the court did consider that the armed conflict in question was international.

[55]The case concerned the killing, in April 1993 by members of the Bosnian Croat military forces, of some 116 Muslim inhabitants of Ahmići, a small village in central Bosnia, the destruction of 169 houses and two mosques.

[56]*Prosecutor* v. *Kupreškić*, Case No. IT-95-16-T, judgement of 12 January 2000, paras. 521 and 522.

[57]The case concerned the firing of Orkan rockets delivering cluster bombs into the Croatian city of Zagreb in May 1995. Although Rule 61 decisions delivered *in absentia* do not carry much weight and later passages of this decision relating to belligerent reprisals are open to severe criticism, this is one of many decisions to affirm the principle, in internal armed conflicts, of civilian immunity.

[58]*Prosecutor* v. *Martić*, 108 ILR 39, 45.

[59]Art. 13 of Protocol II protects the civilian population and individual civilians, not civilian objects.

[60]*Prosecutor* v. *Strugar*, Case No. IT-01-42-AR72, decision of 22 November 2002, para 10.

[61]The case concerned the execution of several thousand Bosnian Muslim men following the take-over by units of the Bosnian Serb army (the VRS) of the UN safe area of Srebrenica in July 1995.

that were framed as either as war crimes or crimes against humanity.[62] It found that murders falling within the meaning of Art. 3 of the statute of the tribunal were committed. Since Art. 3 of the statute does not specifically use the term 'murder', this must be a reference back to common Art. 3 of the Geneva Conventions 1949, which does.[63]

The indictment in the *Galić* case includes counts of attacks on civilians in violation of the laws or customs or war. The accused was the commander of the Sarajevo Romanija Corps of the Bosnian Serb Army from September 1992 until August 1994. According to the prosecution, during this period, the forces under his command and control conducted a campaign of sniping and shelling against the civilian population of Sarajevo.[64] The indictment in the *Strugar* case[65] also contains counts of violating the laws or customs of war by the killing and wounding of civilians in the unlawful shelling of Dubrovnik and Mokosica in the period October to December 1991. Although the indictment is based on the premise that this was an international armed conflict, some of the counts refer to common Art. 3 or Protocol II. The indictment also alleges unjustified devastation, unlawful attacks on civilian objects, destruction or wilful damage to historic monuments and institutions dedicated to education and religion, extensive destruction and appropriation of property and plunder of public or private property.

Art. 13, para. 2, of Protocol II also prohibits 'acts or threats of violence the primary purpose of which is to spread terror among the civilian population'. McCoubrey and White[66] refer to the mortar bombing at the Sarajevo marketplace on 5 February 1994 as 'one gross instance of terror bombardment'. But this may be rushing to judgement. The mere fact that a mortar explodes in a marketplace and kills 68 civilians, while most regrettable, is not, in itself, proof that a war crime has been committed, let alone a terror attack. It would be necessary to establish, first, that it was deliberately fired into the marketplace and, second, that it was done with the requisite intent. No war crime would have been committed if it had been aimed at a military objective but landed in the marketplace owing to a malfunction, for example, or even, perhaps, to the incompetence of the mortar crew.

Forced movement of civilians

Recent conflicts, such as those in the former Yugoslavia, have been blighted by a practice, known by the euphemism 'ethnic cleansing', of forcing civilians of

---

[62] *Prosecutor* v. *Krstić*, 40 ILM (2001) 1346, 1348 (para. 481).

[63] In fact, the court said as much in the *Kupreškić* case, No. IT-95-16-T, judgment of 12 January 2002, para. 647.

[64] Case No. IT-98-29-T. At the date of writing (30 June 2003) the judgment is awaited.

[65] Case No. IT-01-42. At the date of writing (30 June 2003) the trial has not commenced.

[66] H. McCoubrey and N. D. White, *International Organizations and Civil Wars*, Aldershot, Dartmouth, 1995, p. 107.

a different cultural background to move out of the region. In the case of Kosovo, this meant that Kosovo Albanians were forced to leave the country altogether for Albania. Methods adopted for carrying out this practice included shelling their homes, special police operations to round up and expel them and burning their houses to prevent their return. As pointed out to the author when flown by helicopter over central Bosnia in 1996, where one in every two houses was roofless, this was usually due to burning rather than to military operations.

Protocol II provides:

Art. 17. Prohibition of forced movement of civilians

1. The displacement of the civilian population shall not be ordered for reasons related to the conflict unless the security of the civilians involved or imperative military reasons so demand. Should such displacements have to be carried out, all possible measures shall be taken in order that the civilian population may be received under satisfactory conditions of shelter, hygiene, health, safety and nutrition.

2. Civilians shall not be compelled to leave their own territory for reasons connected with the conflict.

The words 'for reasons related to the conflict' are intended to permit the evacuation of civilians in the event of natural disaster, the words 'imperative military reasons' would preclude political reasons[67] and the words 'own territory' relate to the possibility that different parts of a state may be under the control of different parties to the conflict.[68]

Art. 8, para. 2(e) of the ICC Statute makes the following a war crime in internal armed conflicts:

(viii)   Ordering the displacement of the civilian population for reasons related to the conflict, unless the security of the civilians involved or imperative military reasons so demand;

In the *Krstić* case,[69] the tribunal was concerned with the forcible transfer of persons. It held that, although forcible transfer within the boundaries of a state (Bosnia–Hercegovina) did not amount to deportation,[70] it did amount to inhumane treatment.[71]

Military objectives and civilian objects

The Yugoslav tribunal seems, on the basis of the cases cited above, to accept that, even in internal armed conflicts, attacks on civilian objects are prohibited.

[67] *Ibid.*, p. 115 state that the provision for military necessity is 'a practical recognition of the real exigencies of warfare, not an invitation to callous infliction dictated by military convenience'.

[68] ICRC, *Commentary*, paras. 4854, 4855 and 4859.

[69] 40 (2001) ILM 1346, 1356 (para. 532).

[70] Contrary to Art. 5(d) of the Statute of the International Criminal Tribunal For The Former Yugoslavia (ICTY Statute).

[71] Contrary to Art. 5(i) of the ICTY Statute.

In the *Tadić* (jurisdiction) case, the appeals chamber stated:

It cannot be denied that customary rules have developed to govern internal strife. These rules ... cover such areas as ... protection of civilian objects, in particular cultural property.[72]

There is no definition of military objective in the treaties dealing with internal armed conflicts, nor is the term used. Civilian objects are not given general protection in these treaties,[73] only certain objects being singled out for protection under Protocol II.[74]

Nevertheless, in order to be able to give effect to the principle of civilian immunity, it is necessary to distinguish between persons and things it is specifically prohibited to attack and other persons and things. The customary law principles of military necessity and humanity combine to prevent attacks unless there is a legitimate military purpose to be achieved.[75] This is recognized by Art. 3 of the Statute of the Yugoslav tribunal, which lists as war crimes:

(b) wanton destruction of cities, towns or villages, or devastation not justified by military necessity;

(c) attack, or bombardment, by whatever means, of undefended towns, villages, dwellings, or buildings;

(d) seizure of, destruction or wilful damage done to institutions dedicated to religion, charity and education, the arts and sciences, historic monuments and works of art and science;

(e) plunder of public or private property.

Art. 8, para. 2(e) of the ICC Statute makes the following war crimes in internal armed conflicts:

(v) Pillaging a town or place, even when taken by assault;[76]

(xii) Destroying or seizing the property of an adversary unless such destruction or seizure be imperatively demanded by the necessities of the conflict;[77]

In addition, there is a customary law principle that undefended towns, villages, dwellings or buildings may not be attacked.[78]

---

[72] 105 ILR 520 (para. 127).

[73] ICRC *Commentary*, para. 4772, n. 9.

[74] See Protocol II, Arts. 14, 15 and 16.

[75] Solf, in Bothe *et al.*, *New Rules*, p. 670, states that the deletion of Art. 24 (which set out the principle that military operations be directed only against military objectives) from the draft before the diplomatic conference left a significant gap in the text of Protocol II. However, he concludes that a prohibition of attacks on houses, schools and other structures occupied by civilians (unless they have become military objectives) may be inferred from Art. 13. Green considers that one of the aims of Protocol II is to ensure that attacks are limited to military objectives, L. C. Green, *The Contemporary Law of Armed Conflict*, Manchester University Press, 2nd edn, 2000, p. 326.

[76] See also Hague Regulations, Art. 28.

[77] See also Hague Regulations, Art. 23(g).

[78] Hague Regulations, Art. 25.

It follows from the above that, while there is no definition of 'civilian object' in the treaty law relating to internal armed conflicts, it can be inferred that property, other than that of the armed forces or factions, is protected from destruction, appropriation or attack unless there is a necessary military purpose to be achieved. That would preclude gratuitous acts of violence or destruction by way of revenge or 'to teach them a lesson'.

Precautions in attack

There is a customary law principle that, except in cases of assault, where surprise may be of the essence, the commander of attacking forces must do all in his power to give a prior warning of an attack.[79] In addition, all necessary steps must be taken to spare cultural property,[80] hospitals and places where the wounded and sick are collected.[81]

In conflicts to which Protocol II applies, there is no specific rule on precautions in attack[82] but there is an obligation to protect civilians against the dangers arising from military operations.[83] That implies a duty to take precautions to minimize incidental losses,[84] not only from attacks but also from other military operations and means, for example, that 'military installations should not be intentionally placed in the midst of a concentration of civilians with a view to using the latter as a shield or for the purposes of making the adverse party abandon an attack'.[85]

In the *Kupreškić* case, the tribunal further decided that the principle of proportionality also applied in internal armed conflicts so that 'any incidental (and unintentional) damage to civilians must not be out of proportion to the direct military advantage gained by the military attack' and, furthermore, that 'attacks, even when they are directed against legitimate military targets, are unlawful if conducted using indiscriminate means or methods of warfare, or in such a way as to cause indiscriminate damage to civilians.'[86] The tribunal went on to say that, while these two provisions left a wide discretion to belligerents, the elementary considerations of humanity required the rules to be interpreted so as to construe as narrowly as possible the discretionary power to attack

[79]Hague Regulations, Art. 26.
[80]See below.
[81]Hague Regulations, Art. 27.
[82]See Bothe *et al.*, *New Rules*, p. 671, who state that the principle of proportionality as part of the principle of humanity cannot be ignored in construing the provisions of this part of the protocol.
[83]Protocol II, Art. 13, para. 1.
[84]Green considers that one of the aims of Protocol II was to require precautions to be taken to avoid unnecessary or excessive injury to civilians, Green, *The Contemporary Law of Armed Conflict*, p. 326.
[85]ICRC *Commentary*, para. 4772.
[86]Case No. IT-95-16-T, judgment of 12 January 2000, para. 524.

belligerents and, by the same token, so as to expand the protection accorded to civilians.[87]

Protocol II does not include a specific prohibition on indiscriminate attacks. Attacks that were not aimed at a military objective were probably prohibited under customary law.[88] McCoubrey and White[89] are of the opinion that any practice of indiscriminate bombardment would seem to fall foul of the provisions of Art. 13, para. 1, for 'general protection against the dangers arising from military operations'. In any event, it seems clear that if an indiscriminate attack results in disproportionate civilian casualties, the attack would be unlawful anyway.

In the *Tadić* (jurisdiction) case, the appeals chamber took a more robust line, stating: 'It cannot be denied that customary rules have developed to govern internal strife. These rules ... cover such areas as protection of civilians from hostilities, in particular from indiscriminate attacks.'[90]

Precautions against the effects of attacks

The only customary law provision under this heading is the requirement for those under siege to indicate cultural property, hospitals and places where the wounded and sick are collected by distinctive and visible signs, notified to the adversary beforehand.[91]

Cultural property

For states party to the Cultural Property Convention of 1954 and its protocols, these apply, at least with regard to the provisions for the respect of cultural property,[92] to both international and internal armed conflicts,[93] so Chapter 6 should be consulted.

For the remainder, as explained in Chapter 6, customary law requires 'buildings dedicated to religion, art, science, or charitable purposes and historic monuments' to be spared so far as possible during sieges and bombardments, provided they are not being used for military purposes.[94]

---

[87]*Ibid.*, para. 525.

[88]See Chapter 1. To this Bothe *et al.*, *New Rules*, p. 677, would probably have added area bombardments.

[89]*International Organizations and Civil Wars*, p. 105.

[90]105 ILR 419, 520 (para. 127).

[91]Hague Regulations, Art. 27.

[92]According to McCoubrey and White, *International Organizations and Civil Wars*, p. 116, that means Art. 4 of the 1954 convention.

[93]Cultural Property Convention 1954, Arts. 18 and 19; Second Hague Protocol of 1999, Arts. 3 and 22. The Second Hague Protocol applies in its entirety to internal armed conflict (Art. 22).

[94]Hague Regulations, Art. 27.

Protocol II provides:

Art. 16. Protection of cultural objects and of places of worship

Without prejudice to the provisions of the Hague Convention for the Protection of Cultural Property in the Event of Armed Conflict of 14 May 1954, it is prohibited to commit any acts of hostility directed against historic monuments, works of art or places of worship which constitute the cultural or spiritual heritage of peoples, and to use them in support of the military effort.

Art. 8, para. 2(e), of the ICC Statute makes the following a war crime in internal armed conflicts: '(iv) Intentionally directing attacks against buildings dedicated to religion, education, art, science or charitable purposes, historic monuments, hospitals and places where the sick and wounded are collected, provided they are not military objectives.' In the *Tadić* (jurisdiction) case, the appeals chamber stated: 'It cannot be denied that customary rules have developed to govern internal strife. These rules ... cover such areas as ... protection of civilian objects, in particular cultural property.'[95]

Environmental protection

Customary law, common Art. 3 and the ICC Statute have nothing to say, in the context of internal armed conflicts, on the subject of the protection of the environment. It follows that the only protection for the environment, whether natural or manmade, would be that explained in the above paragraph headed 'military objectives and civilian objects'.

Protocol II is more specific, at least in connection with the human environment:

Art. 14. Protection of objects indispensable to the survival of the civilian population

Starvation of civilians as a method of combat is prohibited. It is therefore prohibited to attack, destroy, remove or render useless for that purpose, objects indispensable to the survival of the civilian population such as food-stuffs, agricultural areas for the production of food-stuffs, crops, livestock, drinking water installations and supplies and irrigation works.

Art. 15. Protection of works and installations containing dangerous forces

Works or installations containing dangerous forces, namely dams, dykes and nuclear electrical generating stations, shall not be made the object of attack, even where these objects are military objectives, if such attack may cause the release of dangerous forces and consequent severe losses among the civilian population.

[95] 105 ILR 419, 520 (para. 127).

Criminal responsibility

Prior to the establishment of the Yugoslav tribunal, international jurisdiction had not been exercised in respect of violations of the law relating to internal armed conflict. Even Art. 3 of the statute of the tribunal, which deals with war crimes, does not specifically mention internal armed conflicts. Indeed, much of the language of this article is borrowed from the Hague Regulations. However, in the *Tadić* (jurisdiction) decision[96] the trial chamber considered that it was mandated to apply the laws or customs of war and that this term included the prohibitions of acts committed in both international and internal armed conflicts.[97] It considered that:

It cannot be denied that customary rules have developed to govern internal strife. These rules ... cover such areas as protection of civilians from hostilities, in particular from indiscriminate attacks, protection of civilian objects, in particular cultural property, protection of all those who do not (or no longer) take active part in hostilities, as well as prohibition of means of warfare proscribed in international armed conflicts and ban of certain methods of conducting hostilities.[98]

The appeals chamber went on to confirm that customary international law: 'Imposes criminal liability for serious violations of common Article 3, as supplemented by other general principles and rules on the protection of the victims of internal armed conflict, and for breaching certain fundamental principles and rules regarding means and methods of combat in civil strife.'[99] The decision of the appeals chamber in *Tadić* seemed to surprise international lawyers at the time but it has been regularly followed in other tribunal cases[100] and has been confirmed by the ICC Statue, which treats as war crimes certain acts committed in internal armed conflicts.[101]

Belligerent reprisals

There is no specific prohibition of belligerent reprisals in either common Art. 3 or in Protocol II. Some delegations at the diplomatic conference that negotiated the latter were of the opinion that the rules of such reprisals concerned only

---

[96]The case concerned the treatment of detainees at the Omarska prison camp in the Prijedor region of Bosnia–Hercegovina maintained by Bosnian Serbs. The tribunal may have been influenced by the fact that the Statute of the International Tribunal for Rwanda, adopted by the UN Security Council on 8 November 1994, specifically permits the trial of serious violations of Common Article 3 and of Protocol II.

[97]105 ILR 419, 445. This view was supported by the appeals chamber, 105 ILR 419, 495.

[98]105 ILR 419, 520 (para. 127).

[99]105 ILR 453, 523 (para. 134).

[100]For example by the appeals chamber in the *Delalić* case, 40 (2001) ILM 630, 662 (para. 174).

[101]See Art. 8, paras. 2(c) and (e) of the statute.

relations between states and, therefore, had no place in rules relating to internal armed conflict.[102]

The tribunal in the *Kupreškić* case went further. It expressed the view that: 'While reprisals could have had a modicum of justification in the past, when they constituted practically the only effective means of compelling the enemy to abandon unlawful acts of warfare and to comply in future with international law, at present they can no longer be justified in this manner'[103] and concurred with the view of the International Law Commission, stated in 1995, that reprisals against civilians in the combat zone are prohibited.[104]

Nevertheless, the unequivocal statement on ratification by the United Kingdom, one of the permanent members of the United Nations Security Council, reserving the right to take reprisals, at least in respect of Protocol I, must carry considerable weight, especially as there have been no objections by other states. This silence may indicate an acceptance by states that the doctrine of belligerent reprisals is not dead. Other states may have indicated this view in rather less direct language.[105]

If the doctrine of belligerent reprisals is still alive in customary law, its existence in the law of internal armed conflict, where the treaty rules are silent on the issue, must remain a matter of debate.[106]

---

[102]ICRC, *Commentary*, n. 18 on p. 1372. Green does not comment on this when he states that Protocol II does not forbid the taking of reprisals against cultural property, *The Contemporary Law of Armed Conflict*, p. 326.

[103]Case No. IT-95-16-T, judgment of 12 January 2000, para. 530. Greenwood considers that the reasoning in the case is unconvincing as there is a strong argument that the provisions on reprisals were not codificatory at the time of their adoption in 1977, that they can hardly have acquired customary law status since then and that it was not necessary for the chamber to determine, for the purposes of the case, whether a customary law prohibition existed (C. J. Greenwood, Belligerent reprisals in the jurisprudence of the international criminal tribunal for the former Yugoslavia, in H. Fischer, C. Kress and S. Lüder (eds.), *International Law and National Prosecution of Crimes under International Law*, Bochum, 2001, pp. 539–58).

[104]*Ibid.*, paras. 527–34. Moir, *The Law of Internal Armed Conflict*, p. 242. comments: 'the weight of opinion in favour of the prohibition of belligerent reprisals against civilian populations in all armed conflicts would accordingly seem to be overwhelming and it certainly ought to be the case that such reprisals against civilians are prohibited even during internal armed conflict. Nonetheless, it must be difficult for those involved in armed conflict to disregard the possibility of belligerent reprisals where violations of the law are occurring.'

[105]E.g., the statements on ratification of Protocol I by Germany and Italy. A. Cassese, *International Law*, Oxford University Press, 2001, p. 341, seems to think so too. Commenting on the ban on reprisals in Protocol I, he states: 'the strong opposition of States such as France and Australia, and the misgivings entertained by a number of other States, may lead one to believe that those provisions remained treaty law, and consequently bind only those States which ratify or accede to the Protocol (without entering reservations).'

[106]Kalshoven, who condemns the judges in the *Kupreškić* case of being 'guilty of an attempt to rewrite the law', leaves open the possibility of the resort to belligerent reprisals 'in a conflict that resembles an international armed conflict in all significant aspects' (F. Kalshoven, Reprisals and the protection of civilians: two recent decisions of the Yugoslavia tribunal, in L. C. Vohrah *et al.* (eds.), *Man's Inhumanity to Man*, Kluwer, 2003). See also, Zegveld, *Accountability of Armed Opposition Groups*, pp. 89–92.

Internal armed conflicts, a summary of the rules

The following is an attempt to present the body of law applicable to internal armed conflicts, as discussed above, as a set of rules applicable to all parties to internal armed conflicts.[107] These rules are not based on Protocol II because of the more limited scope of application of that protocol and because with, at the time of writing, 156 ratifications,[108] and some important states not being parties it cannot be said to be of universal application.

1   All combat activity must be justified on military grounds; activity that is not militarily necessary is prohibited.

2   A distinction must always be made between combatants, who may take a direct part in hostilities and be attacked themselves, and non-combatants, who may not take a direct part in hostilities and may not be attacked or used as shields. It is prohibited to direct attacks against the civilian population as such or against individual civilians not taking a direct part in hostilities.[109]

3   It is prohibited to enlist or use actively in hostilities children under 15.[110]

4   Attacks may be directed *only* against objects that make a contribution to the enemy's military effort and hence are of tactical or strategic importance. Warnings of attacks should be given where it is feasible to do so.[111] Incidental loss and damage must be minimized.[112] Undefended towns, villages, dwellings or buildings may not be attacked or bombarded.[113] Civilian property must not be attacked unless it is being used for military purposes. It may not be destroyed unless it is a military objective and it is militarily necessary to do so.[114] It may be requisitioned only for use for necessary military purposes.[115] The environment is also protected by these rules. Pillaging is prohibited.[116]

5   Non-combatants and their property must be spared as far as possible from the incidental effects of military operations.

---

[107]An earlier attempt, on which this is based, was published in A. P. V. Rogers, Civil war, in R. Gutman and D. Rieff (eds.), *Crimes of War*, W. W. Norton & Company, 1999, p. 82. A more detailed set of rules, with commentary, is under development by a group of experts convened by the International Institute of Humanitarian Law at San Remo. It is hoped to publish the results in a manual entitled *The San Remo Manual on the Protection of Victims of Non-International Armed Conflicts*.

[108]Information from the ICRC website: www.icrc.org.

[109]ICC Statute, Art. 8, para. 2(e)(i).

[110]ICC Statue, Art. 8, para. 2(e)(vii).

[111]Hague Regulations, Art. 26.

[112]Geneva Conventions 1949, Art. 3; ICC Statue, Art. 8, para. 2(e)(i).

[113]Hague Regulations, Art. 25.

[114]Hague Regulations, Art. 23(g); ICC Statute, Art. 8, para. 2(e)(xii). For example, to clear a field of fire, or because it is being used as a sniper post.

[115]Hague Regulations, Art. 23(g); ICC Statute, Art. 8, para. 2(e)(xii).

[116]Hague Regulations, Art. 28; ICC Statute, Art. 8, para. 2(e)(v). Pillaging, or plunder, is prohibited even when a town or place is taken by assault. Stealing is an offence in war as in peace.

6 It is prohibited to commit rape, sexual slavery, enforced prostitution, forced pregnancy, enforced sterilization or any other form of sexual violence.[117]

7 Prisoner-of-war status does not arise in internal armed conflicts. Captured persons can be tried under the law of the state where the internal armed conflict is going on for any offences they may have committed against that law. They have the protections listed in para. 8 (below) and under human rights law. Sentences may only be carried out after judgement pronounced by a regularly constituted court, affording all judicial guarantees that are generally recognized as indispensable.[118]

8 Persons who take no active part in hostilities (non-combatants, captured persons, the wounded, sick and shipwrecked) are to be treated humanely and equally, irrespective of race, colour, religion, sex, wealth or similar criteria. Violence to their life and person is prohibited. That means that there must be no murder, mutilation, cruel treatment, torture, or other outrages on personal dignity, or humiliating or degrading treatment.[119] Detainees are to be provided with sufficient food and drinking water, facilities for health and hygiene and shelter from the weather and the dangers of armed conflict.

9 Hostage-taking is prohibited.[120]

10 It is prohibited to deny quarter.[121]

11 It is prohibited to kill or wound by resort to treachery.[122] Ruses of war are permitted.[123]

12 It is prohibited to make improper use of the flag of truce, the red-cross or red-crescent emblems or the military insignia or uniforms of the enemy.[124]

13 Starvation of non-combatants as a method of warfare is prohibited.

14 The wounded, sick and shipwrecked must be collected and cared for.[125] It is prohibited to attack medical buildings and material, medical units, transports and personnel.[126] All necessary steps must be taken to spare, as far as possible, hospitals and places where the sick and wounded are collected.[127] Precautions are to be taken to mark such property or places by the red-cross or red-crescent emblem.[128]

---

[117]ICC Statute, Art. 8, para. 2(e)(vi). Forced pregnancy means the unlawful confinement of a woman forcibly made pregnant, with the intent of affecting the ethnic composition of any population or carrying out other grave violations of international law (ICC Statute, Art. 7, para 2(f)).

[118]Geneva Conventions 1949, Art. 3; ICC Statute, Art. 8, para. 2(c)(iv).

[119]Hague Regulations, Art. 23(c); Geneva Conventions 1949, Art. 3; ICC Statue, Art. 8, para. 2(c).

[120]Geneva Conventions 1949, Art. 3(1)(b); ICC Statute, Art. 8, para. 2(c)(iii).

[121]Hague Regulations, Art. 23(d); ICC Statute, Art. 8, para. 2(e)(x).

[122]Hague Regulations, Art. 23(b); ICC Statue, Art. 8, para. 2(e)(ix).

[123]Hague Regulations, Art. 24.

[124]Hague Regulations, Art. 23(f).

[125]Geneva Conventions 1949, Art. 3.

[126]ICC Statute, Art. 8, para. 2(e)(ii).

[127]Hague Regulations, Art. 27.

[128]Hague Regulations, Art. 27; ICC Statute, Art. 8, para. 2(e)(ii).

15   It is prohibited to subject persons in the power of another party to the conflict to physical mutilation or to medical or scientific experiments of any kind which are neither justified by the medical, dental or hospital treatment of the person concerned nor carried out in his or her interest, and which cause death to or seriously endanger the health of such person or persons.[129]

16   Although it may be necessary to evacuate non-combatants from areas of danger, it is prohibited to move them for discriminatory reasons, or to shield military targets from attack.[130] 'Ethnic cleansing' is prohibited.[131]

17   Cultural property. It is prohibited to attack buildings dedicated to religion, education, art, science or charitable purposes and historic monuments.[132] All necessary steps must be taken to spare, as far as possible, such buildings.[133] Precautions are to be taken to mark such property or places by distinctive and visible signs notified to the enemy.[134]

18   It is prohibited to attack personnel, installations, material, units or vehicles involved in a humanitarian assistance or peacekeeping mission in accordance with the United Nations Charter.[135]

19   Serious violations of the law relating to internal armed conflicts entail individual criminal responsibility.

---

[129]ICC Statute, Art. 8, para. 2(e)(xi).

[130]ICC Statue, Art. 8, para. 2(e)(viii).

[131]Geneva Conventions 1949, Art. 3, International Covenant on Civil and Political Rights 1966, Arts. 6, 7, 16 and 18; European Convention on Human Rights 1950, Arts. 9 and 10.

[132]ICC Statute, Art. 8, para. 2(e)(iv).

[133]Hague Regulations, Art. 27.

[134]Hague Regulations, Art. 27.

[135]ICC Statute, Art. 8, para. 2(e)(iii). This protection only applies so long as such humanitarian or peacekeeping personnel or property are regarded as civilians or civilian objects under the law of armed conflict. They might lose that status, for example, if they became involved in peace enforcement operations.

10

The military lawyer's perspective

The military lawyer's involvement in law on the battlefield may take one or more of several forms: as a negotiator in international conferences, as a writer of military manuals or as an instructor on the law of war, as a legal adviser to a commander or his staff or as a prosecutor in war crimes proceedings. In all these areas he (or she) can make a useful contribution to the understanding and implementation of the law.

Negotiator

At an international conference where treaty texts are being negotiated, the military lawyer may be part of a national delegation. Apart from providing the delegation with technical advice on the law of the war, he ought to be able to bring realism into the debate to ensure that participants are aware of the practical effect of the proposals that are being made; he should also be able to act as a link between the advocates of humanity and the advocates of military necessity in finding common ground, compromise and solutions. He should see that the rules that are being negotiated are capable of being understood, accepted by those to whom they apply and implemented in practice. This will involve endeavouring to make sure that the language is unambiguous and consistent. Here the search for compromise is a severe obstacle to clarity. Treaty texts sometimes contain emotive and politicized language,[1] or loose drafting,[2] or provisions which may be misunderstood if they are not considered in the context of other

---

[1]E.g., Art. 1, para. 4, of Protocol I, which speaks of armed conflicts in which peoples are fighting against colonial domination and alien occupation and against racist regimes.

[2]Such as Art. 51, para. 4(c), of Protocol I, which refers to attacks the effects of which cannot be limited as required by the protocol, so importing elements of proportionality into a rule dealing with distinguishing between the armed forces and civilians. It would have been clearer and more logical for there to have been a separate article dealing with proportionality.

provisions,[3] or provisions which are inconsistent with those of previous treaties,[4] or which lead to uncertainty[5] or whose meaning is downright obscure.[6]

The military lawyer should, at least, be aware of lack of consistency or looseness of drafting and bring it to the attention of the conference so that corrections can be made.

Sometimes these difficulties are caused by a combination of factors: the need to find consensus sometimes leaves room for different interpretations. Pressure of time, late-night sittings, eagerness to clinch a deal after long and hard-fought negotiations also play their part.

An example is Art. 5 of the Mines Protocol to the Weapons Convention. This provides that remotely delivered mines may only be used within an area that is a military objective or which contains military objectives and then only if either they are fitted with neutralizing mechanisms or 'their location can be accurately recorded in accordance with Article 7(1)(a)'. On looking at Art. 7(1)(a) one finds that it provides that the parties to the conflict shall record the location of all preplanned minefields laid by them.

The meaning of Art. 5 is, therefore, opaque. It might be interpreted as meaning that remotely delivered mines without neutralizing mechanisms can only be used for laying preplanned minefields or, perhaps, that they can be used without recording in all cases when such use was not preplanned.

With such widely divergent interpretations possible, the reference to Art. 7(1)(a), therefore, makes no sense at all. It is necessary to examine the negotiating history to find out what the parties to the negotiations intended.[7] The reference to Art. 7(1)(a) was a clumsy attempt by the delegates (including the writer!) suffering from the effects of a late-night sitting towards the end of a busy conference to ensure that remotely delivered mines not fitted with neutralizing mechanisms were to be used only if their location could be accurately recorded. Art. 7(1)(a) was the only provision for the *mandatory* recording of mines, para. 2 being merely exhortatory.

---

[3]E.g. when considering the status of British military advisers to the Kuwaiti armed forces captured by Iraq during the invasion of Kuwait in 1990, it was not enough to consider the Prisoner of War Convention. In fact, their status as *civilian* protected persons was confirmed by the Civilian Convention. See, further, F. J. Hampson, Liability for war crimes, in P. J. Rowe, *The Gulf War 1990–91 in International and English Law*, Routledge, 1993, p. 246.

[4]Because law-of-war treaties are self-standing and do not repeal and replace previous treaties dealing with the same subject matter, their relationship with each other may be difficult, if not impossible, to ascertain, as in the case of the cultural property texts referred to in Chapter 6. The problem is exacerbated by use of similar language in different treaties to mean different things, as in the ENMOD Convention and the ecological provisions of Protocol I.

[5]E.g. the failure to mention in Art. 53 of Protocol I that if cultural property is used for military purposes it loses its protection or the rather loose language of the Cultural Property Convention, which refers to property of great importance, property of very great importance and property of relative importance, see Chapter 6.

[6]E.g. the term 'pre-planned' in the Mines Protocol to the Weapons Convention.

[7]This is set out in full in A. P. V. Rogers, The Mines Protocol: negotiating history, in ICRC, *Symposium on Anti-personnel Mines, Report*, ICRC, 1993.

As agreement on this text had only been achieved at a very late stage after prolonged and intense arguments, nobody wanted to reopen the issue, even when its obscurity became evident.

The military lawyer will also be looking for realistic proposals. During the diplomatic conference at which Protocol I was negotiated, a proposal that stretcher-bearers should carry a red-cross flag was objected to by the medical colonel in the Soviet delegation on the grounds that stretcher bearers need both hands to carry the stretcher and do not have a spare hand for flag carrying! One provision that is regarded by some as unrealistic is the requirement of Protocol I to give effective advance warnings of attacks that may affect the civilian population, unless circumstances do not permit. The writer finds the provision realistic enough. If to do so would endanger the attacker, circumstances probably would not permit the giving of a warning. On the other hand, there is no reason why minefields designed to channel the enemy into a certain direction should not be clearly marked. That would achieve the military aim and at the same time protect the civilian population. It may be possible when one's own territory is under attack to pass warnings through loyal civil channels without endangering the military operation. So much depends on the prevailing circumstances, but it is right that commanders should be obliged to consider the possibility of warnings.

Manual writer

It goes without saying that the manual writer must be a master of the subject matter who can express himself clearly and unequivocally. Where the law is unclear or controversial he should say so, but still provide guidance to readers. In the opinion of the writer, therefore, it would be better to treat civilians working in military objectives as civilians exempt from direct attack but vulnerable to the incidental dangers of an attack on that objective than to describe them as having quasi-combatant status. To do that would only confuse the uninitiated. Even where the treaty texts are straightforward, as in the Geneva Conventions of 1949, practical guidance and practical examples should be provided. Where the treaty texts are complicated, such as the rules on indiscriminate attacks in Protocol I, the texts will need careful explanation.

The writer will also have to consider carefully at whom the manual is aimed.

Obviously, military lawyers prefer to work from the treaty texts, but need explanatory footnotes, or a commentary and cross-references.[8] The latter are especially important. For example, the definition of 'military objective' cannot be looked at in isolation; attention must also be drawn to specific rules on objects such as dams, dykes and nuclear electrical generating stations. Generally

[8]Such as from Art. 78 of Protocol I to Art. 49 of the Civilian Convention.

speaking, though, military lawyers do not need a legal treatise because in practice time will not be available for studying problems in depth. They need to be in a position to give prompt and accurate legal advice. They do not need a learned discussion of whether or not an enemy combatant is to be classed as a military objective; they just need to know that it is permissible to attack enemy combatants. Where the law is controversial, as in the case of economic targets, the manual writer will have to make a decision on the guidance to be given. It may require political clearance. Military lawyers also may need practical examples like specimen rules of engagement.

Specialists, such as those handling prisoners of war, may need a special manual giving practical guidance on how to implement the Prisoner of War Convention, for example, the layout of a prisoner-of-war camp, orders for sentries, censorship, diet or recreational facilities.

Commanders and staff officers require manuals that are written in clear, straightforward and non-legal language, perhaps expressed in the form of a series of rules or propositions. Some rules or propositions will need explanatory examples. The definition of 'military objective' in Protocol I, for instance, will be of limited use to the commander without an explanation of what it means, particularly concepts such as 'in the circumstances ruling at the time', and without concrete examples, particularly in the case of items of a civilian nature such as lines of communication. The circumstances in which an area of land may be a military objective must also be explained. The same is true of the rule of proportionality. Historic examples can help to clarify the meaning and application of the rule. In other cases, manuals may go beyond the treaty texts by laying down practical guidelines or instructions. It would be dangerous to set out the law on reprisals without saying at what level, according to national rules, reprisal action should be sanctioned. Otherwise the doctrine might be seized upon as an excuse for the commission of war crimes. In the case of cultural property, manuals can specify the level at which a decision to waive protection should be taken. The obligation to take precautions in attack can be summarized on the lines suggested in Chapter 4 and checklists can be developed in the light of experience.

Junior officers probably need a pamphlet explaining the basic principles of the law of war.[9] Soldiers and junior non-commissioned officers do not need a manual at all, a brief summary being all that is required.[10] Rules of engagement cards may well suffice. Different cards can be produced for different situations. While parties to the Geneva Conventions and Protocols have a duty to disseminate them, it is left to the parties to decide how best to do so.[11]

---

[9]E.g. The British Army pamphlet, *A Soldier's Guide to the Law of Armed Conflict* (Army Code 71130), 1998.

[10]As in the British forces card JSP 381, Aide Memoire on the Law of Armed Conflict.

[11]See, e.g., Protocol I, Art. 83 and ICRC *Commentary*, para. 3382.

The structure of a manual can be based on the subject matter such as the conduct of combat, occupation, relations between belligerents, and so on[12] or on the tactical situation such as exercise of command, conduct in action or problems arising in support areas.[13] Again, the structure will depend on the readership: military lawyers may prefer the subject matter approach while infantry officers may prefer the tactical approach. Certainly, it would be of advantage to include a 'teeth arm' officer in the editorial team.

Instructor

Protocol I recognizes the importance of legal advisers in providing advice on the instruction to be given to the armed forces on the law of war.[14]

Many of the considerations affecting manual writers apply to instructors too: clarity, firm guidance, tailoring the presentation or course to the audience, special presentations for specialist subjects, practical guidance. Obviously those with first-hand experience of the conduct of combat or operational deployments and the legal problems arising will speak with greater authority. Syndicate work is essential to reinforce points made in formal presentations and should preferably involve the discussion of problems among groups drawn from different disciplines. Best is the inclusion of realistic law of war problems in exercise scenarios. Here the military lawyer can be of great assistance to exercise planners but also to exercise controllers to ensure that legal problems are included in the exercise plans, recognized as such and that action is taken accordingly.

Adviser

Protocol I specifically lays down a requirement for legal advisers to be available to advise commanders about the Geneva Conventions and Protocols.[15]

Like the manual writer, the adviser must be an expert in the subject. The experience of the author is that the adviser will not have the time to acquire the necessary knowledge once the armed conflict, or the state of tension leading up to an armed conflict, has started. Advice is always needed very quickly, often in a matter of hours or at the very most overnight. This does not leave time for learning or research or more than the barest consultation. It means that the adviser must have attended courses and studied the treaty texts, commentaries, law books and military manuals beforehand so that answers to questions can be

---

[12]As in the German manual, *Humanitäres Völkerrecht in bewaffneten Konflikten – Handbuch*, Bundesministerium der Verteidigung, 1992.
[13]As in F. de Mulinen, *Handbook on the Law of War for the Armed Forces*, ICRC, 1987.
[14]Art. 82.
[15]Art. 82.

given almost instinctively. His burden will be eased if checklists have been prepared in peacetime, for example, a list of legal points to be considered when examining target lists or plans of attack or draft rules of engagement or a model memorandum of understanding between allies. He should be aware of the traps inherent in obscure wording of treaty texts and how they should be interpreted. His advice must be practical. The commander or staff or Ministry of Defence officials involved do not, unless they specifically ask for it, want a legal essay with considerations, conditions and reservations. The adviser should have considered all that before preparing his advice. Those who have consulted him will want to know what action they can take within the law and if various courses are open, the advantages and disadvantages of each with recommendations.

It is not enough for the legal adviser to know about the law of war in the abstract. He must also know which countries have ratified or acceded to which conventions and with what reservations or statements. He needs to be aware of the legal background to the conflict, whether or not an armed conflict exists, whether it is an international or non-international armed conflict and between which states or factions, what United Nations Security Council resolutions have been passed and their content, what bilateral or multilateral agreements have been entered into and their effect. Here he may be lacking information because these things will have been dealt with at a higher level, but he must have this information. Without it his advice may be useless.

The legal adviser must also be proactive because legal problems may not be recognized by commanders and their staff. As noted in Chapter 8, commanders must be alert to law-of-war issues and take them into account in operational planning. Here the legal adviser can perform a useful function by briefing commanders about likely pitfalls and in advising them on procedures to be adopted to ensure compliance with the law. He may also be able to make suggestions for reducing the incidental effects of military operations by, say, creating demilitarized zones, or by drawing attention to the worldwide concern for the protection of the environment. For this purpose, the legal adviser must be informed about what is going on, anticipate problems and provide advice in advance. This means that the lawyer must attend briefings so he is aware of the military situation and that he must be accessible to all divisions of the staff of a headquarters, preferably reporting direct to the chief of staff, and not be tucked away in the personnel division or the civil affairs division.

Nevertheless, in the context of multi-national deployments under United Nations auspices or under the auspices of a regional defence organization like NATO, the civil affairs division of a headquarters is becoming increasingly important and busy and may well need dedicated legal staff to negotiate host-nation support agreements and agreements between the contributing nations and resolve legal problems arising from their implementation. Those lawyers can also play a useful part in law on the battlefield in ensuring that the necessary steps are taken to introduce or plan for the precautions against the effects of attacks dealt with in Chapter 5, or for the protection of cultural property dealt with in Chapter 6, identifying legal problems and ensuring that solutions are found.

Finally, the military lawyer has a very important role to play in public relations and media briefings. Allegations and counter-allegations about violations of the law of war, about massacres and atrocities are rife during armed conflict. It is very important that those responsible for making public statements are well informed about the law of war and are quick to correct misapprehensions and false allegations. Likewise, if the enemy are violating the law of war by, for example, placing military objectives close to cultural objects or by using hostages as 'human shields', such violations need to be brought to the attention of the world community. The military lawyer can help in identifying these breaches and explaining the legal background.

When during the Gulf war of 1991 bombs fell on the market town of Fallujah, the RAF spokesman, Group Captain Henderson, was quick to explain that this was due to the malfunctioning of a bomb which was aimed at a bridge, a legitimate target because it was on a main supply line.[16] This was exactly the right thing to do to forestall allegations that the RAF was deliberately bombing civilians. The military lawyer can help to ensure that press lines are legally accurate. He can also draw attention to statements in the media that are legally incorrect and need correction.

Some legal aspects of peace support operations

The Falkland and Gulf conflicts gave rise to very few questions of applicability of the law of armed conflict. The first was a straightforward territorial conflict between two states, fought in and around the thinly populated disputed territory. It did not spread to the home territories of the states concerned. The second involved more states on the coalition side, acting under a United Nations mandate. There were more civilian casualties because of the air and missile attacks against targets in populated areas but again the applicability problem was easily resolved.

Far more difficult from the legal point of view were the conflicts in the Balkans from 1991–95. The applicability problem here was a lawyer's nightmare as the constituent parts of the Yugoslav federation started to break away. First Slovenia and Croatia declared their independence on 25 June 1991. Federal tanks entered Slovenia the following day but a well-planned resistance probably persuaded the authorities in Belgrade that it was not worth following up the incursion and the tanks withdrew. There is little doubt that the fighting that followed in Croatia from late August 1991 to early 1992 and from about April 1992 in Bosnia–Hercegovina (Bosnia for short), amounted to armed conflicts to which international law applied. By the end of 1992 some 8,000 United Nations troops had been deployed to Bosnia to protect aid supplies. In May 1993 the

[16]*The Times*, 19 February 1991.

'safe areas' of Sarajevo, Tuzla, Žepa, Goražde, Bihać and Srebrenica were established[17] and in June the UN protection force (UNPROFOR) were authorized to use force to protect those areas from bombardment or armed incursion[18] though this did not prevent the fall of most of these safe areas, UNPROFOR being vulnerable to hostage-taking. The turning point was probably in mid-1994 when the Muslims and Croats stopped fighting each other. The siege of Sarajevo continued, however, and it was not until May 1995 that the UN gave NATO authority to undertake air strikes against the besieging positions. This resulted in the taking hostage of some UN soldiers and, eventually, the deployment of a 10,000-strong Anglo-French reaction force including artillery on Mount Igman. While that might have helped Sarajevo, it did not prevent Srebrenica and Žepa falling in July. Nevertheless, the successful Croatian operation to recapture the Krajina in early August, the heavy NATO air strikes later that month which forced General Mladić to remove his heavy weaponry from the Sarajevo exclusion zone and the military gains of the Muslim–Croat federation at last paved the way for a peace settlement in the general framework agreement initialled at Dayton and then signed in Paris on 14 December 1995.[19,20]

The difficulty for the lawyers concerned with these events has been in knowing whether to place the conflicts in the category of internal or international armed conflicts. This is an important issue for lawyers, because the law that applies varies enormously according to the applicable law, and is discussed in Chapter 9. To take but one question of concern to UNPROFOR lawyers: 'suppose we are attacked, use armed force in self-defence and the attackers surrender, are they prisoners of war?'. If the conflict is internal, the answer is no; if it is international, the answer might be yes, depending on the separate question of whether the states providing troops to UNPROFOR could be said to be parties to the, or an, armed conflict. Similar questions arose in relation to NATO air and artillery strikes in support of UNPROFOR. It was even being suggested in some circles that you could, in those cases, slip into a state of armed conflict for the duration of the operation and then out again.

There must be a point on the escalatory scale of violence at which troops involved in peace support operations themselves become involved in an armed conflict. Perhaps they do not when using proportionate force in personal self-defence or, for example, when using occasional artillery or air strikes to protect safe areas. But the situation might be different if they had to mount extensive military ground and air operations to protect safe areas or forcibly to regain territory. Whatever the true legal position, on which only a competent tribunal

---

[17]UN Security Council Resolution 824.

[18]UN Security Council Resolution 836.

[19]35 (1996) *International Legal Materials* (ILM) 75.

[20]In preparing this summary the author has been invaluably assisted by Noel Malcolm's book, *Bosnia, a Short History*, Papermac, revised 1996.

could rule, UNPROFOR and NATO personnel would have been well advised to apply the law of armed conflict by analogy so far as the circumstances permitted. For example, persons captured after the use of armed force in self-defence, though not prisoners of war, should be given equivalent treatment until handed over to the appropriate civil authorities.[21] As for air and artillery strikes to safeguard protected areas, even if the law of armed conflict did not strictly apply, it would be sensible for the targeting principles of that law to be applied in practice.

Prosecutor

The prosecutor will have to decide, first, whether the alleged offence should be made the subject of a prosecution at all. If it was a grave breach of the Geneva Conventions, there is a duty to do so under international law.[22] If it was another breach of the law of war, it is suggested that the prosecutor has a discretion but should advise prosecution in the case of serious war crimes not amounting to grave breaches, such as direct attacks on civilians or the civilian populations.[23] In the case of minor violations it would suffice if corrective action were recommended.

In deciding, second, whether an individual is responsible for an alleged war crime arising out of conduct in action and, if so, whether he should be prosecuted, the military lawyer will need to consider the situation as it appeared to the accused at the time in the light of the information available to him at that time. That will involve consideration of the tactical situation, the time available for a decision, the heat of the moment, and so on. Where it is a question of assessing proportionality, it will involve examining very many factors: the method and timing of attack, the weapons available and used and their effect, the orders given by higher authority, the intelligence available about the target and its surroundings, the military gain expected from the attack, the likely civilian casualties and damage and the attack in the context of the operation as a whole. In the case of a commander, the prosecutor will have to consider whether he committed the offence himself as a principal or accessory, or whether he should be charged in respect of his failure to act to suppress or repress offences committed by others.

It is suggested that in the rare case when the law is controversial or obscure, and the accused acted in good faith, the prosecutor will advise no prosecution.

[21] Itself a vexed question, especially in contested areas. Principles of humanity would have prevail if there were good reasons to suspect that the person handed over might be executed witho trial or subjected to inhumane treatment.
[22] See, e.g., Art. 129 of the Prisoner of War Convention 1949 or Arts. 85 and 86 of Protocol
[23] See the classification by Hampson, War crimes, p. 256.

Final remarks

Although some ambiguities remain, and although the law has become complicated, especially with regard to the protection of cultural property, Protocol I provides a useful code of conduct in combat which achieves a reasonable balance between military and humanitarian considerations. Any perceived imbalance between the rights and duties of defenders and attackers can be redressed by applying the rule of proportionality. Of course, Protocol I cannot stand by itself as a document issued to military personnel. It has to be incorporated into military manuals with explanatory commentaries, cross-references and practical guidance, but it does form the foundation for those manuals on the subject of law on the conduct of combat, or law on the battlefield, which previously had been somewhat neglected. Had Protocol I applied to the allied forces in the Gulf war of 1991, it is suggested that they would have had no difficulty in complying with its provisions.

Experience of the last thirty years indicates that one always has to be ready to deal with the unexpected. It seems too short-sighted to say that we can expect now to be prepared only, say, for operations involving light and highly mobile forces. When in the 1970s we, in the United Kingdom, were mainly concerned with the powerful threat from the East, we would not have foreseen the early fall of the iron curtain and the benefits, such as the end of the stalemate in the United Nations Security Council, but also the troubles caused by the breakdown of the Soviet Union. We could not have contemplated the Falklands expedition of 1982 or the conventional operations in 1991 and 2003 against Iraq, culminating in an occupation regime, or the air campaign in respect of Kosovo, or the peace support operations in the Balkans and elsewhere. That means that military lawyers have to be prepared for the unexpected and will have to continue to study the traditional law of armed conflict as well as the law relating to peace support operations and the law relating to military support to the civil authorities.

Works cited

Adler, G. J., Targets in war, legal considerations, *Houston Law Review*, 1980.

Aldrich, G. H., New life for the laws of war, *American Journal of International Law*, 1981.

Aldrich, G. H., Prospects for US ratification of Protocol I, *American Journal of International Law*, 1991.

Alexandrow, E., *International Legal Protection of Cultural Property*, Sofia, Sofia Press, 1979.

Algase, R. C., Islamic law in warfare, *Military Law and Law of War Review*, 1977.

Allen, C., *Thunder and Lightning*, London, Her Majesty's Stationery Office, 1991.

Amnesty International, *NATO/Federal republic of Yugoslavia, 'Collateral Damage' or Unlawful Killings?* June 2000.

Anderson, K., A public call for international attention to legal obligations of defending forces as well as attacking forces to protect civilians in armed conflict, 19 March 2003, www.crimesofwar.org.

Antoine, P., International humanitarian law and the protection of the environment in time of armed conflict, *International Review of the Red Cross*, 1992.

Arbuckle, T., Rhodesian bush war strategies and tactics, *Royal United Services Institute Journal*, 1979.

Austin, J. E. and Bruch, C. E., *The Environmental Consequences of War*, Cambridge, Cambridge University Press, 2000.

Baker, J. R. and Crocker, H. G., *The Laws of Land Warfare*, Washington, US Department of State, 1919.

Barclay, T., *The Law and Usage of War*, London, Constable, 1914.

Barras, R. and Erman, S., Forces armées et développement du droit de la guerre, *Military Law and Law of War Review*, 1982.

Beeston, R., Civilian casualties take on a key role, *The Times*, 11 February 1991.

Bentham, M., Iraqi paramilitaries 'used children as human shields', *The Independent*, 2 April 2003.

Best, G., *Humanity in Warfare*, London, Methuen, 1983.

Best, G., *Law and War since 1945*, Oxford, Clarendon Press, 1994.

Best, G., World War Two and the law of war, *Review of International Studies*, 1981.

Binney, M., Dubrovnik's scars laid bare, *The Times*, 8 February 1992.

Bishop, P., Diehards keep allies at bay, in *The Daily Telegraph, War on Saddam*, London, Robinson, 2003.

Biswas, A. K., Scientific assessment of long-term environmental consequences, in Austin and Bruch, *Environmental Consequences of War*.

Blix, H., Area bombardment: rules and reasons, *British Yearbook of International Law*, 1978.

Bothe, M., The protection of the environment in time of armed conflict, *German Yearbook of International Law*, 1991.

Bothe, M., The Protection of the Environment in Time of Armed Conflict, paper for the Ottawa Conference of Experts, July 1991.

Bothe, M., Partsch, K. J. and Solf, W. A., *New Rules for the Victims of Armed Conflicts*, The Hague, Martinus Nijhoff, 1982.

Bouvier, A., Protection of the natural environment in time of armed conflict, *International Review of the Red Cross*, 1991.

Bouvier, A., Recent studies on the environment in time of armed conflict, *International Review of the Red Cross*, 1992.

Bouvier, A. and Gasser, H. P., Protection of the natural environment in time of armed conflict, paper for the Ottawa Conference of Experts, July 1991.

Boylan, P. J., *Review of the Convention for the Protection of Cultural Property in the event of Armed Conflict*, Paris, UNESCO, 1993.

Brown, B. and Shukman, D., *All Necessary Means*, London, BBC Books, 1991.

Bruderlein, C., Custom in international humanitarian law, *International Review of the Red Cross*, 1991.

Buncombe, A., US army chief says Iraqi troops took bribes to surrender, *The Independent*, 24 May 2003.

Campbell, J., Rings of disaster, *Evening Standard*, 3 July 1991.

Canada, Note on the Current Law of Armed Conflict relevant to the Environment in Conventional Conflicts, paper by the Office of the Judge Advocate General for the Ottawa Conference of Experts, July 1991.

Carcione, M. M., Protection de biens culturels en cas de conflit armé, paper for the sixteenth Round Table of the International Institute for Humanitarian Law, 1991.

Carnahan, B. M., Additional Protocol I: a military view, *Akron Law Review*, 1986.

Carnahan, B. M., Protecting civilians under the draft Geneva protocol, *18 Air Force Law Review*, 1976.

Cartledge, G. J., *The Soldier's Dilemma: When to Use Force in Australia*, Canberra, Australian Government Publishing Service, 1992.

Cassese, A., *International Law*, Oxford, Oxford University Press, 2001.

Cassese, A., *Violence and Law in the Modern Age*, Cambridge, Polity Press, 1988.

Cataldi, A., Child soldiers, in Gutman and Reiff, *Crimes of War*.

Cauderay, G. C., Visibility of the distinctive emblem on medical establishments, units and transports, *International Review of the Red Cross*, 1990.

Clarke, M. H. F., The status of guerrillas and irregular forces, unpublished, 1976.

Clarke, M. H. F., Glynn, T. and Rogers, A. P. V., Combatant and prisoner of war status, in M. A. Meyer, (ed.), *Armed Conflict and the New Law*, London, British Institute of International and Comparative Law, 1989.

Cockburn, P., Bomber crew kills nine in the 'big one' but was Saddam Hussein among them? *The Independent*, 9 April 2003.

Cordesman, A. H., *The Lessons of Afghanistan*, Washington, CSIS Press, 2002.

Craig, D., Should Australia ratify the 1977 protocol additional to the 1949 Geneva conventions? *Defence Force Journal*, 1989.

Cruickshank, D., The raiders of the lost art, BBC 2 television broadcast, 8 June 2003.

Daily Telegraph, *The War on Saddam*, London, Robinson, 2003.

David, E., *Principes de droit des conflits armés*, Brussels, Bruylant, 3rd edn, 2002.

De la Billière, P., *Storm Command*, London, HarperCollins, 1992.

De Mulinen, F., *Handbook on the Law of War for the Armed Forces*, Geneva, International Committee of the Red Cross, 1987.

De Smet, A., General report on civilian support to the armed forces, Brussels Congress of the International Society for Military Law and the Law of War, 1991.

Detter, I., *The Law of War*, 2nd edn, Cambridge, Cambridge University Press, 2000.

De Vattel, E., *Le droit des gens*, 1758.

De Visscher, C., Les lois de la guerre et la théorie de la necessité, *Revue Général de Droit International Public*, 1917.

Dinstein, Y., Siege warfare and the starvation of civilians, in A. J. M. Delisson and G. J. Tania (eds.), *Humanitarian Law of Armed Conflict, Challenges Ahead*, The Hague, Martinus Nihoff, 1991.

Dinstein, Y., *The Defence of Obedience to Superior Orders in International Law*, Leyden, Sijthoff, 1965.

Dowty, A., Sanctioning Iraq: the limits of the new world order, *Washington Quarterly*, 1994.

Doswald-Beck, L. *San Remo Manual on International Law applicable to Armed Conflicts at Sea*, Cambridge, Cambridge University Press, 1995.

Doswald-Beck, L., The value of the 1977 protocols, in M. A. Meyer, *Armed Conflict and the New Law*, London, British Institute of International and Comparative Law, 1989.

Draper, G. I. A. D., Humanitarianism in the modern law of armed conflict, in M. A. Meyer, (ed.), *Armed Conflict and the New Law*, London, British Institute of International and Comparative Law, 1989.

Draper, G. I. A. D., The new law of armed conflict, *Royal United Services Institute Journal*, 1979.

Dufka, C., Children as killers, in Gutman and Rieff, *Crimes of War*.

Dunlap, C. J., Jr., The end of innocence: rethinking noncombatancy in the post-Kosovo era, *Strategic Review*, summer 2000, p. 9.

Dworkin, A., Iraqi television: a legitimate target, www.crimesofwar.org.

Dworkin, A., The Yemen strike: the war on terrorism goes global, www.crimesofwar.org.

Elliott, H. W., Dead and wounded, in Gutman and Rieff, *Crimes of War*.

Evans, M., Freedom of the sky, *The Times*, 5 February 1991.

Falk, R. Evaluating the adequacy of existing international law standards, in Austin and Bruch, *Environmental Consequences of War*.

Falk, R., The environmental law of war: an introduction, in G. Plant, (ed.), *Environmental Protection and the Law of War*, London, Belhaven, 1992.

Falk, R. A. (ed.), *The International Law of Civil War*, Baltimore, The Johns Hopkins Press, 1971.

Fauchille, P., Le bombardement aérien, *Revue Général de Droit International Public*, 1917.

Fenrick, W. J., Attacking the enemy civilian as a punishable offence, *Duke Journal of International and Comparative Law*, 1997, p. 563.

Fenrick, W. J., The rule of proportionality and protocol I in conventional warfare, *Military Law Review*, 1982.

Fenrick, W. J. and van Veen, A. J., Annex VI.B of the Final Report of the UN Commission of Experts established pursuant to UN Security Council Resolution 780 (1992).

Finn, C., The broader implications of the increasing use of precision weapons, *Air Power Review*, spring, 2001.

Finn, C., The employment of air power in Afghanistan and beyond, *Air Power Review*, winter 2002.

Fisk, R., Library books . . . set ablaze, *The Independent*, 15 April 2003.

Fleck, D., Die rechtlichen Garantien des Verbots von unmittelbaren Kampfhandlungen gegen Zivilpersonen, *Military Law and Law of War Review*, 1966.

Fleck, D., Environment: legal and policy perspectives, in H. Fox and M. A. Meyer (eds.), *Effecting Compliance*, London, British Institute of International and Comparative Law, 1993.

Fox, H., Reparations and state responsibility, in P. J. Rowe (ed.), *The Gulf War 1990– 91 in International and English Law*, London, Routledge, 1993.

Garner, J. W., *International Law and the World War*, vol. 1, London, Longman, 1920.

Gasser, H. P., Humanitäres Völkerrecht in Aktion, *Humanitäres Völkerrecht Informationsschriften*, 1991, Bonn, German Red Cross, and Bochum, Ruhr University, 1991.

Gasser, H. P., Some legal issues concerning ratification of the 1977 Geneva protocols, in M. A. Meyer, (ed.), *Armed Conflict and the New Law*, London, British Institute of International and Comparative Law, 1989.

Gehring, R. W., Loss of civilian protection, *Military Law and Law of War Review*, 1980.

Germany, *Der Schutz von Kulturgut bei bewaffneten Konflikten*, Bonn, Federal Ministry of Defence publication Zdv 15/9, 1964.

Germany, *Humanitäres Völkerrecht in bewaffneten Konflikten – Handbuch*, Bonn, Bundesministerium der Verteidigung, 1992.

Germany, Report concerning the execution of the [Cultural Property Convention] by the Federal Republic of Germany, *Military Law and Law of War Review*, 1978.

Goldblat, J., Legal protection of the environment against the effects of military activities, *Bulletin of Peace Proposals*, 1991.

Goldblat, J., The ENMOD Convention: a critical review, *Humanitäres Völkerrecht Informationsschriften*, 1993.

Goldman, R. K., The legal regime governing the conduct of operation Desert Storm, *University of Toledo Law Review*, 1992.

Gonsalves, E. L., Armed forces and the development of the law of war, *Military Law and Law of War Review*, 1982.

Gray, P. W., Dresden 1945 – just another raid, *Air Power Review*, spring 2001.

Green, J. H., The destruction of the abbey of Monte Cassino, *British Army Review*, 1988.

Green, L. C., Book review: law on the battlefield, *Naval War College Review*, summer 1997, p. 130.

Green, L. C., Superior orders and the Geneva conventions and protocols, in H. Fox and M. A. Meyer (eds.), *Effecting Compliance*, London, British Institute of International and Comparative Law, 1993.

Green, L. C., *Superior Orders in National and International Law*, Leyden, Sijthoff, 1976.

Green, L. C., *The Contemporary Law of Armed Conflict*, 2nd edn, Manchester, Manchester University Press, 2000.

Green, L. C., The Environment and the Law of Conventional Warfare, paper for the Ottawa Conference of Experts, July 1991.

Green, L. C., The new law of armed conflict, *Canadian Yearbook of International Law*, 1977.

Greenspan, M., *The Modern Law of Land Warfare*, Berkeley, University of California Press, 1959.

Greenwood, C. J., Belligerent reprisals in the jurisprudence of the International Criminal Tribunal for the former Yugoslavia, in H. Fischer, C. Kress and S. Luder, (eds.), *International Law and National Prosecution of Crimes under International Law*, Bochum, 2001, pp. 539–58.

Greenwood, C. J., *Command and the Laws of Armed Conflict*, Camberley, Strategic and Combat Studies Institute, Army Staff College, 1993.

Greenwood, C. J., Customary international law and the first Geneva protocol of 1977 in the Gulf conflict, in P. J. Rowe (ed.), *The Gulf War 1990–91 in International and English Law*, London, Routledge, 1993.

Greenwood, C. J., War crimes proceedings before the International Criminal Tribunal for the former Yugoslavia, *Military Law Journal*, 1997.

Greenwood, C. J., International humanitarian law and the *Tadić* case, 7 (1996) *European Journal of International Law*, 265.

Greenwood, C. J., Reprisals and reciprocity in the new law of armed conflict, in M. A. Meyer, (ed.), *Armed Conflict and the New Law*, British Institute of International and Comparative Law, 1989.

Gross, M. L., Fighting by other means in the Mideast: a critical analysis of Israel's assassination policy, *Political Studies*, 2003, vol. 51, p.1.

Grotius, H., *De Jure Belli ac Pacis*, 1642.

Hall, W. E., *A Treatise on International Law*, 8th edn by A. Pearce Higgins, Oxford, Clarendon Press, 1924.

Gumbel, A., 1,700 civilians died as US took Baghdad, *The Independent*, 19 May 2003.

Gumbel, A. and Keys, D., US blamed for failure to stop sacking of museum, *The Independent*, 14 April, 2003.

Gutman, R. and Kuttab, D., Indiscriminate attacks, in Gutman and Rieff, *Crimes of War*.

Gutman, R. and Rieff, D. (eds.), *Crimes of War*, New York, W. W. Norton & Company, 1999.

Hamilton, J. D., How Britain helped kill Heydrich, www.theherald.co.uk/perspective/archive.

Hampson, F. J., Belligerent reprisals and the 1977 protocols, *International and Comparative Law Quarterly*, 1988.

Hampson, F. J., Liability for war crimes, in P. J. Rowe (ed.), *The Gulf War 1990–91 in International and English Law*, London, Routledge, 1993.

Hampson, F. J., Means and methods of warfare in the conflict in the Gulf, in P. J. Rowe (ed.), *The Gulf War 1990–91 in International and English Law*, London, Routledge, 1993.

Hanke, H. M., The 1923 Hague rules of air warfare, *International Review of the Red Cross*, 1993.

Higgins, R., International law and civil conflict, in Luard, *International Regulation of Civil Wars*.

Hill, G., Conflict threatens ancient sites, *The Times*, 28 February 1991.

Hine, P., Despatch by the joint commander of operation Granby, second supplement to the *London Gazette*, 28 June 1991.

Holland, T. E., *The Laws of War on Land*, Oxford, Clarendon Press, 1908.

Howard, M., On balance, Bush must go to war, *The Times*, 5 November 1990.

Human Rights Watch, *The Crisis in Kosovo*, undated.

ICRC, *Protection of the Civilian Population against the Dangers of Hostilities*, Report No. 3 to the Conference of Government Experts, Geneva, International Committee of the Red Cross, 1971.

ICRC, *Protection of the Environment in Time of Armed Conflict*, Report for the 48th Session of the United Nations General Assembly, Geneva, International Committee of the Red Cross, 1993.

Infeld, D. L., Precision guided missiles demonstrated their pinpoint accuracy in Desert Storm; but is a country obligated to use precision technology to minimize collateral civilian injury and damage? *George Washington Journal of International Law and Economics*, 1992.

International Criminal Tribunal for the former Yugoslavia, Final report to the prosecutor by the committee established to review the NATO bombing campaign against the Federal Republic of Yugoslavia, 39 (2000) *International Legal Materials* 1257.

Jochnick C. and Normand, R., The legitimation of violence: a critical history of the laws of war, *Harvard International Law Journal*, 1994.

Johnson, D. H. N., The legality of modern forms of aerial warfare, *Royal Aeronautical Society Journal*, 1968.

Kadelbach, S., Zwingende Normen des humanitären Völkerrechts, *Humanitäres Völkerrecht Informationsschriften*, 1992.

Kalshoven, F. and Zegveld, L., *Constraints on the Waging of War*, 3rd edn, Geneva, International Committee of the Red Cross, 2001.

Kalshoven, F., Reprisals and the protection of civilians: . . . decisions of the Yugoslavia tribunal, in L. C. Vohrah, *et al.* (eds.), *Man's Inhumanity to Man*, The Hague, Kluwer, 2003.

Kalshoven, F., The reaffirmation and development of international humanitarian law, *Netherlands Yearbook of International Law*, 1978.

Karsten, P., *Law, Soldiers and Combat*, Westport, Greenwood, 1978.

Keaney, T. A. and Cohen, E. A., *Gulf War Air Power Survey, Summary Report*, Washington, Government Printing Office, 1993.

Keenan, T. P. Jr., Die Operation Wüstensturm aus der Sicht des aktiven Rechstberaters, *Humanitäres Völkerrecht Informationsschriften*, 1991.

Keleny, G., Enshrined in the Geneva Convention is a protection which all PoWs are owed, *The Independent*, 25 March 2003.

Kirby, A., UK to aid Iraq DU removal, BBC news online, 23 April 2003.

Krieger, H. (ed.), *The Kosovo Conflict and International Law*, Cambridge University Press 2001.

Krüger-Sprengel, F., Le concept de proportionalité dans le droit de la guerre, *Military Law and Law of War Review*, 1980.

Kuehl, D. T., Airpower v. electricity: electric power as a target for strategic air operations, *Journal of Strategic Studies*, 1995.

Ladisch, V., 'Stress and duress': drawing the line between interrogation and torture, 24 April 2003, on www.crimesofwar.org.

Lauterpacht, H., The problem of the revision of the law of war, *British Yearbook of International Law*, 1952.

Levie, H. S., The rise and fall of an internationally codified denial of the defence of superior orders, *Military Law and Law of War Review*, 1991.

Luard, E., *The International Regulation of Civil Wars*, London, Thames & Hudson, 1972.

Luttwak, E., Supplies, not troops should be the main target of jets in Kuwait, *The Times*, 16 February 1991.

McCoubrey, H., *International Humanitarian Law*, Aldershot, Dartmouth, 1990.

McCoubrey, H., The Idea of War Crimes and Crimes against the Peace since 1945, University of Nottingham Research Papers in Law, 1992.

McCoubrey, H., The nature of the modern doctrine of military necessity, *Military Law and Law of War Review*, 1991.

McCoubrey, H. and White, N. D., *International Law and Armed Conflict*, Aldershot, Dartmouth, 1992.

McCoubrey, H. and White, N. D., *International Organizations and Civil Wars*, Aldershot, Dartmouth, 1995.

MacIntyre, D., Chilling images 'breach Geneva Convention', *The Independent*, 24 March 2003.

MacIntyre, D., Suicide bomb threats by women are linked to deaths of American soldiers, *The Independent*, 5 April 2003.

Malcolm, N., *Bosnia, a Short History*, London, Papermac, 1996.

Masters, J., *The Road Past Mandalay*, London, Michael Joseph, 1961.

Matthews, T., *et al.*, The secret history of the war, *Newsweek*, 18 March 1991.

Mawhinney, B., Basis and Objectives of the Meeting of Experts on the Use of the Environment as a Tool of Conventional Warfare, paper for the Ottawa Conference of Experts, July 1991.

Meek, A. D., Operation Centre, *British Army Review*, 1994.

Meilinger, P. S., Winged defence, answering the critics of air power, *Air Power Review*, winter 2000, p. 41.

Meron, T., Henry the Fifth and the law of war, *American Journal of International Law* 86, 1992.

Meron, T., The continuing role of custom in the formation of international humanitarian law, *American Journal of International Law* 90, 1990.

Meyer, M. A. (ed.), *Armed Conflict and the New Law*, London, British Institute of International and Comparative Law, 1989.

Meyrowitz, H., Buts de guerre et objectifs militaires, *Military Law and Law of War Review*, 1983.

Middle East Watch, *Needless Deaths in the Gulf War*, New York: Human Rights Watch, 1991.

Milmo, Allied commanders open battle for the airwaves, *The Independent*, 27 March 2003.

Moderhack, R., *Braunschweig, das Bild der Stadt in 900 Jahren*, vol. 1, Brunswick, Städtisches Museum Braunschweig, 1985.

Moir, L. *The Law of Internal Armed Conflict*, Cambridge, Cambridge University Press, 2002.

Moore, J. N., *Law and Civil War in the Modern World*, Baltimore, The Johns Hopkins University Press, 1974.

Morgan, J. H., *The German War Book*, London, John Murray, 1915.

Morris, K., 'Threats' to kill Afghan killing witnesses, BBC news online, 14 November 2002.

Murray, K., US troops face children, and hard calls, in battle, 7 April 2003, www.reuters.com.

Nakhoul, S., Civilians killed in bombing near hospital, *The Independent*, 3 April 2003.

Obradovic, K., La protection de la population civile dans les conflits armés internationaux, in Cassese, A., *The New Humanitarian Law of Armed Conflict*, Naples, Editoriale Scientifica, 1979.

Oeter, S., Methods and means of combat, in D. Fleck, (ed.), *The Handbook of Humanitarian Law in Armed Conflict*, Oxford, Oxford University Press, 1995.

Oppenheim, L., *International Law*, vol. 2, 7th edn by H. Lauterpacht, London, Longman, 1952.

Painchaud, P., Environmental weapons and the Gulf war, paper for the Ottawa Conference of Experts, July 1991.

Parks, W. H., Air war and the law of war, 32 *Air Force Law Review*, 1990.

Parks, W. H., Department of Defence news briefing, 7 April 2003, on www.defenselink.mil.

Payne, S., Tornados lead blitz on Baghdad, in *The Daily Telegraph, War on Saddam*, London, Robinson, 2003.

Pearce, N., *The Shield and the Sabre*, London, Her Majesty's Stationery Office, 1992.

Phillips, G. R., Rules of engagement: a primer, *Army Lawyer*, 1993.

Pictet, J., *Commentary* on the I Convention for the Amerlioration of the Condition of the Wounded and Sick in Armed Forces in the Field, Geneva, International Committee of the Red Cross, 1958.

Pictet, J., *Commentary* on the IV Convention relating to the Protection of Civilian Persons in Time of War, Geneva, International Committee of the Red Cross, 1958.

Pienkny, R., Der Schutz von Kulturgütern bei bewaffneten Konflikten im Lichte jüngster völkererchtlicher Entwicklungen, *Humanitäres Völkerrecht – Informationsschriften*, 1/2003.

Plant, G., Elements of a new Convention for the Protection of the Environment in Time of Armed Conflict, paper for the Ottawa Conference of Experts, July 1991.

Plant, G., Environmental damage and the law of war, in H. Fox and M. A. Meyer (eds.), *Effecting Compliance*, London, British Institute of International and Comparative Law, 1993.

Price, A. R. G., Possible environmental threats from the current war in the Gulf, *Greenpeace*, 2 February 1991.

Rauch, E., Attack restraints, target limitations, *Military Law and Law of War Review*, 1979.

Rauch, E., Conduct of combat and risks run by the civilian population, *Military Law and Law of War Review*, 1982.

Rauch, E., Le concept de necessité militaire dans le droit de la guerre, *Military Law and Law of War Review*, 1980.

Rauch, E., *The Protocol Additional to the Geneva Conventions for the Victims of Armed Conflicts and the United Nations Convention on the Law of the Sea: Repercussions on the Law of Naval Warfare*, Berlin, Duncker & Humblot, 1984.

Risley, J. S., *The Law of War*, London, Innes & Co., 1897.

Roberts, A., Civil defence and international law, in M. A. Meyer (ed.), *Armed Conflict and the New Law*, London, British Institute of International and Comparative Law, 1989.

Roberts, A., Failures in protecting the environment, in P. J. Rowe (ed.), *The Gulf War 1990–91 in International and English Law*, London, Routledge, 1993.

Roberts, A., The laws of war and the Gulf conflict, *Oxford International Review*, 1990/91.

Roberts, A. and Guelff, R., *Documents on the Laws of War*, 3rd edn, Oxford, Oxford University Press, 2000.

Robinson, N. A., Draft Articles with Commentary on a Convention securing Nature from Warfare or other Hostile Activities, paper for the Ottawa Conference of Experts, July 1991.

Rogers, A. P. V., A commentary on the protocol on prohibitions or restrictions on the use of mines, *Military Law and Law of War Review*, 1987.

Rogers, A. P. V., Civil war, in Gutman and Rieff (eds.), *Crimes of War*.

Rogers, A. P. V., Conduct of combat and risks run by the civilian population, *Military Law and Law of War Review*, 1982.

Rogers, A. P. V., Military necessity and the rule of proportionality, *Military Law and Law of War Review Addendum*, 1980.

Rogers, A. P. V., Mines, booby-traps and other devices, *International Review of the Red Cross*, 1990.

Rogers, A. P. V., The defence of superior orders in international law, *Military Law Journal*, 1991.

Rogers, A. P. V., The Mines Protocol: negotiating history, in ICRC, *Symposium on Anti-Personnel Mines, Report*, Geneva, International Committee of the Red Cross, 1993.

Rogers, A. P. V., The use of military courts to try suspects, *International and Comparative Law Quarterly*, 2002.

Rogers, A. P. V., War crimes trials under the royal warrant, *International and Comparative Law Quarterly*, 1990.

Rogers, A. P. V., What is a legitimate military target?, in R. M. Burchill (ed.), *Essays in Honour of Hilaire McCoubrey*, Cambridge, Cambridge University Press, 2004.

Rogers, A. P. V., Wilfulness, in Gutman and Rieff (eds.), *Crimes of War*.

Rogers, A. P. V., Zero-casualty warfare, *International Review of the Red Cross*, March 2000, p. 165.

Rogers, A. P. V., Malherbe, P. and Doppler, B., *Fight it Right* (Model Manual on the Law of Armed Conflict for Armed Forces), Geneva, International Committee of the Red Cross, 1999.

Rooney, B., First strike, in *The Daily Telegraph, War on Saddam*, London, Robinson, 2003.

Rose, M., *Fighting for Peace*, London, Harvill Press, 1998.

Rosenblad, E., Area bombing and international law, *Military Law and Law of War Review*, 1976.

Rousseau, C., *Le Droit des conflits armés*, Paris, Pedone, 1983.

Rowe, P. J., Memorandum to the Foreign Affairs Select Committee, in *The Expanding Role of the UN and its Implications for UK Policy*, London, Third Report from the Foreign Affairs Select Committee, 1993.

Rowe, P. J., *Defence: the Legal Implications*, London, Brassey, 1987.

Rowe, P. J., Response from the United Kingdom Group of the International Society for Military Law and the Law of War to the criminology questionnaire, 1994.

Saalfeld, M., Umweltschutz in bewaffneten Konflikten, *Humanitäres Völkerrecht Informationsschriften*, 1992.

Sandoz, Y., *The establishment of safety zones for persons displaced within their country of origin*, International Committee of the Red Cross, 1995.

Sandoz, Y., Swinarski, C. and Zimmerman, B. with Pictet, J., *Commentary on the Additional Protocols of 8 June 1977 to the Geneva Conventions of 12 August 1949*, Geneva, Martinus Nijhoff, 1987.

Sands, P. and Alexander, D., Assessing the impact, *New Law Journal*, 1 November 1991.

Sassòli, M. and Bouvier, A., *How does Law Protect in War?* Geneva, International Committee of the Red Cross, 1999.

Schachter, O., United Nations law in the Gulf conflict, *American Journal of International Law*, 1991.

Schindler, D. and Toman, J., *The Laws of Armed Conflicts*, 3rd edn, Dordrecht, Martinus Nijhoff, 1988.

Schmitt, M., Book review: law on the battlefield, US Air Force, 8 (1998) *Journal of Legal Studies*, p. 255.

Schmitt, M. and G. L. Beruto (eds.), *Terrorism and International Law: Challenges and Responses*, San Remo, International Institute of Humanitarian Law, 2003.

Schmitt, M., War and the environment: fault lines in the prescriptive landscape, in Austin and Bruch, *Environmental Consequences of War*.

Schwarzenberger, G., *International Law*, vol. II, London, Stevens, 1968.

Schwarzenberger, G., The revision of the law of war, *British Yearbook of International Law*, 1952.

Shany, Y., Israeli counter-terrorism measures: are they 'kosher' under international law?, in M. Schmitt, *Terrorism and International Law*.

Shotwell, C. B., Food and the use of force, *Military Law and the Law of War Review*, 1991.

Sidel, V. S., The impact of military preparedness and militarism, in Austin and Bruch, *The Environmental Consequences of War*.

Skarstedt, C. I., Armed forces and the development of the law of war, *Military Law and Law of War Review*, 1982.

Smith, J. C. and Hogan, B., *Criminal Law*, 7th edn, London, Butterworth, 1992.

Smithers, A. J., *The Man Who Disobeyed*, Leo Cooper, 1970.

Smyth, F., Gulf war, in Gutman and Rieff (eds.), *Crimes of War*, p. 162.

Spaight, J. M., *War Rights on Land*, London, Macmillan, 1911.

Spaight, J. M., *Air Power and War Rights*, London, Longmans, 1924 and 1947.

Spaight, J. M., Non-combatants and air attack, 9 *Air Law Review*, 1938.

Spaight, J. M., The doctrine of air force necessity, undated paper from the United Kingdom Air Ministry archive.

Spieker, H., Martens'sche Klausel, *Humanitäres Völkerrecht Informationsschriften*, 1988.

Stone, C. D., The environment in wartime: an overview, in Austin and Bruch, *The Environmental Consequences of War*.

Stone, J., *Legal Controls of International Armed Conflict*, London, Stevens, 1954.

Strickland, P. C., USAF aerospace-power doctrine, decisive or coercive? *Air Power Review*, spring 2001, p. 17.

Switzerland, *Botschaft über die Zusatzprotokolle zu den Genfer Abkommen*, Berne, Swiss Federal Council, 1981.

Switzerland, *Gesetze und Gebräuche des Krieges*, Berne, Swiss Army Regulation 51.7/II d, 1987.

Szasz. P. C., Study of Proposals for Improvements to existing Legal Instruments relating to the Environment and Armed Conflicts, paper for the Ottawa Conference of Experts, July 1991.

Taubenfeld, H. J., The laws of war in civil wars, in Moore, *Law and Civil War.*

Toman, J., *La Protection des biens culturels en cas de conflit armé*, Paris, UNESCO, 1994.

Usborne, D., US 'psy-ops' division rolls out its weapons of mass persuasion, *The Independent*, 21 March 2003.

United Kingdom, *A Soldier's Guide to the Law of Armed Conflict*, British Army Pamphlet, Army Code 71130, 1998.

United Kingdom, *Kosovo*, Foreign Affairs Committee, Fourth Report, vol. 1, London, The Stationery Office, 2000.

United Kingdom, *Queen's Regulations for the Army*, London, Her Majesty's Stationery Office, 1975.

United Kingdom, *Manual of Military Law*, 7th edn, London, Her Majesty's Stationery Office, 1929.

United Kingdom, *Manual of Military Law*, Part I, London, Her Majesty's Stationery Office, 1972 (reprinted 1992).

United Kingdom, *Manual of Military Law*, Part III, London, Her Majesty's Stationery Office, 1958.

United Kingdom, *Preliminary Lessons of Operation Granby*, House of Commons Defence Committee Tenth Report, Her Majesty's Stationery Office, 1991.

United Kingdom, *Prisoners of War Handling*, Joint Warfare Publication 1–10, Joint Doctrine and Concepts Centre, Ministry of Defence, March 2001 edition.

United Kingdom, *Review of the Results of Investigations . . . and the Involvement . . . of Lieutenant Waldheim*, report by the Ministry of Defence, London, Her Majesty's Stationery Office, 1989.

United Nations, Environment Programme, Post-Conflict Assessment Unit, Report on Depleted Uranium in Bosnia and Hercegovina, revised May 2003, on http:// postconflict.unep.ch.

United States, *Commander's Handbook on the Law of Armed Conflict*, Washington, Department of the Air Force, Pamphlet 110–34, 1980.

United States, *Conduct of the Persian Gulf Campaign*, Washington, Department of Defence interim report to Congress, July 1991.

United States, *Conduct of the Persian Gulf War*, Washington, Department of Defence final report to Congress, April 1992. Appendix O to the report, entitled The Role of the Law of War, is published in 31 (1992) *International Legal Materials*, 612.

United States, Department of Defence, Military Commission Instruction No. 2, dated 30 April 2003, www.nimj.org.

United States, *International Law*, vol. II, Washington, Department of the Army, Pamphlet 27–161–2, 1962.

United States, *International Law – The Conduct of Armed Conflict and Air Operations*, Washington, Department of the Air Force, Pamphlet 110–31, 1976.

United States, *Joint Doctrine for Targeting*, Joint Chiefs of Staff Publication 3–60, 2002.

United States, *Kosovo/Operation Allied Force After-Action Report*, 31 January 2000.

United States, *Law of Land Warfare*, Washington, Department of the Army, Manual 27–10, 1956.

Van Dongen, Y., *The Protection of the Civilian Population in Time of Armed Conflicts*, Groningen, Groningen University, 1991.

Walzer, M., *Just and Unjust Wars*, 2nd edn, Basic Books, 1992.

Waters, G., *Gulf Lesson One: the Value of Air Power*, Canberra, Air Power Studies Centre, 1992.

Westing, A. H., The environmental modification conference of 1991, *Humanitäres Völkerrecht Informationsschriften*, 1992.

Westlake, J., *International Law*, Part II (War), Cambridge, Cambridge University Press, 1913.

Wheaton, H., *International Law*, 7th English edn by A. B. Keith, London, Stevens, 1944.

Witteler, S., Der Krieg im Golf und seine Auswirkungen auf die natürliche Umwelt, *Humanitäres Völkerrecht Informationsschriften*, 1991.

Woetzel, R. K., *The Nuremberg Trials in International Law*, London, Stevens, 1962.

Wortley, B. A., Observations on the revision of the 1949 Geneva 'Red Cross Conventions', *British Yearbook of International Law*, 1983.

Würkner-Theis, G., *Fernverlegte Minen und humanitäres Völkerrecht*, Frankfurt am Main, Peter Lang, 1990.

Zegveld, L., *The Accountability of Armed Opposition Groups in International Law*, Cambridge, Cambridge University Press, 2002.

Index